SURVEY
OF
SOCIAL
SCIENCE

SURVEY
OF
SOCIAL
SCIENCE

SOCIOLOGY SERIES

Volume 5
1845-2244

Social Stratification: Functionalist Perspectives—Z

Edited by
FRANK N. MAGILL

Consulting Editor
HÉCTOR L. DELGADO
UNIVERSITY OF ARIZONA

SALEM PRESS
Pasadena, California   Englewood Cliffs, New Jersey

Library of Congress Cataloging-in-Publication Data
Survey of social science. Sociology series / [edited by]
Frank N. Magill; consulting editor, Héctor L. Delgado.
   v. cm.
   Includes bibliographical references and index.
   1. Sociology—Encyclopedias.   I. Magill, Frank
Northen, 1907-   . II. Delgado, Héctor L., 1949-   .
HM17.S86   1994   94-31770
301'.03—dc20   CIP
ISBN 0-89356-739-6 (set)
ISBN 0-89356-744-2 (volume 5)

CONTENTS

SOCIOLOGY

SURVEY
OF
SOCIAL
SCIENCE

SOCIAL STRATIFICATION: FUNCTIONALIST PERSPECTIVES

Type of sociology: Social stratification
Field of study: Theoretical perspectives on stratification

The functionalist perspective on social stratification proposes that social stratification is inevitable in society and is therefore universal. Generally, functionalist scholars have argued that stratification is both necessary and desirable to ensure that difficult and important positions will be filled by individuals capable of fulfilling the duties associated with such positions.

Principal terms

ACHIEVED STATUS: refers to the assignment of individuals to positions in society based upon their achievements, such as education or the attainment of some skill

ASCRIBED STATUS: refers to the assignment of individuals to positions in society based on intrinsic characteristics, such as birth order, kin network, sex, or race

DIVISION OF LABOR: refers to the manner in which work is allocated in society, with increasing specialization of different tasks/occupations leading to a more complex division of labor

SOCIAL CLASS: a category of group membership that is generally based on one's position in the economic system with respect to economic resources, income, occupational prestige, and educational attainment

SOCIAL PRESTIGE: the esteem with which one is regarded in society

SOCIAL STRATIFICATION: a hierarchical ranking system, often represented as a "ladder," in which there are differences in access to social resources; individuals at the top ranks have more access, while those at the bottom lack social resources; also called structured inequality

Overview

The study of social stratification developed from sociological concerns about social inequality and social classes. In his 1993 book *Inequality and Stratification*, Robert Rothman says that "the study of social class has been a central theme in sociology since its origins in the nineteenth century." According to Rothman, the most important contribution sociology makes to understanding social stratification is in presenting the view that stratification, or inequality, is patterned into societies. For Rothman, these patterns of inequality must be viewed in relation to values and beliefs, social institutions, laws, norms, and patterns of power. These together, he argues, support and maintain social stratification. Sociologists have studied social stratification to understand the extent of its occurrence and the consequences of institutionalized inequality for members of society. In the United States throughout the twentieth century, the leading sociological theory of social stratification has been functionalist.

Functionalist theory, in the United States most often associated with Talcott Parsons, is a theory that is most concerned with how societies maintain order. Generally, functionalist theorists have tended to stress stability, consensus, and integration in society. They view society as similar to the human body with its many organs. Like the body's organs, society's institutions must function properly to maintain the general stability of the entire social system. Parsons, perhaps more than other functionalist theorists, believed that this social order was based upon values shared by members of society.

Parsons differentiated societies as falling on a continuum between ascribed-status-based societies and achievement-based societies. Societies in which individuals were valued based on their family position, sex, race, or other traits of birth are viewed as falling at the traditional end of the continuum. On the other end is modern society, in which a system of rewards is used to aid in fulfilling a complex division of labor. Parsons argued that the more difficult positions that demanded considerable responsibility required a system of rewards to motivate individuals to take them. In his view, stratification—which is, by definition, social inequality—was both necessary and agreeable. Parsons believed that stratification was necessary to provide rewards for people who would take on the additional responsibility tied to difficult positions, and, in his view, stratification was desirable because it allowed the social system to function smoothly.

Parsons' articulation of a functionalist theory of social stratification was further developed by Kingsley Davis and Wilbert Moore in the 1945 landmark essay "Some Principles of Stratification," published in *American Sociological Review*. In their essay, Davis and Moore set forth a notion of social stratification that shared the basic premises elaborated by Talcott Parsons. They said that social stratification was universal (in varied forms), functional, and integral to fulfilling the division of labor.

For Davis and Moore, the reason social stratification, or structured inequality, is necessary lies in society's need to distribute individuals to vital social positions. Furthermore, society must motivate individuals to perform their duties once they have been recruited for positions. Davis and Moore argued that it was necessary and functional for society to have a varied set of rewards in relation to the varied levels of sacrifices required by some jobs. In other words, there are some jobs that require individuals to possess special talents or to develop special skills. These jobs may also require that the individual filling the position works with the utmost care. Therefore, Davis and Moore find it logical that societies have developed a system of rewards whereby those jobs requiring the greatest preparation and responsibility are rewarded more highly than are other positions. The social order has developed a differentiated system of rewards, which has led to social stratification.

Davis and Moore acknowledge that one way of rewarding people is to contribute more to their sustenance and comfort levels. Like Parsons, however, they focus most on social prestige, the rewards that contribute to one's self-respect. As the social order has developed, these rewards have been "built into" the position and have come to be viewed as rights and fringe benefits of the position. Rewards, however, do not necessarily have to be great, simply enough to ensure that individuals will fill the positions that are of great import to the functioning of society. Furthermore, there must be a hierarchy of rewards so that less-important positions are unable to compete with more important positions. Therefore, for positions that require considerable sacrifice and training, such as that of medical doctor, it is essential to reward individuals with a great amount of social prestige to attract them to the positions because training is so extensive and costly.

Davis and Moore were concerned about how to explain variations in social stratification among societies. They believed that variations in stratification systems ultimately developed because of differences in what they called "functional importance" of positions and in the "scarcity of personnel." In other words, a position of great functional importance to one type of society may not be important to a different type of society. For this reason, there may be few individuals to fill a position of great import to one society, while there may be no scarcity in another society because there is not even a requirement for that position. As Davis and Moore saw it, societies are divided into types depending on two sets of features: internal organization and external conditions. The important aspects of internal organization are whether they have a specialized division of labor; whether they are organized around family as their most important connections; sacred authority (in which there is little social mobility for people who are not religious leaders); and capitalism (in which technology and economic activity are most important). The external conditions that influence the form of social stratification are the level of development, because specialization is viewed as a sign of advancement; foreign relations, such as a state of war with other nations; and the size of the society, because smaller societies are assumed to have lower degrees of functional specialization.

In sum, both Parsons and Davis and Moore present a view of structured inequality as being necessary to maintain social order and therefore society's survival, and as being based on general agreement among members of society.

Applications

The functionalist theory of social stratification, influenced most by Parsons and Davis and Moore, has focused on explaining social stratification as a system of rewards resulting in differences in social prestige. Therefore, applications of the theory have generated studies of occupational prestige and income.

In his 1977 study *Occupational Prestige in Comparative Perspective*, Donald Treiman examined the issue of structured social inequality. Treiman examined various occupational prestige hierarchies, arguing in the manner of Davis and Moore and Talcott Parsons that stratification is inherent in complex modern societies. Treiman's study sought to clarify the determinants of prestige for various occupations and to determine whether this ordering operates universally (in all societies).

Using secondary data from a variety of societies, Treiman examined "occupational hierarchies of power, privilege, and prestige" by looking at differences in income, educational level, and prestige. He found that prestige evaluations by students in all countries examined showed considerable similarity despite cultural differences. He also found that education and income are related to each other, as are education and prestige, and prestige and income. Those countries that were highly industrialized, however, had more in common with one another than they did with less-industrialized countries. Treiman also found that there were differences in stratification based on the economic system of the country; for example, the socialist nations in Eastern Europe did vary somewhat from the pattern of stratification found in capitalist societies. Furthermore, Treiman was unable to prove that the work that an individual does determines that individual's status in all societies. For some societies, it is not the work one does but the wealth, family membership, or ethnic identity that affects one's status.

Don B. Cullen and Shelley M. Novick's study "The Davis-Moore Theory of Stratification: A Further Examination and Extension," in the *American Journal of Sociology* 83, no. 6 (1979), also applies functionalist ideas about stratification to research. Cullen and Novick examined occupations to look at the amount of talent they required and the amount of "disagreeability," training, importance, and rewards through prestige and income that they entailed. They found that the amount of talent and training required for a position, and the importance of the position, did affect the levels of income and prestige accorded to that position. When jobs were physically demanding, there was a negative effect on prestige. Overall, Cullen and Novick believed that talent and training differences provide the best explanation of differences in rewards.

Generally, functionalist theories of social stratification have been assumed, as far as public policy is concerned, because they mirror and support the status quo. In other words, it is assumed that individuals at the upper end of the stratification system are there because the positions they hold merit higher rewards than do the positions of those at the bottom. In other words, the functionalist perspective on stratification has been complementary to the notion that U.S. society is meritocratic, that people with the highest incomes and high social esteem have earned them. Furthermore, this line of reasoning may lead to the supposition that those with low incomes and low levels of esteem merit fewer social rewards because of the positions they hold.

In terms of social policy, critics have argued that social mobility is restricted by lack of access to training and education for people on the lower end of the stratification system. The governmental response has been varied, resulting at times in greater governmental support for students' educational expenses but contracting at other times, when students are expected to bear the sacrifice themselves. In the aftermath of the large social movements of the 1960's and 1970's, women and people of color have argued that some positions warrant higher rewards than they are currently given because they are demanding and are of great importance to society. Such premises guide the notion of comparable worth, for example, which seeks to provide higher rewards for jobs that have been feminized, or have been performed primarily by women. Comparable worth proponents argue that positions that women hold are rewarded at lower levels than are those that men hold simply because it is women who fill those positions.

Context

Functionalism is a major theoretical orientation in sociology, dating from the work of Émile Durkheim. In U.S. sociology, this perspective is most often represented by the work of Talcott Parsons, who developed the contemporary functionalist perspective on social stratification. Indeed, functionalism has been the dominant perspective in American sociology throughout the twentieth century. Its major characteristics are a view of society as working to ensure its own survival; a view of social institutions as furthering the maintenance of social order; an emphasis on consensus, or agreement, undergirding the social order; and a belief in the universal applications of these notions. In keeping with these overriding concerns, then, the functionalist perspective on social stratification views this structured inequality as essential to the stability of society, necessary to the smooth functioning of society, based on consensus, and universal to all societies.

Although the functionalist notion of stratification introduced in the middle of the twentieth century was immediately accepted as the prevailing theory of stratification, it was not without its critics. Chief among these was Melvin Tumin, who argued that it was impossible to calculate the "functional importance" of any position in society objectively. According to Tumin, in his 1953 essay "Some Principles of Stratification: A Critical Analysis," "to judge that engineers in a factory are functionally more important to the factory than the unskilled workmen involves a notion regarding the dispensability of the unskilled workmen . . ." In other words, Tumin is saying that in any given line of production, every position is interdependent and is therefore of functional importance. Tumin also argues that, instead of encouraging the use of talent, a rigid system of stratification may suppress the discovery of new talent. This is particularly salient in the areas of training and education. Tumin states that wealth may determine access to training and education, thus depriving large portions of the population of the opportunity to attain those positions that reward training and education. Based on this thinking, Tumin asserted that stratification was dysfunctional to society. He further argued that it cannot be assumed that people actually make sacrifices to get greater amounts of training and education. Instead, he suggested that one might view the ability that some parents have to support their children through college and medical school as a resource that those parents have as a reward for their high positions in the system of stratification.

Other sociologists have debated the functionalist perspective on stratification. In particular, they have been concerned with the proposed inevitability of stratification and the use of consensus on occupational rankings to determine functional importance. For example, Abrahamson et al. argue in their 1976 book *Stratification and Mobility* that the notions guiding this theory are not clearly testable, objective notions. They cite Polish sociologist Wlodzimierz Wesolowski, who argued that the Davis-Moore notion of rewards presupposes that human nature is selfish and greedy, motivated by materialistic desires. Generally, the major debate against functionalist theories of stratification has come from the conflict theorists in sociology.

The conflict-theoretical perspective contrasts sharply with that of the functionalists. Conflict theorists view social inequality as emanating from conflict between social groups in society, in which the most powerful group can shape and impose an unequal system of rewards and punishments. Though they agree that social stratification is universal, they view it negatively, as a practice that inhibits the development of the talents of most of the population by giving unfair advantage to the upper levels of society. Furthermore, conflict theorists do not agree that structured inequality is either agreeable to most of society or inevitable in modern, specialized societies.

The conflict-functionalist debate on stratification was further expanded following the impact of the social movements of the 1960's and 1970's on U.S. sociology. In particular, it was argued by feminist sociologists and some racial minority sociologists that studies of stratification had to include more rigid examination of the roles played by race and gender—ascriptive characteristics—in placing individuals in positions. In fact, Rothman argues, in *Inequality and Stratification*, that "no development has been more salient than recognition that considerations of color and gender are central to a full appreciation of the composition and dynamics of class systems." It is the growing understanding that race, color, and gender have played a central role in determining access to training, education, and positions in society that is posing the greatest challenge to the traditional sociological theory of stratification—the functionalist perspective.

Bibliography

Abrahamson, Mark. "Stratification." In *Functionalism*. Englewood Cliffs, N.J.: Prentice-Hall, 1978. In this chapter, Abrahamson very clearly lays out the functionalist theory of stratification. He discusses, briefly, the origins of American functionalism in the work of the French sociologist Émile Durkheim; then turns to a consideration of Talcott Parsons, Davis and Moore, and W. Lloyd Warner; and then discusses the critics of functionalism.

Abrahamson, Mark, Ephraim H. Mizruchi, and Carlton A. Hornung. *Stratification and Mobility*. New York: Macmillan, 1976. The authors present an overview of the functionalist theory of stratification and its critics in chapter 4, along with a comparison of functionalist theory and conflict theory. This work is geared more toward the scholar of sociological theory than toward the layperson.

Bendix, Reinhard, and Seymour Martin Lipset, eds. *Class, Status, and Power*. 2d ed. New York: Free Press, 1966. The editors have collected the essays of the major theorists in the area of social stratification. In part 1, "Theories of Class Structure," the original essays by Davis and Moore and Tumin, with replies to each other, are included. The original essays are very clearly and succinctly written; even the nonsociologist can easily follow the arguments of Davis and Moore and the criticisms presented by Tumin.

Rothman, Robert A. *Inequality and Stratification: Class, Color, and Gender*. 2d ed.

Englewood Cliffs, N.J.: Prentice-Hall, 1993. Rothman's text presents an overview of class, race, and gender stratification in U.S. society, with a presentation of sociological theories of stratification and other types of stratification. This highly readable text also presents a different side of stratification, including the consequences of one's placement in various positions on the social ladder.

Treiman, Donald J. *Occupational Prestige in Comparative Perspective*. New York: Academic Press, 1977. In this volume, Treiman presents his quantitative study of the international application of functionalist theories of stratification. The analysis is statistical, but nonsociologists can follow his substantive discussion of the dilemmas in functionalist theory and his concluding arguments.

Sharon Elise

Cross-References

Conflict Theory, 340; Education: Functionalist Perspectives, 586; The Family: Functionalist versus Conflict Theory Views, 739; Functionalism, 786; Racial and Ethnic Stratification, 1579; Social Stratification: Analysis and Overview, 1839; Social Stratification: Marxist Perspectives, 1852; Social Stratification: Modern Theories, 1859; Social Stratification: Weberian Perspectives, 1866.

SOCIAL STRATIFICATION: MARXIST PERSPECTIVES

Type of sociology: Social stratification
Field of study: Theoretical perspectives on stratification

Social stratification is the hierarchical arrangement of social groups. Marxist perspectives generally regard modern society as being divided primarily into two classes—the bourgeoisie and the proletariat—on the basis of property ownership or nonownership of property.

Principal terms

BOURGEOISIE: the modern social class, also known as the capitalist class, which owns the means of production, employs wage-labor, and has profit as its source of income

CLASS: a fundamental social group determined by its economic relationship to the means of production in terms of ownership and nonownership and in terms of producing or nonproducing

CLASS CONSCIOUSNESS: an awareness of belonging to a definite socioeconomic class and a conscious sharing of the political interests of that class

CLASS STRUGGLE: the historical conflict between the oppressors and the oppressed; in modern society, the antagonism existing between the bourgeoisie and the working class

EXPLOITATION: the extraction of unpaid labor from the working class

MODE OF PRODUCTION: a distinct structure of economic relations composed of the form of property ownership and the arrangement between the producing and nonproducing classes

PROLETARIAT: the modern social class that is composed of the nonowning working class; the proletariat produces commodities and derives its income from wages that it has obtained in return for its labor

RELATIONS OF PRODUCTION: the structure of economic relations or the way in which people are related to one another in the production process and in terms of property ownership

Overview

Although class theory and the idea of class struggle are associated with the nineteenth century German philosopher Karl Marx, these ideas did not originate with him. He admitted as much in a letter written in 1852: "no credit is due to me for discovering the existence of classes in modern society, nor yet the struggle between them." In fact, Marx never fully set forth a systematic theory of social classes. He did, however, appear to begin a manuscript on social classes that appears at the end of *Das Kapital* (1867; *Capital: A Critique of Political Economy*, 1886), where he stated, following classical political economy, that modern society is made up of three classes: wage-laborers, capitalists, and landowners. They are differentiated by their respective sources of income: wages, profit, and ground-rent. Laborers live on wages, capitalists on profits, and landlords on rent. Marx goes on to say that class differentiation based on sources of revenue would result in an unnecessary multiplication of classes. At this point, the manuscript suddenly breaks off.

In *Der achtzehnte Brumaire des Louis Bonaparte* (1852; *The Eighteenth Brumaire of Louis Bonaparte*, 1852), Marx offers a provisional definition of class: "In so far as millions of families live under economic conditions of existence that separate their mode of life, their interests, and their culture from those of the other classes, and put them in hostile opposition to the latter, they form a class." Thus, economic conditions determine class formation. In addition, classes stand in antagonistic relations with one another.

Generally, Marx understood classes to be economically determined by the difference between the owners of the means of production and the nonowning direct producers. In his words: "it is always the direct relation between the owners of the conditions of production and the direct producers which reveals the innermost secret, the hidden foundation, of the entire social edifice" (*Das Kapital*).

Class differences, therefore, are determined by the mode of production. Marx and Friedrich Engels have divided history into five distinct epochs of production: primitive communism, Asiatic, ancient Greece and Rome, feudal society, and capitalism, or the bourgeois. Of these only the ancient, the feudal, and the bourgeois receive special treatment. Ancient society was based on slavery, feudal society on serfdom, and capitalism on wage-labor.

Each of these societies was divided into two major classes: the oppressors and the oppressed, or the exploiters and the exploited. In every case, the exploiters are made up of those who own the means of production but do not produce. The exploited are those who do not own the means of production but are the direct producers of social goods and services. Because the exploited do not own the means of production, they are forced, in order to live, to work for those who own and control the productive conditions of life. The exploiters live by means of the surplus produced by the exploited. As a result, the social mode of production also reproduces the social relations of production. Thus, the relationship between the exploiters and the exploited is constantly renewed and conserved.

The two fundamental economic classes in modern society, according to Marx, are the bourgeoisie and the proletariat. The bourgeoisie is the capitalist class—the class that owns the conditions of production. The proletariat is the nonowning class that sells its labor to the capitalist class for wages. The capital-labor relationship, therefore, is a wage relationship.

It should be pointed out that Marx never equated all workers with the proletariat. Marx made a distinction, typical of classical political economy, between productive labor and unproductive labor. Productive labor is labor purchased by wages and utilized in the production process to produce commodities the surplus value of which accedes to the capitalist a profit over and beyond the outlay in labor and means of production. Unproductive labor is service that is exchanged for a fee. This service does not yield a profit to the buyer but is consumed. For example, a laborer making pianos in a piano factory undertakes productive labor and is therefore a proletarian. A piano player who is employed to play music at a wedding, although receiving a fee, is not making profit for the employer and is therefore not a proletarian. It is important to remember that, from a Marxist perspective, the proletariat does not include all workers. It should also be understood that capitalist production includes intellectual and cultural production as well as material production. In the words of Hal Draper (1978), "There is a whole sphere of intellectual or mental production that is proletarian."

Capitalist social relations are marked by a distinctive contradiction: the contradiction between social production and private appropriation. The mass production of commodities is produced by masses of laborers working in cooperative forms, yet ownership of those commodities belongs to the capitalist class. This contradiction is the heart of the exploitative relationship.

Jon Elster, a Norwegian philosopher and Marx scholar, insists that class denotes a relationship of exploitation: "class . . . is the collective social expression of the fact of exploitation, the way in which exploitation is embodied in a social structure" (1985). Exploitation is the private appropriation of social labor. Thus, from a Marxist perspective, the ending of exploitation means abolishing the existence of social classes, and particularly, the capital-labor relationship.

This goal implies struggle, but the proletariat will not struggle until it attains a certain level of class consciousness. More than any other Marxist theoretician, György Lukács, a Hungarian Marxist philosopher, attributed crucial importance to the development of class consciousness. In his important work *Geschichte und Klassenbewusstsein* (1923; *History and Class Consciousness*, 1971), Lukács made a significant distinction between actual class consciousness and imputed class consciousness. By actual class consciousness, Lukács means what members of a definite class really think. By imputed class consciousness, Lukács recognizes the fact that while the working class may not actually think correctly about economic reality and political facts (that is, may not have class consciousness), the working class would have class consciousness if it had all the facts; it would then think in a revolutionary manner. Class consciousness refers to the conscious interests shared by members of a class by virtue of their class position. Class consciousness is absolutely indispensable for organization, mobilization, and political activity. The absence of class consciousness is referred to as false consciousness. Trade union activity is the best way to instill class consciousness and to get workers to participate in class struggle, but there is a debate in Marxism regarding whether class consciousness is a necessary feature of class definition or of class conflict.

In *Manifest du Kommunistischen Partei* (1848; *The Communist Manifesto*, 1850), Marx and Engels asserted the idea that class conflict was the driving force of history: "The history of all hitherto existing society is the history of class struggles." Class struggle is the essential relationship between oppressors and oppressed. In modern society, the struggle is the antagonistic relationship between the bourgeoisie and the proletariat. In the *Manifesto*, Marx and Engels claim that the modern epoch "has simplified the class antagonism: Society as a whole is more and more splitting up into two great hostile camps, into two great classes directly facing each other: Bourgeoisie and Proletariat."

The essential interests in this conflict are those involving exploitation and resistance to exploitation. The political interests of the bourgeoisie are to conserve the social relationships based on economic exploitation. The interests of the proletariat are to resist the exploitation of the bourgeoisie and to overthrow a society based on the division of classes. One must be careful to note that these interests are the interests imputed to these classes by virtue of their structural position and not actual conscious interest known to the members of the bourgeoisie and the proletariat.

The struggles between classes constitute one of the major causes of historical societal change. As Jon Elster puts it: "Classes should be defined by what people have to do, not by what they actually do."

Applications

Various questions that have been raised by Marxist social theory have to do with its explanatory power. To what extent does the theory of classes and class conflict help explain historical social changes? Does the Marxist theory of social classes correspond to the actual form of social stratification in modern society? Does the Marxist theory of social stratification apply to all epochs or only to modern capitalism? Are historical changes really explained by the theory of class struggle? Are the bourgeoisie and the proletariat the two major social classes in modern society? What about the middle classes? What about other social forces that account for historical change, such as nationalism, racism, imperialism, and the women's movement?

From 1844 until his death in 1883, Marx grappled with the political economy of capitalist society. He wanted to uncover the logic of capitalism, the motivating forces of modern society. To that extent, his class analysis is basically applicable only to modern capitalist society. The bourgeoisie and the proletariat are social products of the modern industrial era.

Perhaps the most oft-repeated criticism of Marxism is that which questions Marx's theory about the increasing widening in the lifestyles between the bourgeoisie and the proletariat. It is believed that Marx claimed that the working classes would become more impoverished as capitalism progressed. Not only has the gulf not widened, say the critics, but the working classes are better off than ever. Marx, however, was not speaking in absolute terms or in solely materialistic terms. He was speaking in relative and spiritual terms. That is, relative to its output, the return of the working class in the form of wages would decrease. In addition, the world of commodities created by capital does not allow for the full development of human beings as human beings. Instead workers become alienated.

Along similar lines, critics claim that Marx's theory cannot account for the rise of the middle classes. In *Das Kapital*, however, in the unfinished manuscript on social classes, Marx does recognize other strata besides the major social classes. In another work, Marx claims that bourgeois society tends to give rise to new middle classes. In a few places, Marx and Engels claimed that the intermediate strata between the bourgeoisie and the proletariat would disappear. According to Tom Bottomore, the growth of the new middle classes—office workers, technicians, and so forth—interposes between the bourgeoisie and the proletariat a whole range of status groups. Such a range, or continuum, according to Bottomore, based on factors other than property ownership, would deflate the theory of class conflict. Bottomore believes, however, that Marx's theory of classes is less falsifiable than are other theories of social stratification. For example, if one accepts the continuum theory of social stratification, then one has to account for the possibility of nonarbitrary division in the continuum between extremes. Jon Elster (1985) asks the interesting question "When does an individual own enough property to be considered no longer a worker but a capitalist?"

Property ownership in Marxist terms becomes a thorny issue. It is not so simple to divide society into property owners and the propertyless. Corporate property, profit sharing, and other such financial assets pose problems. Do stockholders own property or do they only have entitlements to shares of dividends? Is the source of power in the ownership of property or in the management of property? Although these questions are difficult to answer, it cannot be denied that Marx's fundamental principle is incontestable—the masses of people can only survive by selling their labor power on the market for wages. As long as this remains true, Marxist theory is applicable.

Context

As noted above, Marx did not invent the term "class" or the idea of class struggle. The Marxist idea of social stratification in class terms was rooted in classical political economy on the one hand and in the socialist literature of nineteenth century Europe on the other hand. "Class" and "class struggle" are explanatory terms.

As mentioned above, other historians have used the terms "class" and "class struggle." These terms were used in socialist literature as well as in classical political economy. Political economy centered on the question "What is the source of value?" In the medieval period, the Scholastics spoke of the just price; they believed that remuneration should be proportionate to outlay and effort. For the Mercantilists, value came to be identified with the customary price or the market price. The Physiocrats equated value with agricultural labor or the labor costs in agricultural production. Eventually, political economists began to identify value with production costs in manufacturing. In other words, labor was seen as the creator of social wealth. In their analyses of the economy, Adam Smith and David Ricardo divided society into three major classes: the capitalists, the landowners, and the laborers. Neither writer, however, elaborated on the exploitative relationship existing between the property-owning class and the propertyless working class. This was left to Marx.

Marx, as editor of the *Rheinische Zeitung* between 1842 and 1844, dealt with discussions, proceedings, and debates on such economic questions as wood theft, landed property, the conditions of the peasantry, and free trade and tariffs. It was not until his 1844 critical review of Georg Hegel's *Grundlinien der Philosophie des Rechts* (1821; *Philosophy of Right*, 1875), however, that Marx began to apply historical materialism to the study of society. In that work, Marx set forth the claim that legal relations and forms of state have their origin in the material conditions of life. At that time, Marx also became acquainted with Friedrich Engels, who had published his article "The Condition of the Working Class in England." Marx began using the term "class" in 1844. In his critique of Hegel, he wrote, "A class must be formed which has radical chains, a class in civil society which is not a class of civil society, a class which is the dissolution of all classes . . . the proletariat." In the *Ökonomische und philoso-phische Manuskripte* (1844; *Economic and Philosophic Manuscripts of 1844*, 1947), Marx began a criticism of classical political economy. While agreeing with the idea of classical political economy that society falls into two classes— the property-owners and the propertyless workers—Marx criticized classical political economy for failing to consider the direct relationship between the worker and production. In this relation-ship is found the core of capitalism—the antagonism between the capitalist class and the working class. In 1847, Marx asserted that the capital-labor relationship is the inner contradiction of capitalist society that will eventually culminate in the dissolution of that society.

Max Weber contrasted Marx's notion of classes with his own notion of *Stand*, or status group. *Stand* designates social rank and explains collective action in ways that class alone cannot. Collective action, according to Weber, must be accounted for in terms of the lifestyles and cultures of social groups. The latter not only determine the rise of ideas but also explain group behavior on the basis of honor, privileges, and distinctions attributed to social situations. For Weber, class is only an economic category and explains market behavior exclusively. Weber did not accept class as the sole explanatory force.

Bibliography

Bottomore, T. B., et al., eds. *Classes in Modern Society*. New York: Pantheon Books, 1966. This fine little book is a study of social classes in modern industrial society. Inequality and social hierarchy are considered from a Marxist perspective.

_____ . *A Dictionary of Marxist Thought*. Cambridge, Mass.: Harvard University Press, 1983. This is the only work of its kind. Key terms and important figures in Marxism are dealt with expertly by the top scholars in the field.

Draper, Hal. *The Politics of Social Classes*. Vol. 2 in *Karl Marx's Theory of Revolution*. New York: Monthly Review Press, 1978. This work constitutes a studious and comprehensive look at Marx's theory of proletarian revolution.

Elster, Jon. *Making Sense of Marx*. Cambridge, England: Cambridge University Press, 1985. Elster's book is a critical examination of Marx's major ideas from the point of view of the analytic philosophy.

Tucker, Robert C., ed. *The Marx-Engels Reader*. 2d ed. New York: W. W. Norton,

1978. This is the best paperback anthology of the writing of Marx and Engels. Contained in this volume are letters, economic writings, political analyses, philosophical treatises, and the later writings of Engels.

Michael Candelaria

Cross-References
Conflict Theory, 340; Embourgeoisement and Proletarianization, 633; Marxism, 1127; Racial and Ethnic Stratification, 1579; Social Mobility: Analysis and Overview, 1812; Social Stratification: Functionalist Perspectives, 1845; Social Stratification: Modern Theories, 1859; Social Stratification: Weberian Perspectives, 1866.

SOCIAL STRATIFICATION: MODERN THEORIES

Type of sociology: Social stratification
Fields of study: Maintaining inequality; Theoretical perspectives on stratification

All societies are organized with at least some degree of hierarchy, and most modern societies have rather rigid distinctions between the classes. Theorists have developed a wide range of ideas with which to explain this phenomenon, and some modern theories engage the strengths of both functionalist and materialist (or Marxist) perspectives.

Principal terms

CLASS: a broadly defined category, measured in social and economic terms, that indicates one's access to social resources and other goods as well as one's range of social options in life

DIFFERENTIAL ACCESS TO RESOURCES: the situation in which some people can attain more of a certain good than others can because of social factors that define what different people can receive

PRESTIGE: a measure of the worth of persons as attributed by others and manifested in systems of privilege and respect that function within hierarchies between persons

SOCIAL CONFLICT: the struggle over values and resources between disparate social groups in which groups perceive the goods to be limited and thus seek exclusive control over all or part of the goods

SOCIAL MOBILITY: the ability, through any of a variety of social mechanisms, to replace one's membership in a socioeconomic class with affiliation in another class

STRATIFICATION: a social process by which societies form classes and other distinct categories for persons through differential distribution of goods and resources

STRUCTURED INEQUALITY: systems in which society limits some persons' access to social resources in permanent ways, leaving them unable to attain certain goals valued by the society at large

UNDERCLASS: a class that permanently occupies the lower rungs of a society, with little or no chance for upward social mobility

Overview

One of the more obvious features of any society is its construction of inequality. Any sort of division of labor seems to lead inexorably to differences in power and prestige. Many historians and sociologists have attempted to explain these differences. Ancient philosophers and historians usually justified inequalities by claiming that they stemmed from natural differences between people; such thinking survives to the present day, although this approach is now often recognized as being racist and elitist.

Functionalist sociologists emphasized the inevitability of different tasks existing within a complex society. Since these different tasks are perceived as having different levels of value and pleasantness, functionalists argued, a system of stratification allows a reward system for the inequities. For example, since being a physician takes great skill and energy, physicians rightly receive more financial reward to compensate them for performing this vital and difficult task. Marxist theory took an opposing approach to the problem of stratification, connecting class formation with the unequal acquisition of material goods, property, and power. Some persons possess more goods and wealth than others, and they use this possession to acquire still more; this process leads to increasing conflict and inequality. To many sociologists, both of these theoretical orientations ultimately prove unsatisfactory, because they depict societies as either too harmonious or too self-destructive; in reality, societies persevere and endure, though in sometimes discordant fashion.

Ralf Dahrendorf developed notions of stratification that included both the institutional gains of stratification and the conflict inherent in societal inequalities. He perceived that every society institutionalizes power and that this power enforces societal sanctions in differential ways, creating unequal distributions of resources. Thus, stratification results from the presence of power. Those with power gradually increase their prestige and wealth, but power is not the only social force at work. If the upper classes were to redistribute wealth too unequally, the economy would shut itself down from the imbalance. Thus, the presence of power both creates the class system and sows the seeds of its demise. Societies persist in the dialectic between the classes, with constant redistributions of power creating a continuing flux of goods that define the classes.

In a similar vein, Lewis Coser examined the role of social conflict, arguing that conflict not only is the mark of social dissolution but also produces other social functions, such as the maintenance of social boundaries and the prevention of withdrawal from groups. Conflict sharpens the identity of each group within the society, encouraging it to fulfill its particular function. Conflict, therefore, not only is a factor for change, as different groups compete for and win access to resources, but also maintains the society by balancing the competing groups against one another and encouraging adherence to a specific group. Stratification results from the institutionalization of such necessary and productive social conflict.

Both Dahrendorf and Coser note the investment of all levels of society in maintaining the status quo. The classes are interdependent. The slave owner, for example, depends on the slave for food and economic production; the slave depends on the slave owner for the survival of the economic entity that keeps all of them alive. Thus, both slave and owner share an investment in the perpetuation of the system, even though they participate in the system of structured inequality in very different ways. The interconnection of the stratified class system moves toward stability, but the power differentials result in the constant presence of change. Thus, stratification theory can explain both stability and change in ways preferable to Marxist or functionalist theories alone.

Stratification, therefore, applies to a wide variety of societal phenomena that separate one class from another. In other words, societies can stratify whenever a certain social variable correlates with differential access to resources. Clearly, the United States represents a highly stratified society with a large number of parameters connected to stratified difference. For example, there are clear connections between income and factors such as race, ethnicity, and gender. Language of birth also plays a strong factor in social stratification. Education levels represent another form of stratification, since there is differential access to educational resources and since education in turn produces differential access to larger societal resources such as income; occupation is similarly correlated. In a larger sense, income and wealth are the chief factors in stratification in the United States. With money, one has access to almost any social resource, regardless of education, race, gender, age, or other factors. Analytically, therefore, one can see stratification when any other social variable correlates to income differences between groups of people.

In American society most individuals believe in the possibility of social mobility. Most persons feel that they could better their standard of living, over time, if they could meet the requirements for improving their lot in life. American ideology emphasizes rags-to-riches stories, in which it is possible for anyone to climb the ladder of social success. These expectations may well function as a justification for the system, but they also reflect the real possibility of changing one's own life in the stratification system. The chances for change may be remote, but they are present. The increasing stratification of American society, however, is decreasing the instances of social mobility and thus is creating a more rigidly divided society in keeping with the general tendency for stratification to grow over time.

Applications

The most severe examples of social stratification occur in caste societies. In these settings, one's biography is almost completely determined at birth by the status of one's lineage. After that, one merely lives out the life of the social grouping to which one belongs. There is no opportunity for social mobility, and in many caste systems there is only minimal chance for any sort of consistent or meaningful social contact between members of differing castes. Modern societies do not have caste systems, but some stratified societies exhibit many of the same characteristics.

One might consider as an example what Lewis Coser terms the "greedy institution." This term refers to the social organization that demands undivided commitment from its members. It creates a role set mandating that all of the individual's behaviors conform to the expectations of the institution. Coser develops cases such as a celibate priest's renunciation of other social roles in order to emphasize his servitude to the church. Members of greedy institutions are clear examples of social stratification. Such stratification allows access to some societal goods but not to others; the limits are clearly and rigidly delineated. Furthermore, there are connections between the access to goods and the education and gender of the role participant, if not also race, class, and other factors. Roles within greedy institutions tend toward low social mobility; once one trains for and attains a role within such a social location, it is very difficult to transfer to other roles in the larger society. This example demonstrates many of the aspects of stratification within a group that is somewhat marginalized but still in contact with the wider range of the society's institutions.

The United States has developed a welfare system that provides a social and economic safety net for its citizens; however, according to many experts, the development of the welfare system has generally paralleled the birth of a permanent underclass at the bottom of the system of social stratification. In this case, stratification has occurred along several lines at once. The American underclass consists of a higher proportion of racial and ethnic minorities than other classes within American society. There are also more women than men in the underclass' perpetual poverty. (Throughout the culture, in fact, women tend toward lower earning potential.) Members of the permanent underclass are rarely able to afford the higher levels of education that can increase the opportunities for social mobility, and this relative lack tends to repeat itself through the generations. The chronic unemployment and underemployment within this class result in less acquisition of skills that could result in higher opportunities for employment or significant income. With little preventive health care, this class is more susceptible to debilitating medical problems and to the high costs and reduced income associated with them. Together, it has been argued, these factors produce a self-perpetuating underclass, separated from other classes in American society through a rather rigid social stratification.

Such extensive examples of multivariate stratification occur in complex modern societies with highly evolved systems of hierarchy and privilege in response to the presence of high amounts (even "surplus") of resources. Nevertheless, stratification is a feature of every society. Even hunting and gathering societies undergo social stratification as a result of the differential distribution of goods. In a subsistence economy, the details of stratification involve a very different dynamic. All members of the social economy must work in the production of food, so the division of labor is only slightly differentiated. Everyone farms, gathers food, or fishes, but some individuals learn and practice additional part-time specialties, such as medicine, trade, or religion. These extra occupations frequently produce high amounts of prestige and greater access to resources, so they can lead to the same sort of stratification as that possible in much more complex societies.

Context
Early sociological theories about class included sharp differences between Marxist and functionalist views. Functionalism emphasized the ways in which different classes contribute to the stability of society as each class maintains its own niche within the overall social structure. On the other hand, the Marxist and materialist views concentrated on the differential distribution of resources and access to wealth. They identified this inequity as the cause of a struggle between self-interested classes. Modern stratification theories made possible a synthesis of these extremes.

Functionalism believes norms and values to be more influential than power in determining human action. According to functionalism, norms work in a stabilizing fashion within a system of equilibrization, whereas nonfunctionalist theories see norms as socially negotiated through power systems that operate as means of social control. Likewise, human agency, which allows variation as well as historical change, is discounted. This exacerbates functionalism's overly stable view of society, which was a problem in functionalist theories about class. On the other hand, Marxist views were quite capable of explaining change. By viewing class relations as conflict over a limited amount of material goods and the means of their production and reproduction, Marxist theories demonstrated how differences produce class conflict and thus change involved in redistribution of resources. Both extremes were problematic. Societies change in ways that functionalism could not well explain, yet class divisions have a tendency to maintain their inequality much more tenaciously than Marxist theory could tolerate.

Subsequent theories of stratification have solved the dilemma between these opposing theoretical views by emphasizing the ability of classes to maintain conflicting interests through antagonistic but interrelated participation in the larger society. These macrosociological views allow for the integration of stability and change, antagonism and functional maintenance into a larger perspective. Thus, such theories have explanatory power over both stable and changing social systems.

The future of stratification theories lies within a growing ability to explain the different factors that lead to social division and structured inequality. In American society, the creation of a permanent underclass involves economic, educational, political, and racial factors. Stratification theories must be able to sort through these many issues and explain the wide range of social experiences that exist in complex, stratified societies.

Bibliography

Coser, Lewis A. *Continuities in the Study of Social Conflict*. New York: Free Press, 1967. This book details certain refinements of Coser's social conflict theories in the decade after the publication of his classic book, *The Functions of Social Conflict* (1956). He pays more attention here to issues of violence and deviance, and he develops further the theoretical connections between his own work and that of Marx and Émile Durkheim. He also draws some conclusions about sources of social conflict at the time of his writing.

_____ . *The Functions of Social Conflict*. Glencoe, Ill.: Free Press, 1956. This book offers what is arguably twentieth century American sociology's classic study of conflict. Coser builds chiefly from the earlier work of Georg Simmel and develops a thorough sociological interpretation of the destructive and functional results of social conflict.

Dahrendorf, Ralf. *Class and Class Conflict in Industrial Society*. Stanford, Calif.: Stanford University Press, 1959. This was Dahrendorf's first large foray into the field of class and conflict. Beginning with Marx's class analysis, he explains and critiques the Marxist view before attempting his own construction. His theory of classes in "post-capitalist society" have proved to be of great significance within sociology.

_____ . *Essays in the Theory of Society*. Stanford, Calif.: Stanford University Press, 1968. This anthology contains many of Dahrendorf's classic theoretical statements and thus provides a larger methodological context for his development of social conflict. Dahrendorf criticizes the dominant functionalist models for their inabilities to deal with conflict and change, among other issues. Though it can be difficult reading because of its heavily theoretical orientation, it is an excellent resource for in-depth work in sociology and offers some particularly pertinent remarks about the origins of inequality.

_____ . *The Modern Social Conflict: An Essay on the Politics of Liberty*. New York: Weidenfeld & Nicolson, 1988. This contribution by Dahrendorf details applications of his social conflict theories for a new time, specifically examining the ramifications of social conflict theory for understanding the politics of industrial and international development. He also comments on the nature of social conflict apart from class theory.

Eisenstadt, S. N. *Social Differentiation and Stratification*. Glenview, Ill.: Scott, Foresman, 1971. Eisenstadt analyzes patterns of social stratification in a range of modern societies. China, Russia, and India form the context for special examples. The author's macrosociological perspective proves profitable in the investigation of class, elites, mobility, and equality.

Jackson, John A., ed. *Social Stratification*. London: Cambridge University Press, 1968. Though this anthology shows its age, it contains some excellent articles on stratification and class formation, with strong contributions by Erik Allardt, W. G. Runciman, S. N. Eisenstadt, and Edward Shils. There are also articles offering specific analyses of Britain, West Germany, Poland, and Australia.

Lenski, Gerhard E. *Power and Privilege: A Theory of Social Stratification*. New York: McGraw-Hill, 1966. Lenski's contribution contains sharp theoretical insights, especially concerning the connections of technology and economy. Of special value is the author's careful analysis of stratification systems in a range of historical societies from hunting and gathering societies through modern, late-industrial economies.

McNall, Scott G., Rhonda F. Levine, and Rick Fantasia, eds. *Bringing Class Back in Contemporary and Historical Perspectives*. Boulder, Colo.: Westview Press, 1991. This anthology offers a variety of poststructuralist views on class, conflict, and ideology. Most of the examples are American, with some additional studies on Europe. The articles feature extensive bibliographies current to 1991, so this book functions as an excellent starting point for in-depth research into the concepts and ideologies of class and stratification.

Rossides, Daniel W. *Social Stratification: The American Class System in Comparative Perspective*. Englewood Cliffs, N.J.: Prentice-Hall, 1990. This thorough textbook provides an understanding of the basic factors of stratification, such as economics, class systems, education, health, occupation, gender, ethnicity, and race. Examples include American and, to a lesser extent, Soviet societies. A highly useful study for information about class differences and the process of class stratification, especially in modern American society.

Jon L. Berquist

Cross-References

Age Grading and Age Stratification, 27; Caste Systems, 198; Conflict Theory, 340; Functionalism, 786; Racial and Ethnic Stratification, 1579; Racism as an Ideology, 1586; Social Stratification: Analysis and Overview, 1839; Social Stratification: Functionalist Perspectives, 1845; Social Stratification: Marxist Perspectives, 1852; Social Stratification: Weberian Perspectives, 1866.

SOCIAL STRATIFICATION: WEBERIAN PERSPECTIVES

Type of sociology: Social stratification
Field of study: Theoretical perspectives on stratification

The pioneering German sociologist Max Weber showed how the many layers and ranks in capitalistic Western societies are defined by people's skills, credentials, market relationships, and property ownership—and by other determiners of stratification such as status and party. Weber rejected Karl Marx's view that the class conflicts inherent in capitalism were simplistic and could be resolved by socialism.

Principal terms
BOURGEOISIE: the middle-class, property-owning social class
BUREAUCRACY: a goal-focused administrative system emphasizing specialized duties, fixed rules, hierarchy or rank, and chain of command
CAPITALISM: an economic system featuring private or corporate ownership, investment free from state control, and a free market system that controls prices, production, and distribution
ENTREPRENEUR: an investor who undertakes a business venture
IDEAL TYPE: an abstract case or situation; a hypothetical construct that makes it possible to generalize about real social experiences
RATIONALIZATION: in the Weberian sense, using formal procedures and rules (as in a bureaucracy) instead of informal, spontaneous patterns
SOCIAL MOBILITY: the capacity to improve one's class standing
SOCIAL STRATUM: a level of society based on class, race, or economic condition; stratification thus means division into layers or levels
VERSTEHEN: empathic (interpretive) understanding; Weber's main goal as a social analyst

Overview

Social "stratification" is an imperfect analogy because it suggests that the many layers of society—representing its identifiable groups—are like the stacked strata in geological formations. No one wants to be at the "bottom of the heap," yet some always are, because they lack power, money, property, respect, status, or marketable skills. Theorists study the makeup of society by identifying and defining the many social strata that exist and by explaining their origins, causes, features, and effects. The writings of the renowned German sociologist Max Weber (1864-1920) shed light on many aspects of social stratification.

Throughout history, societies have exhibited various systems of layered subdivision based on cultural values and economic organization. While historians and anthropologists focus on the past, sociologists examine modern Western societies, whose dominant economic patterns have been capitalistic. Weber's own interests ranged broadly over past and present, but his ideas have direct, ongoing implications for studies of modern social stratification.

Weber discussed all three major forms of social stratification: classes, castes, and estates. A class is defined in the *International Encyclopedia of Sociology* (1984) as "a form of social stratification in which allocation to, membership of, and relationships between classes are governed by economic considerations rather than law (as in *estates*) or religion and ritual pollution (as in *caste*)." Before the Renaissance, the established division into three estates (commoners, nobility, and clergy) officially described social organization in Europe. Social class, the most important factor in the stratification of modern free societies, was an aspect of some early societies—the Romans used the term to differentiate degrees of wealth—but its modern sense dates from the Industrial Revolution in the eighteenth century, when the capitalist system of social organization solidified in Western Europe. The prominence of the middle class and entrepreneurship are characteristic of capitalism.

As Wolfgang Mommsen (1989) points out, the sociological results of the advance of modern industrial capitalism are the focus of much of Weber's writing. Weber thoroughly described the complex ways in which capitalistic societies subdivide themselves into socioeconomic classes, combining the viewpoints of economist and sociologist in his analysis of stratification. Discussing what he called "rational bourgeois capitalism," Weber showed how people's economic behaviors determined their social ranking; "rational" is a complex and ambivalent modifier, suggesting "quantifiable," "calculating," "sensible," "systematic," and "opportunistic." Such aspects of the economic market as distribution and consumption of goods dominated Weber's theory of stratification: People can improve their social standings in a mobile society by having marketable goods and services, and by exploiting the existing system in order to market them profitably.

In *Wirtschaft und Gesellschaft* (1922; *Economy and Society*, 1968), Weber defines and analyzes three overlapping class categories: property classes, which are determined by property ownership; commercial (or acquisition) classes, which are determined by the marketability of services, goods, and skills; social classes, which are characterized by social mobility and a sense of community (involving shared lifestyles and ideas about honor). Yet another of Weber's systems for categorizing class included four types: the working class; the petite bourgeoisie; specialists and intelligentsia (propertyless technicians, civil servants, and "white-collar" workers); and classes that are privileged because they have "property and education." The complexity of Weber's multiple classification systems is apparent.

Weber noted that members of classes do not always have a sense of class membership but do often act collectively in their own interests. Property ownership or the lack of it is, for Weber, the main determinant in class membership, but he notes that other determinants of social stratification include types of property that people own, the types of income they yield, and the types of services that individuals provide. Weber sees community power as being affected not only by class but also by status groups and parties. The former have prestige; the latter have memberships that may cut across economic, status, or class lines.

The origins of capitalism in Weber's view are closely tied to the "Protestant," or "work," ethic, an example of idealism that has practical implications. Capitalism itself, once in force, exerts social determinism, for people must adapt to the roles that the system creates: management, middle managers, and workers; producers and consumers; monopolists and outsiders; haves and have-nots; property owners and the landless.

Though hierarchical power structures have always existed in societies, the capitalistic bureaucracy is a distinctly modern feature of Western society that, Weber thought, would always limit ideal democracy. New elite groups would constantly be emerging in the modern bureaucratic systems according to which businesses and governments operate.

Applications

Merely by looking around, one can easily demonstrate Weber's basic belief that the multiple social categories in modern societies are defined by complex economic factors. Many of Weber's own examples of social stratification, however, come from historical situations and analyses of historical class conflicts. In those early prototypes, one can often see analogies with modern situations, whether or not Weber points them out specifically.

In his *General Economic History* (1966), Weber notes that the ancient Roman "knighthood" was a social group operating, in effect, according to the principles of "modern rationalistic capitalism." The group analyzed market opportunities and responded to "mass demand," finding ways to meet "mass need." Group members detected various unmet needs of the state and then offered to meet them, for a price—by lending money, for example, to support government ventures. These knights were in conflict with the "official" Roman nobility.

Modern examples of "rationalistic capitalists" who can move quickly into new positions of high social rank include movie stars, rock stars, sports superstars, and television personalities, whose status comes from their ability to provide services that society values.

More generally, Weber shows how in earlier societies the traditional aristocracy—dominant patrician families—gradually lost power to the rising populace, the future middle class. This segment of the population included not only entrepreneurs and artisans but also knights with "status pride." Conflicts between the various bourgeois classes and the status classes inevitably emerged—and they continue to do so in modern times. Middle-class families, for example, may encourage their children to pursue lifestyles that are at odds with the values of the superstars whom the general culture idolizes. In countries such as Great Britain, clashes may occur between traditional aristocrats (who may not have money) and the newly rich (who lack traditional status).

In modern societies, families with both wealth and "family charisma" (such as the Rockefellers and Kennedys in America) enjoy class advantages that grow from more than just the family's economic status. The idea of "charisma" is one of Weber's contributions to sociology and to the modern vocabulary describing social influence. The power of the Kennedy family, particularly, can be attributed partly to the "charismatic" appeal of John Kennedy. Similarly, the "charisma" of superstars such as Elvis or the Beatles or Madonna is an important aspect of their socioeconomic power and cultural prestige.

As a sociologist of religion, Weber studied societies such as India in which the caste system operates. Weber specifically compared the ancient Indian system to the newer one in the American South (of the period c. 1910-1920), with its "white" and "black" coach cars and waiting rooms. American attempts at social integration since Weber's death have effectively eliminated the rigid element of caste, but many class differentiations remain to divide peoples of various colors, statuses, and economic conditions—supporting Weber's doubt that a fully democratic or "classless" society can ever emerge. Still, as Weber notes, the marketability of one's skills becomes a main determiner of social standing, so those born into families without property or status can "rise" if they use the capitalistic framework shrewdly to cultivate skills that are in demand. The emergence of a "black middle class" in the United States since World War II illustrates this pattern.

Weber's analysis of Judaism provides a different historical example of social stratification. Jews lived in caste-free societies but were ritually separated from all other classes. In the stratified context in which Jewishness first coalesced, Weber detected various social groups—desert Bedouins, city-dwelling patricians, artisans, merchants, and so on. Important in the uniquely emerging self-concept of the Jews was the idea of *berith*, an "oath-bound league." Since the Jews' pact was essentially with God, Weber believed that they enjoyed the stability that religious orders have traditionally exhibited—as opposed to the more volatile political alliances that have tended to come and go throughout history. In Weber's analysis, the early pattern of exile and the development of an intellectual tradition further contributed to the peculiar social history of the Jews. The shift of Jews into their "rational capitalistic" roles as the moneylenders of Europe was a later development in their cultural odyssey.

Julien Freund, in *The Sociology of Max Weber* (1968), explains Weber's notion that any socioeconomic group can be closed (like that of the Jews) or open. Historically, among the closed groups were the guilds, which functioned as monopolies. Within the groups, various levels (apprentices and masters, for example) established social stratification. Social strata such as "peasants, nobles, traders, liberal professions," and religious fraternities have traditionally had specific economic functions. Modern groups that are still relatively closed include those of physicians, lawyers, college teachers, members of Congress, and street gang members. It is possible, however, to enter into any of these groups by "rationally" working toward that end.

Trying to exemplify what the term "middle class" (or bourgeoisie) means in the Weberian sense is difficult. The group can be defined by separating out the "positively privileged property classes" (which live from income derived from their property), on the top end, and "negatively privileged" classes (including debtors, the poor, outcasts), on the bottom. People left "in the middle" are those who own various kinds of property or have marketable abilities from which they draw their livelihoods. The American middle class comprises many subcategories. Weber shows that, although a main factor in determining one's social class is the market value of what one does or owns, various status factors move beyond pure economics. Thus, priests, ministers, and college professors—who belong to the economic middle class because they are paid for marketable services—tend to have status that transcends economic class.

Context

Among Weber's important general concepts, according to Martin Albrow (1990), are the principles that people's actions in society can be understood best by looking at their motives, and that people are always self-responsible, are influenced by ideas, and are constrained by dominant patterns of social organization—which establish both opportunities and limits. These almost self-evident principles belie the complex ways in which Weber explored their implications.

After an early university career in economics, Weber was for two decades a private writer and scholar—following a mental breakdown in 1897. In his last several years, he resumed public life as a university professor of sociology at Vienna (1918) and Munich (1919), writing numerous pieces on a vast array of interconnected subjects—economics, history, law, philosophy, religion, and sociology. Most of his unfinished works were published posthumously. His major writings include *Die Protestantische Ethik und der Geist des Kapitalismus* (1904; *The Protestant Ethic and the Spirit of Capitalism*, 1930) and *Wirtschaft und Gesellschaft* (1922; *Economy and Society*, 1968). As Donald G. MacRae (1974) emphasizes, certain unique features of Weber's sociology—including his concern with bureaucracy—can be explained by examining the sociopolitical features of German society before and after 1900. Harvard professor Talcott Parsons' *The Structure of Social Action* (1937) helped to spread Weber's ideas and fame outside Germany.

Weber's historical and comparative studies of expansive institutional patterns are unequaled and remain influential. His subtle writings tend to use self-defined terminologies, however, and are hard to summarize. Hans H. Gerth and C. Wright Mills, in *From Max Weber: Essays in Sociology* (1946), observe that Weber's German sentences are built like Gothic castles. Disagreements about the meaning, accuracy, and value of Weber's ideas abound, and all generalizations about his views risk inaccuracy, especially because he was himself skeptical about the capacity of sociology to get at the truth.

Weber believed that "real" truth lay only in the actions of single individuals, that "social reality" did not really exist. He believed, however, that the use of "ideal types" could help scholars approximate social reality. This important proposal helped to establish the general investigative methodology that modern sociologists use. Weber also helped sociologists to clarify the position of their discipline (an "inexact" science) relative to the natural sciences, in which laboratory experimentation can verify or refute findings. As the "father of interpretive sociology," he saw the paradox in sociology that one must be objective in studying facts but must also exhibit sympathetic understanding (*Verstehen*). Thus, he helped to bridge the gap between positivists—who stressed the objective, scientific aspects of sociology—and more humanistic, subjective, or ingeniously creative scholars.

Weber's views are often compared to those of two other important sociological theorists, the French sociologist Émile Durkheim (1858-1917)—who followed the positivist views of Auguste Comte—and the German social thinker Karl Marx (1818-1883). Weber differs with Marx, but their differences are often oversimplified.

While Marx focused on class conflict and the inevitable triumph of the proletariat (or worker) over the bourgeois (the middle class or management level), Weber correctly envisioned the continued march of capitalism, with its stratification patterns based mostly on economic status. By 1893, Weber predicted that capitalism, as a modern revolutionary force, would destroy traditional social structures, but his attitude toward its advance was ambivalent. He disagreed with Marx's main conclusions but shared his concern over the alienation and unethical exploitation of the worker in the capitalistic system. Weber's writings sometimes view social causality under capitalism as being uncontrollable and inevitable—a perspective with which Karl Marx might have agreed.

By 1990, the collapse of socialism as a system of socioeconomic organization in the old Soviet Union and its satellites had renewed an interest in Weber's analysis of social stratification as a function of market economics. Capitalism and bureaucracy, as Weber predicted, had not disappeared, but rather had gained almost universal dominance. Thus, like others, Alan Sica argues in *Weber, Irrationality, and Social Order* (1988) that Weber's ideas continue to be relevant.

Bibliography

Albrow, Martin. *Max Weber's Construction of Social Theory*. New York: St. Martin's Press, 1990. A British university scholar's important, readable book on the meaning of Weber's ideas. Studies Weber's life, works, and times.

Käsler, Dirk. *Max Weber: An Introduction to His Life and Work*. Translated by Philippa Hurd. Chicago: University of Chicago Press, 1988. A wide-ranging, insightful book about Weber's contributions to the methodology of sociology. Includes well-indexed historical examples of social stratification that Weber discussed in various contexts.

MacRae, Donald G. *Max Weber*. New York: Viking Press, 1974. This short book in the Modern Masters series tries to cut through the complexities to get at the heart of Weberian sociology. It is generally useful but does not discuss class stratification directly.

Mommsen, Wolfgang J. *The Political and Social Theory of Max Weber: Collected Essays*. Chicago: University of Chicago Press, 1989. Includes pertinent essays on Weber's "dialogue" with Marx; bureaucracy and bureaucratization; and Weber's modern relevancy.

Poggi, Gianfranco. *Calvinism and the Capitalist Spirit: Max Weber's Protestant Ethic*.

Amherst: University of Massachusetts Press, 1983. Tries to summarize the ideas of Weber's two-part essay *The Protestant Ethic and the Spirit of Capitalism*, arguing that Weber's ideas are not diametrically opposed to those of Marx. Indexed discussions of the bourgeoisie, entrepreneurs, the manorial system, and monasticism explore various aspects of social stratification.

Weber, Max. *Basic Concepts in Sociology*. Translated and introduced by H. P. Secher. 5th ed. New York: Citadel Press, 1968. Discusses topics with implications for social stratification, including "legitimate authority," "aggregate" and "communal" social relationships, "open" and "closed" relationships, "corporate groups" ("political" and "religious"), and "power and domination."

_____ . *General Economic History*. Translated by Frank H. Knight. New York: Collier Books, 1966. Weber's historical overview analyzes class conflicts at various stages of history, the rise of modern capitalism, and modern social groupings based on economic functions.

_____ . *The Protestant Ethic and the Spirit of Capitalism*. Translated by Talcott Parsons, with a foreword by R. H. Tawney. New York: Charles Scribner's Sons, 1958. This classic interpretive work about modern society and the idealistic forces that shaped its patterns of economic and social organization is central in the Weber canon and is often included in college curricula. Weber found close connections between Calvinistic religion (with its "work ethic") and economic progress in Western societies.

_____ . *The Theory of Social and Economic Organization*. Edited and introduced by Talcott Parsons. Translated by A. M. Henderson and Talcott Parsons. Glencoe, Ill.: Free Press, 1947. The long introduction helps to clarify this important primary text, whose last chapter ("Social Stratification and Class Structure") is particularly pertinent.

Wrong, Dennis, ed. *Max. Weber*. Englewood Cliffs, N.J.: Prentice-Hall, 1970. A volume in the Makers of Modern Social Science series. Most relevant are the essays on capitalism (and its connections to Protestant ideology) and bureaucracy.

Roy Neil Graves

Cross-References

Capitalism, 191; Class Consciousness and Class Conflict, 271; Conflict Theory, 340; Marxism, 1127; Social Stratification: Analysis and Overview, 1839; Social Stratification: Functionalist Perspectives, 1845; Social Stratification: Marxist Perspectives, 1852; Social Stratification: Modern Theories, 1859; Traditional, Charismatic, and Rational-Legal Authority, 2064.

SOCIALISM AND COMMUNISM

Type of sociology: Major social institutions
Field of study: The economy

In theory, socialism (in which the state owns the means of production) is an intermediate stage between capitalism (in which individuals own the means of production and exploit those who must work for them) and communism (in which all goods are communally owned and are available to all as needed).

Principal terms
> CONFLICT THEORY: a theory that holds that certain groups dominate other groups; according to conflict theory, most of the divisiveness found in society can be explained in terms of the battle between the "haves" and the "have nots"
> MASS MOVEMENT: a situation in which a group holds a consensus about norms and values relative to a society's political, economic, and/or social system
> NORMS: behavioral rules ranging from mores, which are almost sacred, to folkways, which may be violated with impunity
> SOCIAL STRATIFICATION: the division of society into groups according to various criteria
> STRUCTURAL-FUNCTIONALIST THEORY: the theory according to which society is held together by the sharing of ideals and values; the theory holds that society is a system of interrelated parts

Overview

In theory, many forms of socialism exist. Some socialists believe that the state should control all means of production and all property; others argue that only the major industries should be nationalized—for example, banking and the extractive industries that drain natural resources. Some socialists argue for a strictly centralist government, while others find room for much decentralization and thus allow local governments some control. Some call for a "command" economy, while others simply want a government that regulates a "guided" economy. Communism, however, lacks such diversity of definitions. Communists demand unconditional state ownership of the means of production. Furthermore, while some socialist doctrine calls for the education of society and voluntary socialism, communists view such a concept as romantic drivel and openly advocate class warfare and the victory of the proletariat. Additionally, many socialists believe in the necessity of the state, while true Marxist Communist doctrine holds that one day the state will simply "wither away" because it will no longer be needed.

Yet despite such definitions, laypeople are sometimes confused because some scholars use the terms "socialism" and "communism" interchangeably. When they do, they are usually referring to their common aspect: Both doctrines promote state control and regulation of the means of production. This idea is opposed to the concept of pure capitalism, in which, at least in theory, the state owns none of the means of production.

The term "socialism" has its roots in the Europe of the 1830's, when the word was coined to describe the philosophies of such intellectuals as Robert Owen of England and F. M. C. Fourier and Comte Henri de Saint-Simon of France. Owen was a successful, wealthy industrialist. Having humanitarian concern for his workers, he advocated a competition-free cooperative movement that would be devoted to the physical and spiritual well-being of all members of the working class. Owen attracted adherents even in the United States, where several Owenite communities (such as New Harmony, Indiana) were founded.

While early European socialist theorists came principally from England and France, by the 1840's the baton had passed to Germany, among whose socialist advocates were the radical followers of G. W. F. Hegel, such as Ludwig Feuerbach, Moses Hess, Karl Grun, and Bruno Bauer. The year 1848 saw a major expansion of the socialist view. After the failed European revolutions of that year, Karl Marx and Friedrich Engels published *Manifest du Kommunistischen Partei* (1848; *The Communist Manifesto*, 1850). They chided earlier thinkers, calling them romantic idealists, utopian dreamers, and social quacks. Marx and Engels introduced what they called "scientific socialism," which stressed economics as a motivating force in history. According to Marx and Engels, the members of the industrial working class (the proletariat), because they were so cruelly exploited, would become self-conscious, would eventually recognize their collective oppression, and would revolt and conquer the capitalists. Such a revolt—the inevitable outcome of the historical process—might well occur, said Marx, simultaneously in many different parts of the world. When the workers were victorious, the state would own all the means of production and all land. Soon, the state itself would wither away, leaving nothing but a contented "commune" behind.

Marxist communism as it operated in the twentieth century was refined by the Russian revolutionaries Vladimir Lenin and Leon Trotsky. Lenin, for example, did not believe that the proletariat could bring about a revolution on its own; instead, a cadre of professional revolutionaries would be needed to guide the working class toward its goals. In fact, Lenin guided well; largely as a result of the dislocations caused in Russia by World War I, Lenin's Bolsheviks came to power in Russia in 1917 with the promise of "peace, bread, and land." In the World War I era, communism was also embraced by reformers in various other European states, but only in Hungary, with the Bela Kun government, did the movement appear likely to become a success—and even Kun's regime lasted only for a matter of months.

Applications

From 1917 to the World War II era, various states—such as Sweden and Norway—evolved into a mixed socialist/capitalist system, but no new Bolshevik governments sprang up. All that changed, however, as Russian troops "liberated" Eastern Europe. Soon, communist governments, supported by the Soviet Union, came to power in Poland, Hungary, Czechoslovakia, Romania, and elsewhere. In the post-World War II era, communism made gains in the Far East, with China adopting communism in 1949; the movement also succeeded in North Korea and, eventually, in French Indochina.

A study of "romantic" socialism and Marxist communism proves beneficial for various reasons. First, because militant communism failed as a movement, it does not follow that capitalism is automatically the best economic and social system. Human greed drives the capitalist order. Furthermore, even in the days of the "free market" economy, it must be realized that no true free market exists. In fact, most capitalist countries have political economies that have always been managed or manipulated for the benefit of the capitalist class. Second, the study of Marxism is still valid for those sociologists and historians who grapple with the conflict between the consensus theory (or "structural-functionalist" theory) and the conflict theory of societal organization. Consensus sociologists argue that the majority of people in a society voluntarily share common ideas about values, mores, and norms and that such sharing provides the social cohesion necessary to hold a society together. Social, economic, and political changes, when they come, come slowly—and they come only when a new consensus has emerged.

Some sociologists and historians, however, support the conflict theory, which holds that the most important factor in the social order is that some groups or individuals absolutely dominate other groups and individuals. Conflict theorists tend to ignore consensus, arguing that groups in power manipulate educational systems, the communications media, law, government, and the economy—all to achieve a popular attitude that helps to keep the elite in power.

Historic examples of the conflict theory in action abound, and they seem to undercut the structural-functionalist theory that was held by such notable twentieth century sociologists as Talcott Parsons. Consider, for example, the bloody European revolutions of 1830 and 1848 and the massive upheavals of the nineteenth century's industrial era, wherein agents of capitalism were forever at odds with oppressed industrial laborers. In the United States alone, scores of major strikes occurred between the 1870's and 1920. Legal authorities and industrialists usually suppressed such strikes violently.

A discussion of various issues may be useful in illustrating the consensus versus conflict debate. One issue regarding which there are differences of interpretation is that of social stratification. Some structural-functionalists would compare the social system to a biological organism. They believe that the social system operates in the same way that the human body operates: It needs all of its internal and external parts to work together to form a highly complex whole. Functionalists argue that when a "function" is no longer necessary (the manufacture of covered wagons in the automobile age, for example), roles will automatically change. In an era of more complex technology, formal education might lag behind the needs of business firms that are on the cutting edge of that technology. In such a situation, businesses might set up their own training schools or government might come to the rescue with more funding for programs that teach the complex technology so that the new parts fit into an integrated whole.

Students of socialism and Marxist communism are conflict theorists. They would, for example, replace the capitalistic inequalities of wealth with a more balanced distribution of wealth for the common good. Furthermore, they champion more social programs and social equality than do the defenders of capitalism—programs such as basic health care for all; equal opportunity education; and the right of all to have decent housing, adequate food, and meaningful jobs for the sake of the common good.

Conflict theorists, most of whom lean in the direction of socialism, stress the divisive strains of the capitalistic system. They see people and interest groups fighting among themselves for maximum benefits and profits. They maintain that society is held together by coercion—the "haves" rule the "have nots"—because some groups have more power and authority and are able to enforce what they say is the necessary order; they can then force their views on less powerful groups that disagree. Many thinkers believe that such struggles could be mitigated by socialism. Recent trends in the United States appear to support the ideas of conflict theorists. From the 1970's to the present, the income gap between the rich and the poor has widened dramatically. In 1969, as outgoing president Lyndon B. Johnson was still fighting a War on Poverty with his Great Society programs, the number of people living below the government's definition of the poverty line reached a low of 11 percent; when Johnson had taken office in late 1963, the figure had stood at 25 percent. By the early 1990's, some 25 to 30 percent of Americans were again living in poverty.

As the world neared the twenty-first century, it became clear that limited socialism (and liberal reform) was a success in many countries. In the post-World War II era in Western Europe, for example, democratic socialism won converts in such countries as England and France, and its public following, despite setbacks, grew as time passed. In those countries, reforms eventually came that seemed to mirror the mixed socialist/capitalist economies already established in such countries as Sweden and Norway. Militant communism, however, failed: The Soviet Union simply collapsed from within. The courageous statesman Mikhail Gorbachev managed the Russian crisis as the state crumbled, allowing his people more self-government in the form of "limited" democracy and more economic freedom as well. He also worked to establish friendly relations with the United States, just as his successor Boris Yeltsin and other Russian leaders continued to do after Gorbachev fell from power.

Soon, other states behind the Iron Curtain threw off communist domination and established new Western-oriented governments. A new, if somewhat uncertain, age had dawned. Of the remaining communist states in existence, China was probably the most viable, but even communist China moved toward a limited free market economy. It is likely that, in the future, many countries will move toward a blend of socialism and capitalism. Ideally, capitalistic countries would move to the left, while communist countries would move to the right.

Contemporary socialists and sociologists now share a bias against the utopian philosophies of earlier thinkers such as Owen and Fourier. Both socialists and sociologists now believe that change and its pace depend on the starting point; in other words, the range of alternatives open to societies is limited by the starting point—the kinds of resources that are available, the degree of differentiation, and other factors as well. What sociologists call structural constraints socialists call objective conditions. Certain chosen paths impose on society certain imperatives. For example, the rise of industrialism necessarily brought in its wake the rise of a new technical class, a new educational system, a different view of capital and capital formation, and an increasing structural differentiation that required a more complex society, more social coordination, and so on.

Context

There is a close association between socialism and sociology. Both terms came into use in France in the 1830's, and both approaches grew in response to the rise of industrial capitalism. Such responses were most fully developed by Auguste Comte, whose "positive politics" and "positive philosophy" stressed the conscious, rational regulation of the human environment. Although such later thinkers as Herbert Marcuse rejected Comte's ideas about social laws because such laws would stifle society's evolution and stifle change in the future, Comte's work, like that of Marx, is a starting point for all who wish to join the debate. Still, most later sociologists such as Émile Durkheim broke with Comte; Durkheim tried to build a foundation for a nonpositivist, scientific sociology.

Max Weber also grappled with Comte's positivism, and he finally came to advocate for society a type of "general science" with many positivist overtones. He shared with Marx an overriding concern for the fate of human beings in the face of unrestrained capitalism. Weber made the case for individual freedom and autonomy in a capitalistic world where there was increasing bureaucratization and mechanization; Marx, however, swore allegiance to the proletariat because it would be the means of bringing about human emancipation in the face of unrestrained capitalism. Although in much of his writing Weber disagreed with Marx, he nevertheless took Marxism as his starting point and thereby emphasized the importance of Marxist theory. Most of Weber's work, therefore, can be considered a prolonged commentary on Marx. For example, Weber's *Die Protestantische Ethik und der Geist des Kapitalismus* (1904; *The Protestant Ethic and the Spirit of Capitalism*, 1930) began with Marxist accounts of the origins of capitalism, but his sociology of religion challenged the Marxist emphasis on the materialist view of human history.

In the modern era, Marxists who have practiced proletarian social science have hesitated to accept Western sociologists who, according to their Marxist critics, practiced only bourgeois social science. Marxist theory has come to be a major sociological paradigm that reaches into academic disciplines such as economics, history, anthropology, and literature.

Today, Marxist thought challenges both structural-functionalists and sociologists who embrace the conflict theory. More and more, functionalists stress social "equilibrium," study static aspects of society, and give historical processes and historical explanations short shrift; conflict theorists, however, rally around the processes of historical change and evolution, stressing not static society but changing society.

Overall, most evolutionists try to comprehend the historical growth and change of society from its beginnings to its present forms. Some evolutionists stress episodic history; that is, major watersheds in society (industrial society versus postindustrial society, for example).

One criticism of socialism/communism and of the sociologists who grapple with these concepts is that, for the most part, the state is still emphasized—the state's power and its use of that power. True socialism, however, is more than state reform or state ownership of the means of production. True socialism involves personal "lifestyles" and asks individuals to begin an entirely new way of life that stresses cooperation and sharing. Such change obviously includes a different set of values and norms from those that presently hold sway in capitalistic countries. True socialism would do the greatest good for the greatest number, whereas capitalism, in the main, still stresses a "survival of the fittest" mind-set wherein the individual, not the group, is most important. Capitalism stresses the correctness of greed, whereas true socialism would try to overcome greed.

Some modern reformers still seek the utopian dream, but it would seem that a new type of human being would have to be manufactured before such a utopian scheme could successfully function. Because of the amazing human capacity for greed, the utopia that some people still seek remains far away.

Bibliography

Bottomore, Tom. *Sociology and Socialism*. New York: St. Martin's Press, 1984. This volume is an excellent, in-depth treatment of the relationship between sociology and socialism (and communism). It examines, among other things, competing paradigms of sociology, Marxism, the capitalist state and Max Weber's views of it, and the working class in relation to socialism.

Broom, Leonard, and Philip Selznick. *Sociology: A Text with Adapted Readings*. 4th ed. New York: Harper & Row, 1968. This wide-ranging textbook covers the most relevant aspects of sociology and also provides selected readings from the early work of some of the major figures in sociology and related fields, such as Émile Durkheim, Margaret Mead, and Frank Tannenbaum.

Craib, Ian. *Modern Social Theory: From Parsons to Habermas*. New York: St. Martin's Press, 1984. Craib's work covers many aspects of social theory and has sections on Marxism, conflict theory, and structuralism. Craib also includes a detailed "Bibliography and Further Reading" section at the end of every chapter.

Marx, Karl, and Friedrich Engels. *The Communist Manifesto of Karl Marx and Friedrich Engels*. Edited by D. Ryazanoff. New York: Russell & Russell, 1963.

_____ . *Selected Works of Karl Marx and Friedrich Engels*. Moscow: Foreign Languages Publishing House, 1962. The two volumes listed here present the philosophy of Marx and Engels, the founders of what they called "scientific" socialism, and their thinking about communism, which they believed would inevitably follow socialism.

Mills, C. W. *The Marxists*. New York: Dell, 1970. Mills's relatively brief work is one of the best treatments of the sociological views of Marx. A sociologist himself, Mills emphasized that aspect of Marx's thought. This well-written book will be especially useful to students and nonprofessional readers.

Parsons, Talcott. *The Structure of Social Action.* New York: McGraw-Hill, 1937. Valuable for its own contribution to the field of sociology, this volume also contains one of the best secondary interpretations of the ideas and the bodies of work left by Max Weber and Émile Durkheim.

Weber, Max. *The Protestant Ethic and the Spirit of Capitalism.* Translated by Talcott Parsons. London: Allen & Unwin, 1930. Weber was very much a student of Marxism, but he took many positions that were critical of Marxism. For example, Weber held that Marxism was "one-sided" and that ideas, especially religious ideas, had a necessary place in social analysis.

Wilson, Everett K. *Sociology: Rules, Roles, and Relationships.* Homewood, Ill.: Dorsey Press, 1966. Although this volume is somewhat dated, it is very readable and has excellent name and subject indexes. The work is footnoted, and each chapter has a selected bibliography for further reading.

James Smallwood

Cross-References

Capitalism, 191; Class Consciousness and Class Conflict, 271; Marxism, 1127; Political Sociology, 1414; Social Change: Functionalism versus Historical Materialism, 1779; Social Stratification: Analysis and Overview, 1839; Social Stratification: Marxist Perspectives, 1852; Social Stratification: Modern Theories, 1859.

SOCIALIZATION: THE FAMILY

Type of sociology: Socialization and social interaction
Field of study: Agents of socialization

Socialization is a continual learning process through which an individual becomes acquainted with the social customs of a group of people. In the family, socialization is accomplished through the application of a combination of learning methods and parenting styles.

Principal terms

CULTURE: the total lifestyle that a group of people hold in common, including intangible qualities such as values and standards and tangible products such as art and technology

LEARNING THEORY: a suggested explanation of how people learn

PARENTING STYLE: one's approach to rearing children; based on the amount of affection and control exhibited by the parent

SOCIALIZATION AGENT: a source of socialization; the persons or means that instruct or impart information, either formally or informally

SUBCULTURE: a portion of a broader culture that is set apart by certain unique characteristics

Overview

Socialization is a dual process in that it involves a teacher (or agent of socialization) and a learner, the person undergoing the socialization process. One person, group, or institution imparts information through training or education, and another person learns and internalizes the information. Socialization is the continuing process through which an individual becomes acquainted with the social customs of a group of people and accepts the group's attitudes and behavior. It is through socialization that children learn to participate in the various roles of their culture and subculture so that they can become full-fledged members of their society as adults.

The socialization process typically encompasses learning and adopting all aspects of group life that a person needs to know in order to establish interrelationships and associations with individuals and organizations. What one needs to know varies from group to group. Yet, according to human development specialists Carol K. Sigelman and David R. Shaffer, there appear to be three goals of socialization that cross cultural boundaries: survival, economic success, and self-actualization. In order to be able to attain these three goals, an individual is involved in a continuous process of learning values, standards, attitudes, language, skills, opinions, beliefs, roles, behaviors, goals, customs, expected behaviors, obligations, and responsibilities. Absorbing all these aspects of life shapes the individual and defines the range of the person's present and future thoughts and actions.

The family is almost always the first place that an individual encounters the socialization process, and the family and parent(s) are widely recognized as the primary agents of socialization. Although socialization is a lifelong endeavor, childhood is a time of concentrated socialization. It is during childhood that primary socialization takes place. This consists of basic indoctrination into a value system, language, and concept of the world. In addition to primary socialization, anticipatory socialization in childhood occurs. Anticipatory socialization is training for future roles. An example would be taking music lessons as a child in anticipation of being involved in a school marching band.

Since socialization is a continuing process, a third kind of socialization, referred to as developmental socialization, occurs as the person grows and has new experiences, learns new skills, and comes in contact with people that think and act differently. Gerald R. Leslie and Sheila K. Korman, in *The Family in Social Context* (1985), suggest that because learning how to be a part of the group is so dramatic and noticeable in children, there is a tendency to think that such learning ceases after adolescence. Adults and the elderly continue to learn, however, and are active participants in socialization. There may be times in one's life when it is necessary to relearn how to fit into a particular group or to learn how to fit into a new group. Examples include joining the military, marrying into a family of a different culture, changing religions, and coming to terms with a disability. Learning to adapt to a new environment, group, and lifestyle is referred to as resocialization.

To accomplish primary socialization, a child's parents use differing parenting styles. Socialization methods used by family members and other adults for primary, anticipatory, or developmental socialization (or for resocialization) can be examined through various learning theories. Social learning theory, which views learning as occurring through observation, modeling, and imitation, is certainly applicable to socialization.

Yet socialization through observation and imitation is only a partial explanation of how children acquire information about fitting into the adult world. At times, more specific and direct training happens; this may occur through either classical or instrumental conditioning. Through classical conditioning, individuals come to understand how events in their lives are related. Technically, classical conditioning refers to a neutral stimulus becoming associated with a stimulus that already produces a response. For example, a small child's trip to the doctor's office, itself a neutral event, may be accompanied by the painful experience of an inoculation. Particularly after this happens more than once, the child may come to fear going to the doctor. On the other hand, a child could come to associate going to the doctor with a toy given at the end of the visit and might then look forward to the visit.

In instrumental or operant conditioning, either a weakening or strengthening of behavior may occur because of positive or negative reinforcement. All behavior is reinforced, either purposefully or unintentionally. For the purposes of socialization, a parent may use rewards to produce a desired trait in a child. A parent may award stars to be placed on a child's personal hygiene chart for tooth-brushing behavior, for example. In this example, the parents are hoping that the reward of the stars will help develop a habit or strengthen a behavior in the child. Unintentional reinforcement also occurs during the socialization process. A busy parent may only half listen to a child's conversation, for example, thus conveying a message that children's thoughts and feelings are unimportant.

Applications

Socialization of children by adults, a major responsibility of the family, is accomplished with varying degrees of effectiveness. According to family specialist William J. Goode, effective socialization is facilitated by six major elements that may characterize the parent-child relationship: warmth, nurturance, and affection toward the child; the child's identification with the person doing the socializing; parental authority; consistency; freedom; and communication.

Warmth, nurturance, and affection are necessary from the moment the child is born. According to James Garbarino, infants will attach to their primary caregivers regardless of the level of nurturance and caring exhibited by the adult. Therefore, the kind of attachment that develops warrants attention. Sigelman and Shaffer report that secure attachments formed during infancy may lead to future positive interactional abilities and intellectual growth. Secure attachments are facilitated when a parent understands and responds to the baby's personal signals and when a parent sincerely likes and enjoys interacting with the child. Child development specialist Urie Bronfenbrenner believes that development—including cognitive, emotional, moral, and social—is more completely realized when the child experiences a relationship with one or more adults who have a lifelong and total commitment to the child.

The mother and the father can share equally in this secure relationship through nurturing. Research reported by Hilary M. Lips and by Sigelman and Shaffer demonstrates that fathers are comfortable and competent in the role of nurturing and providing warmth and affection. Thus, quality infant-parent relationships are not necessarily tied to the mother. Mothers and fathers do tend to spend their time with the infant differently. Fathers are more likely to play with the child, while mothers typically spend a larger portion of their time in primary care duties such as feeding. While the time spent by mother and father may be characterized differently, both are equally important in the socialization of the child.

Parenting style is associated with the quality of nurturance provided to the child, and it subsequently affects the quality of socialization. Sigelman and Shaffer integrate the available information on parenting styles into a model with a freedom/restriction dimension and a warmth, nurturance, and affection dimension. In the 1960's, psychologist Diana Baumrind developed a characterization of three main types of parenting styles: authoritarian, authoritative, and permissive. Sigelman and Shaffer used Baumrind's typology in describing their freedom/restriction dimension.

Authoritarian parenting is characterized by arbitrary, rigid rules and regulations; parents expect absolute obedience, and punishments are applied when the child is not doing as the parent wishes. An "I said so" attitude prevails. Children may interpret authoritarian homes as lacking warmth and affection. Authority and control are of utmost importance, and personal freedom is curtailed.

In an authoritative parenting style, authority is central but is accompanied by reasons and explanations. Limits are provided, yet warmth, affection, and attention to individual differences and development are provided. There is flexibility and consideration of each person's needs when making decisions. Children are included in decisions when possible, and freedom with responsibility is encouraged.

A third style, permissive parenting, is the absence of rules except for those involving personal safety. Children are allowed to go their separate ways, and individual freedom is highly valued. While love and affection may be there, they may not be communicated. Making one's own decisions is prized.

These parenting styles can be viewed as a continuum, with authoritarian and permissive at the extreme ends and authoritative in the middle. Warmth, nurturance, and affection appear in varying amounts in each style. Since all families and parents are unique, individual parenting styles will be found all along the continuum.

The second factor related to effective socialization is identification with the person doing the socializing. The child first identifies with the parent(s) and siblings in the family. According to Garbarino, a child forms a sense of self-awareness around the age of two. Self-identification is in large part facilitated through observational learning, modeling, and imitation. Parenting style, however, is also related to identification formation in children. Authoritarian parents may rely more on rewards and punishments to reinforce identity-forming behaviors. Garbarino suggests that children from authoritarian homes therefore may not consider certain options related to self-awareness.

Flexible and positive homes (homes whose style falls within or near the authoritative parenting style) produce children or young people who successfully formulate a definition of self. This may be related to findings that identity formation is facilitated by an atmosphere of warmth and emotion. Furthermore, as child development specialists Judith A. Schickedanz, David I. Schickedanz, Karen Hansen, and Peggy D. Forsyth report, children view parents who help them solve problems as desirable role models. The permissive parenting style is more likely to depend completely on observational learning and imitation. Parents with a permissive approach to child rearing believe that many of the things considered to be aspects of socialization—teaching and learning attitudes, values, morality, and so on—should be the child's own decision.

Parental authority is the third factor in the socialization process; the application and character of that authority appear to be crucial. Authority that is characterized by negativism may lead to incomplete identity formation. Again, the authoritative parenting style, emphasizing authority balanced with reason and consideration of others, produces the most positive results. What appears to be the crucial factor regarding application of authority is that of perceived total parental acceptance of the child.

Consistency is the fourth factor Goode noted as facilitating effective socialization; consistency is important in two ways. First, when imitation is the primary form of learning, it is important that parents are consistent in their lifestyle and in what they expect of children's behavior presently and in the future. Children imitate what they see more than what they are told.

Consistency is crucial in providing guidance. Generally this entails treating a behavior with the same level of attention each time it occurs. Immediate reinforcement is important for changing a behavior; however, partial reinforcement (acknowledging certain actions at unpredictable times or introducing the element of surprise) also tends to encourage change. Sigelman and Shaffer recommend continuous reinforcement (consistency) for changing a behavior and partial reinforcement for maintaining the change.

A fifth quality fostering socialization is freedom. The amount of freedom given a child is associated with parenting style, and the most desirable characteristics or end products of socialization are directly linked to the authoritative approach. The authoritarian style represents the least freedom, and permissive parenting represents the most. Authoritative parenting typifies a balance of limits and freedom.

Finally, effective socialization is facilitated through positive communication. Positive communication skills include explanations, supportive statements and actions, demonstrations of empathy, and clear statements of instructions or problems. Again, the authoritative parenting style emerges as the one most likely to employ positive communication skills.

Context

Socialization of the young is one of the central functions of the family, but it is not the only one. The family unit has additional functions and responsibilities, both for society and for individual family members. These responsibilities or functions are generally agreed to include procreation and regulation of sexual activity, maintenance of health and safety, economic provision and responsibility, and affection and emotional support.

In all cultures, families engage in the socialization of the young. While socialization may be a function of all cultures, however, it is not implemented the same way in all. The desired results may also be different. Psychologists David White and Anne Woollett report that the goals of socialization in Western families may include independence, autonomy, and even high achievement. On the other hand, in some cultures the qualities of obedience, dependence, and passivity are more highly valued.

Studying socialization is not the domain of sociology alone. In *Human Socialization* (1969), Elton B. McNeil suggests that all the social sciences are interested in socialization; only the specific focus is different. Human ecologists/home economics might be interested in the interrelationship of the parent and child, the psychologist in the internal experience of the person, the historian in how socialization is affected by place in history, and an economist in the effects of poverty on socialization. The sociologist might emphasize the impact of individual socialization on society, and an anthropologist could examine the differences in socialization by cultures.

While the family is considered the most important socialization agent for the child, sociologists David B. Brinkerhoff and Lynn K. White suggest that with the increased use of day care and early childhood education centers, some of the responsibility for early socialization has been transferred from the home. A parent can exercise some control by choosing a day care facility carefully. Child care expert Janet Gonzalez-Mena reports that as long as the family can find a day care center that adheres to the same values and behavior expectations of the parent(s), there is relatively high satisfaction with the child care. When the day care staff is insensitive to the cultural differences within its own clientele, however, there is a chance for misinterpretation, miscommunication, and role confusion for the child.

The family also affects socialization—primary, anticipatory, and developmental—and resocialization by applying minimal or maximum control over external socialization agents in the child's life. During primary socialization, when the parent or parents are still making the bulk of decisions for the child concerning television viewing, reading, choice of religion, table conversation, friendships made, and so on, the control of the socialization process is greater. This control is displaced as the child matures and is able to make his or her own decisions. Parents typically feel that effective socialization has taken place when the late adolescent or young adult is able to take his or her place in society.

Bibliography

Bronfenbrenner, Urie. "The Parent/Child Relationship and Our Changing Society." In *Parents, Children, and Change*, edited by L. Eugene Arnold. Lexington, Mass.: Lexington Books, 1985. This book combines sources from anthropology, psychiatry, folklore, medicine, and theology on how the family can expect to be affected by technological, social, economic, and biological advances.

Garbarino, James. *Children and Families in the Social Environment*. 2d ed. New York: Aldine de Gruyter, 1992. Interdisciplinary essays concerning family and child development issues and how they relate to society as a whole. Systems theory is the basis for Garbarino's interpretation.

Gonzalez-Mena, Janet. *Multicultural Issues in Infant Care*. Mountain View, Calif.: Mayfield, 1993. Practical information is provided on how to minimize insensitivity to multicultural differences in early childhood programs, including day care and nursery school settings. Respect for all cultures is the underlying theme.

Goode, William J. *The Family*. 2d ed. Englewood Cliffs, N.J.: Prentice-Hall, 1982. A comprehensive look at the family as a social group. Research and historical data complement the chapters. Focuses on the family as a subgroup in society.

Leslie, Gerald R., and Sheila K. Korman. *The Family in the Social Context*. 6th ed. New York: Oxford University Press, 1985. A comprehensive look at the family covering cross-cultural, historical, and contemporary family issues. It is research-based but includes useful information on family theory.

Lips, Hilary M. *Sex and Gender: An Introduction*. 2d ed. Mountain View, Calif.: Mayfield, 1992. Research into the similarities and differences between males and females in a wide variety of personal and societal situations. Every attempt has been made to cross culture boundaries.

Schickedanz, Judith A., David I. Schickedanz, Karen Hansen, and Peggy D. Forsyth. *Understanding Children*. Rev. ed. Mountain View, Calif.: Mayfield, 1992. An introductory college text in child development. The child from infant to adolescent is discussed with research information and applications provided. A glossary is included.

Sigelman, Carol K., and David R. Shaffer. *Life-Span Human Development*. Pacific Grove, Calif.: Brooks/Cole, 1991. A topical approach to all ages is employed in this introductory human development college text. Practical applications of research and illustrations are included.

White, David, and Anne Woollett. *Families: A Context for Development*. London: Falmer Press, 1992. This book is written for beginning students but will also be interesting to those who work professionally with the family.

Diane Teel Miller

Cross-References

Cultural Norms and Sanctions, 411; The Family: Functionalist versus Conflict Theory Views, 739; Gender Socialization, 833; The Looking-Glass Self, 1099; Parenthood and Child-Rearing Practices, 1336; Political Socialization, 1407; Socialization: The Mass Media, 1887; Socialization: Religion, 1894; Socialization and Reference Groups in Race Relations, 1900.

SOCIALIZATION: THE MASS MEDIA

Type of sociology: Socialization and social interaction
Field of study: Agents of socialization

Mass media socialization refers to the manner in which mass media institutions such as television, film, magazines, radio, and newspapers contribute to the individual's socialization in terms of behaviors, attitudes, role expectations, value structures, and belief systems.

Principal terms
> CULTIVATION HYPOTHESIS: the study of the extent to which the mass media, and particularly television, cultivate distorted perceptions of social reality
> MAINSTREAMING: the process in which an individual, through extensive exposure to mass media, is moved from the margins of society to its center in terms of values and beliefs
> MEDIA EFFECTS TRADITION: the history of systematic inquiry by sociologists and mass media researchers into the effects of the mass media on such things as socialization, voting behavior, and attitudes toward violence
> MODELING: the observation of symbolic behaviors by an individual which results in the acquisition of these behaviors
> SOCIALIZATION: the continuing process in which people learn both the rules and norms of a society and how to interact with and be participants in that society

Overview

Socialization, the process in which the individual is integrated as a functioning member of society, is carried out by social institutions such as the school, the church, and the family. Although these forces, among others, are central to an individual's explicit socialization, the mass media are often the implicit teachers of societal norms, expectations, values, and beliefs. The mass media socialize people not only through the lessons they teach but also by providing topics of conversation and common experiences that they can share with others, thereby creating the mediated background against which socialization takes place.

Although most sociologists agree that socialization—particularly media socialization—occurs constantly throughout people's lives, research indicates that the mass media are an especially significant social force in the lives of children and adolescents. This is because the media provide young people with "scripts" for living that explain the types of behavior that are acceptable and appropriate in various situations, create expectations about the kinds of consequences that are likely to follow from certain behaviors, and define the numerous contingencies that can operate in given situations.

Researchers argue that television, in particular, influences social behavior by shaping the expectations and norms that children hold regarding various behavioral situations. Perhaps more significant, however, is the claim of many psychologists that children's perceptions of social reality itself are largely dependent on socially mediated information, the most predominant sources of which are the mass media.

Although debate still exists about the extent of media impact as a socializing agent, it is generally accepted that mass media exert the most influence either when reinforcing existing attitudes and expectations about normative behaviors and beliefs developed originally through direct experience and/or interpersonal influence, or when providing normative information about situations which was not previously available to the individual. For example, one 1972 study found that children from rural and suburban areas claimed that they were more likely to use television for information about how to behave with African Americans than were children from city environments who relied upon direct experiences instead. The mass media, in other words, either reaffirm what people already "know" or fill in the gaps in our socialization process. It is important to note, however, that when the messages sent by the mass media contradict information either derived from direct experience or from significant interpersonal sources, the effects of these messages, although significantly reduced, are not completely eliminated.

The role modeling of observed symbolic behavior is one way in which individuals develop a repertoire of interpersonal behaviors. A theoretical model that explains behavioral acquisition through observation of symbolic behavior is Albert Bandura's social learning theory. According to social learning theory, the individual learns new behaviors not only by performing those behaviors (rehearsal) but also by observing others perform them (modeling). In fact, the repetitive trial-and-error method of learning is often unnecessary or impractical in the acquisition of skills when it is possible to observe symbolic behavior.

Many researchers agree that the mass media are a powerful source for social learning through observation of symbolic behavior. Television and film, for example, expose viewers to many "backstage" behaviors, allowing them to experience the private emotions and motivation of role occupants to whom they might not normally be exposed. These portrayals provide "unique opportunities to increase understanding of others' perspectives and the ability to predict how others may behave in similar real-life situations." Studies indicate, in fact, that viewers may make use of information gained from television characters when faced with situations that are similar to those experienced by those characters.

There are a number of factors that reinforce the likelihood that children and adolescents will model mass media behaviors. Bandura and other researchers have found, for example, that if the media role model is rewarded for a portrayed behavior, the child's performance of the behavior increases. If, however, the role model is punished for performing the behavior, the child's subsequent performance will decrease. In addition, the more realistic the portrayal, the greater the perceived similarity between the child and the media role model, the greater the similarity between the media performance situation and the child's performance situation, the more frequently and consistently the behavior is portrayed, then the more likely the child is to model the behavior and view it as appropriate. For example, when parents watch television with children and remark on television's portrayals of violence as inappropriate or unrealistic, the attitudinal and behavior influence of those portrayals are reduced.

While Bandura's work explains the mass media's effect on behavioral acquisition in children, another important mass media researcher, George Gerbner (1986), focuses on how the mass media, and television in particular, socialize people by cultivating certain beliefs and values. Even though television cultivates a distorted perception of social reality, Gerbner argues, the more television one watches, the more likely one is to espouse these values and beliefs. This is particularly true, Gerbner explains, in heavy television viewers' perception of the world as a "mean and scary" place. This is primarily a result of the amount of violence that is shown on American television.

Gerbner's most relevant finding regarding the socialization process, however, has to do with what he calls television's mainstreaming effect. According to Gerbner, heavy television viewers become "mainstreamed" in that they develop common outlooks or viewpoints about the world that bring them into the mainstream of American society. Thus, television socializes, for better or for worse, a more homogeneous, or "middle of the road," population.

Applications

Researchers have explored a number of different issues and topics surrounding mass media socialization, some of the more prominent of which have been the effects of media portrayals on such things as gender socialization, stereotyping, expectations of family life, and perceptions of and predisposition toward violence.

Gender socialization is one area in which the mass media have had a demonstrated influence. It has been argued that television, in particular, provides children and adolescents with a vast array of same-sex models to learn from and emulate. Some researchers, for example, "maintain that once children recognize that their gender identity is stable and invariant, they will begin to imitate the activities and behaviors exhibited by same-sex models on television" (Gerbner et al., 1986) and that boys are more likely than girls to identify with same-sex characters. According to Gerbner, this phenomenon has been demonstrated in the finding that "children's gender role perceptions and expectations generally conform to the stereotypes of television." In addition, some research suggests that children who are heavy television viewers are more likely to prefer sexually stereotypical toys and activities. Gender stereotypes are not true only for children; research indicates that the more individuals watch television, the more likely they are to express stereotypical attitudes regarding gender (Gerbner et al., 1986).

The impact of mass media on family socialization has been another area of study. Mass media research indicates, for example, that media families are used by viewers as models for their own behavior in families. A mid-1970's sociological analysis of marital and family roles in situation comedies, for example, concluded that television, as far back as the 1950's, was an "important vehicle for teaching nonmarried viewers about marital obligations and role expectations." According to George Gerbner, "the seductively realistic portrayal of family life in the media may be the basis for our most common and pervasive conceptions and beliefs about what is natural and what is right. This may be problematic in that researchers have claimed, among other things, that the mass media reinforces traditional and stereotypical division of labor in the family.

A particularly well-studied area is that of the effects of mass media portrayals of violence on perceptions of violence, attitudes toward violence, and predisposition toward aggressive and/or violent behavior. The central finding regarding children and media violence is that "children who see a great deal of violence on television are more likely than children who see less to engage in aggressive play, to accept force as a problem-solver, to fear becoming a victim of violence, and to believe that an exaggerated proportion of the society is involved in law enforcement. These conclusions remain true when held constant for IQ, social status, economic level, and other variables" (Comstock et al., 1978).

Although some of the socialization lessons that people learn from the media may be antisocial, such as perceptions of the appropriateness of aggressive behavior or stereotypical views of women's role in the family, the prosocial nature of mass media must not be overlooked. A significant amount of research concerned with the impact of mass media actually indicates that many mass mediated messages are predominantly prosocial. Although the mass media often provide images that make individuals feel inadequate, films and television shows often give audience members a chance to be "a fly on the wall" observing, for example, someone else's "family." Thus, the media often provide positive or prosocial models that validate communication behaviors. They offer examples of communication behaviors, roles, and issues that help audiences better understand their own communication patterns, perceptions, and beliefs.

Despite their particular focus, most researchers on the mass media's effect on society either generally conclude or speculate that the media "teach—however misleadingly—norms, status positions, and institutional functions" (Elkin and Handel, 1984). The mass media are certainly a powerful vehicle of socialization.

Context
As early as 1968, Herbert Mead argued that the mass media had taken over the parental role of raising America's youth. By the mid-1970's, some sociologists declared that television had become the primary socializing agent, superseding both church and parents. By 1980, Gerbner and his associates suggested that the mass media provide "touchstones by which we gauge our experiences." In 1987, Taylor asserted, "Few contemporary forms of storytelling offer territory as fertile as television for unearthing changing public ideas . . . TV speaks to our collective worries and to our yearning to improve, redeem, or repair our individual and collective lives."

Despite these declarations, after more than forty years of research on the effects of the mass media, particularly television, on society, researchers still disagree about the extent of the impact of such things as television violence, portrayals of pornography, and the link between the mass media's influence on attitudes and behavior. Early research into mass media effects, for example, argued that the mass media had only limited or minor impact on individual behaviors. This was the case, researchers claimed, because people usually selectively exposed themselves to messages that supported preexisting beliefs ("selective exposure"), rationalized messages that were incongruent with their beliefs ("cognitive dissonance theory"), or relied on interpersonal sources of information rather than media sources ("personal influence theory"). If the media had any influence, it was asserted, their influence was disseminated through opinion leaders rather than directly ("two-step flow").

These limited effects findings, however, were in direct contradiction with the 1960's findings of experimental psychologists such as Albert Bandura, who argued that media portrayals of violence and aggression had a profound impact on children's predisposition toward aggressive behavior. Later laboratory studies of violence in the 1960's and 1970's found support for Bandura's work, but a lack of nonexperimental data kept these findings from receiving wide acceptance until the late 1970's. Additionally, while some researchers argued that media violence caused aggression, others asserted that media violence did the opposite, acting as a catharsis, or release, for the individual's aggressive impulses.

Other researchers, such as Gerbner, avoided making claims about the behavioral impact of the mass media, preferring instead to focus, in the 1980's, on the mass media's effects on attitudes and beliefs. Even today, what might be considered Gerbner's modest claims regarding the mass media as a "mainstreaming" force of socialization are debated by sociologists and mass media researchers alike.

In summary, most analysis of mass media's role as an agent of socialization has come from sociology and mass communication in the form of experimental research, survey research, and content analysis of large quantities of data. This work has established baseline understandings of, for example, the predominance of certain roles, models, expectations, and interaction patterns in the media and in society. There is a growing interest, however, in research that qualitatively explores audiences' interpretations and use of media portrayals by placing those interpretations into situational, cultural, sociological, and ideological contexts.

Negotiation theory, based on the work of members of the British school of cultural studies (Stuart Hall, Charlotte Brunsdon, David Morley, John Fiske), has been a particularly dominant approach in the analysis of mass media's impact on attitudes and behaviors. Negotiation theory addresses the process by which individuals, as members of cultures, negotiate meaning in their interaction with the mass media and other cultural phenomena. Critics explore how individuals' own life experiences shape their responses to the visual, verbal, and acoustic signs and codes in discourse. Critics ultimately argue, with differing degrees of emphasis, that the individual's response to the mass media is neither completely idiosyncratic nor completely universal, neither completely free nor completely bound. In other words, both individual experiences and socio-ideologically significant messages (those that contextualize the media discourse in the contemporary condition and in the dominant, more enduring ideological forces in society at large) interact to shape meaning. The point of debate for various critics lies in describing the balance between structure and freedom in the discourse and in reconciling audience freedoms with audience constraints in meaning-making.

Bibliography

Bandura, Albert. *Social Learning Theory*. Englewood Cliffs, N.J.: Prentice-Hall, 1977. Bandura is the central figure in the development of social learning theory. This book describes his theoretical framework and summarizes the available research up to the mid-1970's.

Comstock, George, et al. *Television and Human Behavior*. New York: Columbia University Press, 1978. A significant review of most of the research up to 1977 on television and its link to human behavior. Covers such areas as the mass media's effect on political and psychological socialization as well as the potential prosocial and antisocial implications of mass media socialization. Chapter 8, "The Psychology of Behavior Effects," is particularly relevant to a discussion of the mass media's socializing influence.

Elkin, Frederick, and Gerald Handel. *The Child and Society: The Process of Socialization*. 4th ed. New York: Random House, 1984. A primer on the socialization process that focuses on children and adolescents. Includes a discussion of the mass media as a significant force in the socialization process.

Gerbner, George, et al. "Living with Television: The Dynamics of the Cultivation Process." In *Perspectives on Media Effects*, edited by Jennings Bryant and Dolf Zillman. Hillsdale, N.J.: Lawrence Erlbaum, 1986. Provides a clear explanation of the "cultivation hypothesis" and a thorough review of the findings of Gerbner and his associates regarding the effects of the mass media, particularly television, on attitudes and beliefs.

Morley, David. *The Nationwide Audience: Structure and Decoding*. London, England: British Film Institute, 1980. This book deals with attempts by Morley, a major figure in the British cultural studies tradition, to measure qualitatively British audiences' uses and interpretations of the mass media, particularly television. A good introduction to negotiation theory as a model of mass media socialization.

Pearl, D., L. Bouthilet, and J. Lazar, eds. *Television and Behavior: Ten Years of Scientific Progress and Implications for the Eighties*. Rockville, Md.: U.S. Department of Health and Human Services, Public Health Service, Alcohol, Drug Abuse, and Mental Health Administration, National Institute of Mental Health, 1982. A comprehensive anthology of social/scientific research on the effects of the media.

Perloff, Richard. "Social Effects of the Media." In *Mass Media: Process and Effects*, edited by Leo W. Jeffres. Prospect Heights, Ill.: Waveland Press, 1986. Perloff provides a readable summary of the stereotypes fostered by the mass media and the effects of these portrayals on role modeling and the cultivation of attitudes and beliefs. He summarizes and critiques both Bandura's and Gerbner's work on media socialization. Perloff also reviews the research on the impact of the mass media on children's cognitive development and the research on the impact of media violence and pornography.

Susan Mackey-Kallis

Cross-References

Gender Socialization, 833; High Culture versus Popular Culture, 870; Legitimation of Inequality: The Mass Media, 1061; Socialization: The Family, 1880; Socialization: Religion, 1894; Socialization and Reference Groups in Race Relations, 1900; Workplace Socialization, 2202.

SOCIALIZATION: RELIGION

Type of sociology: Socialization and social interaction
Fields of study: Agents of socialization; Religion

Religious socialization is the process through which people learn to engage more deeply in the verbalizations, actions, and institutions of a religion which provides them with a sense of meaning and belonging. While the process of religious socialization is similar to socialization into other groups, what one recognizes as a religion will determine one's understanding of religious socialization.

Principal terms
> CIVIL RELIGION: the recognition of the values of one's culture or nation as the ultimate values of one's life
> CONVERSION: the acceptance of a religion as one's own
> ROLE: what one does and says to be part of a group, and what a group needs one to say and do to ensure the group's survival
> SECULARIZATION: the process whereby religion loses its legitimizing role in society
> SOCIALIZATION: the process through which one learns the culture of one's society or group and thereby becomes a full participant in it; adopting the roles necessary to be a member of a group

Overview

The concept of religious socialization is complicated by what one understands to be the meaning of the word "religion" and is best approached, from a sociological point of view, by reference to a different concept: that of the "religious group." The discussion in this "Overview" section will therefore define the latter term before considering the relationship of religion to religious socialization in the "Applications" and "Context" sections that follow.

Every religious group has a way of speaking about that which is important to it; sociologists refer to this as "verbalization." Verbalizations are found in stories handed down from generation to generation, significant books, songs, and creedal formulas. What is common to these verbalizations is that they use words to express the religious reality. Every group also has a way of doing that which is important to it, and sociologists refer to this as "action." Action has two major subdivisions: moral or ethical behavior, and rituals. For example, every religious group has a way of ritualizing birth, marriage, and death. Every religious group conducts regular gatherings to mark special occasions and times of year. Finally, every group has a way of assuring that the words and actions are systematized and that the group itself is organized, a process known as "institutionalization." The institutional element is the organizational structure or skeleton that assures that the words and actions have a coherent form or pattern from day to day and from generation to generation.

Religious socialization, then, is the process through which people learn to engage more deeply in the verbalizations, actions, and institution of a religion. Anyone who becomes a member of a religious group learns how to say the religious words, perform the religious actions, and acknowledge the accepted pattern for religious life sanctioned by its institution. The recognition and description of the actual socialization process will depend on which religious group one is attempting to describe. The socialization process of Baptists, for example, is different from that of Roman Catholics because the two institutions have different concepts of membership: Baptists believe in adult baptisms; Catholics, in infant baptism. Hence, one becomes a Baptist through a deep experience of Jesus as Lord and Savior (recognized in the ceremony of adult baptism), whereas one becomes a Catholic when faith itself becomes part of one's life through infant baptism. A description of the socialization of the Baptist will see the born-again experience as a significant marker of one's entry into the group; Catholics' socialization process is more gradual, with conversion usually described as a lifelong process. The socialization process is well under way by the time one is baptized as an adult in the Baptist church; in the Catholic church it usually begins with one's infant baptism.

If one puts aside membership considerations, one can describe religious socialization in terms of group development theory. For this description to be accurate, one must take for granted that the person undergoing religious socialization has been born into a family environment in which religion forms an important part. Most people are socialized into a religion through the religion of their parents. Some reject the religion of their parents and become part of another religious group, but in both cases the socialization process will follow roughly the same pattern. Early in life (or at the beginning of one's religious socialization, if one rejects the family's religion and becomes religiously socialized later in life), one learns how to act or behave in the religious manner; for example, in church one learns when to stand, sing, be quiet, or respond to the religious leader. One learns the words of a prayer uttered before meals. One learns the rituals and behaviors performed on significant festive days. Socialization into the family, therefore, often includes socialization into the religion of that family.

One next learns how to feel about what one does. Parents, friends, teachers, religious leaders, and others teach how it feels to say, "I am a sinner," "Love thy neighbor," or "Praise God." Prayer before meals incorporates the words and the feelings of thanks and gratitude. Feelings become associated with behavior.

In addition to doing and feeling, socialization involves thinking. Religious socialization gradually instills the ideas and concepts associated with what one does and feels. One begins to arrange these ideas and abstractions in certain common ways. "God," for example, becomes more than a word or sound that one utters, developing first into a feeling and then into an idea—one that can be discussed, questioned, argued about, and clarified. In the process of thinking and clarifying, one begins to recognize that one's religion defines certain ideas as correct ideas, certain behavior as correct behavior. One becomes socialized into the norms of the group, accepting as normal the ideas and behaviors that have been sanctioned by the religious group.

Some individuals continue their religious socialization by taking leadership positions within the religious group. These positions will require them to be able to adjust the group to changing conditions. They will become accustomed to recognizing the behavior, emotions, ideas, and norms that are sanctioned and projecting new ways for these to occur. In order to deal with life's changes, they come to understand various ways that religion may be verbalized, enacted, and institutionalized. A successful leader is one who enables the religious group to adjust its socialization process to changing times—for example, to stresses and changing conditions in the society in which it is situated—and thus to ensure the survival of the religious group.

Conversion, the process of accepting a religion to be one's own, can take place either in the context of the family or in the context of another group; one can be converted to the religion of one's parents or to another religion. Generally, conversion is a religious socialization experience that is associated with the individual who is older and is making choices consciously and actively, rather than passively accepting the status quo; conversion is therefore more often associated with a change, either in one's attitude about one's existing religion (that is, a reaffirmation or renewal of one's faith) or to a different religion. More often than not, one discusses "conversion" as the latter experience, but in its broadest sense, the conversion experience has played an increasingly important role in the latter half of the twentieth century as individuals have sought new, or renewed, sources of values to direct their lives.

Sociologists have advanced different theories of the reason people undergo religious conversion. Although structural sociologists (who consider people's choices as a by-product of social forces arising from social organization) are not often interested in the individual's reasons for conversion, they do identify some ways in which society's structure, specifically religious organization, contributes to this process. Some studies have supported the theory that disruptions in the individual's life (stresses such as marital problems, loss of a loved one, or being fired from one's job) tend to precede the conversion experience. Social connections with members of the new religious group can create another social force toward the conversion. Similarly, the severing of ties with or membership in a former religious group (or the lack of any such ties in the first place) creates another force toward conversion. Finally, family values expressed by parents during the potential convert's childhood (such as the importance of service to community or the need for a spiritual dimension to one's life) may lead individuals to convert to a religion that meets these needs, reiterating the importance of family in the religious socialization process. Situations in which the conversion process involves departure from the cultural mainstream to enter a cult is another interest of structural sociologists.

Unlike structural sociologists, action theorists are more concerned with the individual's search for moral meaning as a force in the religious socialization process. Action theorists see religious conversion primarily as a product of the individual's need to cope with life's problems or to find spiritual meaning in life, rather than as a product of social forces imposed from without. Likewise, the creation of religious meaning is often the result of the individual's own initiative, a conscious decision to live life in service of a code of values.

Applications

The real-world application of religious socialization depends on one's definition of religion. Religion is difficult to define, especially because most believe that they know what it is but have a difficult time pinning it down in words. North American culture, for example, has roots in Christian religion. Its principal features are God, the Bible, the Ten Commandments, attending church on Sunday, and experiencing God. Many sociologists unwittingly accept this cultural (Christian) definition of religion in their work. For them, religious socialization is a process in which one comes to a gradual realization of God and of what God has told human beings to say, do, and expect. Those who do not believe in God cannot be a member of a religion; they would be said to follow a philosophy or a "way of life."

Even many sociologists who do not believe in God accept these cultural presuppositions descriptive of what a religion is: God, a sacred book, commandments, prayer, and religious experience. If people have these, then they are seen to be religious; if they do not, they are secular (nonreligious). This definition of religion is culture dependent.

Many sociologists of religion do not accept such a narrow definition of religion. They look at all the religions of the world and claim that what is common to all of them is an involvement with, and recognition of, the supernatural. The supernatural, from this perspective, is that which is beyond and not subject to what human senses and ordinary knowledge reveal. Religious socialization, then, is an acknowledgment of the roles that one should play in the face of this supernatural reality. Certainly, this view of religion recognizes many of the religions that existed before the sixteenth century; however, if one accepts this definition of religion, many styles of life that have been adopted in opposition to supernaturalism would be dismissed as philosophies and ways of life. Consequently, some theorists find a need for a broader definition of religion.

Such a definition has been posited: A religion is a group of people who share an ultimate point of view. This view enables them to make sense of personal and universal existence. Religious socialization, in this context, is the process by which we share with others the common conviction of ultimacy. As long as we share verbalizations, actions, and institutions that provide us with a sense of wholeness and a way of understanding our existence, we may be said to be participating in a religion. Another way of articulating this definition of religion is that all people hold a point of view—a position from which they see and act in this world. This point of view has a physical component (people take up space), a social component (they live within a group of other people), an emotional component (they feel life in a way that is unique, different from others), and an intellectual component (they think slightly differently from others). When this point of view is their only way of understanding and dealing with life—when it becomes the ultimate viewpoint—then it is their religion. From this perspective, everyone has a point of view and therefore everyone is religious.

This definition of religion enables sociologists to understand a pluralistic world in which there are many competitors for ultimacy which seek people's total dedication. Such a definition also allows new religions to be incorporated into sociological models and compared with older religions. At the same time, it acknowledges that various competitors for people's limited energies seek to convert them to a particular way of life and are constantly engaged in the process of attempted socialization and conversion.

In the past, the role of religion was to legitimize the truths, morals, and institutions of a society. The religions that did so, such as Christianity, no longer perform this function to the degree they once did. The question could be asked, granted the foregoing broad definition of religion, "What does legitimize our laws, literature, and institutions?" That which legitimizes our culture may be seen as a civil religion. All people enter into a civil religion at birth and are socialized into it. A society's schooling, work, sports, politics, and media all play a part in the process of socialization into civil religion. An example of civil religion is nationalism—when one's nation becomes one's ultimate value.

To know people's religion and the socialization process whereby they enter more deeply into that religion is to know who they are and what motivates their thoughts and actions. Much sociological research investigates whether people are religious, using norms derived from the first and second definition of religion. Little sociological research exists which attempts to discover those deeper concerns, words, and actions suggested by the third, broad definition of religion.

Context

Sociologists, and most social scientists, find it difficult to incorporate the absolute nature of religion into their disciplines. Religions seek truth through faith, through address to a supernatural, non-empirical authority, whereas social scientists seek answers in the empirical world. If one defines religion in the sense of either a traditional institutionalized religion (Judaism, Christianity, Islam) or a supernatural one (as a significant number of sociologists do), then one might conclude that religion is having less and less influence in the modern world. Those sociologists who accept this view claim that today's North American society is a secular one in which religion has lost its legitimizing role and thus its influence over society. If, on the other hand, one extends the definition of religion to that broadest definition identified earlier—an ultimate point of view shared by a group of people—then the status of religion and religious socialization is much different and will be approached differently by sociologists. The future directions of research in the sociology of religion and religious socialization will therefore largely depend on the refinement of sociology's definition of religion.

Bibliography

Bellah, Robert N. *The Broken Covenant: American Civil Religion in Time of Trial.*

New York: Seabury Press, 1975. Bellah's foundational book began a decade-long discussion about the religion of the United States.

Berger, Peter, and Brigitte Berger. *Sociology: A Biographical Approach.* New York: Basic Books, 1972. Chapter 17, "Values and Ultimate Meanings," is an excellent review of socialization from the perspective of the broad definition of religion. This chapter describes how one is socialized into religions that offer ultimate answers to the meaning of life but do not necessarily appeal to the supernatural.

Johnstone, Ronald L. *Religion in Society: A Sociology of Religion.* 3d ed. Englewood Cliffs, N.J.: Prentice-Hall, 1988. Chapter 3, "Becoming Religious," treats religious socialization from the supernaturalist point of view.

Kohlberg, Lawrence, Charles Levine, and Alexandra Hewer. *Moral Stages: A Current Formulation and a Response to Critics.* Basel, Switzerland: Karger, 1983. Kohlberg claims that moral development happens outside religious development. His stages of moral development challenge those theories that claim that religion, in the traditional institutional and philosophical senses, is necessary for a moral society.

Luckmann, Thomas. *The Invisible Religion.* New York: Macmillan, 1967. Luckmann provides a description of what kind of new religion is developing to replace the supernaturalist religions.

Stokes, Kenneth, ed. *Faith Development in the Adult Life Cycle.* New York: W. H. Sadlier, 1982. Stokes's book is based on his work as head of a project that uses the methodologies of social science to investigate how people enter more deeply into religious life.

Wuthnow, Robert. *The Restructuring of American Religion.* Princeton, N.J.: Princeton University Press, 1988. A description of the socialization process outside the traditional religious institutions.

Nathan R. Kollar

Cross-References

Christianity, 231; Civil Religion and Politics, 259; Religion: Functionalist Analyses, 1603; Religion: Marxist and Conflict Theory Views, 1610; Secularization in Western Society, 1700; Socialization: The Family, 1880; Socialization: The Mass Media, 1887; The Sociology of Religion, 1952.

SOCIALIZATION AND REFERENCE GROUPS
IN RACE RELATIONS

Type of sociology: Racial and ethnic relations
Field of study: Theories of prejudice and discrimination

The concept of reference groups helps to explain the dynamics underlying inter-group behavior. It emphasizes the individual's use of salient groups as role models—by either referring to them at crucial moments, joining them, or being socialized into them. Among the effects of reliance on reference groups can be an ethnocentric outlook on life that leads to social conflict.

Principal terms

ETHNIC GROUP: a group that is defined by reference to such cultural characteristics as its religion and language; ethnic groups are self-conscious social units

ETHNOCENTRISM: the tendency for groups to regard their own culture as superior to that of outsiders

MAJORITY GROUP: the group in a society that is socially and politically dominant

MINORITY GROUP: a group which, because of relative powerlessness, experiences discrimination; other features include distinguishing characteristics, endogamy, and, often, small size relative to society's dominant group

PLURALISTIC SOCIETY: a society consisting of large numbers of people from different racial and ethnic backgrounds

RACIAL GROUP: a group that is defined socially, based on physical (biological) features which a particular society deems to be relevant

SOCIALIZATION: the process whereby individuals acquire their society's norms and values

Overview

Since its inception many decades ago, the concept of reference groups has found a number of applications in the social sciences because of its ability to illuminate certain motives underlying human action. Among the more important of these applications has been its use in the race relations field to help explain the dynamics underlying prejudice and discrimination. Because these phenomena are such deeply rooted and persistent problems, much effort has been applied to understanding their genesis. Sociologist Tamotsu Shibutani, in 1955, carefully discussed some of the implications inherent in the concept of reference groups. He argued that one can find at least three such implications. First, reference groups may be seen as standards which actors use to gauge their definition of particular situations; that is, individuals, in attempting to interpret unfamiliar situations, often emulate groups whose orientation they find influential. Individuals ask themselves, "What would x do in these circumstances?" Second, reference groups may be viewed as groups in which an actor desires to participate. Third, reference groups are groups whose viewpoint constitutes an actor's frame of reference. This implication, though similar to the first, differs in an important way: It implies a continuous socialization into the culture of the reference group, whereas the former does not. In the former usage, the idea is that at crucial moments, the individual will turn to his or her understanding of the reference group for guidance. In the latter, this orientation is more or less permanent, since the individual is constantly submerged in the norms and values of the reference group. It would not occur to the person that any other course of action is possible. Shibutani argues that the third meaning of reference groups is most important because of its association with culture and socialization.

Seen from the point of view of culture, reference groups are an outcome of the process of socialization. In this process, the norms and values of particular groups are inculcated into individuals such that they become their own. They reflexively act and feel as do others in their particular group. The group's frame of reference becomes one's own. The individual is able to anticipate the attitudes and feelings of others in the group because the individual is like them. Racial and ethnic groups are among the most important of the groups into which individuals are socialized, since they often generate intense in-group loyalty, and, hence, conflict. As reference groups, they are especially important in plural societies with their multiplicity of racial and ethnic groups. In such societies, the desire for social advancement can heighten racial and ethnic consciousness. Consequently, it becomes relatively more difficult to resolve conflicting group interests, since in-group members are unable (or unwilling) to take the viewpoint of others in competing racial or ethnic groups. The respective frames of reference are often too far apart to allow a rapprochement.

Paradoxically, plural societies can also undermine the particularistic leanings that lead to racial and ethnic conflict. By definition, these groups are not the only ones that exist in plural societies; there are many others. Significantly, some of these—such as occupational groups, classes, and religious groups—cross-cut racial and ethnic groups. Since individuals can belong to numerous groups at the same time, they might find that they have conflicting reference groups. The norms and values predominating in one group might conflict with those in another. For example, a racially conscious individual might harbor negative sentiments toward members of another race; however, he might also belong to a religious group which teaches that such feelings are wrong. Similarly, an individual might dislike members of a competing ethnic group but might find herself working closely with members of that ethnic group. As psychologist Gordon Allport has shown, close cooperation of this sort tends to undermine negative racial and ethnic sentiments. The task of reference group theory in circumstances such as those just noted is to predict which set of affiliations will win out in the end. According to Shibutani, this might depend on such factors as the individual's commitment to the respective groups or the depth of the interpersonal relationships that have developed in the groups. The expectation is that the reference group to which the individual is most deeply committed will be relatively more influential in guiding behavior.

Some sociologists say that reference groups are crucial to individuals in modern pluralistic societies such as the United States because they provide a frame of reference through which individuals make sense of the world. It is virtually impossible to imagine the nonexistence of reference groups, since they are the natural outgrowth of the process of socialization. Through this process, individuals assume that the norms and values of the groups into which they have been socialized are standard for all groups. Reference group formation, therefore, is inherently ethnocentric. Pluralism, however, can offset this ethnocentrism by providing individuals with the opportunity to belong to competing reference groups.

Applications

As noted in the previous section, the concept of reference groups is useful for explaining conflict in plural societies. One example of this is the situation to be found in former colonies. In many such societies, there exists a pattern of ethnic stratification in which, as the colonial rulers give up power, indigenous elites approximating them in culture (and sometimes in color) rise up to take their place. At the same time, the groups that traditionally resided at the bottom of colonial society remain subordinated. Thus, the end of colonialism, far from radically restructuring these societies, tends to maintain the status quo; indigenous elites, like the colonial masters before them, tend to despise the groups that reside at the bottom of the society. The concept of reference groups provides a clue as to how this pattern might be explained.

The former British colonies of the West Indies provide an example. Traditionally, these territories have exhibited a tripartite social structure quite unlike the sharp racial dichotomy to be found in the United States. Whereas Americans, relying on the "one drop rule," have tended to classify individuals with even remote black ancestry as "black," the West Indian countries have recognized three distinct social strata: a tiny white (and largely foreign) elite residing at the top of the society, a middle stratum made up of mixed-race individuals, and a large group of blacks (who constitute the bulk of the population) residing at the bottom of the society. Social status varied from top to bottom according to color and occupation. As was the case in the United States, "blackness" was denigrated and blacks were discriminated against. There was a crucial difference, however, since mixed-race individuals (who would be considered "black" in the United States) were recognized as constituting a distinct social category. Also, as historian Douglas Hall has shown, the idea existed that upward mobility could partially offset the stigma of black skin. Thus, the concept arose that "money whitens." This meant, essentially, that as upwardly mobile blacks adopted British culture more fully, they became increasingly "acceptable" to the British elite. This elite, therefore, constituted a reference group for the whole society. Their viewpoint, through socialization, became the prism through which blacks—mixed and unmixed—viewed the world. Writers such as Diane Austin and Gordon Lewis have shown that the family and the education system are the two most important institutions for transmitting

British culture. They argue, further, that the effectiveness of this transmission can be seen in the fact that West Indians overvalue educational credentials and "proper behavior" (such as forms of speech), and they evince deep class consciousness.

In the postcolonial period (formally inaugurated with Jamaica's independence in 1962), the British presence declined, but British culture remained very influential. As they withdrew from the region, the mulattoes, Syrians, and Jews who bore the closest physical resemblance to the British gradually occupied the elite position formerly occupied by the British. One aspect of this ethnic succession was the wholesale adoption of the antiblack stereotypes that had formerly been held by the British. The new elite's thorough inculcation into British culture meant that few other reference groups could rise to challenge the traditional way of viewing the world. Thus, the actual withdrawal of the British from the islands had little effect on racial attitudes. British culture acted as a conservative force to perpetuate existing inequalities even after the physical removal of the original British reference group. One could say, therefore, that race relations in the West Indies (and a number of other former colonies) cannot be understood without grasping the historical importance of reference groups.

In a similar vein, psychologist Jeff Howard and physician Ray Hammond have argued that the concept is useful in explaining underachievement among African Americans in the educational system. They argue that this problem stems from blacks' fear of competing intellectually because of stereotypes of black inferiority that have been broadcast by the majority group. For Howard and Hammond, the majority group is a reference group which establishes certain criteria for what will be defined as "success" and which undermines the confidence of African Americans by sowing doubt about the capabilities of African Americans. The majority group is able to do this because, by definition, majority groups exercise political, social, and cultural dominance in the societies in which they exist. Minority groups, on the other hand, are subordinated and face an uphill fight in getting their point of view to prevail.

If one bears in mind Shibutani's discussion of reference groups, one can see that writers use the term in different ways. For example, Shibutani wishes to confine the term to groups that provide an automatic frame of reference to individuals because of socialization. The analysis of West Indian racial attitudes, however, implies that reference groups serve as standards for making judgments, are groups which others aspire to join, and provide a frame of reference for upwardly mobile West Indians. Thus, in the West Indian context, the concept of reference groups embraces the full complement of meanings outlined by Shibutani. On the other hand, as used by Howard and Hammond, the term implies only the idea of groups that provide standards of judgment—in this case, intellectual. Therefore, one always needs to examine the context in which the term is used to determine its full meaning.

Context

The concept of reference groups was coined in the 1940's by the psychologist H. H. Hyman to explain how individuals evaluate their status. He reasoned that they could do this by using other people as reference groups. Hyman found that individuals' estimation of their status varied according to the particular group that was being used as a comparison group. Subsequent work by sociologists Robert K. Merton and A. Katt (1950) added the two other interpretations of reference group already mentioned: They are groups that others aspire to join and groups that organize an individual's frame of reference.

Reference groups must be seen within the context of two other important concepts: the social construction of reality and plural society. As discussed by the sociologist W. I. Thomas, the former term refers to the idea that the patterned interactions making up social structure are based largely on the selective perception of which social facts are important and which are not. This historical process involves the arbitrary selection of these criteria and their establishment as the basis of regularized social action. Once these criteria are chosen, people take them for granted and behave as if they have always been in effect. Moreover, the interaction that is based on these criteria is hardly questioned. While this view of society implies a static situation involving preknowledge of norms and values, social interaction is, in fact, dynamic. Individuals are constantly encountering situations in which norms are not obvious, and participants in these situations must negotiate the rules guiding interaction. One aspect of this process of negotiation is the use of reference groups as guides in the construction of rules of engagement in hazy social situations.

The possibilities for these types of situations arising increase as societies become more technical and more plural. This leads to the possibilities of individuals belonging to multiple groups and encountering unfamiliar situations. Both these possibilities create the need for guidelines to help in decision making. Belonging to multiple groups—for example, being a black immigrant from Africa and working as an engineer—can lead to the problem of deciding which identity will take precedence: the racial identity that stems from being black in America, the ethnic identity that stems from having an African background, or the class identity that stems from occupation and education? How an individual resolves such conflicts might well revolve around which reference group he or she views as being most salient. Living in a plural society also increases the number of encounters that individuals have with members of different groups. These encounters are potentially anxiety-producing, since cultures vary widely. Quite likely, an individual's response will be strongly affected by salient reference groups. For example, immigrants to the United States sometimes adopt negative stereotypes of groups already living here, even though they have previously had little experience with these groups. This prejudice can be explained by viewing it as a learned response deriving from native groups which the immigrants view as reference groups.

Bibliography

Allport, Gordon W. *The Nature of Prejudice*. Cambridge, Mass.: Addison-Wesley, 1954. A classic overview of prejudice and discrimination that is required reading for anyone interested in this field. Allport covers many of the most important aspects of the subject of race relations in a clear and accessible style.

Austin, Diane J. *Urban Life in Kingston, Jamaica: The Culture and Class Ideology of Two Neighborhoods.* New York: Gordon and Breach Science Publishers, 1984. Austin compares two neighborhoods in Kingston, Jamaica, in an attempt to analyze differences in middle-class and working-class culture. She concludes that Jamaican society exhibits high levels of class consciousness, deriving from the history of British colonialism. This is especially evident in Jamaicans' overvaluing of educational credentials.

Hall, Douglas. "The Ex-colonial Society in Jamaica." In *Patterns of Foreign Influence in the Caribbean,* edited by Emanuel de Kadt. London: Oxford University Press, 1972. Historian Hall gives an overview of social and political life in postcolonial Jamaica, showing both the shifts in power that have taken place between various racial/ethnic groups and the factors that have remained unchanged.

Lewis, Gordon K. *The Growth of the Modern West Indies.* New York: Monthly Review Press, 1968. In this important work, Lewis discusses British West Indian history from the eighteenth century to the 1960's. Although a large book, it is well worth reading for the many insights Lewis brings to the history of this region.

Merton, Robert K., and A. Katt. "Contributions to the Theory of Reference Group Behavior." In *Studies in the Scope and Method of "The American Soldier,"* edited by Robert K. Merton and Paul F. Lazarsfeld. Glencoe, Ill.: Free Press, 1950. Merton and Katt extend the concept of reference groups to include groups that others aspire to join and groups that shape the perceptual field of others.

Shibutani, Tamotsu. "Reference Groups as Perspectives." *American Journal of Sociology* 60 (May, 1955): 562-569. Shibutani's discussion of reference groups is incisive and informative. He discusses the various meanings of the term and argues that it is best understood as groups that provide a frame of reference for individuals. In this way, he ties the concept to culture and socialization.

Milton D. Vickerman

Cross-References

TYPES OF SOCIETIES

Type of sociology: Social structure
Field of study: Key social structures

Societies differ in the ways in which their members earn a living, particularly in the ways in which food is procured. These differences lead to markedly different social, economic, and political structures, as well as to very different attitudes toward resource use.

Principal terms

BARTER: the exchange of goods for other goods without the use of money or any other standardized medium of exchange

COERCIVE AUTHORITY: the right of a ruler, as recognized by the society as a whole, to exercise force to implement a policy

COLONIALISM: a system in which one country controls another for economic exploitation

CONSENSUS: unanimous or almost unanimous agreement, usually achieved through persuasion

CULTURAL EVOLUTION: a set of theories that maintain that there are regularities to long-term sociocultural change, resulting in a sequence of similar stages through which most cultural traditions pass

EGALITARIAN SOCIETY: a society whose members have essentially the same social status

KIN GROUP: a group of individuals who have a common ancestry and consider themselves a corporate entity, often organizing activities and acting as an economic unit

OCCUPATIONAL SPECIALIZATION: the condition in which individuals gain their primary livelihood in a relatively specialized way and then exchange the goods or services produced for those of other specialists

REDISTRIBUTION: the collection and reallocation of goods, particularly food, by a ruler, sometimes to consolidate political control

Overview

It is common to distinguish six types of society on the basis of how most people gain a livelihood: hunting and gathering, horticultural, agrarian, pastoralist, industrial, and postindustrial. Societies are systems that are designed in part to facilitate the everyday tasks of their members, and societies of each type usually share features that are related to their primary mode of livelihood.

Hunting and gathering societies collect their food from nature, with minimal control of what types and quantities of foodstuffs are available. Hunting and gathering includes actively hunting animals, trapping animals, fishing in its many forms, collecting shellfish, and collecting wild plants for food. Although hunting often has been considered the most important input into hunting and gathering economies, plant gathering almost always is the quantitatively predominant input. The fact that hunting typically is a male activity and plant gathering typically is the work of women, reflects a gender bias common among both hunting and gathering societies and the scholars who have studied them. The primary exception to the predominance of plant gathering is in the Arctic, where plant foods are simply unavailable in appreciable quantities and animal foods have to be the dietary mainstay.

The common image of hunting and gathering as time-consuming and precarious is only partly correct. Richard Lee's studies (1979) among the !Kung Bushmen of Africa show that the time spent hunting and gathering is considerably less than that spent by farmers and others. Yet hunter-gatherers are largely at the mercy of their environment and have few opportunities to increase either the amount of food or the reliability of its yield from year to year. Hunter-gatherers often have engaged in practices that provide some measure of control, such as burning areas to increase edible species or to increase forage for game, but these activities have limited effects.

Consequently, hunter-gatherers typically must live in relatively low densities and in small communities to avoid overtaxing the resources of their environments. In addition, they must move with the seasons—often five to ten times a year—to avoid depleting resources below the point at which they can recover and to take advantage of seasonal variations in resource availability. Sometimes a community breaks into smaller groups for the lean season, reuniting in a season of greater plenty.

This frequent movement means that the accumulation of material goods is limited and private ownership usually is rare. Land, too, is considered to belong to everyone, although the legitimate use of certain tracts may be allocated to particular kin groups. The movement of goods takes place largely through kin sharing or barter (the exchange of goods for other goods).

There are no specialized occupations among most hunter-gatherers; every man is a hunter and every woman a gatherer. Formal leadership is very limited, and many hunting and gathering communities have no formal leader; others have a nominal leader with no authority to make decisions for the group, a leader who leads by example and the ability to mold consensus. Hunting and gathering societies are essentially egalitarian, with few status differences among individuals.

Horticultural societies gain most of their living through the small-scale production of domesticated plants, although they may supplement their diets with hunted or gathered foods. Like hunter-gatherers, horticulturalists live in low densities and in small villages. A horticultural community may stay at a village for twenty years until local resources (such as soil and firewood) are depleted, at which time it will move to a new site. Land typically is owned communally, either by the community as a whole or by its component kin groups.

Horticultural societies have few specialists; everyone is a gardener. There usually is a community leader who works through consensus. A leader with unpopular ideas is simply ignored, and another leader emerges through informal processes. Their settled lifestyle permits horticulturalists to accumulate material goods, encouraging personal ownership. Although kin exchange remains important, barter takes on increasing importance.

Agrarian societies also grow crops, but they differ from horticultural societies in the larger scale of their production. Agriculturalists grow crops in more specialized manners, often in large fields rather than gardens, tilling with plows rather than hoes. Individuals in agrarian societies often specialize in one or a few crops, which means that they are dependent on other individuals for the other foodstuffs they require.

This developing occupational specialization is seen in other arenas; specialists may make tools, clothing, and other goods to be sold. This growing web of specialists ties society together in a new way, which influential sociologist Max Weber called "organic," with each member dependent on many other members for everyday needs. Kin-based exchange becomes less important, the exchange of goods occurs predominantly through barter and cash purchase, and private ownership becomes standard. The old egalitarian system breaks down, and some people begin to amass wealth. Permanent towns with many goods and a few rich people become the norm.

This increased complexity both permits and demands stronger leadership, and leaders with coercive power emerge. They may be called "chiefs," "kings," or "pharaohs," but these rulers all share the power to enforce their will. The greater the coercive authority, the greater the bureaucracy that is required to ensure that the ruler's will is carried out. Some rulers gather produce together and redistribute it to their subjects, withholding food and other essentials to ensure obedience.

Pastoralist societies are those that gain their primary livelihood from the herding of domesticated animals. Pastoralists must live in low densities and small communities, lest their herds destroy pasturage too rapidly. For the same reason, they must travel almost constantly in search of new grazing lands.

Pastoralists have a unique relationship with settled agriculturalists. The pastoralists cannot produce either the quantity or variety of products necessary to maintain a satisfactory lifestyle, so they regularly trade with agriculturalists; in addition, they may take advantage of their superior mobility to raid agriculturalists, seizing the goods they desire. In this manner, some individuals become wealthy, possessing too many goods to continue their nomadism, abandoning the strenuous life of pastoralism to become sedentary agriculturalists in towns. At the same time, poor town-dwellers may opt to join pastoralist groups in hopes of improving their situations. This intimate relationship has been documented and analyzed closely by Fredrik Barth and others.

Pastoralists range from kin-based communities with weak leadership to feudal societies with strong, coercive leaders overseeing a bureaucracy. Some pastoralists, such as the Mongols, have conquered large empires, though it is difficult to maintain an empire without settling into an agrarian lifestyle.

Industrial societies build on an agrarian base, changing the ways in which goods are made. Industrial societies use factories and mass production, rather than the small-scale craft production of earlier times. These factories require a sufficiently large and prosperous middle class to finance them and to consume many of the goods that they produce, since the output of goods must increase to make factories financially viable. Industrialization began in Europe in the late 1700's and has spread throughout the world.

Industrial societies intensify many of the trends seen earlier, leading to larger settlements, more important cash economies, stronger government, and a more specialized agricultural base. In addition, they provide a vehicle for vertical mobility, enabling those born with little to aspire to great wealth. They also provide jobs for unskilled laborers, creating another sector of purchasers of goods.

This focus on material production produces ecological and social crises of various sorts. Resources dwindle, industrial by-products pollute air and water, and cast-off products clog landfills. Some factories have exploited children and the poor shamelessly, and conditions in factories and associated communities often have produced poor health and despair.

Postindustrial societies are those few that have been able to shift much of their industrial focus into the processing of information. Industrial manufacturing remains important, but increasing numbers of workers provide services, manage accounts, write software, and otherwise process information. Postindustrial societies have developed only since World War II, and it is unclear how far the industrial base can be replaced with information-processing occupations. To the extent that this is possible, some of the ills associated with industrialization can be reduced.

Applications

The foregoing typology of societies is primarily of descriptive and theoretical importance. Its primary application lies in the societal conflicts that are associated with colonialism.

Although societies of different types have been in contact for millennia, the greatest conflicts developed in the centuries following the European voyages of exploration in the 1500's. The hunger of Europeans for land and resources led to the colonial exploitation of vast areas, particularly the Americas, Australia, and parts of Africa. In these places, the agrarian and industrial societies of Europe had a clear economic-military advantage, and the European colonists usually were able to force conquered peoples to do their bidding.

In North America, for example, European Americans attempted to rationalize the seizing of Native American lands by stating that those lands were not being used efficiently. As those who appropriated the lands accurately noted, there were no Native American cities, factories, gold mines, or (in most areas) extensive fields. For an industrial society, such land use could be considered wasteful, but for the hunting-gathering and horticultural societies of native North America, it was not only appropriate but also necessary.

Colonial conflict between societies of different types has continued into the late twentieth century. The deforestation of the Amazon rain forest, for example, has been progressing since the eighteenth century, and the Native American inhabitants of the forest have been forced onto increasingly cramped reserves. The reserves are mostly far too small to permit the continuation of the traditional hunting-gathering and horticultural lifeways of these people, and they increasingly have joined the ranks of unskilled, disillusioned, and exploited miners and loggers, destroying the very landscape that formerly nurtured their ways of life.

It is perhaps noteworthy that Western opposition to the destruction of the Amazon rain forest has been based primarily on the deleterious effects of that destruction on the world climate (particularly the enhancing of the greenhouse effect and global warming) and the extinction of plant species with potential for medicinal use. It was only the recognition of effects on industrial and postindustrial societies that sparked widespread concern.

By recognizing the needs of the various types of societies, governments and individuals can take the first step in the difficult job of balancing different societies' demands in these intersocietal conflicts. Deciding which society's needs are more pressing is not an easy thing, and the ethical basis for such decisions can be formulated only if a clear understanding of each type of society and its distinctive needs has been established.

Context

Although generations of earlier scholars had been aware that different types of societies existed, Lewis Henry Morgan, in the mid-nineteenth century, was the first to place these societies in an analytic framework. He established an influential scheme of cultural evolution that passed from "savagery" (hunting-gathering) to "barbarism" (horticulture and pastoralism) and on to "civilization" (agrarian-industrial societies). He systematically linked mode of subsistence to societal characteristics for the first time and produced a rationale for the evolution of increasingly complex types of societies.

One reader of Morgan was Friedrich Engels, who brought modified versions of Morgan's scheme to his collaboration with Karl Marx. Together, Engels and Marx developed another cultural evolutionary scheme, again based largely on mode of subsistence, which was slightly reconceived and renamed "mode of production."

In the nineteenth century, the various fields of the social sciences—particularly sociology and anthropology—were less clearly differentiated than they became in the twentieth century, and many of the great early figures are claimed by both disciplines. As they diverged, sociology focused on Western society and anthropology focused on small-scale, non-Western societies. Consequently, more anthropological studies than sociological studies have dealt with hunter-gatherer, horticultural, agrarian, and pastoralist societies, and anthropologists have made most of the twentieth century advances in the study of types of societies.

Anthropologists such as Marshall Sahlins and Elman Service (1960) have continued the cultural evolutionary school of thought, discussing the relationship between mode of subsistence and, particularly, political systems. They defined four types of sociopolitical stages that correlate roughly with subsistence mode. The "band" is restricted largely to hunter-gatherers and has no formal leader; the "tribe" is largely restricted to horticulturalists and has a consensual, noncoercive leader; the "chiefdom" usually is found among agrarian or pastoralist societies and has a coercive leader who rules directly; and the "state," which is found in large-scale agrarian or industrial societies, requires a bureaucracy to assist a coercive leader in administering a large domain. Postindustrial societies were defined after the completion of Service and Sahlins' work, but they, too, are ruled by states. Service and Sahlins argued that the stages lead naturally from one to the next, producing a typical sequence of evolutionary stages within a cultural tradition. Many scholars believe that population increases cause a society to pass into a new stage.

Another school of research focuses on cultural ecology, the relationship between environment and culture. Cultural ecologists usually focus closely on a single society, trying to relate their customary usages to the efficient exploitation of their environment. Cultural ecologists such as Richard Lee and Julian Steward have studied particular societies, concentrating on such issues as how much time and effort have to be expended to gain sustenance with the given subsistence mode, what social and political structures make the extraction and distribution of food and other materials efficient, and what social events serve to legitimize values that are critical to that way of life. Some ecologists take a further step and try to find commonalities among societies of the same type.

Bibliography

Barth, Fredrik. *Nomads of South Persia*. Boston: Little, Brown, 1961. This excellent treatment, based on the author's extensive fieldwork among the Basseri, documents a classic example of the interplay between nomadic pastoralists and sedentary agriculturalists, including economic interdependence and the movement of individuals between the two lifestyles.

Chirot, Daniel. *Social Change in the Modern Era*. San Diego, Calif.: Harcourt Brace Jovanovich, 1986. This discussion of industrial and postindustrial societies focuses on their economic, social, and political development.

Lee, Richard B. *The !Kung San: Men, Women, and Work in a Foraging Society*. Cambridge, England: Cambridge University Press, 1979. A classic work of cultural ecology, this is one of the last pieces of research to analyze a functioning hunter-gatherer society; the !Kung no longer live a hunting-gathering existence. This book's treatments of gender roles and efficiency are superb.

Lenski, Gerhard. *Human Societies: A Macrolevel Introduction to Sociology*. New York: McGraw-Hill, 1970. This fine textbook devotes chapters to discussions of societal classification schemes and descriptions of various types of societies. It is useful in spite of the fact that it was written before the development of postindustrial societies. Its discussions of the development of cultures from an evolutionary perspective are particularly good.

Morgan, Lewis Henry. *Ancient Society*. New York: H. Holt, 1877. Republished by several publishers, this work is the culmination of Morgan's researches into the relationship between subsistence and culture. His earlier works were more influential at the time this work was published, but this work brings together his major ideas on the subject.

Sahlins, Marshall D., and Elman R. Service, eds. *Evolution and Culture*. Ann Arbor: University of Michigan Press, 1960. A classic work whose significance is belied by its small size, this book reinvigorated the search for regularities of cultural evolution. Some of the references to "laws of cultural development" are a bit dated, but the general linkage of modes of subsistence to other aspects of culture remains as fresh as ever.

Russell J. Barber

Cross-References

Agrarian Economic Systems, 60; Communal Societies, 297; Culture and Technology, 443; Horticultural Economic Systems, 903; Hunting and Gathering Economic Systems, 909; Industrial and Postindustrial Economies, 940; Industrial Societies, 953; Postindustrial Societies, 1446; Rural Societies, 1673.

SOCIOBIOLOGY AND THE NATURE-NURTURE DEBATE

Type of sociology: Origins and definitions of sociology
Field of study: Sociological perspectives and principles

Sociobiology refers to the application of the principles of evolutionary biology to the study of the social behavior of organisms, including humans. Sociobiologists often focus on the adaptive significance of social behavior and thus consider the contributions of an organism's environment (including social and cultural factors) and its biology (genes) to social behavior.

Principal terms
ADAPTATION: the process in which a trait—either genetic or socio-cultural—tends to increase the fitness of its possessors relative to the other members of the population; also, the functional interdependence of an organism (genes) and the environment
BEHAVIORAL PREDISPOSITION: a genetically based tendency to behave according to, or to be socialized along, certain general sociocultural patterns
EVOLUTION: the change over time of the proportion of a population's members who possess a certain trait or traits
FITNESS: the measure of an individual's success in contributing genes to future generations relative to that of the other members of a population
INCLUSIVE FITNESS: the sum of the fitness derived from one's own reproductive activities plus those of one's blood relatives (who possess and may contribute common genes)
NATURAL SELECTION: the differential contribution of genes to the next generation by the members of a population on the basis of differential fertility and mortality
REPRODUCTIVE SUCCESS: one's relative success in producing offspring that survive to reproduce in the future generation

Overview

Rather than being a distinct discipline, sociobiology comprises the work of numerous scholars from such disciplines as sociology, anthropology, psychology, neurobiology, ethology, zoology, and primatology who incorporate the principles of evolutionary biology within the study of the social behavior of humans and other organisms. Although research that may be considered sociobiological has been conducted for some time, "sociobiology" and its application to human social behavior—human sociobiology—came into prominence with the 1975 publication of entomologist Edward O. Wilson's book *Sociobiology: The New Synthesis.* The "new synthesis" of human sociobiology, according to sociologist Joseph Lopreato, refers to the marriage of theories of sociocultural behavior and modern evolutionary theory.

The roots of sociobiological theory may be traced to nineteenth century naturalist Charles Darwin's theory of evolution by natural selection. Darwin was aware of economist Thomas Malthus' observation that the growth of populations tends to outpace the growth of the supply of the resources upon which the population is dependent. He argued that competition for scarce resources generally occurs and results in some members of a population being more successful than others in terms of survival and reproduction. He reasoned that the differential abilities of the members of a population to survive and reproduce reflect variations in the traits possessed by the members—that is, some members of a population have traits that are adaptive, given the environmental conditions. Darwin went on to argue that if traits that are adaptive in one generation are heritable and continue to yield a survival and reproduction advantage to their possessors in future generations, the proportion of the population possessing the adaptive traits will increase.

This process, the differential survival and reproduction among the members of a population on the basis of the possession of different and heritable (genetically influenced) traits, is known as natural selection. Numerous examples of evolution by natural selection pertaining to human physiology are evident, including the development of opposable thumbs, bipedalism, and large, complex brains. Following the logic of natural selection, these traits developed and became prominent within human populations because of advantages they conveyed to their bearers in the form of enhanced survival and reproduction. Sociobiologists contend, in essence, that because the human brain—the seat of an individual's cognitive and behavioral functioning—has developed across the millennia through evolution by natural selection, this process has shaped human behavioral traits as well.

In order to characterize the influence of natural selection on behavior, sociobiologists have derived a general principle, commonly referred to as the maximization principle. Lopreato has stated this principle as follows: "Organisms tend to behave so as to maximize their inclusive fitness." The maximization principle is the cornerstone of the sociobiological theory of human nature, human nature being the set of behavioral tendencies or predispositions that characterize the members of the human species. Maximizing one's inclusive fitness entails, in part, contributing more of one's genes to future generations than do other members of the population. The tendency to maximize one's inclusive fitness thus reflects the competitive aspects of natural selection. On the surface, it seems to paint a selfish portrait of human nature. Yet sociobiologists have found in the maximization principle a possible basis for cooperative behavior. One's inclusive fitness can be increased by contributing any copies of one's genes to future generations; therefore, behavior in accordance with the maximization principle may involve helping or cooperating with those who share common genes: one's blood kin. Since most siblings have about half of their genes in common, one could increase one's fitness by helping to increase the reproductive success of one's siblings. Given that throughout most of human existence human societies were structured largely around kin groups, the saliency of this aspect of the maximization principle to the evolution of human societies becomes evident. Following the logic of the maximization principle, sociobiologists have proposed models of human nature consisting, in part, of such behavioral predispositions as reciprocation, an explanatory urge, a need for recognition, and territoriality.

Sociobiologists contend that behavior is at least somewhat influenced by biology. In contrast, many sociologists contend that human behavior is largely determined by learning, the environment, and other external factors; these factors are collectively called "nurture." For example, gender researcher Jean Lipman-Blumen contends that children generally assume so-called normal gender-specific behaviors because they were taught or socialized to do so, not because they are biologically predisposed to some different behaviors.

How can researchers tell whether biology influences behavior? The clearest evidence would come from genetic research, but in many respects this field is still in its infancy. Nevertheless, some studies have suggested that genes influence at least some aspects of behavior; the mental disorder schizophrenia is one example. Another approach is to compare the behaviors of separately reared but genetically identical twins. Some of the best research here was conducted by psychologist Thomas Bouchard, who found many remarkable similarities between twins who shared a common nature but not a common nurture. Bouchard concluded that genes substantially contribute to such behaviors as religiosity, political orientation, and intelligence. In the light of such findings, Daniel Koshland, biologist and editor of the journal *Science*, has remarked that the nature-nurture debate is basically over. Sociobiologists appear to be at least partially justified in their claims of the influence of biology on behavior, but it bears noting that the extent and magnitude of this influence remains largely unspecified.

Applications

One of the major tasks undertaken by sociobiologists is to characterize the interplay of nature and nurture. To clarify the sociobiological enterprise and the interaction of nature and nurture, the class of phenomena known as cultural universals may be considered. A cultural universal is a cultural attribute that is found in virtually all societies. Anthropologist George Murdock, after examining a vast array of historical and ethnographic data, has identified dozens of cultural universals, including an incest taboo, kin groups, kinship nomenclature, status differentiation, and courtship rituals. Sociobiologists view such uniformity as evidence of a commonly held human nature. The widespread existence of these cultural traits, they argue, could not be wholly capricious. Wilson, for example, argues that "few of these unifying properties can be interpreted as the inevitable outcome of either advanced social life or high intelligence." Sociobiologists contend that these common cultural traits reflect deep-seated, biologically based behavior predispositions that have evolved within human neuroanatomy to reflect some of the basic directives of the maximization principle.

The universal phenomenon of the incest taboo may be taken as an example. The specific details of the taboo vary somewhat between and within cultures, but, in general, this term refers to an aversion to and culturally supported prohibitions against

y

marrying or mating with someone who is a close blood relative. Social scientists have often wondered why such a trait would prevail across the diverse range of cultures. Some anthropologists have argued that the incest taboo developed as a means of avoiding intrafamilial conflicts that might arise if incestuous relationships were commonplace; thus it acts to sustain family integrity. Yet explaining the avoidance of incestuous relationships in terms of cultural factors alone seems inadequate in the light of sociologist Joseph Shepher's research indicating the persistence of incest avoidance in a social environment void of cultural prohibitions against incest.

Sociobiologists, in contrast, propose a deeper explanation for the incest taboo that could conceivably operate in conjunction with the one noted above. They reason in the following manner. Each person has twenty-three pairs of chromosomes on which their genes reside. About half of each pair are inherited from one's father, and the other half come from one's mother, so in a sense, a person has two copies of most genes. Among the millions of genes residing in the chromosomes of the average individual are about four that can produce lethal effects. Most people do not suffer the effects of the lethal genes because these genes are usually superseded by their nonlethal complements. Because closely related kin share a greater than average amount of their genes in common, however, there is a heightened risk that offspring resulting from their mating will inherit the same lethal genes from both parents and thus have a greatly reduced chance of surviving and reproducing. Therefore, incestuous mating practices would be likely to decrease one's fitness and would thus oppose the basic tendency suggested by the maximization principle. Sociobiologists suggest that an aversion to mating with one's close relatives may be a behavioral trait that became prevalent across the millennia by means of evolution by natural selection. Furthermore, sociobiologists suggest that the various cultural sanctions discouraging incest may reflect cultural evolution following a trajectory based on biological evolution.

The cultural universals pertaining to kin groups and kinship nomenclature may also be considered. It has been widely documented that a basic institution characterizing human societies is the kin group or family. Furthermore, some set of titles or names (such as aunt, cousin, mother, and brother) is used within these societies to specify the relationships among family members. A host of sociocultural factors have been suggested as explanations of these common occurrences. For example, it has been suggested that families exist because they perform a variety of functions such as being reproductive units, socializing and nurturing the young, and being units of economic production. Sociocultural explanations of the kinship nomenclature often focus on the possible benefits accruing from such a classification system. Incest avoidance, for example, would be aided by clear identification of family members.

Such accounts for the universal existence of kin groups and kinship nomenclature are often incorporated into sociobiological explanations of these phenomena, but sociobiologists search for a deeper level of explanation. They view families as adaptive mechanisms; that is, through providing their participants with resources, nurturance, socialization, and the like, a family can enhance its participants' survival and reproduction.

The universal phenomenon of kinship nomenclature is probably closely related to the concept of inclusive fitness. Kin have a greater than average portion of their genes in common, and sociobiologists suggest that the possession of common genes facilitates cooperation. The extent of this genetic relatedness varies between kin. On the basis of basic Mendelian genetics, for example, the coefficient of relatedness between a parent and child or between two siblings is about 0.50. The coefficient for grandparent-grandchild is 0.25, and that for cousins is 0.13. Therefore, if one were to behave in accordance with the maximization principle, one would be more likely to cooperate with those to whom one was more closely related. Kinship nomenclature, in short, may provide a readily accessible representation of the genetic similarity between family members and hence may facilitate behavior in accordance with the maximization principle.

Context

The relevance of evolution to sociology has long been acknowledged by such prominent social theorists as Karl Marx, Vilfredo Pareto, Talcott Parsons, and George Homans, but its popularity among sociologists has varied over the years. The noted historian Carl Degler carefully chronicled the varying levels of acceptance of evolutionism among American social scientists and concluded that much of the waxing and waning has been attributable to shifts in ideology. Sociologist Joseph Lopreato offers an excellent example of this point. He notes that many of the social Darwinists of the late nineteenth and early twentieth centuries were immersed in a swell of capitalist ideology that characterized the United States at that time. He contends that many of these social Darwinists were more indebted to economist Adam Smith than to Charles Darwin.

Sociology was characterized by a different, liberal wave of ideology at the time of the publication of *Sociobiology: The New Synthesis*. Despite many sociobiologists' explicit recognition of the importance of both biological and sociocultural factors to human social behavior, some sociologists viewed sociobiologists as their opponents in the old nature-nurture debate. Any notions that humans' evolutionary past and biology contributed to human behavior in the present were generally discounted, explicitly or implicitly. Many sociologists considered humans and their behavior to be exclusively the products of environmental influences, social interactions, the sociocultural system, and the like. Degler argues that sociologists' dismissal of nature was attributable largely to a desire for humans to be completely malleable (thus facilitating a resolution to the social turmoil of that era) rather than to any discovery of facts that indicated the irrelevance of biology to human social behavior. Indeed, the assertion by sociobiologists that genes influence at least some aspects of human behavior earned them accusations of being social Darwinists and extreme ideological conservatives. Furthermore, it may not be too amiss to note that some sociologists viewed sociobiology as an attempt by biologists such as Wilson to overtake the domain of their discipline.

Sociobiology has gained more support among sociologists since the 1970's. Although many sociologists would still take issue with Koshland's declaration of the end of the nature-nurture debate, others have found persuasive the research upon which Koshland's position is based. Sociobiology's increasing acceptance is probably attributable to a number of other factors as well, not the least of which are the careful and fruitful sociobiological endeavors undertaken by such noted social scientists as Alice Rossi, Melvin Konner, Jane Lancaster, and Joseph Lopreato. Also, numerous professional journals and organizations have been formed to advance and publish interesting, high-quality research in the field. Given these facts and the tremendous progress being made toward the precise specification of the contributions of genes to behavior, it seems likely that sociobiology will continue to gain prominence within sociology in the years to come.

Bibliography

Alexander, Richard D. *The Biology of Moral Systems*. Hawthorne, N.Y.: Aldine de Gruyter, 1987. In this book, Alexander adopts a sociobiological perspective to discuss the development and future of moral systems among human populations. Alexander discusses such wide-ranging topics as altruism, the rights of children and parents, and the arms race.

Barash, David P. *Sociobiology and Behavior*. New York: Elsevier, 1977. This is a well-written text that introduces some of the complex aspects of sociobiology, including elements of population biology, genetics, reproductive strategies, and ecology, and makes them quite accessible. The second edition, published in 1982, reflects numerous significant changes and is recommended.

Dawkins, Richard. *The Selfish Gene*. New York: Oxford University Press, 1976. This book provides lucid discussions of DNA, genetic inheritance, population biology, and the implications of the basic principles of these topics to human nature, the growth of the human population, and mate selection. Although written for a popular audience, this book has been influential in academic circles as well.

Degler, Carl N. *In Search of Human Nature: The Decline and Revival of Darwinism in American Social Thought*. New York: Oxford University Press, 1991. Degler's book offers a thoughtful history of the nature-nurture debate within American social science. Especially interesting are the numerous insights into the influences of general social events, movements, and attitudes on relative emphasis of nature and nurture in the work of prominent social scientists.

Lopreato, Joseph. *Human Nature and Biocultural Evolution*. Boston: Allen & Unwin, 1984. This book represents one of the most ambitious and thorough attempts to incorporate modern evolutionary biology into sociological theory. Lopreato, a sociologist, is quite appreciative of the importance of culture and quite knowledgeable about evolutionary biology; these traits are evident in the richness of the model of human nature contained in this book.

Lumsden, Charles, and Edward O. Wilson. *Promethean Fire: Reflections on the Origin of Mind*. Cambridge, Mass.: Harvard University Press, 1983. This book offers a theory of gene-culture coevolution written for a popular audience. It is based on a highly technical book by the same authors entitled *Genes, Mind, and Culture: The Coevolutionary Process* (1981). Provides an interesting view of the interdependent evolution of the human brain, mind, and culture.

Wilson, Edward O. *On Human Nature*. Cambridge, Mass.: Harvard University Press, 1978. Although somewhat controversial and dated, this excellent book was the recipient of a Pulitzer Prize and much acclaim in the scientific community. Wilson integrates modern evolutionary theory, data from a variety of animal species, and numerous cross-cultural observations in this exploration of the foundation of human nature.

Arlen D. Carey

Cross-References

Cultural Norms and Sanctions, 411; Deviance: Biological and Psychological Explanations, 532; Gender Inequality: Biological Determinist Views, 826; The Incest Taboo, 934; Personality: Affective, Cognitive, and Behavioral Components, 1356; Personality Development: Erikson, 1362; Personality Development: Freud, 1368; Population Size and Human Ecology, 1428; Socialization: The Family, 1880.

SOCIOLOGICAL RESEARCH: DESCRIPTION, EXPLORATION, AND EXPLANATION

Type of sociology: Sociological research
Field of study: Basic concepts

The conducting of sociological research may involve a number of different approaches, either performed separately or in conjunction with one another. Describing, exploring, and explaining social phenomena are among the most common goals of research; they require different procedures and are intended to produce different types of results.

Principal terms
CONCEPTUAL CONSTRUCT: a type of phenomenon or variable that cannot be directly measured
COVERT RESEARCH: a type of field research in which subjects are unaware of the true identity of the researcher
DEPENDENT VARIABLE: the experimental variable that is a result or by-product of the independent variable
INDEPENDENT VARIABLE: the experimental variable that is typically under the control of the researcher
NATURALISTIC OBSERVATION: in contrast to laboratory research, studies in which subjects are observed in the environment in which they live, with little or no intervention on the part of the researcher
OBSERVER BIASES: beliefs or attitudes of a researcher that can alter the outcome of research by interfering with collection of accurate data or objective analysis of the data
OPERATIONAL DEFINITION: a description of a variable according to how the operations on it will be measured
QUANTITATIVE MEASURES: types of measures that attempt to categorize and summarize observations through the assignment of numbers

Overview

Sociology is a behavioral science that studies human social phenomena. Among the social phenomena that are commonly explored are social institutions (such as religious denominations), human relations, belief systems and values, and social movements. As is true with other sciences, sociology has as its foundation a strong emphasis on research. In order for sociology to continue to grow and evolve as a discipline, it must be continuously infused with new ideas, and research plays an important role in creating new ideas.

There are a plethora of research strategies that may be implemented in the attempt to discover new knowledge. One of the important considerations in choosing a research strategy is the amount of previous research that has been done on the topic being studied. The goals and purposes of studies may vary widely depending on how much has already been learned about a topic. Most research falls into one (or more) of three categories: the description, exploration, or explanation of social phenomena.

Earl Babbie, a practitioner of social science research, states in his book *The Practice of Social Research* (1992) that the description of situations and events is a central purpose of research. He goes on to say that the process of describing events scientifically is very different from the informal or casual methods of observation that most people use on a day-to-day basis. In order to obtain good descriptions of situations or events, observations must be careful, precise, and representative. Most informal observations are based on too few instances for any conclusions drawn to be valid. In addition, no adjustments are made regarding how the data are collected to counteract any observer biases that might be in effect.

Two important characteristics apply to descriptive research. One of these entails defining exactly what will be described. For example, a sociologist might want to study whether a particular group of people could be considered a "religious" congregation. The sociologist would need to decide how this will be determined; he or she would need to translate the conceptual construct "religious" into an operational definition—into behavior that can be publicly observed. For example, "religious" could be operationally defined as involving regular prayer to a god and conformity to a particular set of teachings. The use of such a definition would make it possible for a researcher to categorize a group as religious or nonreligious.

A second characteristic of descriptive research involves the measurement of specific events or observations. Typically, observations are recorded using quantitative measures. This implies that events are recorded as numbers on some kind of scale. For example, the variable "altruism" could be operationally defined as the degree to which an individual offers assistance to a person standing next to a disabled car. A rating system to measure altruism could conceivably look something like this: A score of 0 would be assigned to people who offered no assistance of any kind; a score of 1 would be assigned if someone stopped and said they would call for help when they arrived at their destination; and a 2 would be given for offering to take the person to the nearest telephone. Although this simple rating system is not perfect and does not cover all possible gradations by which someone could be judged to help another person, it is an attempt to quantify an abstract variable.

Exploration as a purpose of research differs considerably from descriptive research. Rather than emphasizing how events should be defined and measured, exploratory research attempts to unearth new facts in an area that has received little, if any, systematic study. Since not much is known about the area that is being studied, exploratory research can be both difficult and exciting. It can be difficult because, in the initial stages, it is usually not possible to identify the important independent and dependent variables that should be studied; there may be considerable guesswork in the early stages. In addition, once the decision has been made to study a set of variables, one may need to develop novel methods to define, organize, and measure them.

Exploratory research can be an exciting process in that it requires a researcher to draw on his or her creative energies to think about a particular topic in new and unique ways. Exploratory research tends to be less structured and well planned than other types. This can add to the excitement of doing research; as one proceeds, it may be necessary to revise the methods that have been employed. In addition, there is always the hope that something significant will arise from the enterprise of studying a new area. Babbie states that exploratory research is done primarily for three reasons: to enable a researcher to understand better a relationship among variables, to find out how feasible it would be to conduct a more carefully thought out study, and to refine the methods that would be necessary to conduct such a study.

Another purpose of research is to explain how things work. Explanatory research goes beyond merely describing and exploring events. Some of the primary goals of conducting explanatory research involve examining the antecedents and consequences of events. It is important not only to learn what the antecedents and consequences are but also to try to determine cause-and-effect relationships. In order to do this, it is usually necessary for the researcher to have control over the independent variables. A carefully thought out procedure is also essential. Thus, much of the research done in terms of explanatory research is in the form of experiments.

Applications

Research is often done with more than one purpose in mind. For example, it is common for a researcher to engage in a study that serves both descriptive and exploratory purposes. There are, however, particular research strategies that tend to be suited to each of the three purposes mentioned above.

Research that primarily describes events and behaviors includes studies focusing on people within their natural environment. In a classic study by John Griffin described in his book *Black Like Me* (1961), Griffin, a white man, colored his skin to take on the appearance of a black man. He traveled throughout the South, documenting his experiences—especially those involving racial discrimination. He then described his experiences, observations, and perceptions in narrative form. The purpose of this research was descriptive in nature—he wanted to gain insight into how he would be treated differently by whites after his skin was dyed.

Field research is a strategy that is frequently used for exploring a new area. David L. Rosenhan, in a field study, studied mental health professionals' ability to distinguish the "sane" from the "insane." Rosenhan published the article "On Being Sane in Insane Places" in *Science* (1973) based on this research. He sent eight psychologically stable individuals to twelve different mental institutions to see whether they would be admitted as patients. Each pseudopatient went to an institution under an assumed name and a false occupation (this was necessary since three of the pseudopatients were psychologists and one was a psychiatrist, and if this were known they might have been given special treatment). The pseudopatients told the admitting staff that they had been hearing voices that appeared to say the words "hollow," "empty," and "thud." All pseudopatients were admitted and diagnosed as "schizophrenic" or "manic-depressive." From the moment the pseudopatients gained entrance into the institutions, they began to act in a completely normal manner. They took notes on a daily basis of the staff members' behaviors. Although Rosenhan was shocked that all his assistants (as well as himself) were admitted, he was even more dismayed that the pseudopatients' "insanity" was never questioned by the staff.

The pseudopatients were released from the hospital anywhere from seven to fifty-two days later. Exploratory research, such as this example, can be filled with risks. None of the pseudopatients truly expected to be admitted, let alone to have to stay an average of nineteen days in the hospital before the mental health professionals declared them well enough to be released. Rosenhan's ground-breaking exploratory study underscored the problem of separating the normal from the abnormal with conventional diagnostic procedures. Rosenhan applied the results of this study to the broader issue of psychological labeling. He pointed out that categorizing an individual as having a particular mental illness can be misleading and, in many instances, harmful.

Research as explanation can be seen in a study by Lee A. Rosen, a behavioral science researcher, and his colleagues entitled "Effects of Sugar (Sucrose) on Children's Behavior," published in the *Journal of Consulting and Clinical Psychology* (1988). Rosen wanted to test the truth of a commonly held belief that eating or drinking foods containing large amounts of sugar has a detrimental effect on children's behavior. In other words, he wanted an explanation of the relationship between sugar intake and behavior. Over a period of fifteen days, he studied forty-five schoolchildren. The children were told that they would be eating breakfast at school. Rosen divided the children into three groups, which received different amounts of sugar in their breakfasts. During the first five days, one group ate a breakfast containing no sugar. A second group ate a breakfast with 6 grams of sugar, and a third ate a breakfast containing 50 grams. For each of the experiment's three five-day periods, the children were assigned to different groups. The children were observed each day according to measures such as fidgeting, changes in activity levels, vocalization, and aggressive behavior. An assortment of cognitive and performance measures was used to test their ability to concentrate and perform tasks. Neither the children nor the people collecting the data knew the amounts of sugar given to each group.

Rosen found that, contrary to common belief, sugar seemed to have no significant effects on the children's behavior. Sugar therefore did not provide an explanation for children acting in excited, disruptive, or aggressive ways. As an alternative explanation, the researchers suggested that the behavioral effects commonly associated with sugar may be the result of certain activities (such as parties) at which large amounts of sugar are consumed. The excitement of the activities themselves may contribute to disruptive behavior.

Context

It is impossible to pinpoint exactly when the field of sociology began to identify description, exploration, and explanation as purposes for research. Sociological research strategies grew out of methods originally developed and refined within the natural sciences. Historical records are filled with documented cases of descriptive, explorative, and explanatory research. Many of these studies lacked the level of sophistication seen in modern-day studies; nevertheless, many of them provided valuable insights into understanding the world. One notable series of descriptive observations was made by Galen (120-200 C.E.), a physician for five years to the gladiators who fought in the Roman Colosseum. Galen treated the wounds of the survivors and began to make important observations regarding head injuries and their impact on behavior. He began to notice that certain kinds of head wounds in certain areas of the head produced specific kinds of speech and processing problems. This descriptive research eventually led to the belief that the mind originates in the brain, not in the heart.

Royce Singleton, Jr., Bruce Straits, Margaret Straits, and Ronald McAllister, in their book *Approaches to Social Research* (1988), make the point that experimentation procedures (which include exploratory and explanatory strategies) were used long before the techniques were recognized by the scientific community. As noted earlier, field research is a common exploratory method. The authors point out that there is a general consensus that anthropologists—followed shortly thereafter by sociologists—first developed and then legitimized this approach to research. Franz Boas and Robert Park were among the early pioneers of field research during the late nineteenth century and the beginning of the twentieth century. Boas, noted for his research in cultural anthropology, emphasized the importance of circumventing one's Western cultural biases by living among the group one is studying for an extended time and acquiring their perspective. On the other hand, Park, who taught for a number of years at the University of Chicago, was influential in encouraging students to use the city as an alternative laboratory—to study people where they lived.

Field research originated in the desire to find answers to questions that could not be brought into a laboratory setting successfully. In the examination of human behavior, the artificial nature of explanatory laboratory research can hinder, rather than aid, understanding. Studies of foreign cultures, complex social relationships, and secretive sects lend themselves to field research rather than to laboratory experimentation.

Early sociological research techniques used data collection procedures that were almost entirely composed of informal notes. A long narrative describing a sequence of behaviors was not uncommon. There was a gradual move toward the use of more "objective" techniques such as standardized rating scales, behavioral check lists, and structured surveys within the latter part of the nineteenth century. These methods were created in order to quantify better the observations being made. Once behaviors could be quantified, specific behaviors could be assigned numbers. Specific behaviors could then be subjected to the statistical analyses commonly used in quantitative research. This improved approach to data collection helped field experimentation methods play a significant role in the social and behavioral sciences.

Bibliography

Babbie, Earl. *The Practice of Social Research.* 6th ed. Belmont, Calif.: Wadsworth,

1992. This comprehensive volume is characterized by an informal writing style that explains complex research concepts in a way that a novice can understand. The purposes of research are set in a much broader context.

Baker, Therese L. *Doing Social Research*. New York: McGraw-Hill, 1988. Gives the reader a general introduction to field research, observational studies, data collection methods, survey research, sampling techniques, and other topics that will help the reader distinguish good field experiments from those that are poorly constructed. Many examples of descriptive, exploratory, and explanatory research studies are mentioned.

Berg, Bruce L. *Qualitative Research Methods for the Social Sciences*. Boston: Allyn & Bacon, 1989. In order to understand better the different purposes of research, it is important to understand the differences between quantitative and qualitative research. This book discusses not only the different types of research but also the different methodological considerations necessary to conduct them.

Griffin, John H. *Black Like Me*. Boston: Houghton Mifflin, 1961. This excellent book is a narrative of the author's experiences traveling around the United States observing how people react to him after he adopted the appearance of a black man. This monumental field study, which contributed to an understanding of social prejudice, provides the reader with an excellent example of the significance of and need for conducting descriptive research.

Rosen, Lee A., et al. "Effects of Sugar (Sucrose) on Children's Behavior." *Journal of Consulting and Clinical Psychology* 56 (August, 1988): 583-589. This is the explanatory research mentioned in the entry that performed a much-needed and well-controlled study on the effects of sugar on behavior. The study has some methodological drawbacks, but it nevertheless appears to be one of the best studies done on this topic.

Rosenhan, David L. "On Being Sane in Insane Places." *Science* 179 (January, 1973): 250-258. Rosenhan describes his research of psychiatric facilities after he and his associates assumed the identity of psychiatric patients. This paper is an interesting and provocative example of explanatory research. It also raises the question of the dangers of conducting covert research as well as the dangers of psychological labels.

Singleton, Royce, Jr., Bruce Straits, Margaret Straits, and Ronald McAllister. *Approaches to Social Research*. New York: Oxford University Press, 1988. This well-written text discusses various aspects of field experimentation, such as selecting a research setting, gathering information, how to get into the field, and when a field study should be adopted. The chapter on experimentation can be used to contrast "true" experiments with field studies.

Bryan C. Auday

Cross-References

THE HISTORY OF SOCIOLOGY

Type of sociology: Origins and definitions of sociology

Sociology took form as an academic discipline and applied science in the late nineteenth century with the rise of the social and behavioral sciences. Ideas and theories about societal institutions, social structures, and the relation of persons to groups dates to antiquity. The development of American sociology reflects the influence of French, German, British, and American thinkers who evolved from nineteenth century systematizers to twentieth century specialists.

Principal terms

CRITICAL THEORY: a school of thought developed in Frankfurt, Germany, during the 1920's that employed the early humanistic ideas of Karl Marx to criticize positivism and scientific Marxism

FUNCTIONALISM: an approach that explains social institutions by the functions they provide or the consequences that they yield

PHENOMENOLOGY: an approach that emphasizes the socially constructed nature of knowledge, especially knowledge of everyday life

POSITIVISM: the view that sociology should model itself in method and theory after the physical sciences and that all knowledge can be hierarchically arranged

QUANTITATIVE METHODS: techniques that attempt to measure in an objective fashion aspects of social structure, social groups, and social opinions; these methods often involve surveys

SOCIOBIOLOGY: an influential perspective since the 1970's derived from evolutionary biology and seeking to understand social phenomena through biological, especially genetic, explanations

STRUCTURALISM: an orientation that places an emphasis on the relations among social elements rather than on the elements themselves

SYMBOLIC INTERACTIONISM: a set of ideas developed at the University of Chicago during the 1920's that emphasized the importance of meaning, language, and learning to take the role of the other in the development of the self

Overview

Sociology is one of the social sciences, along with anthropology, psychology, political science, and economics. It studies the origin and development of human society by examining the social organization and structure of society, its principal institutions (the family, school, religion, politics and government, health care, and economy), collective behavior, and interactions (relations between individuals and between the individual and society). Sociology became a discipline in the late nineteenth century. Previously, ideas and theories about society had been discussed widely in philosophical, political, and theological contexts.

In the nineteenth century, books appeared that offered a systematic approach to the study of society. The emphasis was on the logical and cohesive arrangement of known facts about society combined with a particular philosophical or theoretical orientation. Among the principal thinkers in this "systematics" period of the history of sociology was Auguste Comte (1798-1857), a French theorist sometimes described as the "father of sociology." He coined the term, and he argued for a hierarchical arrangement of the sciences with sociology at the top (a form of positivism). Also influential during this period was Herbert Spencer (1820-1903), a British systematist who authored a three-volume work entitled *Principles of Sociology* (1876, 1882, 1896) in which he reasoned that all societies develop in a similar manner following principles of evolutionary theory.

In addition to the systematically qualitative sociology of the nineteenth century, a quantitative tradition developed. Social statistics on suicides, prostitution, unemployment, and other topics came to be treated as social facts—facts to be explained by societal factors rather than as merely the aggregate of individual behavior. Later, survey research methods for discerning opinions and attitudes were developed, as were techniques to assure the representativeness of the survey sample and to analyze relationships among opinions and demographic data (techniques of statistical correlation). In the latter part of the twentieth century, quantitative methods assumed a major role in sociological research.

Another quality of nineteenth century American sociology was the influence of psychological analysis, resulting in the discipline of social psychology. As developed from the social rather than the psychological end, social psychology has considered the influence of the group on the individual and on those circumstances in which behavior may be unique to social context. The "interactionists" among the social psychologists have emphasized the "meaning" that the situation has to the individual as the determiner of behavior.

By 1905 the American Sociological Society (later the American Sociological Association) was formed. Earlier societies had been formed in France in 1894 and in England in 1903. Professorships, journals, departments, and doctoral programs devoted to the field began to proliferate, although for many years sociology professors often shared a department with anthropologists or scholars in some other social science. The sociological opinions of Comte and Spencer were best represented in the United States by Lester F. Ward (1841-1913), who is regarded as the earliest American systematic sociologist. He distinguished between "pure" and "applied" sociology and thought that social betterment could be brought about by an active scientific process.

Several individuals occupy special positions in the development of sociology. Among them is Émile Durkheim (1858-1917), a nineteenth century French sociologist who helped establish sociology as an independent discipline and science. He is best remembered for his works *De la Division du travail social* (1893; *The Division of Labor in Society*, 1933) and *Le Suicide: Étude de sociologie* (1897; *Suicide: A Study in Sociology*, 1951). In the latter, Durkheim argued, on the basis of suicide statistics from many different countries, that what appeared as individual decision making (taking one's own life) could be better understood in terms of the qualities of the society and times in which one lived. "Social facts" should be explained by social factors, Durkheim believed. Why one particular person takes his or her own life might be explained by psychology, but the overall rate of suicide could not be. Durkheim also wrote other influential works on sociological methods and on the sociology of religion.

Max Weber (1864-1920) was an influential German sociologist who held professorships at various universities. He was plagued by nervous illness, and he died prematurely of pneumonia. His most widely read work is *Die Protestantische Ethik und der Geist des Kapitalismus* (1904; *The Protestant Ethic and the Spirit of Capitalism*, 1930), in which he examined the forces that shaped modern capitalism, particularly the hierarchical institutional and bureaucratic structures. As the title suggests, he argued for the central role of Protestantism, which he believed provided the model for viewing work as a "calling," with its associated aspects of duty and obedience. Hard work, he said, was viewed as rewarded by wealth. In Weber's view, Protestantism "invented" achievement motivation. Weber also made contributions to sociological methodology.

The ideas of Karl Marx (1818-1883) were also influential in sociology. Marx argued for a social basis of consciousness and placed emphasis on social class as a relevant variable in understanding a person's behavior, motivation, and ideology. Marxism rationalized the focus on the social in understanding the behavior of the individual and placed emphasis on the particular historical circumstances. Marx also emphasized the social and political nature of knowledge, a theme that was developed by later twentieth century sociologists. His best works, with those of Durkheim and Weber, are regarded as among the great classics in sociology's history.

Another important sociologist of the nineteenth century was William Graham Sumner (1840-1910), who offered the first American course in sociology at Yale University in 1876 and became known for his work *Folkways* (1907), which treated customs and mores (socially accepted patterns of behavior) from a social Darwinist perspective. He coined the term "ethnocentrism" to describe the preference people have for the viewpoint and folkways of their own group. Albion Woodbury Small (1854-1926) promoted the development of sociology at the University of Chicago, where the first doctoral program was begun in 1893, and in 1895 he founded the first journal in the United States devoted exclusively to sociology, the *American Journal of Sociology*. Charles A. Ellwood (1873-1946) is credited as the founder of sociological social psychology, although Edward A. Ross (1866-1951) was the first sociologist to author a book entitled *Social Psychology* (1908). Ross wrote widely on other sociological topics and was for many years a professor at the University of Wisconsin.

During the 1920's and 1930's, sociology expanded through increased specialization and controversy over method. Some sociologists chose essentially historical methods, others comparative techniques (in which social organization in different cultures might be contrasted), and many others a case-study method focusing on a particular social organization (ranging from a small group, such as a street gang, to an entire small town or city). Still others preferred quantitative methods in which systematic surveys would sample people's beliefs and behaviors. A small number of sociologists emphasized the subjective and meaningful nature of human behavior and tried to employ phenomenological methods.

In Germany the "Frankfurt school" developed around a group of philosophers and social theorists associated with the Frankfurt Institute for Social Research. Beginning in the late 1920's, they developed systematic criticisms of positivistic theories. The views of the Frankfurt school are termed "critical theory" and reflected a neo-Marxist approach combined with German traditions of reason as contained in the philosophy of Georg Wilhelm Friedrich Hegel. Among the important members were Theodor Adorno, Max Horkheimer, and Herbert Marcuse.

Georg Simmel (1858-1918) was a German philosopher who developed the "formal" school of sociology. He believed that the processes which sociologists study, such as conflict, competition, and the formation of alliances, could be examined independently of the particular contexts in which they occurred (such as schools, churches, and political parties).

The views of George Herbert Mead (1863-1931) were also influential during this period. He taught at the University of Chicago as a philosopher and developed the social behaviorist perspective, which argued that the self is a product of interaction with others. His contributions were mainly to the field of social psychology and the social nature of language, gesture, and mind.

Two leading sociologists who exerted a strong influence following World War II were Talcott Parsons and C. Wright Mills. Parsons was for many years associated with Harvard University and the prewar development of sociology at Harvard, where he chaired the doctoral dissertations of many of the subsequent leaders in the field. Several phases of Parsons' career may be distinguished, but his development of "social systems theory," in which the relationship between the individual and group is understood in terms of the role the person occupies and the social expectations associated with the role, has been enormously influential, especially in social psychology. Mills is best known for his works (such as *The Power Elite*) which describe the ways in which ruling classes exert their influence. His writings were influential not only in academic sociology but also as revolutionary texts for the social unrest in the United States in the 1960's. In the latter decades of the twentieth century, sociology saw an increasing development of subspecialties, an emphasis on quantitative technique, and the influence of European theorists such as Claude Lévi-Strauss, Jürgen Habermas, and Michel Foucault.

Applications

Applications of sociological methods and knowledge have developed over time. The effort to explain suicide is a useful example, for it was one of the earliest undertakings by Durkheim. In his classic 1897 work *Suicide* he used statistics from various countries in an attempt to understand what social facts might account for differences in their suicide rates. While he identified social conditions that made a difference (for example, being unmarried and a Protestant), he noted that such social statistics could not explain the choice of suicide by an individual. To understand the behavior of a particular person, he recommended examining the "personal stamp" evident in the actions associated with the suicide.

His view contrasts with those of the Chicago school of sociology, which, under the influence of Mead during the 1920's, sought a more psychological explanation of suicide rates. In addition to social statistics on suicide, an examination of case studies and personal histories was utilized. These could reveal the meaning of the act of suicide for the individual. An effort was made to understand the actions of particular persons, rather than only the gross differences in rates among countries or subpopulations.

Modern sociologists have criticized the early reliance on governmental statistics in the study of rates of suicide. Instead, they have gathered independent data and analyzed it with statistical techniques called multivariant analysis. Hundreds of possible influences on the decision to take one's own life can be examined, and the degree to which each individually and collectively predicts the choice of death can be precisely quantified. Such studies often involve extensive interviews with persons who knew the deceased, and they may include hundreds of cases of suicide. The mass of data studied, the numbers of persons involved in its collection, and the sophistication of the techniques used in its analysis would have been unimaginable in the late nineteenth century when sociologists first took up the topic.

Context

An extensive history of sociology would need to trace the development of exchange theory and interactionism and examine the perspectives of structuralism, functionalism, positivism, and Marxism. It would also look at the refinement of quantitative techniques, including modern techniques of surveying by telephone, demographic analysis, and increasingly sophisticated statistical techniques. Such a history would also include an examination of the broad nineteenth century ideas (many stemming from the works of Marx and Charles Darwin) that strongly influenced the origins of sociology and continue to affect the discipline. Although evolutionary explanations of social behavior existed before Darwin's watershed work *On the Origin of the Species* (1859), Darwinian evolutionary theory provided a foundation both for social Darwinism and for the field known as sociobiology that developed in the later twentieth century.

Modern sociology has developed a wide range of interests. Some sociologists have devoted their work primarily to theory building and analysis, whereas others have focused on the application of sociological methods in governmental agencies and private industry. The dramatic social changes and violent events that took place in the twentieth century have provided extensive social actions and behavior for sociologists to study. The mass of quantitative data now routinely gathered by modern governments at all levels has provided unending data for sociological examination. Mass culture is transmitted over worldwide communication systems, leading to collective behavior of a magnitude unknown during sociology's formative years. The development of complex social systems, such as the health care industry, and ever-changing technology assures that the methods and theories that sociology has developed over its history will continue to find individual and collective behavior that is in need of study and understanding.

Bibliography

Barnes, Harry Elmer. *An Introduction to the History of Sociology*. Abridged ed. Chicago: University of Chicago Press, 1966. This is a collection of essays which trace the development of sociology up to World War II. Each chapter focuses on an influential sociologist, most of them twentieth century scholars.

Bottomore, Tom, and Robert Nisbet, eds. *A History of Sociological Analysis*. New York: Basic Books, 1978. A massive book of essays on selected topics in the history of sociology. The emphasis is on themes (such as Marxism, structuralism, and functionalism) rather than personalities.

Manicas, Peter T. *A History of Philosophy of the Social Sciences*. Oxford, England: Basil Blackwell, 1987. A broad discussion of the theoretical and philosophical aspects of the social sciences as they have developed since the nineteenth century, with selected discussion of sociological concepts.

Martindale, Don. *Prominent Sociologists Since World War II*. Columbus, Ohio: Charles E. Merrill, 1975. The focus of this short book is on theorists influential since the end of World War II. Max Weber, Talcott Parsons, C. Wright Mills, and Pitirim A. Sorokin are given extensive coverage.

Maus, Heinz. *A Short History of Sociology*. New York: Philosophical Library, 1962. This history approaches sociology geographically by describing developments in North America, Europe, and Latin America, with additional chapters on Great Britain, Germany, Belgium, and Eastern Europe.

Ross, Dorothy. *The Origins of American Social Science*. Cambridge, England: Cambridge University Press, 1991. This book places the history of sociology in the United States within the context of the other social sciences, such as anthropology and psychology, as they developed during the late nineteenth century.

Sahakian, William S. *History and Systems of Social Psychology*. 2d ed. Washington, D.C.: Hemisphere, 1982. A lengthy and detailed work that emphasizes the social psychological developments in sociology.

Swingewood, Alan. *A Short History of Sociological Thought*. New York: St. Martin's Press, 1984. A history of sociological ideas, with excellent coverage of Marxism, positivism, functionalism, and structuralism.

Terry J. Knapp

Cross-References

1932

SOCIOLOGY DEFINED

Type of sociology: Origins and definitions of sociology
Field of study: Sociological perspectives and principles

Sociology involves the study and understanding of human interaction. As people live their lives in relation to others—for example, in a family or at school—how they perceive themselves and others and how they act is a consequence of the types of interactions and expectations that occur in a given setting. Sociology analyzes how various group structures are organized, how they work, and what meaning individuals bring to and get from the groups in which they live.

Principal terms
NORMS: standards of conduct that exist within a particular sociological group or social system
ROLES: behavioral expectations related to positions (statuses) held by individuals in any particular group; identified by related clusters of behavioral norms
SANCTIONS: rewards or punishments that shape and reinforce norms and roles
SOCIAL SYSTEM: the institutions of large subgroups that exist within a culture or society and which help to govern behavior
SOCIOLOGICAL GROUP: two or more individuals who are part of a defined membership and who meet regularly with purpose
STRATIFICATION: the unequal distribution, within a particular culture or social system, of power, privilege, and economic resources and opportunities

Overview

Social scientists seek to understand why people behave as they do. For the sociologist, study centers on people as they interact with one another. This definition is tremendously broad, but it must be, because sociologists study a wide range of groups and human interactions. Macrosociology encompasses the study of large groups, for example, such as entire societies; microsociology, conversely, examines very small groups. Sociology may be broken down into a number of fields. Among them are the study of major social institutions (such as the family, education, religion, and medicine); social structure and the inequalities that result from various types of social stratification; the processes of social change; prejudice, discrimination, and race relations; deviance and crime; and gender roles and inequality.

In addition, it is important to realize that a number of different theoretical frameworks have evolved since sociology came into its own in the nineteenth century. These large-scale theories have strongly influenced, even determined, the ways sociologists view people and their societies. Functionalism emphasizes the need for societies to run relatively smoothly in order to meet the needs of its members. Conflict theory, on the other hand, stresses the underlying competition and struggle between those in power and society's subordinate groups. A third major approach, interactionism, studies small-group interaction and emphasizes the meanings that various types of behavior carry.

Sociologists employ a variety of research techniques in their work. One of the principal ways sociologists gather information about people is simply through observing what their subjects are doing. They also conduct interviews, use questionnaires and surveys, and study demographic information. After a sociologist has gathered enough information for it to be representative of the group under study, analysis is conducted. When conducting an analysis, sociologists try to discern patterns in the information gathered. Either patterns of attitude or patterns of behavior might be the focus of interest. Sociologists then make careful generalizations about the likelihood of these patterns occurring in other, similar settings.

Examining two of the basic concepts sociologists use in their study of human interaction can provide further insight into the sociological approach. The first of these is the relationship between norms and rules; the second is the concept of roles. One of the most basic areas of sociological analysis involves norms. Norms refer to the standards of behavior that are expected and accepted within a particular group. To understand the full implications of how this concept works, it is helpful to compare norms with rules. Whereas norms tell what the standard of conduct actually is in any group, rules delineate what conduct ought to be. The intent of a rule is that the behavior it is addressing will become the standard of conduct—a norm. Simply stating a rule, however, does not guarantee that it will become an actuality or a norm. For example, an office may have a rule that its employees must arrive at 8:00 A.M. Observation or interview, however, may reveal that employees do not adhere to the rule but instead arrive by 8:30 A.M. In this case, the norm is arrival by 8:30, even though the rule is different. Many rules do become norms, but many do not.

Norms within groups can emerge naturally, or they may be shaped or imposed by a group leader. In his study of deviance, sociologist Howard Becker explored how a group's norms and perceptions of deviance are imposed on others. In Becker's classic book *Outsiders: Studies in the Sociology of Deviance* (1963), he provides an especially insightful discussion of "moral entrepreneurs"—people who create and enforce rules. Becker uses this discussion to support his thesis that deviance is the product of enterprise, and that rule-making and application are essential; otherwise deviance would not exist.

A second area of analysis involves the roles or positions that people assume in groups. Roles are defined by expected behavior associated with a particular position. Everyone in the group has virtually the same, or shared, expectations for each role. Sociologist Erving Goffman, in his book *Encounters: Two Studies in the Sociology of Interaction* (1961), refers to the relationships among roles as "reciprocal ties" that delineate the rights and responsibilities of the various positions within the group. Even though each individual brings his or her own interpretation to the role, conformity to shared expectations results in smooth operation within the group. Although not all behavior is role-related, much of it is, and considerable sociological investigation and analysis have centered on particular roles and how those are interpreted in different groups, cultures, or times. Whether studying small groups such as families or schools or large groups such as entire societies, sociologists work extensively with the concepts of norms and roles.

The self-fulfilling prophecy, a theorem proposed by sociologist W. I. Thomas and discussed by Robert K. Merton in his classic work *Social Theory and Social Structure* (1949), illustrates the complex relationships between roles and norms while identifying their application. Of Thomas' theorem, which states that if people define situations as real, then they are real in their consequences, Merton wrote:

> The first part of the theorem provides an unceasing reminder that men respond not only to the objective features of a situation, but also, and at times primarily, to the meaning this situation has for them. And once they have assigned some meaning to the situation, their consequent behavior and some of the consequences of that behavior are determined by the ascribed meaning.

Thus, the perceived meaning of a situation affects role definitions, which affect interactions. These, in turn, are subject to become norms for those engaged in the situation. Merton carefully points out that, in this the original definition of the situation is false, yet the new behaviors that are evoked cause the originally false conceptions to become true. Merton believed that this theorem is present in the everyday lives of all people and that understanding it could assist in explaining the dynamics of daily interaction, including racial and ethnic conflict.

Applications

Sociological study and analysis has been applied to almost every area of human endeavor. Frequently, sociological study results in increasing people's awareness of patterns of behavior which might otherwise go unnoticed. Sociological findings have also been consulted and applied by government as it tries to understand and to redress grievances and inequities that exist in society. In fact, societal institutions have sometimes adjusted their practices and policies to achieve more equitable treatment of individuals. One major social institution that has been strongly affected by sociological studies is education.

In the early nineteenth century, education emerged as one of the most important institutions for the American public. Viewed as a means for white males of any class to achieve political, social, and economic equity, schools began to define a new role for themselves. This role expanded after the landmark Supreme Court decision in 1954 of *Brown v. Board of Education*, in which segregation was held to be unconstitutional. This decision, bolstered by Title VI of the 1964 Civil Rights Act, forced schools to desegregate.

Desegregation had implications for admission, curriculum, and career placement of African Americans. Probably the best-known study of desegregation is the Coleman Report, conducted by researcher James Coleman in the mid-1960's. The purpose of the study was to evaluate, ten years after the *Brown v. Board of Education* decision, the education of minority students compared with that of white students. To highlight a few of Coleman's findings, he discovered that all minority students except Asian Americans scored lower on tests at each level; that the socioeconomic makeup of the school and the home backgrounds of students in the school had the most significant impact on academic achievement; and that white students had more access to college preparatory curricula.

Nearly twenty years later, sociologist Jeanne Ballantine, in her book *The Sociology of Education* (1983), presented evidence of continued discrimination against African Americans and students of other racial or ethnic origins. She explored the practice of schools of placing students into different curriculum tracks, tracks which ultimately led to professional or manual occupations in adulthood. Ballantine found that 53 percent of the students who were qualified to be placed in the upper, college-preparatory, tracks were in the lower track. Race and/or socioeconomic background appeared to be the deciding factor. The discrimination which tracking demonstrated and perpetuated continued into the 1990's. Evidence of its detriment was so over-whelming that all fifty state governors agreed to abolish the practice as they enacted educational reform.

Other than racial minorities, women represent the most prominent group that has struggled for equity in education and in the workplace. Sociologists have long been interested in how social and economic inequalities have perpetuated social stratification involving women, but it has only been since the 1980's that sociologists have extensively examined the relationship between education and gender-based socio-economic stratification.

In her article "Where Are the Female Einsteins? The Gender Stratification of Math and Science" (included in Jeanne Ballantine's 1985 book *Schools and Society*), sociologist Donna Kaminsky contends that social, cultural, and educational factors combine to steer women away from taking mathematics and science courses in school. First, many young women still view being a wife, mother, and/or homemaker as the primary female role. Young women also view science and math careers as stereo-typically isolated, impersonal, and unwomanly. Finally, young women are led to perceive a lack of future usefulness in taking courses in math, science, or computer technology.

In another example of the effect of schooling on life opportunities, sociologists Elsie Moore and A. Wade Smith examine both race and gender in their article "Sex and Race Differences in Mathematics Aptitude: Effects of Schooling" (in the second edition of Ballantine's *Schools and Society*, 1989). They found significant differences between males and females and between blacks and whites regarding arithmetic reasoning and mathematic knowledge scores on aptitude tests. This differentiation precludes pursuit of career opportunities in the sciences and math.

Context

Sociology, as a discipline of study, is said to have been founded by Claude-Henri de Rouvroy (comte de Saint-Simon) and Auguste Comte in the early 1800's. Initial study in the discipline looked at the stages of development of entire societies. Since then, sociology has evolved to include the examination of interaction in smaller groups, some of which are as small as two persons (such groups are referred to as dyads). As with all social and physical sciences, sociology uses theories to organize and explain the world in which humans live. Theories can be considered thought systems that are supported by ideas, propositions, and assumptions that researchers have about the world. Concepts, or ideas, are used to create connecting frameworks for various assumptions and propositions. Sociological theories are concerned with explaining the structure, organization, function, and interaction of groups, institutions, and social systems.

Two broad theoretical frameworks that dominated much of twentieth century sociology are functionalism and conflict theory. More recent approaches have also evolved, however, most notably interpretive theory and critical theory. In an effort to clarify the distinctions among all these theories, some sociologists have divided them into two perspectives: transmission theory, which includes functionalism and conflict theory, and transformation theory, which includes interpretive theory and critical theory. In her book *Women Teaching for Change* (1988), Kathleen Weiler describes the distinction between these two theoretical perspectives as reproduction versus production. In other words, people and social systems act either to reproduce existing societal conditions and structures or work to produce or create the society in which they live.

Transmission theory (including functionalism and conflict theory) examines how social structures are copied, or reproduced, from generation to generation, regardless of the influences of different groups in society. Max Weber, Talcott Parsons, and Émile Durkheim were foremost in developing and using functional theory to analyze societies. Key questions include how institutions are organized, who has decision-making power, and who is responsible for performing the work. Functional analysis focuses on such areas as the transmission of cultural norms and values and the distribution of goods and services. A major premise of functionalist theory is that each of the components must be healthy and in good working order or the entire system is put in jeopardy. Also central to functional theory is the idea that an institution or social system works best when it is in a state of balance or equilibrium. It assumes a state of consensus among its members and views conflict as disruptive to the required and desirable balance. Some sociological theorists criticize functional theory for these reasons.

Karl Marx, Georg Simmel, and Ralf Dahrendorf were the principal theorists in the development of conflict theory. Their work examined how different groups in society are in conflict with one another over power and privilege. Most simply, this theory contends that those groups who have money and positions of opportunity and power want to maintain things the way they are. Those groups who do not have these privileges are seen as being in constant conflict with those that do. In his central works, Marx provided a comprehensive and provoking examination of capitalism in modern industrial English society and heavily criticized this structure for exploiting the poor masses in order to increase the wealth and power of a few. Marx and other conflict theorists viewed economic organization and its purposeful unequal distribution of property and resources as the major source of societal conflict.

In contrast to social transmission theories, social transformation theories focus on how societies or institutions might be transformed or produced by individuals who take an active role in creating the world in which they live. The two dominant social transformation theories—interpretive theory and critical theory—are rooted in phenomenology, which analyzes social systems in terms of how meaning is constructed by participants within the group. Interpretive theory emphasizes the study of small groups, and sociologists obtain information for their analysis through observation, interviews, and descriptions provided by participants. These techniques, referred to as ethnomethodology, were adapted from anthropological modes of inquiry. Research within interpretive theory has been heavily influenced by the work of Herbert Blumer, author of *Symbolic Interactionism: Perspective and Method* (1969); Blumer was instrumental in using objectivity and qualitative research to study the symbolic meanings of interaction.

Like interpretive theory, critical theory is rooted in phenomenology and ethnomethodology. Critical theory, however, combines both macro- and microanalyses of social systems and includes the influence of sociopolitical forces. Critical theory has been widely applied to the study of education and is historically rooted in the work of social theorists who worked at the Institute for Social Research in Frankfurt, Germany. Those of the Frankfurt school, along with Italian Marxist Antonio Gramsci and the Brazilian educator Paulo Freire, have been instrumental in developing current critical analyses. Critical theory examines schools both within a historic context and in the light of the sociopolitical ideologies that dominate society.

Bibliography

Becker, Howard, ed. *The Other Side: Perspectives on Deviance.* New York: Free Press, 1964. Organized into three sections, this edited work looks at deviance with regard to its place in society and in personal interactions, and in terms of its role and structure. The reader will come away with an understanding of the nature and complexity of deviance, one of the central issues of sociological inquiry.

Goffman, Erving. *Encounters: Two Studies in the Sociology of Interaction.* Indianapolis: Bobbs-Merrill, 1961. Any reader will obtain an appreciation for sociological analysis from the two classic essays included here. The first, which takes fun seriously, analyzes the dynamics and importance of games. The second is equally relevant and interesting, as Goffman examines roles—what they are, how they work, and how to understand them.

Lyman, Stanford M. *The Black American in Sociological Thought.* New York: Putnam, 1972. Representative of the merit and importance of sociology as a tool of inquiry and analysis, Lyman's work provides an excellent presentation of race relations theory and racial evolution. The text and its analyses are more relevant than ever to understanding the modern multicultural world.

Merton, Robert K. *Social Theory and Social Structure*. Enlarged ed. New York: Free Press, 1968. Although difficult in its treatment of theories, this is a readable and classic work. Merton gives the reader a historical context while making major contributions to the field as he discusses theoretical sociology, structure, the sociology of knowledge, and the sociology of science.

Steiner, Gilbert. *The Futility of Family Policy*. Washington, D.C.: Brookings Institution, 1981. Although norms and legislation regarding families continue to change, Steiner's book provides a clear and comprehensive understanding of how policy is created around issues. Provides an essential foundation for understanding issues, events, and political responses.

Denise Kaye Davis

Cross-References

Conflict Theory, 340; Functionalism, 786; Interactionism, 1009; Microsociology, 1192; Sociobiology and the Nature-Nurture Debate, 1913; The History of Sociology, 1926; The Sociology of Knowledge, 1946.

THE SOCIOLOGY OF EDUCATION

Type of sociology: Major social institutions
Field of study: Education

The sociology of education is the study of the institution of education. Sociologists examine the functions education fills for a society and explore the role of education in preparing citizens for adult life. School life is a central focus; sociologists study how schools contribute to the socialization of children and how schools function as organizations. They also study the role of education in stratification.

Principal terms
   EDUCATION: the formal teaching of a culture's skills, knowledge, and values from one generation to the next
   FORMAL ORGANIZATION: a large collection of people whose activities are specifically designed for the attainment of explicitly stated goals
   HIDDEN CURRICULUM: a set of unwritten rules of behavior taught in school to prepare children for academic success and social relations outside school
   SOCIAL INSTITUTION: patterned behaviors and social structures that fulfill societal needs
   SOCIAL STRATIFICATION: a social system in which groups are ranked hierarchically and have unequal rewards or resources

Overview

Sociologists who study the educational institution look at the roles of education in various societies. In preindustrial societies, children are educated by their family members through informal interaction and socialization. Children generally do not attend school, which is a more formal approach used in industrial societies. The educational institution meets several basic needs of societies. First, education helps to teach future citizens about the culture in which they live. They are taught their culture's values, beliefs, knowledge, and language. They are taught what it means to be a member of their society. Second, education helps to reinforce the socioeconomic power structure. In the United States, for example, educators prepare students for their places in the capitalist system. This system involves a relatively small number of people who control the resources and a larger number of people who work for those in power.

Third, schools help to select and allocate talent. Schools socialize children from different social classes differently in order to prepare them for their future places in the social structure. For example, educators commonly assign students to different tracks, such as the general track, the vocational track, and the college-preparatory track; in the process, they segregate students largely by social class. Although efforts have been made to provide greater equality of educational opportunity, students in the college-preparatory track still are more likely to come from middle- and upper-class family backgrounds than are students in the other tracks. Fourth, schools teach students self-discipline. Students are taught the rules they need to follow in order to fit into the larger society. This process is accomplished through the hidden curriculum, an informal set of processes and rules that reinforce the basic rules (such as the need to line up or to raise a hand to be recognized). Fifth, schools teach children the basic skills they need to survive as members of a society, such as reading, writing, thinking, and mathematics. Schools in the United States have been criticized for poor performance in this area, especially when American students are compared with those from other countries. For example, about one-third of U.S. young adults in the 1990's cannot read at even an eighth-grade level.

Sociologists also look at schools as formal organizations. Schools share many of the characteristics of other formal organizations, such as corporations, hospitals, and even prisons. Schools have a division of labor in which trained specialists perform specific jobs. The English teacher, for example, does not typically also teach physics. Schools have many rules and other standard operating procedures. There are dress rules, disciplinary rules, and rules on how much of the curriculum teachers must cover. Teacher Bel Kaufman provided a detailed account of such rules and their negative effects for students, teachers, and parents in one New York high school in her book *Up the Down Staircase* (1964). Schools also have a hierarchy of authority; a chain of command exists that details who is responsible to whom. At the local level, the school board is typically at the top of the hierarchy, followed by the superintendent, principals, teachers, and students. Sociologist David Rogers detailed the negative consequences of such a hierarchy in his book *110 Livingston Street: Politics and Bureaucracy in the New York City Schools* (1968).

Sociologists also look at the informal structure in schools. While the formal structure meets the needs of the organization, the informal structure meets the needs of the organization's members. For example, schools vary in their predominant social classes, a difference that affects the nature of informal interactions. Different schools often emphasize different values, such as athletics or academics. Students may form themselves into different cliques, or groupings, according to particular interests or social classes. A school's informal climate may also be affected by more formal structural arrangements such as class size, more "open" classrooms, and discipline standards.

Applications

Sociological research on education is applied in several ways to better understand schools and students and to provide possible solutions to problems in the educational system. Sociologists have studied high school dropouts, for example. Nearly one-third of ninth graders do not graduate from high school, and most major cities have dropout rates of 50 percent or higher. The high dropout rate has major implications for both individuals and society. The difference between the lifetime earnings of a typical dropout and a typical graduate exceeds $300,000. Reducing the dropout rate would increase personal incomes and revenues obtained through taxes, decrease the social costs of welfare and crime, and reduce the unemployment rate.

Sociologist Theodore Wagenaar summarized the research on high-school dropouts in *Research in the Sociology of Education and Socialization* (1987). The reasons cited most often by dropouts for the decision to drop out pertain to school, particularly poor grades and a dislike for school. Additional reasons vary by gender; males note economic or work issues, and females note family issues. Having a job tends to matter to male dropouts, and marriage and pregnancy tend to matter to female dropouts. The dropout rates for females and males are similar. The rates for minorities are at least one-third greater than for whites, a statistic that may reflect class differences, since studies show higher dropout rates for lower-class students. Lower-class students do not have the same socialization experiences as middle- and upper-class students. For example, lower-class parents spend less time with their children, talk about school less often with their children, and hold lower expectations for their children. Minorities and lower-class students may also experience discrimination in the schools. For example, they are less likely to be placed in the college-preparatory track and generally receive a poorer-quality education.

Dropouts have significantly lower self-concepts and tend to believe that they have little control over their lives. Particularly critical is the fact that dropouts tend to select as friends other young people who are alienated from school. This peer culture supports the potential dropout in making such decisions as skipping school and doing less homework. As a result, potential dropouts experience increased difficulty with teachers and principals and are disproportionately punished, reinforcing the decision to drop out. Dropouts also tend to feel less socially integrated into the schools, as evidenced by their lower involvement in extracurricular activities.

School factors are also relevant. Smaller schools offer more personal attention to students and suffer fewer disorders. Students in small schools are more satisfied with their educational experiences and show greater involvement in the school and in the educational experience. Larger schools also tend to generate feelings among teachers of less control and less personal responsibility. An orderly school environment, a clear rewards system, and a drive for academic excellence also help to reduce dropout rates. Support services such as counseling are also important.

This research has implications for reducing dropout rates. The persistent effects of family background suggest that early intervention in school is needed to target potential dropouts and to provide appropriate school- and community-based action. Potential dropouts need intensive support—both academic and personal—in the early elementary grades. Communities, schools, and employers can work together to provide social structures and opportunities for social interaction in order to reduce the social isolation and normlessness that commonly characterize potential dropouts. Clear and fair rules, low student-to-teacher ratios, enhanced counseling services, training and work experience, teachers who accept personal responsibility for their students, teacher involvement in decision-making, and strong parental involvement and support also help to reduce dropout rates. These factors underscore the central roles schools play in the socialization of youth.

Another application of sociological studies of education involves efforts to provide equality of educational opportunity to students from all social classes, races, and genders. Schools often function to reproduce the existing social class system, but societal values of individualism and hard work as bases for moving up the social ladder mean that schools need to provide equal opportunities for doing so. The Supreme Court ruled in 1954 that segregated education was inherently unequal, and the Civil Rights Act of 1964 prompted greater desegregation of U.S. schools. The first nationwide study of school inequality was performed by sociologist James S. Coleman and published as *Equality of Educational Opportunity* (1966). Coleman found substantial differences between mostly black schools and mostly white schools in such things as funds spent per student, ages of school buildings, quality of library facilities, teacher characteristics, and class sizes. More surprising, he found that such school characteristics had little effect on learning. Most critical for school success was the student's social environment, which included the attitudes and behaviors fostered by family members and peers.

Coleman's report led the U.S. courts to determine that every student had the right to attend a school with a particular proportion of advantaged students. Since minority students were typically more disadvantaged than white students, the courts mandated the busing of students to achieve greater equality of minority composition in the schools. Busing was very successful in reducing school segregation, but it created considerable opposition from both blacks and whites, leading to the eventual abandonment of the practice in the 1980's. Some think that busing contributed to "white flight," causing white parents to remove their children from urban public schools by sending them to private schools or by moving to the suburbs. Coleman's report also led to compensatory "enrichment" programs designed to enable disadvantaged students to have some of the experiences of more privileged students.

Sociologists studying education also study gender socialization. Schools often promote gender stereotypes, oversimplified but strongly held ideas about the appropriate characteristics of females and males. The educational institution reflects and reinforces the beliefs and values of the larger society. For example, the illiteracy rate for females is much higher than the rate for males in most developing parts of the world. In elementary school, boys are encouraged to solve problems, while girls are more likely to be given answers. Teachers encourage boys to work independently but encourage dependency among girls. Junior-high-school teachers tend to use very different adjectives to describe boys and girls, such as "curious" for boys and "calm" for girls. Although girls' academic performance exceeds boys' into high school, it drops thereafter, as young women begin to conform to expectations for lower performance. Also, females tend to realize that males do not react positively to bright females. Females' occupational plans and values increasingly conform to societal expectations as they move through high school; their interest in science and mathematics drops considerably. Textbooks in both elementary and high school still show males and females performing traditionally expected roles. In college, females tend to talk less in class and to receive less encouragement from professors to contribute to class discussions.

Sociologists have identified strategies that may help to reduce schools' contributions to gender-role stereotyping. Some sociologists advocate changing the sex composition of the predominantly female elementary teaching force in order to provide early role models of both women and men. Others call for the use of gender-neutral instructional materials. Research shows, for example, that females perform higher on mathematics story problems when the figures in the story are female. A cooperative learning environment in which males and females work together has also been shown to help capture and maintain females' interest in science and mathematics. In their book *Failing at Fairness: How America's Schools Cheat Girls* (1994), researchers Myra and David Sadker suggest girls-only education as one approach to reducing the negative effects of girls' school experiences. Studies show that girls in single-sex schools achieve more, have higher self-esteem, and are more interested in mathematics and science than girls in co-ed schools are. Some co-ed schools have begun experimenting with single-sex classes in science and mathematics to bolster females' performance. These suggestions for reducing gender stereotypes address the social context in which children learn and show how important that context is.

Context

Sociological attention to education began around the end of the nineteenth century, shortly after the discipline itself emerged. In the late 1800's, Émile Durkheim was the first to suggest the importance of a sociological approach to education. Early sociological efforts in the United States focused on solving educational problems posed by massive immigration, rapid urbanization, and the development of a large educational system. The term "sociology of education" emerged in the 1920's as sociologists took a more scientific interest in education, gathering data and observing in schools to better understand how schools worked as social systems. With the publication of Willard Waller's *The Sociology of Teaching* (1932), the field became more widely recognized. Waller examined the different goals and orientations of teachers and students and suggested the development of extracurricular activities to enhance students' commitment to school. While the next few decades saw less sociological interest in education, the 1960's saw increasing interest, as sociologists focused both on the role of education in society and on the inner workings of schools. James S. Coleman, for example, studied the informal friendship groups that characterize high schools in his book *The Adolescent Society: The Social Life of the Teenager and Its Impact on Education* (1961).

Sociologists have taken several approaches to the study of education. Some have stressed looking at the bigger picture by studying how the educational institution helps to meet the basic needs of a society and fits in with the larger social structure. Some have noted how schools have become places where those in power wish to make sure that their views and values are taught. Still other sociologists have looked inside schools to study how they operate sociologically. These researchers study such things as how children play at school, how students cope with school demands, and how males and females react differently to the school experience.

Sociological attention to education has helped to broaden the understanding of schools and education by looking at the social context within which schools exist and by describing aspects of school life that were previously ignored. Sociologists have increasingly turned to cross-cultural studies of education to better understand the role of education in society. They continue to study how education contributes to social stratification; they also have devoted increased attention to the social contexts that schools create for students by looking at such issues as school reorganization (such as the creation of schools without grade levels). Moreover, sociologists increasingly focus on how school experiences differ by race and social class, and they make suggestions for improving the school experiences of minority and lower-class students. Sociologists also examine how the growth of technology alters the social structure of schools. Finally, sociologists consider the implications for schools of an increasingly global society.

Bibliography

Ballantine, Jeanne. *The Sociology of Education: A Systematic Analysis*. 3d ed. Englewood Cliffs, N.J.: Prentice-Hall, 1993. Ballantine emphasizes a systems perspective, which should be particularly useful as sociologists increasingly examine schools in a global society. She describes the role of education in stratification and provides an excellent review of educational reform and change.

Freedman, Samuel G. *Small Victories: The Real World of a Teacher, Her Students, and Their High School*. New York: Harper & Row, 1990. Freedman provides an insider's perspective on daily life in a school. Although not written by a sociologist, the book adds much to the knowledge of how the social contexts of schools affect the daily lives of teachers and students.

Kozol, Jonathan. *Savage Inequalities: Children in America's Schools*. New York: Crown, 1991. Kozol acted as an observer in many schools throughout the United States. He delivers a sharp criticism of the inequalities students experience as a result of race and social class. He provides many specific examples.

Mulkey, Lynn. *Sociology of Education: Theoretical and Empirical Investigations*. Fort Worth, Tex.: Harcourt Brace Jovanovich, 1993. Mulkey provides an excellent overview of how sociologists study education. She outlines the various approaches to the field and reviews empirical studies.

Sadker, Myra, and David Sadker. *Failing at Fairness: How America's Schools Cheat Girls*. New York: Charles Scribner's Sons, 1994. The Sadkers provide a detailed and insightful look into the inner workings of America's schools and focus on how schools work against girls' development. They propose several strategies for reducing the negative effect of schools, including single-sex schools.

Sizer, Theodore. *Horace's Compromise: The Dilemma of the American High School*. Boston: Houghton Mifflin, 1984. Sizer has spent many years working at various levels in the public school system. He examines what is wrong with American high schools and offers a detailed prescription for improving them.

Theodore C. Wagenaar

Cross-References

Compulsory and Mass Education, 309; Education: Conflict Theory Views, 579; Education: Functionalist Perspectives, 586; Education: Manifest and Latent Functions, 593; Educational Credentials and Social Mobility, 600; Educational Inequality: The Coleman Report, 607; Educational Vouchers and Tax Credits, 614; Interactionism, 1009; School Desegregation, 1686.

THE SOCIOLOGY OF KNOWLEDGE

Type of sociology: Origins and definitions of sociology
Field of study: Sociological perspectives and principles

Sociology of knowledge is the field of sociological theory that studies how human knowledge—especially knowledge used in everyday life—is created and maintained in the course of social life. The field seeks to explain how a society organizes its culture into certain categories and passes them from one generation to the next.

Principal terms
INSTITUTIONALIZATION: the process by which people develop habitual patterns of behavior and categories of thought that make social relations orderly and predictable
LEGITIMATION: the justification or explanation created by members of the social group to maintain the habitual patterns and categories that have been reified in their society
LIFE-WORLD: the world of daily life along with the corresponding knowledge needed to exist in it; a world and knowledge shared by members of a society or social group
REIFICATION: the process by which habitual patterns of behavior and categories of thought are apprehended by members of society as if being external to them and having a life of their own
SOCIAL CONSTRUCTION: the ability of human groups to create and maintain the knowledge in their cultural heritage
TYPIFICATION: a shared idea about a relationship or a category that focuses on its generic characteristics

Overview

Sociology of knowledge is the field of sociological theory concerned with the social construction and maintenance of everyday knowledge. To sociologists of knowledge, the world that is shared by all members of a group, the life-world, is filled with routines that determine how those individuals perceive and categorize things and relations around them. The life-world is a human construction; it is created by the group yet it acts upon the group as if it has a "life of its own."

According to sociologists of knowledge, the physical world, the empirical reality, is related to but distinct from the social world, the life-world. Whereas reality in the empirical world consists of relationships between variables which lead to natural consequences (for example, the physical process leading to rain), the social world apprehends that reality through the meanings and interpretations that the social group adds to it (a group may deem rain to be the result of God's will, an imbalance in the bow of the heavens, or a blessing from mother earth).

Sociologists of knowledge are interested in documenting how the influence of social location or social context affects the way groups perceive reality and build their knowledge of everyday life. To these scholars, external events cannot be completely explained by the ideas of any group because that group always perceives those events through the eyes of its collective tendencies and habits. In adapting to a certain environment, the group develops categories of thought and habitual patterns of behavior that delimit the way it further relates to the empirical world. People are not generally aware that they construct the social world in which they live. They tend to take the world "out there" for granted. Because knowledge of it is transmitted from one generation to the next, the life-world seems to have a life of its own. Its components seem prearranged, standing on their own, independent of "observers."

Sociologists of knowledge, however, argue that the reality that human beings encounter is always influenced and guided by their social location or context. In order to survive and adapt to their environment, humans create both material and ideal products: technologies to deal with the acquisition of food and shelter, laws to regulate disputes, and values to instill a sense of group solidarity. Those patterns of behavior and categories of thought are institutionalized, thereby becoming the way of life of a group. They are typifications—recipes for dealing with life situations such as being a spouse, buying a television, taking a test, and so on.

Once institutionalization takes place, the categories and patterns of behavior become expected and therefore seem to "act upon" the individual members of the group. The typifications seem to acquire an external force. To be able to live in social groups, individuals adopt this shared world of knowledge and pass it on from one generation to the next. That is the process known to sociologists of knowledge as reification—the process by which the cultural creations of a group are perceived by the group as a part of the overall reality, as "the way things are." To maintain reification, groups create systems of ideas that justify or legitimate "the way things are."

In the life-world, the stock of available knowledge provides the means to interpret the past and present and to help determine the shape of things to come. Thus, middle-class individuals may be socialized into a lifestyle of tastes quite different from those of upper-class people, members of a certain ethnic group may perceive reality in terms that are quite different from those of another ethnic group, and Protestants may celebrate a different set of life events from the ones celebrated by Hindus or Muslims.

Sociology of knowledge was brought to the English-speaking world by Karl Mannheim and Alfred Schutz. Mannheim developed his work in England; Schutz lived in the United States. Given the spread of Marxism in Europe after World War II, Mannheim's work centered on the function of ideology in society. His work redefined ideology as not simply the collective thought of an opposing group (as when the British pointed to German war propaganda as ideology while ignoring their own propaganda or calling it something else), but as the whole of any group's collective thought. Mannheim suggested that all human thought is socially located and therefore influenced by social context. He also argued, however, that certain groups are more capable of transcending their own narrow position than others are. According to him, in the process of interacting with other groups, a group may change and alter its ideological stand to better manage the compromises, coalitions, and conflicts that arise in everyday life.

Mannheim's work was heavy with political preoccupation as a result of the conditions under which the author was writing. It was only with the work of Alfred Schutz that sociology of knowledge lost its political edge and became a field involving the study of everyday life. Born in Vienna, Schutz immigrated to the United States in 1938. He joined the faculty of the New School for Social Research. Free from the political struggles in Europe, Schutz was able to dedicate his sociological analysis to the study of everyday life. Perhaps his most important contribution to sociology of knowledge was the change in the focus of the field. To him the task was no longer the debunking of political discourse but the study of modern life in general. Schutz introduced sociology of knowledge to American sociologists in the book *The Phenomenology of the Social World* (1967). He argued that the world of daily life (the life-world) is not private, but intersubjective. In this shared world there is a stock of knowledge passed from one generation to the next that provides individuals with parameters to guide their lives and to fit in society. The life-world is composed of typifications that are partly shared by individuals, depending on the groups to which they belong in a given society. To Schutz, only a small part of an individual's knowledge is derived from personal experience. Much of what people use in everyday life comes from assimilating the typifications accepted by their groups. The less one knows of a situation, the more likely one is to use the generalizations shared by one's group to categorize it.

In the work of two of Schutz's students, Peter L. Berger and Thomas Luckmann, sociology of knowledge gained its most mainstream presentation in American sociology. Quite familiar with the current American sociological schools of thought of their time, Berger and Luckmann used Schutz' ideas and a blend of Durkheimian, Weberian, and Marxian synthesis to expand the focus of the field to the study of modern society at large. Their book, *The Social Construction of Reality* (1966), discusses modern society as objective and subjective reality. In other words, they explain how categories of thought and habitual patterns of behavior are constructed by members of society and then gain a life of their own, acting upon and restricting the lives of their creators. It was through Berger and Luckmann's book that the discussions of institutionalization, reification, and legitimation were brought into mainstream sociology in the United States.

Applications

The insight that knowledge is always determined by the social context has helped sociologists to be better equipped to study social life without assuming that all individuals are free and disinterested in apprehending reality. One application of such knowledge comes in the realm of politics. For example, conditions that may be tolerable for the group in power may be intolerable for those being oppressed. For example, Martin Luther King, Jr., wrote a letter from his jail cell in Birmingham,

Alabama, explaining to the white clergy of the town why the black leadership could not wait for "gradual" reforms. To the white ministers, who had not experienced prejudice and discrimination, the Christian duty was to "render unto Caesar" and wait for slow change. To the black ministers, who, along with their congregations, suffered harsh discrimination, the Christian call was to fight injustice to bring about drastic change.

The determination of knowledge by context is also outlined by sociologist Karl Mannheim in his book *Ideology and Utopia* (1936). Written on the eve of World War II, the book documents how the vested interests of different political groups—liberals, conservatives, and radicals—make it difficult for them to agree on a common definition as to the causes of any social problem, to develop a common strategy on how to solve it, or to share similar motivations for addressing the problem. Furthermore, Mannheim shows that the group in power at any given time tends to sustain the status quo and determines what is and is not politically feasible.

Mannheim argues that all points of view in politics are partial, because historical totality (the whole of the life-world) is always too comprehensive to be grasped. Since the points of view of liberals, conservatives, and radicals emerge from the same general social context, and since their partial views represent slices of the whole picture, understanding the totality of politics means seeking a synthesis—finding different ingredients from all three points of view that will produce a balanced, relatively realistic view of the whole. In other words, since in practice various groups will always highlight or emphasize certain truths at the expense of others, it is left to the body of professionals who analyze opinion-making (those in academia or the news media, for example) to help the population see the truth amidst the propaganda.

Another application of the sociology of knowledge is seen in a book discussing Third World development, Peter L. Berger's *Pyramids of Sacrifice* (1976). Sociology of knowledge is used by Berger to demonstrate how the major economic models used to bring development to Third World countries (capitalism and socialism) exact a steep price from those nations without delivering on their promises. This occurs because the models are created by cliques of politicians and intellectuals who are likely to ignore the insights of local meanings, knowledge, and context. Failing to take into account local everyday knowledge, capitalism and socialism both demand that Third World nations sacrifice for the promises of a more equitable and safe future that never seems to arrive. Berger suggests that any policy directed toward development needs to take into account local knowledge to be successful.

Berger uses the examples of Brazil and China to show how both models (capitalist and socialist) are willing to sacrifice one or more generations for the sake of creating a developed nation. The problem is that both sets of sacrifices are justified by the imported theories; they structure life in such a fashion that both Brazilian and Chinese populations act as if such definitions were the only true possibility and had a life of their own in determining the steps needed for economic development.

Insights from the sociology of knowledge are also applied to the study of religion. Sociologists of knowledge study religion as both a social product and a contributor to the maintenance of everyday knowledge. In the book *The Sacred Canopy* (1967), Berger argues that human beings create religion by projecting certain characteristics cherished by their group onto the gods they worship. Those characteristics give the gods a feeling of familiarity that makes them appear as if they have a life of their own. Once the religious community accepts the gods as having a life of their own (existing independently from the group), it comes to believe that the gods are capable of establishing the kind of behavior that is acceptable or unacceptable among individuals in the religious community. Berger discusses how, after reification, the religious beliefs of a religious community legitimate the way of life of its individual members and reinforce their shared image of the gods.

Context

As a field of sociological theory, sociology of knowledge is a product of European scholars, specifically of the German academic world of the 1920's. During the period between the two world wars, there was a dramatic rise in radical politics in Germany. Fascists and communists fought for the heart and soul of the country. Ideological pamphleteering, rhetoric, and propaganda escalated on both sides. For German scholars of the period, the question of ascertaining the truth and clarifying the amount of distortion in the claims of political fashions was more than theoretical speculation.

Sociology of knowledge was heavily influenced by the work of historian Wilhelm Dilthey. Dilthey argued that social truth is always situational, that the way one looks at human events is relative because it depends on one's social location. Living in Germany during its surge of ideological nationalism, Dilthey believed that certain ideas have the upper hand on reality because of the social forces that validate them in the eyes of the social group in a given historical period.

Max Scheler, a sociologist at the University of Cologne and one of Dilthey's students, was responsible for the application of Dilthey's historical approach to sociological analysis. Following Dilthey's insights, Scheler created a sociological field that he called *Wissenssoziologie* ("sociology of knowledge"). To separate fact from fiction, reality from political propaganda, Scheler claimed that the two realms— the realm of the ideal and the realm of the real—exist in parallel but are not totally identified. In the end, empirical reality regulates the conditions for the appearance of certain ideas and ideologies in history. In his opinion, it was sociology of knowledge's basic task to isolate and identify the connection between the "real" and the "ideal."

Scheler claimed that external events are not the unfolding of ideologies in the real world (such a claim would be made by the Nazi Party later on, arguing that its platform was the fulfillment of Germany's manifest destiny). Rather, he said, ideologies have a greater or lesser chance of unfolding in the presence of certain external events. Scheler also called attention to the power of ideology in everyday life by showing how, because it precedes the individual, human knowledge (be it in the form of values, ideas, or ideologies) it appears to be the natural way of looking at the world. The creation in Germany of the Nazi youth corps and the commitment of its participants to the Nazi Party confirmed Scheler's theoretical insight.

Bibliography

Berger, Peter L. *Pyramids of Sacrifice*. Garden City, N.Y.: Doubleday, 1976. Berger applies concepts from sociology of knowledge to the study of politics and social change, specifically to their relationship to Third World development. He compares the promises of the two main economic models—capitalism and socialism—and views their results, respectively, in Brazil and China.

_____. *The Sacred Canopy*. Garden City, N.Y.: Doubleday, 1967. In this book Berger applies the insights from sociology of knowledge to the study of religion in modern life. The book addresses specifically the problem of maintenance of religious beliefs in a society in which religion no longer seems to have a central role.

Berger, Peter L., and Thomas Luckmann. *The Social Construction of Reality*. Garden City, N.Y.: Doubleday, 1966. Berger and Luckmann expand on Alfred Schutz's work, bringing sociology of knowledge into the study of modern society in general. The book discusses the processes of institutionalization, reification, and legitimation as well as their functions in modern society.

Mannheim, Karl. *Ideology and Utopia*. New York: Harvest/HBJ, 1936. Mannheim's book was the first work in sociology of knowledge published in the English language. Although a political study, the book contains many of the field's sociological insights. The last chapter is Mannheim's own description of sociology of knowledge as a field of study.

Schutz, Alfred. *The Phenomenology of the Social World*. Evanston, Ill.: Northwestern University Press, 1967. This book is one of the major works in the field of sociology of knowledge to be published originally in the United States. It contains the seeds of all the major concepts and insights developed later by others.

H. B. Cavalcanti

Cross-References

THE SOCIOLOGY OF RELIGION

Type of sociology: Major social institutions
Field of study: Religion

The sociology of religion examines sacred ideologies and associated social practices from an objective and empirical perspective. In contrast with theology, which grapples with the claims of truth made by various religions, sociological analysis considers the social behavioral implications of religious activity, with particular emphasis on its effects on social integration and social change.

Principal terms
ASCETICISM: the practice of self-denial of pleasure so as to achieve greater spiritual purity
FUNCTION: a sociological concept that designates how a particular social element serves (either openly or in a hidden manner) to enhance the larger social whole
IDEOLOGY: a set of ideas, beliefs, and attitudes that provides legitimation for particular patterns of social behavior
INTEGRATION: the binding or holding together of various parts of a social whole, a process frequently viewed by sociologists as "problematic" rather than automatic
LEGITIMATION: a social belief that serves to justify a particular social pattern of behavior by rendering it meaningful
PHENOMENOLOGY: the study of everyday social life in terms of the central role played by human consciousness in social interaction and the "social construction of reality"
RELIGION: a unified system of sacred beliefs and corresponding social practices
SACRED: a social classification of phenomena that includes extraordinary and awe-inspiring events and processes distinct from the everyday, mundane aspects of social life
THEODICY: a religious belief that provides a meaningful explanation to an otherwise inexplicable trauma or undesirable event, thereby strengthening the established legitimations of a given social order

Overview

The sociology of religion is a major subfield within the discipline of sociology. Classical sociological theorists considered religion to be a crucially important area of social investigation. Émile Durkheim, for example, defined religion as a system of sacred beliefs and practices shared by a community of followers such as a church. In contrast to the established tendency to see religious practice in personal and individualistic terms, Durkheim wished to stress the social reality of religion. He believed that even the most profoundly personal religious experiences obtain their human meaning through socially shared symbols that are based in a particular cultural context.

The sociology of religion has carried the basic issues of sociological inquiry into the sphere of sacred belief systems. The question "How is social order possible?" is of paramount concern to sociology. Durkheim ultimately answered this question, in part, through his pathbreaking work in the sociology of religion, in which he asserted that religious behavior serves the socially necessary function of enhancing social cohesion. Through the ritual practices associated with sacred beliefs, social communities are strengthened or "integrated" to a degree that would otherwise be difficult to achieve.

Other functions of religion implied in Durkheim's work include its ascetic character, which encourages self-discipline and self-sacrifice in favor of meaningful and orderly moral conduct. Religion further tends to instill euphoria into the otherwise mundane circumstances of everyday life, providing positive and desirable feelings that are otherwise not reliably present. This in turn revitalizes existing social institutions, enhancing the eagerness of social participants to maintain existing social patterns and promulgate them to their children through socialization.

Having identified the various social functions that religion serves, Durkheim concluded that religion could ultimately be seen as a process whereby "society worships itself." Sacred beliefs essentially embody the moral binding of socially ordered, human collectivities. This conjecture led to Durkheim's concern that the breakdown of sacred beliefs in the context of rapid social change and increasing specialization in the division of labor could create major problems for social stability. Durkheim believed that only by the formation of new sacred belief structures could society continue to maintain harmony and continual growth.

Durkheim's work initiated the functionalist approach to the sociological study of religion. Karl Marx is responsible for consolidating the critical perspective on sacred ideologies and practices. Through forming his own critique of Hegelian philosophy, Marx accepted much of Ludwig Feuerbach's materialist critique of religion. According to Feuerbach, religion is essentially a human projection in which people create and then worship supernatural entities that are in reality based firmly in their collective imagination. Feuerbach believed that the immense power that humans attribute to supernatural entities is actually a mystical and indirect reflection of the vast creative potential rooted in the human species itself. Feuerbach concluded that once this "secret" is discovered, atheism becomes the ultimately desirable human condition because it signifies a sober look at the human potential to pursue higher forms of social life.

Marx was greatly influenced by Feuerbach's materialist critique of religion and synthesized it into his critical view of exploitation in class societies. From Marx's perspective, religion is an "opiate of the masses" because it tends to mystify and obfuscate people's awareness of unjust social structures and preach acceptance of the status quo rather than its revolutionary transformation. Marx greatly influenced the sociology of religion by emphasizing the need to consider critically the social implications of religious practice and the intimate relationship between religion and social change.

Max Weber further explored the relationship of religion and social change by his critical engagement with Marxism. Weber helped to show that religion helps to legitimate social orders. In doing so, however, Weber showed that religion can also become an autonomous force for social change. By researching in tremendous detail the dynamics of change within religious ideologies, Weber hypothesized that changing beliefs in history converge upon human actors in a way that can bring about collective social change. Ultimately, Weber attempted to illustrate this process by arguing that the Protestant ethic (the "work ethic") as an ideological upsurge within Christianity, decisively helped to bring about the rise of capitalism.

The work of Weber, Marx, and Durkheim helped to set the theoretical parameters for the sociology of religion. Modern sociologists of religion, operating almost entirely within the theoretical permutations established by classical sociological theory, have set about the task of systematizing the subfield. Much work has been dedicated to understanding the organizational dynamics of religious communities, the institutional characteristics of religion, and religion's relationship with other human institutions. Sociologists have also developed more methodologically rigorous means of elaborating and verifying sociological theories of religion. The worldwide resurgence of religious movements that began during the 1970's led to a renewed interest in the sociology of religion. Contemporary theorists have been forced to grapple with the reality that religion can both contribute to social harmony and stability and promote destabilization and change.

Applications

The sociology of religion has produced various seminal studies that have attempted to create a general paradigm for the subfield. Peter L. Berger's *The Sacred Canopy: Elements of a Sociological Theory of Religion* (1967) is one of the most widely cited works that attempt to synthesize classical sociological theories into a working framework for scientifically approaching religion. Despite its many strengths, however, Berger's work displayed substantial weaknesses.

Berger's framework was developed from an earlier work he coauthored with Thomas Luckmann (*The Social Construction of Reality: A Treatise in the Sociology of Knowledge*, 1966), in which they attempted to demonstrate the importance of using phenomenological sociology as the basis for a general "sociology of knowledge" which in turn could serve as the central paradigm for all sociological analysis. Although Berger and Luckmann's work was initially received with great acclaim, numerous critics subsequently argued that their phenomenological approach placed too much emphasis upon subjective meanings in explaining social interaction while failing to account adequately for such objective aspects of social reality as power relations. Its shortcomings notwithstanding, Berger and Luckmann's perspective is useful in "knowledge-intensive" areas of everyday life such as religion.

Berger, a strong religious believer, asserts that the sociology of religion must rigidly "bracket" any questions concerning the ultimate "truth" or validity of religious activity. By remaining "disinterested" in theological questions, the analyst is free to consider the ways in which religion forms part of the process of "world building." This detached approach is essential to the sociology of religion and echoes the tradition of Max Weber's "value-free" approach as well as that of Alfred Schutz, the founder of phenomenological sociology.

From Berger's perspective, the social reality of everyday life is "socially constructed" through patterns of symbolic meanings which became shared in social interaction. According to Berger, all social orders are precarious because they are essentially arbitrary historical creations that are subject to modification and change. The stability of social orders therefore requires a distinctive set of reinforcing symbols that, once collectively shared, can provide ongoing support for a social status quo. Such meanings constitute a special form of humanly constructed knowledge known as legitimations, which specifically seek to explain and justify other existing sets of meanings associated with an established social order.

Berger points out that legitimations have both a normative and a cognitive character. Their cognitive character deals with "what is"—with explaining how it is that the world exists. Their normative character, in contrast, refers to a belief in "what ought to be"—an explanation of how things should properly be done. By exhibiting both of these traits, legitimations help to maintain the socially constructed world. When legitimations are woven together into a complex system of beliefs, they provide a "higher reality" in which the everyday real world can be placed into a meaningful context, a sacred and cosmic frame of reference. In this, religion ultimately constitutes the highest expression of shared social legitimations.

Because legitimations are themselves precarious and subject to breakdown, they require constant reenactment through ritual practice. Perhaps the greatest threat to legitimating beliefs, and therefore to social orders themselves, is chaotic or traumatic events such as death and natural catastrophes, which by their inexplicable nature can lead to serious challenges to the established set of legitimated social meanings. A specialized set of legitimations known as theodicies are frequently employed to defend the social order from such challenges.

A theodicy specifically seeks to explain an apparently inexplicable event by placing it into a meaningful context. This helps to alleviate the strain being placed on the established system of legitimation, thereby protecting the social status quo. In animistic religions, for example, a prolonged drought can be explained by the human collectivity's fall from favor with the nature god. A series of remedial rituals is employed as a practical theodicy which allows social participants to reharmonize themselves with nature, thus addressing what is believed to be the source of the problem.

Berger shows how monotheistic Christianity employs a particularly sophisticated kind of theodicy that seeks to address challenges that emerge in times of severe adversity. Rather than attempting to answer the trauma-induced question directly, Christianity employs a strategic theodicy that challenges the very right of the traumatized questioner to pose the question. Thus, the question "How could God allow such a thing to happen?" becomes addressed by a theodicy which asks in turn, "Who are you to question the motives of the all-knowing Creator?"

While Berger's framework amply illustrates many of the key concepts within the contemporary sociology of religion (such as legitimation and theodicy), it has nevertheless been subjected to numerous critiques. His inability to conceptualize the dynamics of social power adequately leaves issues such as class-based, race-based, and gender-based oppression unaddressed at best and trivialized at worst. More recent studies have attempted to rectify these weaknesses by exploring the contributions that neo-Marxist and feminist perspectives can make to the field. In addition, considerable cross-fertilization from liberation theology has generated excitement within the discipline.

Context

The sociology of religion dates back to the concern which the earliest sociologists displayed for understanding the key role played by sacred belief systems. Auguste Comte, the French founder of sociology, saw within religion a developing intellectual sensibility that contained the seeds for what he predicted would eventually lead to a rational pursuit of enlightened morality. Comte's "social dynamics," or theory of social change in stages, postulated evolutionary relationships between religious beliefs, morality, and social order. Ultimately, Comte attempted to form a scientifically based "church of positivism" in which he was the "high priest." His work is generally regarded to be most important for its influence on other key French thinkers, such as Émile Durkheim.

Durkheim was extremely influential in establishing the academic jurisdiction of sociology. He gleaned from Comte an understanding of religion's role in sustaining the social order and went on to postulate the indispensable role that religion plays in maintaining social "integration" or harmony. In his last major work, entitled *Les Formes élémentaires de la vie religieuse: Le Système totémique en Australie* (1912; *The Elementary Forms of the Religious Life: A Study in Religious Sociology*, 1915), Durkheim attempted to show how collective social processes in primitive societies require the binding effects that religion provides. Rather than becoming less important in modern societies, Durkheim argues that the increasing specialization of modern societies requires religious beliefs in order to maintain social integration. The functionalist approach that Durkheim pioneered has remained prominent ever since, influencing contemporary sociological theorists such as Talcott Parsons and Robert K. Merton.

Max Weber's *Die Protestantische Ethik und der Geist des Kapitalismus* (1904; *The Protestant Ethic and the Spirit of Capitalism*, 1930) has likewise been extremely influential in the sociology of religion. Weber, a German sociologist, sought to show that ideas, as part of a "superstructure," could have dramatic effects upon society's "infrastructure," or material base, in the course of history. This argument opposed Marx's view that the superstructure generally reflected changes in the infrastructure.

Weber's work had a great impact upon Alfred Schutz, his German contemporary, who integrated Weberian concerns into the phenomenological philosophy pioneered by Edmund Husserl. Schutz's phenomenological interpretation of Weber was the principal inspiration for Peter L. Berger's attempt to reintegrate the sociology of religion more squarely into the mainstream of sociology.

Marx's critical conception of religion spawned generations of neo-Marxist theorists who in general viewed religion as a "false consciousness" or an obfuscatory ideology in the context of exploitive social orders. Marx's sociology of religion began with his "Economic and Philosophic Manuscripts of 1844," which forms a part of Marx's collected works, published in 1932. Like other aspects of his work, it has profoundly affected social life itself. Beginning in the 1960's, theologians in Latin America, and later in Africa and Asia, were influenced by Marxist concepts. The infusion of Marxist concepts into the lexicon of the spiritual leaders of popular grass-roots political movements helped spur the development of the movement known as liberation theology. This upsurge of religious activism has been instrumental in galvanizing revolutionary movements in Latin America and elsewhere. Ironically, this has forced many neo-Marxists to revise Marx's nineteenth century assertion that religion serves only as the "opiate of the masses."

Bibliography

Beckford, James A. *Religion and Advanced Industrial Society*. London: Unwin Hyman, 1989. An interesting theoretical analysis which argues that the sociology of religion has been largely relegated to the periphery of sociology. The author contends that the theoretical imagery of classical sociology showed ample interest in religion but remained immersed in assumptions concerning the rise of industrial societies in a way that rendered the study of religion in advanced industrial societies problematic.

Berger, Peter L. *The Sacred Canopy: Elements of a Sociological Theory of Religion*. Garden City, N.Y.: Doubleday, 1967. This widely cited work attempts to outline a general model for the sociology of religion. Because of its phenomenological approach, however, it has been widely criticized for its inability to provide a critical view of religion, particularly in terms of an analysis of social power relationships.

Berryman, Phillip. *Liberation Theology: Essential Facts About the Revolutionary Religious Movement in Latin America and Beyond*. New York: Pantheon Books, 1987. A social case study of liberation theology written from a critical sociological perspective. Strongly sympathetic to the movement, the author seeks to introduce readers to the wide-reaching social implications of radicalized religious currents that challenge the established orders of Latin America.

Hargrove, Barbara. *The Sociology of Religion: Classical and Contemporary Approaches*. 2d ed. Arlington Heights, Ill.: Harlan Davidson, 1989. A very accessible introduction to the sociology of religion that examines the nature and function of religion, its cultural basis, the relationship between institutionalized religion and other key social institutions, and the dynamics of religious change.

Homan, Roger. *The Sociology of Religion: A Bibliographical Survey.* New York: Greenwood Press, 1986. An excellent resource for those seeking to do research in the sociology of religion. Following a brief overview of the primary and secondary literature, a substantial annotated bibliography of key works in the field is presented.

McGuire, Meredith B. *Religion: The Social Context.* 2d ed. Belmont, Calif.: Wadsworth, 1987. A survey of the sociology of religion that examines all major areas within the field, including consideration of the role that religion plays in promoting social stability and social change. Key articles and annotated book citations are identified at the end of each chapter. A brief appendix gives tips on doing a literature search in the sociology of religion.

Turner, Bryan S. *Religion and Social Theory.* 2d ed. London: Sage Publications, 1991. A theoretical treatise for advanced students focusing on the challenges that feminist and postmodern theories pose for the sociology of religion. The author explores problematic concepts such as theodicy and secularization, positing that a "sociology of the body" that builds upon the "philosophical anthropology" advanced by Peter L. Berger and others may be a fruitful means of advancing the field.

Yinger, J. Milton. *The Scientific Study of Religion.* New York: Macmillan, 1970. A comprehensive and interdisciplinary approach to religion, stressing the interconnections between the sociology, psychology, and anthropology of religion. This book provides an excellent beginner's guide for the serious student of religion and includes chapters on the organizational, political, and economic factors that interrelate with religious institutions.

Richard A. Dello Buono

Cross-References

Liberation Theology, 1081; The Protestant Ethic and Capitalism, 1533; Religion: Beliefs, Symbols, and Rituals, 1598; Religion: Functionalist Analyses, 1603; Religion: Marxist and Conflict Theory Views, 1610; Religion versus Magic, 1617; Religious Miracles and Visions, 1623; Socialization: Religion, 1894.

SPOUSE BATTERING AND VIOLENCE
AGAINST WOMEN

Type of sociology: Sex and gender

Throughout the life span, women are disproportionately subject to a variety of actions intended to inflict physical or psychological harm; when violent abuse occurs within a marital relationship, it is referred to as spouse battering.

Principal terms

CHILD ABUSE: the psychological, physical, or sexual maltreatment of a person under the age of eighteen in which the child's welfare, health, or safety is endangered

CHILD NEGLECT: negligence or deprivation regarding the provision of care for a child (a person under eighteen years of age)

DOMESTIC ABUSE AND VIOLENCE: mistreatment, injurious actions, or the abuse of power occurring in the home

PHYSICAL ABUSE: the use of physical force to cause bodily harm

PSYCHOLOGICAL ABUSE: verbal and nonverbal acts that impair another person's healthy psychological development

RAPE: the act of forcing or coercing another individual into having sexual intercourse; rape may involve an abuse of power or may involve physical force or threats

SEXUAL ABUSE: any exploitation or misuse of a person for another person's sexual gratification

SPOUSE OR PARTNER BATTERING: physical, psychological, or sexual mistreatment that occurs in a relationship between married individuals or those in a sustaining partnership

Overview

Abusive and violent acts against women come in many forms. When such an act occurs against a person under the age of eighteen, it is called child abuse. Actions that exploit and misuse women sexually are termed sexually abusive. Finally, when abuse and violence are directed against women in the context of a marriage or other sustaining partnership, spouse battering or partner abuse is said to occur. This type of abuse is usually subsumed under the more general term "domestic abuse and violence."

These three types of abuse and violence—domestic abuse, sexual abuse, and child abuse—are linked in a number of ways. First, while males do suffer from all three forms of abuse, victimization of females in these ways is considerably more prevalent, both currently and historically. Second, all three abusive types are frequently "crimes of silence": The victims are usually constrained by a variety of factors from exposing their perpetrators, victims' reports are often not believed and are denied credibility, and criminal conviction (in comparison to the frequency of the crimes) is quite unlikely. Finally, these three forms of abuse frequently coexist: Child or domestic abuse is often sexual in nature, and child abuse is more likely to occur in homes where domestic abuse is occurring. An examination of the nature of domestic abuse and violence, sexual abuse, and child abuse and the statistical prevalence of these violations not only supports the aforementioned statements but also demonstrates the magnitude and severity of these abuses.

Incidents of domestic abuse and violence are the most common but least reported of all crimes. There are four basic types of domestic abuse: economic, physical, psychological, and sexual. All four types have a common theme: the misuse of power and control in a relationship. Economically, domestic abuse occurs when money is withheld, jobs are denied, or careers are interfered with. Physical types of domestic violence include hitting, choking, shoving, and assaults with objects. Verbal and emotional erosions of self-worth such as name-calling, constant criticism, humiliating remarks, and threats to personal safety, beloved objects, or pets constitute the psychological category of domestic abuse. Domestic sexual abuse occurs when sexual gratification is gained by one partner without the other partner's willing, rational consent or when it results in the other person (usually the woman) being demeaned or belittled. While all four types of domestic abuse and violence leave deep and long-lasting scars in the lives of the victims, physical abuse poses the greatest danger to the immediate health of the victim and therefore deserves special attention.

Physical domestic violence in its primary form, male violence against females, is, in the view of many people, the most serious of crimes against women. Former Surgeon General C. Everett Koop described domestic violence as women's number one health problem in 1984. His successor, Antonia Novello, agreed, commenting that domestic violence causes more injuries to women than muggings, rapes, and car accidents combined. She claimed that every five years as many women are killed by domestic violence as soldiers were lost in the Vietnam War—58,000. James McDermott has estimated that as many as 4 million women suffer from incidents of domestic abuse each year. It has been estimated that nearly a third of all women who go to a physician in need of medical care are victims of domestic violence. Finally, Marilyn Gardner, in 1992, reported the most sobering of these statistics: While 4 percent of male murder victims were murdered by their wives or girlfriends, 33 percent of women victims were murdered by their husbands or boyfriends. Death is frequently the culminating result of years of physical abuse of women.

Sexual abuse of adults can occur in a variety of forms, from the act of disrobing to actual sexual intercourse. One thing that all forms of sexual abuse have in common, however, is that a person is less than 100 percent in agreement with engaging in acts with another person. Rape (forcible sexual intercourse) is usually the most violent form of sexual abuse. The statistics on rape are staggering. Twenty percent of American women have been raped, a woman is raped every six minutes, and the rate of rape is increasing four times as fast as the overall crime rate, according to a 1991 Senate report by Mitch McConnell. Results from several studies in the early 1990's revealed similarly astonishing statistics regarding the lack of justice meted out to rapists. Ninety percent of rapes are not reported in spite of (or because of) the fact that in 70 percent of the cases the rapist is known by the victim. Only 33 percent of reported rapes lead to an arrest, only two of every 1,000 rapes lead to a conviction, and only 29 percent of convicted rapists are sentenced to one or more years in jail.

Child abuse is generally considered a topic distinct from violence against women, but it is important to consider it briefly here, as some of the same issues are involved. The prevalence of child abuse in the United States is frighteningly high; a 1991 article by Senator Christopher Dodd in the *Congressional Record* reported that in 1990, 2.5 million children were officially found to be victims of abuse and neglect. Furthermore, an estimated 3.3 million children witness domestic abuse each year. These child witnesses have been found to be 1,500 percent more likely to be abused or neglected than the general population. A 1993 study by the National Center of Child Abuse Prevention reported the following breakdown in regard to types of child maltreatment: neglect, 49 percent; physical abuse, 27 percent; sexual abuse, 16 percent; and psychological abuse, 8 percent. There is one type of child maltreatment in which there is a major gender difference—sexual abuse. The *National Center of Child Abuse Prevention* reported in 1993 that while the number of male victims is usually estimated around 10 percent of the total number of male children, estimates of female victims range from 15 to 38 percent. Males are much more frequently reported than females as perpetrators.

An examination of domestic violence, particularly spouse battering, can provide insight into the factors that generate and maintain violence in the home and can give indications as to how to alleviate this situation. Spouse battering is usually characterized by abuse and violence that is unidirectional, from the batterer to the battered. Frequently one or both people in the abusive relationship fail to recognize how dysfunctional the relationship truly is, perhaps because of having been reared in a violent home themselves. It is, therefore, a critical first step in dealing with spouse battering to inform people about the characteristics of this form of domestic violence. Numerous sources of information, from YWCA battered-women programs to books such as Ginny NiCarthy's *Getting Free: A Handbook for Women in Abusive Relationships* (1986), have compiled lists of characteristics of both the victim and victimizer in a battering relationship.

Signs of being battered usually include several symptoms tied together by the common threat of fear: fear of being physically assaulted, fear of being humiliated or embarrassed, fear of losing control or freedom, fear of doing anything wrong in the eyes of one's spouse, fear of what will happen if one does not rescue or cover up for one's spouse, and, perhaps most important, fear of what will happen should one ever try to leave the relationship. Signs of being a batterer often involve aspects of power: asserting power through physical force, temperamental outbursts, or verbal threats; keeping power by controlling finances and one's partner's behavior and decisions; lowering one's partner's sense of power through humiliation and criticism; and expressing power insecurity through jealousy, drug abuse, or obsessive overprotec-tiveness of the partner.

Numerous factors that contribute to the creation of spouse battering have been described in books such as *Terrifying Love* by Lenore Walker (1989) and *The Dark Side of Families: Current Family Violence Research* by David Finkelhor, Richard Gelles, Gerald Hotaling, and Murray Strauss (1983). These factors can be condensed into three categories: familial (especially family background), situational (current conditions), and personal (personality characteristics). *The Dark Side of Families* sheds some light on the ways people's family backgrounds can place them at greater risk for entering a battering relationship. The book reports that 48 percent of battering victims were subjected to early and repeated sexual molestation. Furthermore, two-thirds of all battered women came from homes with high rates of violence. Current situational factors that contribute to spouse battering include alcohol and other drug abuse; low financial, occupational, and educational status; and high levels of marital conflict. Finally, certain personality characteristics have been identified as playing a role in generating spouse abuse: impulsiveness, possessiveness, and a high need for power on the part of the batterer; poor self-image, lack of assertiveness, and overde-pendency on the part of the battered.

One of the more puzzling questions to the average person regarding spouse battering is, "Why does the woman stay in the abusive relationship?" The answer is complex and multifaceted. Fear is usually at the root of what keeps a woman from leaving a batterer. There are many links in the chain of fear that is involved, links based on realities rather than on paranoid imaginings. The ultimate feared reality, according to Laurie Schipper, director of a shelter for battered women, is death: A woman who leaves a batterer stands a 75 percent greater chance of being killed than a woman who stays. Too many women have learned that no-contact orders, police arrests, and even battered women's shelters are no guarantee of safety. Fears regarding various aspects of well-being also abound. A woman considering leaving an abusive relationship may be asking herself a number of agonizing questions: What will happen to my children; how can I leave a man I still love (a majority of victims do still love their partners); how will I survive financially; and am I personally capable of making it on my own? Battering usually lowers self-esteem and confidence.

One useful theoretical framework for understanding domestic violence and, in particular, why a battered spouse stays is called "the cycle of violence." This frame-work proposes a three-phase circularity of behavior in abusive relationships. In the first phase, there is a buildup of tension, anger, and conflict. During the second phase, this buildup is released in the actual abusive act(s). In the third phase, apologies, forgiveness, and promises to do better give the temporary appearance of a healed relationship. Unfortunately, this "good" time in the relationship may serve only to increase the likelihood of the cycle being repeated. Good intentions and false hopes are not sufficient to break the cycle. While the third phase has been questioned and criticized because of its name ("the honeymoon phase") and its absence in many abusive relationships, it is nevertheless true that many spouse-battering situations, particularly those that involve physical violence, can be adequately characterized by this threefold conception. Many victims have gained much-needed insight into their own abusive relationships when presented with this theoretical perspective.

Understanding spouse battering is a necessary, but not sufficient, step in dealing with it. Action must be taken on at least three fronts—legislatively, therapeutically, and attitudinally—to redress the situation. Legislatively, tougher laws and vigorous prosecution are needed to protect people from being battered. Therapeutically, psychological healing and reform are needed for the victims and perpetrators, respectively. Support services, such as adequate sheltering, are also crucial for victims to overcome their abuse. Attitudinally, global changes in increasing people's respect and valuation for one another and decreasing society's tolerance for any level of abuse in relationships—especially male-female relations—are essential.

Context

Attitudes toward women that facilitate an abusive environment for women have been documented throughout history. An ancient written record (dating from 2400 B.C.E.) states that if a man's wife was verbally abusive to him, he had the right to engrave her name on a brick and knock her teeth out with it. The Latin language reveals that thousands of years later the man still dominated his wife; the Latin root of "family" is "familia," meaning "a group of slaves belonging to a man." More than a dozen centuries after the fall of the Roman empire, a codification of English common law by William Blackstone in the 1760's demonstrated that the lot of married women had changed little. The "rule of thumb" became official English law, meaning that a husband had the right to beat his wife as long as any stick or object used was no thicker than his thumb. Thus for thousands of years women were viewed more as marital property than as marriage partners.

Although feminists of the nineteenth and early twentieth century cried out against the evils of spouse battering, it was not until the 1970's in the United States that solid reform began to occur. Antirape groups were gaining momentum in effecting positive changes regarding sexual assaults, and it was a natural outgrowth of this movement to move into advocacy for battered wives. The 1970's witnessed many firsts for helping battered women. In 1971, the first hotline was established (in St. Paul, Minnesota); in 1974, the first shelter for battered women was opened (also in St. Paul), and in 1977 Oregon became the first state to provide a mandatory arrest law for batterers. In 1979, in her book *The Battered Woman*, Lenore Walker introduced the concept of "the battered woman syndrome."

The 1980's and 1990's have seen a growing societal intolerance of violence against women, particularly of spouse battering. Research from numerous studies, such as *Behind Closed Doors* (1980), the first national study of battering, was used by legislatures in every state to press for better protective measures for victims of spouse abuse. Results were significant. For example, in 1967 in dealing with domestic violence, police were instructed to make arrests only as a last resort, according to the training manual of the International Association of Chiefs of Police. Twenty years later, more than half of the nation's police departments had adopted the opposite policy: In domestic violence disputes, officers should make an arrest unless a very good reason against it can be documented. The medical community also took a more aggressive stance against domestic violence during these two decades. C. Everett Koop, in 1984, was the first surgeon general to single out domestic violence as a major health problem. In 1992, the American Medical Association issued guidelines for screening all female patients for signs of domestic abuse.

Significant gains by women and their advocates against all forms of violence have been made since 1970. A statistical examination of the same years since 1970, however, demonstrates a marked *increase* in violent crimes against women. In addition to this disturbing statistical trend, there has been, especially in the early 1990's, a growing backlash against victims of certain types of violence. Many legal and psychological authorities have mounted campaigns to impugn the credibility of child abuse, rape, and domestic violence victims. Thus, the task of those who stand opposed to violence against women is twofold: to stop the perpetrator's violence and to obtain justice for the victim.

Bibliography

Finkelhor, David, Richard Gelles, Gerald Hotaling, and Murray Strauss, eds. *The Dark Side of Families: Current Family Violence Research*. Beverly Hills, Calif.: Sage Publications, 1983. A collection of essays by noted researchers on several subjects related to violence in the family. The book contains a mixture of research studies and theoretical perspectives on wife abuse, child abuse, sexual abuse, and marital rape. A strong scientific treatment of violence in families.

Jones, Ann, and Susan Schechter. *When Love Goes Wrong: What to Do When You Can't Do Anything Right*. New York: HarperCollins, 1992. This book is intended to help battered women better understand their experiences with controlling partners. Numerous personal stories are offered. Activities designed to help women clarify their abusive situations and practical advice aimed to rectify those situations are presented.

NiCarthy, Ginny. *Getting Free: A Handbook for Women in Abusive Relationships*. 2d ed. Seattle: Seal Press, 1986. This is an excellent self-help book for women in abusive relationships. All sorts of self-help tools are set forth in the context of helping to lead a woman through the many decisions to be made in leaving an abusive partner.

Walker, Lenore. *The Battered Woman*. New York: Harper & Row, 1979. A landmark volume on the subject of wife battering. The influential cycle of violence theory is explained in detail and exemplified with many stories of victims of domestic violence. An excellent examination of the factors that generate and maintain abusive relationships.

_____. *Terrifying Love*. New York: Harper & Row, 1989. The "battered woman syndrome" is used to explain how and why some battered women kill their abusers. An examination of the legal, psychological, and social ramifications of such acts is presented. A strong point of this book is Walker's provision of personal insights and experiences from her years serving as an expert witness in court cases involving battered women.

Kathleen A. Chara
Paul J. Chara, Jr.

Cross-References

Child Abuse and Neglect, 218; The Family: Functionalist versus Conflict Theory Views, 739; Health Care and Gender, 858; The Incest Taboo, 934; Rape, 1592; Sexism and Institutional Sexism, 1728; Violence in the Family, 2157; The Women's Movement, 2196.

STANDARDIZED TESTING AND IQ TESTING CONTROVERSIES

Type of sociology: Major social institutions
Field of study: Education

Standardized tests, including intelligence tests, are widely used and, many argue, misused in modern society. They are generally intended to measure individuals' abilities or aptitudes in various subject areas. Controversies include the uses to which test results are put and whether intelligence tests truly measure intelligence.

Principal terms
APTITUDE TESTS: tests intended to predict future performance
ETHNIC GROUP: a group distinguished principally by the cultural heritage shared by the group
GROUP TEST: a test that may be administered to a number of individuals at the same time by one examiner
INDIVIDUAL TEST: a test that can be administered to only one person at a time because of the nature of the test and/or the maturity level of the examinees
INTELLIGENCE TESTS: tests intended to provide an understanding of the bases of a person's performance or to predict what that person will do in the future
MINORITY GROUP: any group of people, not necessarily a numerical minority, who have been socially disadvantaged
STANDARDIZED TESTS: tests given, usually nationwide, under uniform conditions and scored according to uniform procedures

Overview

Testing is an integral part of education. Most persons who have been educated formally have participated in some aspect of testing as a means of evaluating their performance. The results of standardized testing can have profound effects on people's lives, as such tests help determine who passes from one grade to the next, who is admitted to special programs, who enters college, who receives scholarships, who is accepted into graduate school, and who is promoted on the job.

There are several kinds of standardized tests, including intelligence tests, aptitude tests, and achievement tests. Intelligence tests measure analytical and general thinking skills. Aptitude tests measure mental functioning in various subjects or areas. Achievement tests are used to measure skills and information taught in the average American classroom. Testing is a multimillion dollar industry in the United States, with group intelligence tests being used primarily in business and in schools.

Standardized tests are usually used nationally. They are administered under uniform conditions and are scored according to uniform procedures. Most often group admin-istered, they include such tests as the California Achievement Test (CAT), Scholas-tic Aptitude Test (SAT), Comprehensive Test of Basic Skills (CTBS), Metropolitan Achievement Test (MAT), Standard Achievement Test (SAT), Iowa Test of Basic Skills (ITBS), Graduate Record Examination (GRE), National Teachers' Examination (NTE), Law School Admissions Test (LSAT), and Dental Aptitude Test (DAT). One of the most popular and frequently used aptitude tests is the Scholastic Aptitude Test. The SAT comprises a verbal section to measure reading comprehension and vocabu-lary and a mathematical section to measure to measure quantitative abilities closely related to college work. This test is used as a common national standard for evaluating students.

The purpose of tests such as the SAT and others listed above is to determine "achievement," how much a person has gained or learned in a given content area or span of time, or "aptitude," which is a measure meant to predict performance. Thus, standardized achievement tests provide information about students' academic gains, whereas standardized aptitude tests attempt to provide information about a person's potential performance in certain academic pursuits or endeavors.

Intelligence tests are standardized tests used to determine a person's ability to acquire and use knowledge for solving problems and adapting to the world. Standard intelligence tests include the Wechsler Preschool and Primary Scale of Intelligence (WPPSI), Wechsler Adult Intelligence Scale-Revised (WAIS-R), Wechsler Intelli-gence Scale for Children, third edition (WISC-III), and the Stanford-Binet Intelligence Scale.

The most famous and probably most frequently used of these standardized intelli-gence tests are the Stanford-Binet test and the Wechsler series. The Stanford-Binet Intelligence Scale consists of a variety of mental tasks arranged by age level. The person's mental age and intelligence quotient (IQ) are determined by the summing of credits for the successful completion of tasks at each level. Test performance is expressed by a single score, which represents a highly verbal measure of general mental ability. The Wechsler intelligence tests are organized by subtest as opposed to age level. Each test contains a Verbal Scale, composed of five or six subtests, and a Performance Scale, which is composed of five subtests.

The dimensions of intelligence that may be measured on a standardized intelligence test include verbal, reasoning, spatial, memory, and quantitative abilities. Thus the information provided by intelligence tests includes a person's abilities in vocabulary memory, mathematical ability, and visual and spatial skills. Intelligence test scores predict future academic behavior and job success in the workplace and have been found to correlate with many other variables.

There are at least three controversies that surround the use of standardized tests, particularly standardized intelligence tests: the controversy concerning reliability and validity; the controversy about possible bias in the tests that affects the performance of minorities; and the controversy over how the tests are used. Reliability in testing refers to the extent to which a test is consistent in measuring what it measures. Validity refers to the extent to which a test measures what it is supposed to measure. Those who do not support the use of standardized tests point out that testing may not adequately portray how much students know.

The fact that minority groups, such as African Americans, American Indians, and Latinos, tend to perform relatively poorly on standardized tests has been a cause for serious concern. Charges have been made that the tests are biased in favor of students from middle-class backgrounds, who are primarily white. Considerable research has examined this problem, and much of it has found ways in which such tests contain subtle bias (almost certainly unintended, at least by the late twentieth century) against ethnic minorities and against females. The makers of standardized tests have taken a variety of approaches to charges of bias; they have both denied that such bias exists and redoubled efforts to create tests that do not contain bias. It is a difficult challenge: Creating a test that does not contain some cultural assumptions (ranging from assumed background knowledge to language use to expected thought patterns) is virtually impossible. The hope is that most assumptions that are discriminatory against particular groups can be eliminated.

A third controversy surrounding standardized testing focuses on the uses to which test results are put. SAT scores, for example, are often tremendously important in colleges' decisions concerning which students to admit. If the tests are indeed biased, then the use of their results in this way actually constitutes an act of discrimination. Standardized tests have also been used to determine people's access to advanced placement programs, scholarship and other financial aid programs, jobs, and job promotions. The denial to minority students of programs that could benefit them increases their risk of falling victim to truancy, dropping out of school, alcohol or drug abuse, or street crime.

Applications

In spite of the controversies surrounding standardized tests, they are still widely used and are supported by many educators and other professionals. One argument used in support of such tests is that they are, even if flawed, "better than nothing." In other words, in formulating such tests, experts in their field have at least made attempts at objectivity. The alternative, supporters say, would be more subjective decision making by educators and employers. This might well leave minorities in a worse position—even more vulnerable to discrimination. Another argument is that testing should be an on-going part of schooling and that standardized tests do measure certain skills that society has deemed important. Since a goal of education is to help students acquire skills needed to become productive members of society, these tests can be seen as measuring a culturally important goal of education.

Standardized tests can also be used, supporters argue, for increasing the accountability of teachers: ensuring adequate emphasis on basic aspects of education (reading, writing, and math skills), reducing teacher bias and prejudice, and improving coordination among the curricula of different grade levels. Required standardized testing can help to ensure that academic standards are maintained.

The controversies over testing have led to many developments in the testing industry itself, including attempts by test-making agencies to address bias in testing, the practice of combining standardized tests with other measures in decision making, and educational efforts to improve performance on standardized tests. As an attempt to address and alleviate bias in testing, test-making agencies employ professionals who read and critique tests for content and items which may discriminate against a person because of ethnicity, race, or gender. Items that are questionable may be either discarded or reworked.

The practice of employing other measures in decision making so as to give less weight to the use of test results is another way that the standardized test controversies have been addressed. As opposed to using test scores alone as a means of making decisions such as who passes from one grade to the next, who is admitted to a special program, who enters college, who receives scholarships, who is accepted into graduate school, and who is promoted on the job, other information such as teacher recommendations, classroom observations, examination of work samples, parent recommendations, and written essays are used to help make these important decisions. In the case of college admissions, teacher recommendations could be considered along with SAT scores when decisions are being made regarding funding for college. If students' scores on the SAT are borderline or low but are counterbalanced by high teacher recommendations, they might not be excluded from funding.

Finally, the controversy surrounding the use of standardized tests, including intelligence tests, has been addressed by educational efforts to improve personal performance on standardized tests. There are numerous training books, materials, and systematic courses which may be taken to aid students' performance on such measures as the SAT. Practice in using materials that aid problem solving and using materials similar to those used on the actual tests may help students' performance on standardized tests.

Context

Intelligence tests were the first standardized tests developed, and early tests were far from objective. In the nineteenth and early twentieth centuries, intelligence tests (first developed in Europe) were often used to justify the "survival of the fittest," and tests and their interpretations were demonstrably skewed toward proving that white Europeans were the mentally fittest. Cultural bias was rampant. The situation has improved dramatically, but the fact that controversy swirls around standardized tests indicated that there is still a long way to go. Among the cultural factors that have been studied with regard to test results are family influences and the role of race or ethnicity.

Standardized testing controversies should be understood as being related to the influence of the family in American society. Research has shown that there is considerable variation from family to family both within and between different races and socioeconomic statuses. There are many events in the family that affect intellectual functioning. Many of these events are social, but they also include viral infections, unrecognized head injuries, and forms of nutritional deprivation based on individual inabilities to metabolize otherwise normal quantities of specific nutrients; all these elements influence intellectual ability and thus performance on standardized tests.

Deficiencies in the mother's womb or disadvantageous configurations in families may severely depress IQ scores, according to Miles B. Storfer in *Intelligence and Giftedness* (1990). For example, black women tend to become mothers at earlier ages than white women and tend to have more closely spaced births. Their children's IQ scores are likely to be affected adversely. Research continues on parental treatment, biological differences, and socioeconomic differences as influences occurring within the context of the family that might affect a person's standardized test and intelligence test performance.

The IQ scores of Americans rose steadily and rapidly during the twentieth century. Generally, blacks, Hispanics, and American Indians score about one standard deviation below Anglo-Americans and Asian Americans, while Jews outperform all other groups on standardized measures of intelligence. According to Storfer, research indicates that the IQ gap that has existed between blacks and whites is decreasing. He argues that efforts to improve the health and early education of lower and lower-middle classes have caused the reduction in the size of this gap.

Bibliography

Kline, Paul. *Intelligence: The Psychometric View*. New York: Routledge, 1991. This handbook summarizes research studies that focus on the nature of intelligence and related human abilities. Included are topics such as the history of the concept of intelligence and ways to measure intelligence. Definitions of statistical and technical terms are presented in a clear and readable fashion.

Mitchell, James V. *The Ninth Mental Measurements Yearbook*. Lincoln: University of Nebraska Press, 1985. This book is an encyclopedia of tests in many topic areas. There is a description of the tests' purposes, appropriate age range, critiques of the tests, number of pages, and time limits.

Sternberg, Robert. *Intelligence Applied*. Edited by Jerome Kagan. San Diego, Calif.: Harcourt Brace Jovanovich, 1986. In this book, which is a training program based on the triarchic theory of intelligence developed by the author, effective strategies one should use when solving various types of problems, including science insight problems and analogies, are explored. Sternberg also offers his definition of intelligence.

Storfer, Miles B. "The Black/White IQ Disparity: Myth and Reality." In *Intelligence and Giftedness*. San Francisco: Jossey-Bass, 1990. The author states that claims of the genetic inferiority of blacks have been countered by gains in the IQ scores of black Americans in the past fifty years. The gap in IQ scores of blacks and whites can be addressed through improvements in health and in the early education of persons in the lower and lower middle classes.

Woolfolk, Anita E. *Educational Psychology*. Needham Heights, Mass.: Allyn & Bacon, 1993. This book blends theory, research, and practice in a very meaningful way. Topics include socioeconomic differences, race and ethnicity, bilingual education, and gender differences, all of which are pertinent to the topic of standardized and intelligence testing.

Debra A. King-Johnson

Cross-References

THE STATE: FUNCTIONALIST VERSUS CONFLICT PERSPECTIVES

Type of sociology: Major social institutions
Field of study: Politics and the state

The concept of the state is of vital importance to sociologists, given the power it exercises in society. The functionalist perspective views the state as an institution that carries out necessary activities that preserve and perpetuate the social system. The conflict perspective views the state as an arena of struggle in which various groups struggle for power.

Principal terms

CONFLICT PERSPECTIVE: a theory that views conflict as being a ubiquitous force in shaping arrangements between social classes and competing groups in society

FUNCTIONALIST PERSPECTIVE: a theory that focuses on the way the various parts of society work together to maintain stability and order in the social system as a whole

INSTRUMENTALIST THEORY OF THE STATE: a theory that holds the state to be a tool or instrument of the ruling class

PLURALISM: a theory that views power as being dispersed among competing groups in society

POWER ELITE: a term used by C. Wright Mills to identify those at the top of the power structure who formulate policy designed to perpetuate their own interests

RELATIVE AUTONOMY OF THE STATE: the thesis that views the state as exercising some level of independence from the dominant classes, enabling it to negotiate with and grant concessions to the dominated classes in society

STATE: a powerful institution that holds the legitimate monopoly on the use of force in society

STRUCTURALIST PERSPECTIVE OF THE STATE: a theory that looks at the character of the dominant and dominated classes in society and their relationship to the state

Overview

The significance of the state in modern society can be traced to the pervasive role it plays in private and public life. In *Political Theory and the Modern State* (1989), David Held points out that the state conditions our social existence from the issuance of the birth certificate to the signing of the death certificate. The functionalist and the conflict perspectives delineate the powerful role that the state plays in society from divergent theoretical traditions.

The functionalist perspective is greatly indebted to the work of the German sociologist Max Weber (1864-1920). Weber defined the state as that agency in society which holds the legitimate monopoly in the use of physical force and violence. The state's ability to exercise coercion is rooted in rationally created laws and rules. In addition, the state acts to preserve law and order by building a consensus regarding norms, values, and beliefs that perpetuate the orderly functioning of society as a whole. In practice, the state performs two primary functions: preserving law and order and holding the legitimate monopoly of force and violence in reserve for use in the maintenance of social stability when law and order are challenged.

According to the functionalist perspective, the state performs other functions that seek to promote the long-term maintenance of the social system. Among these functions are the collection of taxes and their allocation to programs and projects deemed important by society, and the enactment and codification of laws through the legislative, executive, and judicial branches of government. The state acts as an arbitrator in the allocation of resources—for example, to education, scientific research, health, housing, social welfare programs such as Social Security and Medicare, and national defense. The state formulates regulations regarding the operation of economic and commercial activities on the domestic and international level. It also enters into agreements with other states in the formation of diplomatic ties, trade relations, military arrangements, and alliances.

While acknowledging the functionalist characteristics of the state, the conflict perspective, drawing on the writings of the German social thinker Karl Marx (1818-1883), views the state as existing largely to protect and promote the interests of the dominant or ruling class in society. In *Manifest du Kommunistischen Partei* (1848; *The Communist Manifesto*, 1850), Marx argued that all class societies beyond the level of primitive communism (hunting and gathering societies) are divided into social classes, with a ruling class dominating the other classes. The state comes into existence with the rise of surplus food production, the emergence of social classes and class conflict, and the division of labor in society. Any state may be considered the state of the ruling class. Historically speaking all states are different, depending on the class that rules the society. For example, in ancient societies, the ruling class comprised the masters who ruled over the slaves. In a feudal society the aristocracy (nobility) rules over the serfs, and in a capitalist society the bourgeoisie (the capitalists) rule over the proletariat (the working class) and the middle classes.

Two different approaches characterize the conflict perspective: the instrumentalist and structuralist approaches. The instrumentalist approach draws its arguments, in part, from Marx's position in *The Communist Manifesto* that the modern capitalist state is the executive committee that manages the interests of the capitalist ruling class. The structuralist approach draws its arguments from Marx's writings in *Der achtzehnte Brumaire des Louis Bonaparte* (1852; *The Eighteenth Brumaire of Louis Bonaparte*, 1852), in which he argued that the state exercises relative autonomy or some measure of independence from the ruling class. Here the ruling class is seen as being not a monolithic entity but one that is internally divided by competition and conflict over its economic, political, and ideological interests. Instead of a unified ruling class, there are dominant classes that are divided into fractions of capital (such as finance capital, industrial capital, and manufacturing capital) that seek to promote their interests at the political level.

British political scientist Ralph Miliband uses the instrumentalist approach in his work *The State in Capitalist Society* (1969) to evaluate and critique the functionalist perspective that holds the state to be a neutral arbitrator among social classes in society. Miliband establishes a link between members of the capitalist ruling class and their participation in the state through the holding of positions and offices at the highest levels. He goes on to note that the ruling class owns and controls the means of production and does so through personal ties of power and influence with the personnel of the state. In short, he perceives the state as working to maintain and defend the power and privilege of the capitalist ruling class by promoting its interests and preserving the status quo. Hence, the state is regarded as being an instrument or tool wielded by the ruling class to protect and promote its interests to the exclusion of the interests of the other classes in society (such as the working class and the middle class). The instrumentalist approach portrays the ruling class as a monolithic entity that is internally united in its political, economic, and ideological interests.

In contrast to the instrumentalist approach, Nicos Poulantzas, a Greek sociologist who taught in France, advances the structuralist view of the state in his work *Pouvoir politique et classes sociales de l'etat capitaliste* (1968; *Political Power and Social Classes*, 1973). He develops the thesis that the state exercises relative autonomy, or some degree of independence from the control of the dominant classes. Poulantzas argues that, in this way, the state is better able to serve the interests of the dominant classes. The state, for example, unifies a capitalist society through its exercise of hegemony (leadership and domination in society). Given the divergent economic interests and competition that continuously separate the dominant classes from one another, the state must also act as a cohesive factor that unites these different dominant classes at the political level in order to promote their long-term political and economic interests. While organizing the political interests of the dominant classes, the state works to disorganize and short-circuit the political interests of the dominated classes. The state is able to grant concessions to the dominated classes—the working and middle classes—and to various interest groups, such as environmental, women's, business, and ethnic groups—that go counter to the immediate interests of the dominant classes. In doing so, it actually perpetuates the long-term interests of the dominant classes, the capitalist system, and the status quo. Examples of concessions include the eight-hour work day, the minimum wage, worker safety regulations on the job, environmental protection, civil rights, voting rights, and the increasing of income taxes on the wealthy. Finally, the state mediates the level of class conflict in society by intervening directly through legal, political, and economic means to ameliorate crises in order to sustain the long-term interests of the capitalist system.

Applications

The functionalist view of the state is clearly expressed through the pluralist position.

Pluralism argues that modern democratic society is not dominated by a ruling class, a powerful elite driven by class interests. Society is not seen as being driven by class conflict over the production, accumulation, distribution, and utilization of scarce resources. Instead, society is viewed as being based on consensus—agreement on common norms and values. The state is regarded as being a neutral arena in which various interest groups, pressure groups, and lobby groups (business and professional organizations, trade unions, trade associations, consumer groups, environmental organizations, and foreign governments) vie with opposing groups and interests to have their own positions expressed through the formation of law and social policies. In effect, the policies that the government pursues are not the policies of class-based and ruling class interests; rather they are the by-products of interest groups. The result is that no single group or class can claim to have control of the government or the state.

The conflict perspective in its instrumentalist version was effectively applied to the study of the American power structure by sociologist C. Wright Mills in *The Power Elite* (1956). Mills argues that there is a "power elite" that exercises control over the function of the government. This power elite is composed of three sectors: the corporate elite, the executive branch of government, and the military establishment. Mills argues that the power elite is composed mainly of white Anglo-Saxon Protestants (WASPs) who share similar social backgrounds and interests, come from wealthy families, have attended prestigious prep schools and universities, belong to exclusive clubs, have personal ties with one another, and intermarry within their class. There is considerable circulation among the top positions within these three sectors: high-ranking retired military officers join large corporations, business leaders take high positions in government either through appointment or election to high office, and retired political leaders join large corporations. The words that best describe this relationship are those delivered by President Eisenhower in his farewell address to the nation, in which he cautioned against the rising influence of the "military-industrial complex."

The structuralist approach within the conflict perspective of the state has been applied by sociologist Rhonda Levine to study the New Deal policies enacted in the United States in the 1930's to ameliorate the economic crisis that the nation faced. In her book *Class Struggle and the New Deal* (1988), Levine builds on Poulantzas' work. Arguing that the state exercises relative autonomy apart from the dominant classes, she discusses how the state was able to mediate between the conflicting interests of the dominant classes and the discontent of the working class to fashion the policies that launched the creation of the New Deal programs and the welfare state. In order to protect the interests of capital and the capitalist system, the state fashioned policies that in the short term were detrimental to some of the interests of the dominant classes; however, it set the foundation for the long-term interests of the dominant classes by stabilizing the capitalist system as a whole.

Context

Prior to the 1960's, sociology in general neglected the study of the state. This was partly because of the pervasive influence of functionalist theory in the United States.

Functionalism, as expressed through pluralism, reinforced the view that the state was a neutral entity in society. Power was perceived as being dispersed throughout society with no centralized power structure, power elite, or dominant ruling classes running the affairs of government. Individuals working through the democratic process and through collective action competed with other individuals and groups to have their positions expressed in governmental policy. Given this viewpoint, the state was defined as not being particularly important to the political process. Furthermore, social classes (as agencies of change in society) and class conflict were displaced by a greater emphasis on the role of individuals as agents of change. Class conflict was transformed into competition between various individuals and societal groups. The events of the 1960's, however, such as the Civil Rights movement, the women's movement, the war in Vietnam, and the independence and revolutionary movements around the world, brought the role of the state as a powerful force in society to the forefront.

The publication of Miliband's *The State in Capitalist Society* and Poulantzas' *Political Power and Social Classes* and the ensuing debate between their viewpoints created considerable interest in the conflict perspective on the state. Their work opened up new theoretical approaches to exploring the character and workings of the capitalist state and the capitalist system as a whole. In the 1980's, conflict and functionalist theorists began to call for bringing the state back to the center of sociological analysis. Since then, more and more sociologists, political scientists, political economists, historians, and anthropologists have sought to study and understand the relationship between the state and society.

Bibliography

Held, David. *Political Theory and the Modern State*. Stanford, Calif.: Stanford University Press, 1989. A thorough and well-written work that covers the development of political theory from Aristotle to modern democracy. The book is an excellent source for the functionalist and conflict perspectives on the state, democracy, and the limits of the state.

Levine, Rhonda. *Class Struggle and the New Deal*. Lawrence: University Press of Kansas, 1988. An excellent book that utilizes the relative autonomy thesis of the state. It demonstrates the role the state played in the formation of the New Deal in the 1930's. It has an excellent bibliography that includes government documents, library collections, and business publications that pertain to the New Deal.

Marx, Karl. *The Eighteenth Brumaire of Louis Bonaparte*. New York: International Publishers, 1963. Originally written in 1852, this is Marx's concrete analysis of class struggle in France, where various capitalist classes, the proletariat (the working class), and middle classes clashed with one another, thereby precipitating the events that brought Napoleon III to power through a coup d'état.

Marx, Karl, and Friedrich Engels. *The Communist Manifesto*. New York: New York Labor News Co., 1948. One of the major political documents that has earned Marx international fame. Originally published in the critical year of 1848, when France and other parts of Europe were on the brink of working class revolutions.

Miliband, Ralph. *The State in Capitalist Society*. New York: Basic Books, 1969. In
this book, Miliband challenges the functionalist and pluralist views that power is
diffused throughout society. In addition, he argues for an examination of the state
as constituting an economic, political, and cultural reality in capitalist society.
Mills, C. Wright. *The Power Elite*. New York: Oxford University Press, 1956. The
classic work by C. Wright Mills that made the term "power elite" a popular concept
for defining three powerful sectors—corporate leaders, the executive branch of
government, and the military—said to run the affairs of government. In the 1960's,
this group was referred to as the "establishment."
Poulantzas, Nicos. *Political Power and Social Classes*. Atlantic Highlands, N.J.:
Humanities Press, 1975. A major pathbreaking work that set a new theoretical
standard for study on the nature of the capitalist state. Originally written in French
in 1968 and first translated in 1973, this work propelled Poulantzas to international
fame. Poulantzas develops highly sophisticated analyses that give new insights into
politics, social classes, capitalism, and the state. Three other important works by
Poulantzas should be noted: *State Power Socialism* (1978), *Classes in Contemporary Capitalism* (1975), and *Fascism and Dictatorship* (1974).
Weber, Max. "Politics as a Vocation." In *From Max Weber: Essays in Sociology*, edited
by H. H. Gerth and C. Wright Mills. London: Kegan Paul, Trench, Trubner, 1948.
This essay, given as a speech by Weber at Munich University in 1918, was originally
published in 1919. It is a masterful work in which Weber discusses the legitimate
monopoly of force and violence that resides in the state, forms of domination and
leadership, political parties, the feudal system, and government.

Basil P. Kardaras

Cross-References

Authoritarian and Totalitarian Governments, 153; Capitalism, 191; Democracy and
Democratic Governments, 483; Marxism, 1127; The Nation-State, 1282; Political
Socialization, 1407; Political Sociology, 1414; Power: The Pluralistic Model, 1484;
The Power Elite, 1491.

STATUSES AND ROLES

Type of sociology: Social structure
Field of study: Components of social structure

> *The related concepts of status and role are central to all studies of social organization and stratification. Stated most simply, status refers to an individual's position in a social structure, whereas role refers to the behavior that is expected of someone who occupies a given status.*

Principal terms

FORMAL SOCIAL ORGANIZATION: the behavioral organization of those individuals occupying particular paired statuses such as doctor and patient

ROLE ANTICIPATION: a perception and prediction of how most individuals who are occupying a social position will behave

ROLE EXPECTATION: a belief about how any individual who is occupying a particular status ought to behave

ROLE PERFORMANCE: the actual behavior of most individuals who occupy a particular status

SOCIAL GROUP: a set of individuals who interact in patterned ways, who share a culture that includes role expectations of how group members ought to behave, and who create a "boundary" by identifying with one another

STATUS: any particular position in a social structure

Overview

The way sociologists use the word "status" differs from the way the word is commonly used. Most people use it to mean "prestige" (as in the phrase "status symbol"). To sociologists, however, a status is any particular position that an individual holds in a social structure. The term, therefore, may refer to a wide range of positions and situations. Examples of statuses include such categorizations as student, mother, parent, child, friend, waiter, corporation president, farmer, husband, wife, male, female, physician, and patient. A role is the collection of behaviors, attitudes, privileges, and obligations that society associates with a particular status and expects of someone with that status. For example, someone with the status of "friend" is generally expected to be helpful, loyal, and considerate toward those who consider that person a friend.

Sociologists distinguish between ascribed status and achieved status. Ascribed status is a status with which one is born. A person, for example, is born either male or female, is born into a particular ethnic group, and may be born of rich or poor parents. Another type of ascribed status is contingent upon one's place in the life cycle (the statuses of child, adolescent, and so on). Achieved status, on the other hand, refers to a status that one acquires through effort or choice (such as becoming a college graduate or a parent or working in a certain occupation). These two classifications are closely related, however, because in any existing society, one's ascribed status affects the life chances one has to attain certain achieved statuses.

The statuses that people occupy and the related roles that they play are inextricably tied to the concept of social structure or organization. A structure is anything that consists of distinct or distinguishable parts that have a relationship to the other parts. Such relationships determine many of the aspects of the overall structure. A status cannot exist in isolation; it can only exist within the overall framework of a social organization. In other words, relationships among statuses in society are required for the idea of "status" to make sense.

The word "organization" can be used interchangeably with "structure"; organization connotes a pattern, system, or structure—something that is put together in some systematic way. Whatever is organized functions to accomplish certain things in a relatively effective way. Sociologists consider several forms of organizations or structures; two of these are informal and formal organizations. Statuses and roles are primarily important in formal organizations. Informal organization refers to the organized behavior that is characteristic of a specific set of individuals. In an informal structure, the parts are seen as individuals, and social ranking and individuals' behaviors are unique to the particular set of individuals involved. Formal organization, on the other hand, refers to the organized behavior that exists among categories of individuals—those who occupy particular statuses. Formal organization does not mean explicit or codified organization; rather, it directs attention to the underlying common forms of behavior.

A role, the organized behavior that is associated with a status, contains three distinguishable components: role expectation, role performance, and role anticipation. A role expectation is a statement of how an individual—any individual—who occupies a status ought to behave. It is a rule of conduct. In its emphasis on how one "should" behave, it is also a moral statement. Thus, for example, teachers should grade students objectively, and doctors should not take advantage of their patients. Some role expectations may be written down as policies or regulations; others exist only in peoples' minds. The fact that role expectations exist does not mean that status occupants are completely constrained in their behavior. Some expectations specify a range of appropriate behavior. In some aspects of interactions, no significant expectations exist. Further, expectations vary in their moral force. Some are strongly held, others much less so.

Thus, it is expected that a teacher should teach, but the definition of "teaching" is rather vague. If a teacher told her class jokes or conversed with her students about motion pictures for class after class, then she would not be conforming to what most people would define as acceptable teaching practices. On the other hand, lecturing and discussing assigned reading both fall within the range of acceptable conduct.

Role performance, then, refers to the actual behavior of those who occupy a particular status. In invoking this notion, the sociologist claims that all or most of those who occupy a particular status tend to act in roughly similar ways. These roughly similar ways constitute role performance. Thus, most college professors meet their classes at the allotted times, give assignments, evaluate student achievement, treat students without favoritism, and so on.

At the same time, there is some "slippage" in the conduct of status occupants; that is, actual behavior may deviate to some degree from the shared expectations. Thus, many college students perceive that their professors devote too much time to their own research and not enough time to teaching; many professors believe that a sizable number of their students are only interested in being graduated and are not interested in the subjects they are studying. These beliefs or perceptions are role anticipations. A role anticipation is a prediction or perception of how those or most of those who occupy a particular status will behave. Included in the concept of role anticipation is a recognition of the fact of minor degrees of deviation—of the sense that few individuals totally live up to their obligations. These minor deviations become tolerated or accepted but are also frequently noted.

All human interactions occur between individuals who are each occupying some status; therefore, each person brings to the interaction an idea of what is to be expected from it. The only time an individual can be free of a status (and therefore of role expectations) is when he or she is alone. Many statuses are typically paired with another status. For example, one can only occupy the status of teacher when interacting with someone who is occupying the status of student. A teacher may interact with a student's parent, but then a somewhat different (although related) pair of statuses is involved: teacher-of-student and parent-of-student. Thus, many statuses can only coexist with a single other status or, at most, a few other statuses.

Applications

Status and role are theoretical concepts, invoked and defined to help interpret social behavior and to provide an understanding of social life. They do not constitute a social theory to be tested. They are not specific ideas to be applied only in particular contexts. Rather, they appear—implicitly if not explicitly—in a broad range of studies. Although the terms may not always be used, in nearly every investigation or analysis descriptions of behavior emerge, some of which are in effect descriptions of formal organization, roles, and statuses.

A few examples will illustrate this point. In a study published in 1956 as *Union Democracy*, researchers Seymour Martin Lipset, Martin Trow, and James Coleman studied the International Typographers Union (ITU). They wondered what factors were involved in making the ITU one of the few truly democratic labor unions. They noted that, among other things, the ITU had a custom of having its union president serve only one term. This custom was found to be sustained by a strong role expectation. Another illustration can be found in *American Odyssey* (1984), a study by Michel S. Laguerre of Haitians in New York City. Laguerre found that many Haitians, when ill, go to physicians (typically, to Haitian doctors). At the same time, however, they also seek folk healers. This practice is supported by expectations transmitted from generation to generation. Even some well-educated and Westernized Haitians respond to such traditional expectations.

A third illustration concerns Charles L. Bosk's study of surgical residents, *Forgive and Remember* (1979). He discusses what he calls "normative errors." These occur when residents deviate from the role expectations held of them by the senior medical staff. The major expectation is that the residents will follow an implicit rule that states: "No surprises." The senor staff members want to be informed of any significant data about, and changes in, their patients who are being cared for by the residents. A resident who fails to inform an attending physician of an adverse medical development in one of the attending physician's patients is severely reprimanded. Bosk distinguishes normative errors from what he calls "quasi-normative errors," which, for example, would be deviations from the expectations held by a specific surgeon. Thus, normative errors are related to formal organization, while quasi-normative errors emerge from the informal organization in the hospital.

Although every social interaction occurs between individuals who are occupying some status, the status occupants have some freedom. To a greater or lesser degree, they can make decisions and act on those decisions. For example, an individual who is a lawyer is not constrained in the choice of which automobile to buy. He may say to himself: "As a lawyer, I need to make a good impression, so I should trade my automobile in for a new one every two or three years." In saying this he is responding to what he sees as an expectation—perhaps only self-created, but an expectation nevertheless. At the same time, however, there are other lawyers who will not think this way and who will make decisions free of any self-imposed ideas of what a lawyer "should" do.

Occupying a status over a sustained period of time can have a pronounced psychological effect on an individual. He or she comes to develop a particular worldview—a sense of self, particular attitudes, values, and beliefs—which may result from experiences in occupying the status. None of these may be explicit role expectations associated with a particular status. Nevertheless, they may become like expectations in that individuals interact with others who occupy the same status; in so doing, they come to acquire shared views and beliefs, all of which are consonant with the demands placed on those in that status.

Context

The *Oxford English Dictionary* states that the first known use of the word "status," which comes from the Latin word meaning "to stand," was in 1693. The first use of "role" was in 1606, and it came from the French word meaning "the part played by an actor." An early body of work that provided a setting for the emergence of the concepts of status and role was research focusing on norms, folkways, and mores. These phenomena, discussed in *Human Society* (1952) by Kingsley Davis and in *Folkways* (1906) by William Graham Sumner, can be seen as role expectations associated with the status of citizen of a society.

The contemporary usage of status and role are thought to have come from Ralph

Linton's use of the terms in *The Study of Man* (1936). To Linton, status is a collection of rights and duties; role is the "dynamic aspect of status." It is what an individual does when occupying a status. As others have done since, Linton distinguishes between ascribed statuses and achieved statuses.

A more recent body of related work concerns the examination of interaction from a dramaturgical perspective—attempting to analyze interactions as instances of particular types of drama in which, for example, if the interaction is like a tragedy presented on stage, the real-life interacting individuals are playing roles that have tragic features. Erving Goffman discusses this concept in *The Presentation of Self in Everyday Life* (1959).

Other contexts for these ideas are found in various elaborations on the notions of status and role. There is role conflict, for example, which is the situation of an individual facing two or more conflicting expectations (such as the physician with a patient who demands a particular medication, which the physician believes is inappropriate and ineffective). Role strain is a situation in which the demands are excessive (as for the resident in medicine who finds that he or she is expected to work twenty hours without a break). A status set is the set of statuses through which a particular individual moves. A role set consists of the various other statuses that are tied to one of the statuses of an individual (the role set of a lawyer would include client, judge, fellow lawyer, parole officer, and so on). Role segmentation is the resolving of role conflict by allotting each set of expectations to a situation different from that of any other set. Role sequence is an individual's "movement" over time from playing a role one way to playing a role another way. Role gradations represent the movement of an individual through a sequence of statuses for which the associated roles vary only a little from one status to the next. Status inconsistency is the situation in which the rank of one status of an individual is greatly different from the rank of another of his or her statuses (for example, the bricklayer who has a Ph.D.).

Bibliography

Bosk, Charles L. *Forgive and Remember*. Chicago: University of Chicago Press, 1979. This well-written study of how surgical residents are trained in the practice of surgery—learning both the techniques of surgery and the appropriate ways of interacting with their superiors—covers issues related to statuses and roles in a hospital setting.

Goffman, Erving. *The Presentation of Self in Everyday Life*. Garden City, N.Y.: Doubleday, 1959. This, like Goffman's other books, has been quite influential. It has a useful discussion of performances, which conveys the dramaturgical perspective on role-playing.

Linton, Ralph. *The Study of Man*. New York: Appleton-Century, 1936. This book by a distinguished anthropologist was used by students both in sociology and anthropology. A central chapter concerns status and role.

Lipset, Seymour Martin, Martin Trow, and James Coleman. *Union Democracy*. Glencoe, Ill.: Free Press, 1956. A classic study from which one can learn much about the way sociologists think and perform research. In dealing with a very important substantive problem, it offers thoughtful ideas and findings concerning role expectations.

Sumner, William Graham. *Folkways*. Boston: Ginn and Company, 1906. This early sociological study of customs and laws presents much information relevant to the concepts of status and role. It still has much to offer the reader of today who is interested in the nature of society.

Dean Harper

Cross-References

Dramaturgy, 566; Interactionism, 1009; Microsociology, 1192; Organizations: Formal and Informal, 1316; Role Conflict and Role Strain, 1655; Social Groups, 1806; Social Mobility: Analysis and Overview, 1812.

STEREOTYPING AND THE SELF-FULFILLING PROPHECY

Type of sociology: Racial and ethnic relations
Field of study: Theories of prejudice and discrimination

Stereotyping is a mental process in which generalized beliefs about a group are assigned to all members of that group. Stereotypes, regardless of how invalid they may be, tend to be rigidly held. When people are confronted with society's stereotyped views of how they are expected to behave, they may actually begin to behave that way; this phenomenon is known as a self-fulfilling prophecy.

Principal terms

DISCRIMINATION: any behavior that reflects acceptance or rejection of a person based solely on the person's membership in a specific group

OUT-GROUP: any group of which a person is aware but is not a member

PREJUDICE: an unfavorable, unfair, or intolerant attitude toward another group of people

SCHEMA (*pl.* SCHEMATA): a mental program or template based on experience that helps people identify and categorize persons, events, or things

SELF-FULFILLING PROPHECY: a situation that occurs when other people's expectations for a person lead him or her to act in ways that confirm those expectations

STEREOTYPE: a specialized schema that assigns a structured set of beliefs or characteristics to all members of a group

Overview

Stereotyping is a particular form of social typing involving rigidly held beliefs that are frequently based on incomplete or erroneous information. Stereotyping involves generalizing the identifying characteristics of groups (such as Latinos, blacks, women, homosexuals, or obese people) and applying those generalizations to individual members of the group. Common examples of stereotyping include such widespread notions, held at various points in time, that Italian people are passionate, Irish people fight and drink, women are very emotional, and obese people are jolly. A central problem with stereotyping is that it involves overgeneralizing: A stereotype is unfairly and rigidly applied to individuals on the basis of identification with a group regardless of whether the individual (or even the group as a whole) actually behaves in that way.

A stereotype can be seen as a form of schema—a mental map or program that helps a people make sense of their environment. Schemata help the brain organize and simplify information about people, things, and situations so that people can recognize them readily. The use of schemata is crucial in mental development; children develop schemata as required to think and become familiar with the world. For example, when a young child sees a bird, a parent will tell the child, "That is a birdie," and explain that birdies hop, fly, and go "tweet-tweet." The child then assumes that all birdies have these characteristics. As the child matures, he or she learns that not all birds have all these characteristics, so the initial schema is amended to encompass new examples.

The process of schema development usually serves humans well, but sometimes it causes problems when people overgeneralize or erroneously assign specific characteristics to all members of the conceptual group. Often a prototypical schema is developed that contains a single, well-defined model describing all members of a group even though there is great variability among group members. When this occurs in stereotyping the attributes or behaviors of other human beings, it can cause a number of problems. One problematic aspect of stereotyping is that stereotypes are most likely to develop when people have strong feelings for or against some identifiable group, and particularly when they have a compelling need to view that group as inferior or threatening. Stereotypes, once formed, are often difficult (if not impossible) to change. Stereotypes are frequently drawn from a small number of people from a larger group, and such a small sample can often be misleading. The choice that one group makes as to what constitutes the defining characteristics of another group are likely to be self-serving more than grounded in objective reality.

Stereotyping, therefore, is related to prejudice. It involves expectations placed on members of a particular group because of a preconceived, generalized idea of that group. Like other forms of prejudice, it frequently (but not always) serves the function of making one group feel superior to another. Stereotypes permeate societal views in myriad ways. There are gender stereotypes, for example, such as the concept that men are competitive, logical, and ambitious, whereas women are sensitive, quiet, and nurturing. Mentally ill people are often stereotypically thought of as dangerous to others, when this is rarely the case. People with disabilities are often automatically seen as unable to participate fully in society. Everyone has stereotypes embedded in his or her consciousness. The crucial thing is to be aware that they exist and to attempt not to let them prejudicially influence one's attitudes and behaviors toward others.

Stereotypes pervade the media, and various "watchdog" groups are quick to protest when members of their group are portrayed as offensive stereotypes. Frito-Lay once used a cartoon character called the Frito Bandito to sell its chips on television until publicized protests from Mexican Americans forced the company to abandon it. Another stereotypical image, seen regularly in television dramas and films in the 1980's, was the "disturbed" Vietnam War veteran. Films and television programs have traditionally presented stereotypical characters precisely because they automatically fit into viewers' existing stereotype schemata, allowing instant emotional reactions on the part of viewers. The negative side of this is that the tremendous power of film and television is used (intentionally or unintentionally) to reinforce stereotypes.

All stereotypes contain the essential ingredients for creating self-fulfilling prophecies. The central aspect of the self-fulfilling prophecy is the stereotypical expectations held regarding the members of a particular group; in fact, the word "prophecy" here essentially means expectations. Expectations of a person's behavior based on his or her membership in some group (such as an ethnic or gender category) can either be positive or negative. One common gender stereotype is that boys are better at math than girls are. The self-fulfilling prophecy that may occur (and, experts say, has in fact occurred) because of this belief develops because parents and teachers encourage boys to excel in math more than they encourage girls. Boys receive more careful instruction and are subtly told that it is appropriate for them to be good at math; therefore, they do indeed begin to excel. In a self-fulfilling prophecy, a stereotypical trait that was originally overgeneralized and invalid becomes "true" because of the expectations and behavior of others toward the person or group toward whom the stereotype is directed.

Applications

The power of people's expectations is great and has been documented in many studies. Robert Rosenthal and others have amply demonstrated how teachers' positive expectations for their students can result not only in improved performance but also in increases in measured intelligence (although it should be noted that the degree to which intelligence tests truly measure "intelligence" has been hotly debated).

In a 1968 study by Rosenthal and Lenore Jacobson, teachers were told that certain students would show marked academic improvement during the school year (the students, who were dubbed "bloomers," were actually chosen at random). Because of the way these students were treated by their teachers, they did indeed show more improvement than other students of equal ability. Their IQ scores rose about four points higher than those of other students.

In many studies after Rosenthal and Jacobson's, when teachers have been given information that causes them genuinely to believe that children have significant growth potential (whether they actually do or not), the teachers have engaged in behavior that encourages and reinforces growth in the children. Teachers have been observed to direct more questions to these children, to give them more time to respond, and to react more approvingly to their contributions. Other studies have indicated that teachers form expectations even for very young students based on the children's parents' economic status. The implications for society are enormous, since it would appear that the success of young children in school and perhaps later in life is largely a function of what significant others believe about them and communicate to them. It must be noted, however, that not all studies show teacher expectations to determine student achievement. Some sociologists have concluded that only some teachers form rigid expectations of students' potential; many others seem to be open and flexible and are able to alter their expectations as students display growth.

Just as positive expectations can have beneficial effects, so negative expectations can have disastrous effects. In the South before school desegregation, there was a commonly held belief among whites that blacks were intellectually inferior. This belief (stereotype) bolstered the acceptance of separate schools for blacks and whites. Black schools received far less funding than white schools. Whites rationalized that since blacks were inferior intellectually it was not sensible to waste money attempting to educate them at the same level of intensity and sophistication as whites. School underfunding led to lower-quality education for black students and consequently to lower levels of academic achievement for black students. In other words, a self-fulfilling prophecy occurred: Beliefs led to actions that exacted behavior consistent with the original beliefs.

Much experience suggests that people are very faithful and efficient communicators of their stereotype-driven negative expectations for others. Carl Word and his colleagues found that the manner in which employment interviewers interact with job candidates can have a telling effect on candidate performance in an interview. For example, when interviewers sat farther away from the black candidates (a nonverbal indication of one's desirability or worth), made more language errors with them (a verbal indication of one's believed intelligence and ability), and spent less time interviewing them (another nonverbal indication of personal worth), the black candidates fared measurably less well in their interviews. When experimental conspirators playing the interviewer role subsequently treated white candidates in the same fashion, the white employment candidates also fared poorly—they became more nervous and were judged less effective. The results of this experiment provided compelling evidence of the destructive effects that stereotype-driven expectations and behavior can have.

Need-driven stereotypes of out-groups and minorities are often based on little or no objective data or experience; principal sources are often hearsay and anecdote. Moreover, because stereotypes are so rigidly held, people tend to view a person belonging to another group selectively and to discard evidence that does not fit the stereotype. If, based on hearsay and anecdote, one develops a stereotype of Latinas as having fiery tempers, one will carefully note and mentally record the occasion one witnesses that confirms such behavior, while rejecting or ignoring the many times the expected behavior is not manifest. (Occasions that do not fit the stereotype may be simply shrugged off as "exceptions that prove the rule.")

When one uses isolated instances of expected behavior to affirm one's stereotypes, one is using "illusory correlation"—that is, asserting a relationship that does not really exist. Stereotypical beliefs about out-groups are ordinarily built on empirically non-existent grounds, maintained by the least little bit of affirming evidence, and defended against change because of the holders' strong need to believe the stereotype.

The need to hold a stereotype in the face of evidence against it can be illustrated by a true anecdote involving a Mexican American woman. "Maria" has a dark complexion (mestiza) and dark hair. At one point in her career she worked in an office in which the majority of the personnel were often overt and verbal with their prejudice. They harassed the one black woman in the office, for example, with sexually oriented and insulting notes. They also made open (although not necessarily loud) remarks about "niggers, spics, and chinks." Maria is an excellent worker, attractive, and though reared in the barrio, speaks flawless, unaccented English.

Over a period of time, an interesting phenomenon began to occur. She became more respected, liked, and accepted, although the tenor of the prejudicial conversations and remarks directed at others did not change. Eventually her coworkers began to make clearly prejudiced remarks about out-groups—including her own—directly to her, no longer recognizing her obvious membership in that group. This anecdote indicates what happens when a member of a stereotyped group fails, over time, to fit the behavioral stereotype of the group: The prejudiced person develops a kind of selective blindness, excludes the nonstereotypical member from group membership, and continues maintaining the original stereotype. Such mental processes demonstrate why it is extremely difficult to dispel need-based stereotypes.

Context

To a considerable degree, human belief drives human behavior. Any belief about other people (whether correct or erroneous, positive or negative), if strongly held and clearly expressed, can have an effect on the behavior of others. Stereotypes about out-groups have certainly existed since evolution first granted humans the ability to form and express them. The term "stereotype" itself derives from the printing technology of the early nineteenth century; it originally referred to a plate made from a printing surface, and it eventually came to mean any rigidly held or clichéd image or idea.

The scientific study of stereotypes and the effects of expectations (or prophecies of behavior), however, is a phenomenon of the second half of the twentieth century. In the largest sense, it may be seen as an outgrowth of the interest in understanding racism and prejudice that developed after World War II. In the late 1940's, the horrifying realization that the Nazis had systematically put to death more than six million people on the basis of their religion (Jews) or ethnicity (other groups, including Gypsies, were also marked for execution) led social scientists to believe that there was an overwhelming and immediate need to uncover the causes of such hatred and prejudice and to ensure that such an event could never occur again.

The teacher expectations study by Rosenthal and Jacobson is considered a classic sociological experiment. Their findings, published as *Pygmalion in the Classroom: Teacher Expectation and Pupils' Intellectual Development* (1968), spawned considerable interest in the area of stereotyping and self-fulfilling prophecies. Also in 1968, sociologist Robert K. Merton, in his edited volume *Contemporary Social Problems*, provided a concise definition of the self-fulfilling prophecy: a "*false* definition of the situation evoking a new behavior which makes the originally false conception sound true." Considerable research on stereotypes and self-fulfilling prophecies appeared in the 1970's.

If the dominant group in a society believes that a particular out-group is violent or wanting in some way, society may communicate its expectations for them in a number of ways—it may simply deny the group progress and sharing of resources (typically blaming the group for its own dilemma), or it may go so far as to segregate the group socially or confine it physically. Expectations communicated by word or action can eventually lead to tremendous frustration that may erupt in violence. Because the likelihood of altering the expectation-behavior relationship is small, the most reasonable goal for social scientists is to harness the power of human belief and find ways to motivate people to adapt the power for beneficial purposes. This could, ideally, lead to improved child rearing within the family, improved results from the education system, and better relations between cultures. There is much for society to gain. On the other side of the coin, however, it is unlikely that humankind will ever completely eliminate those conditions that tend to promote prejudice and stereotypical thinking, so intergroup strife is virtually certain to continue.

Bibliography

Aronson, Elliot. *The Social Animal*. 3d ed. San Francisco: W. H. Freeman, 1980. An excellent social psychological commentary on a variety of topics, including a chapter on prejudice. That chapter details the causes of prejudice, the nature of stereotypes, and their self-fulfilling nature. This book is widely used by both academicians and laypersons. Contains footnotes and an extensive index but no bibliography.

Cooper, Harris M., and Thomas L. Good. *Pygmalion Grows Up: Studies in the Expectation Communication Process*. New York: Longman, 1983. A thorough assessment of all the prior research pertaining to the effects of teachers' expectations for students on student behavior and school performance. Contains footnotes and bibliography.

Fiske, Susan T., and Shelley E. Taylor. *Social Cognition*. Reading, Mass: Addison-Wesley, 1984. A widely cited text on social cognition. Includes significant sections on schema formation, stereotype development, belief persistence, and the self-fulfilling prophecy. Contains an extensive bibliography and an index but no footnotes.

Mack, Raymond W. *Race, Class, and Power*. 2d ed. New York: American Book Company, 1968. A compilation of essays providing comprehensive sociological treatment of topics including minorities, race, social structure, prejudice, discrimination, and stereotyping. Contains detailed footnotes and supplemental bibliographies for each chapter.

Rothman, Robert A. *Inequality and Stratification: Class, Color, and Gender*. 2d ed. Englewood Cliffs, N.J.: Prentice-Hall, 1993. Has a number of germaine passages pertaining to stereotyping, the historical roots of certain stereotypes, and the perpetuation of stereotypes through such mechanisms as humor. Contains excellent lists of additional readings as well as name and topic indexes.

Ronald G. Ribble

Cross-References

THE STRUCTURAL-STRAIN THEORY OF DEVIANCE

Type of sociology: Deviance and social control
Fields of study: Social implications of deviance; Theories of deviance

The structural-strain theory of deviance is an explanation of the violation of social norms that emphasizes the psychological pressure caused by exclusion from legal means of achieving success. This theory emphasizes the destructive consequences of social and economic inequality. It provided the intellectual underpinnings of both the largest delinquency prevention program ever attempted and the War on Poverty in the 1960's.

Principal terms

ANOMIE: normlessness; a stressful psychological condition associated with rapid social or personal change in which the sufferer loses confidence in authority structures and their rules

CASTE SYSTEM: a hierarchical social arrangement in which people are assigned the same status as their parents and have no possibility of changing status through personal achievement

CONFLICT SUBCULTURE: a distinctive subgroup in lower-class neighborhoods whose members engage in nonutilitarian violence because neither legitimate nor illegitimate opportunities for success are readily available

CRIMINAL SUBCULTURE: a distinctive subgroup in lower-class neighborhoods in which techniques of crime and values supporting criminal behavior are taught and opportunities to engage in crime are provided

DISORGANIZED NEIGHBORHOOD: a lower-class residential area in which there are neither sufficient legitimate jobs nor sufficient jobs in criminal organizations to employ most residents who are able to work

MOBILIZATION FOR YOUTH: the largest delinquency prevention program attempted to date; it was located in the Lower East Side of Manhattan in the 1960's and was organized around principles of structural-strain theory

RETREATIST SUBCULTURE: a distinctive subgroup in lower-class neighborhoods whose members have given up trying to succeed and use drugs to escape from the pain of failure

Overview

The structural-strain theory of deviance emphasizes the relationship between inequality and violation of social norms. Poverty alone is not viewed as the cause of deviance. Rather, the cause is the frustration that many poor people experience when they compare their own condition to the condition of middle-class people.

The "structural" component of this theory emphasizes the stable, hierarchical nature of Western democratic societies. The large concentrations of poor people, the common pattern in which poverty continues in families from one generation to the next, and the failure of many hard-working poor people to escape from poverty contrast sharply with the ideology of democratic societies. In a democracy, all people supposedly have an equal chance to succeed, regardless of their parentage, and hard work is rewarded by financial success.

Strain theorists assume that nearly all members of American society, including poor people, share middle-class standards of success that emphasize, above all else, the acquisition of material wealth. When poor people accept "middle-class measuring rods" as valid criteria for their own accomplishments, they inevitably appear to be failures. That sense of failure causes poor people to experience distress beyond the practical difficulties of managing their lives on low incomes. The structural-strain theory of deviance explains the deviance of poor people as a response to the frustration they feel from their "failure" according to middle-class standards.

The eighteenth century French social philosopher Émile Durkheim provided the theoretical foundation for structural-strain theory. In *Le Suicide: Étude de sociologie* (1897; *Suicide: A Study in Sociology*, 1951), Durkheim explained a fundamental difference between humans and other animals: Humans have the unique capacity to imagine a better existence, regardless of their present condition. Since biology does not place a limit on human desires, the task of limiting those desires falls to society. In caste societies, people could be happy because they could achieve "success"; it was defined differently for members of each caste. They could not even attempt to achieve success by the standards of a higher caste. With the destruction of caste systems and the development of democratic societies, the socially imposed limits to people's aspirations were lifted. This freedom has produced a situation in which success can be achieved only relative to other people's achievements, because no absolute standard can be defined. One theorized result of this is a condition called anomie, in which social norms seem no longer to apply.

In his key article "Social Structure and Anomie" (1938), sociologist Robert K. Merton took Durkheim's concept and applied it to American society. He found that all people were encouraged to achieve monetary success but that many people lacked legitimate means to achieve that success. Merton saw deviance arising from the mismatch between culturally approved goals and institutionalized means to attain those goals. Merton described five possible personal adaptations to this mismatch.

First is conformity, living a conventional life involving acceptance of both culture goals and institutionalized means. Second is innovation, accepting the culture goals but substituting alternative (sometimes criminal) means of obtaining them. Third is ritualism, giving up on the culture goal of material success but continuing to live and work in conventional ways. Fourth is retreatism, rejecting both culture goals and institutionalized means, sometimes escaping into drugs or alcohol. Fifth is rebellion, renouncing conventional goals and means and substituting new goals and means.

Structural-strain theory has been applied most extensively to juvenile delinquency.

Sociologist Albert K. Cohen, in *Delinquent Boys* (1955), reported on a delinquent subculture among working-class males. He found that members of this subculture embraced middle-class standards of work and success. Their socialization, however, left them without the skills necessary to compete successfully with members of the middle-class. Their decreased ability to succeed produced strain, so many of them joined with other people who experienced the same strain to form a delinquent subculture. Within this subculture, delinquent activities were characteristically "non-utilitarian, malicious, and negativistic." Cohen hypothesized that "reaction forma-tion"—a forceful rejection of middle-class values to hold off their appeal—was behind the destructive nature of lower-class delinquency.

The most politically influential application of strain theory to delinquency was offered by sociologists Richard A. Cloward and Lloyd E. Ohlin in their book *Delin-quency and Opportunity* (1960). Their argument was similar to Cohen's. They found three subcultural adaptations to the strain produced by blocking opportunities. The first was that the criminal subculture existed in neighborhoods that had criminal organizations. Within those organizations children learned how to be delinquent and were given opportunities to succeed through crime. The second was that the conflict subculture existed in "disorganized" neighborhoods, where there were neither legiti-mate nor illegitimate opportunities. Under such conditions boys formed fighting gangs whose major interest was in staking out and defending their "turf." A boy could achieve success in this subculture by being a brave and skillful fighter. Finally, these disorgan-ized neighborhoods also spawned a retreatist subculture composed of youths who turned to drugs and alcohol as a was of dealing with their failure in both legal and illegal activities.

Applications

Among sociologists, structural-strain theory has been of interest primarily to those concerned with the relationship between poverty and delinquency. Sociologists inves-tigating other forms of deviance have largely ignored this theory.

By far the largest-scale application of structural-strain theory was in the Mobiliza-tion for Youth program, a delinquency prevention program on New York's Lower East Side in the 1960's. The unifying principles of Mobilization for Youth were contained in Cloward and Ohlin's book *Delinquency and Opportunity*. The explicit strategy of this program was to reduce delinquency by expanding legitimate opportunities in the following ways: by improving education through better teacher training and new preschool programs; by creating jobs through a new Youth Service Corps, a Youth Jobs Center, and better vocational training; by organizing lower-class neighborhoods through new neighborhood councils and a Lower East Side Neighborhood Associa-tion; by providing services to youths, such as by assigning detached workers to gangs and establishing an Adventure Corps and a Coffee Shop Hangout; and, finally, by providing counseling to families through new Neighborhood Service Centers.

President John F. Kennedy, having adopted "the New Frontier" as his campaign slogan, sought ways to deal with social problems such as delinquency. He appointed the President's Committee on Juvenile Delinquency and Youth Crime in May, 1961. The leadership of the committee worked with the Ford Foundation, for whom Cloward and Ohlin worked as consultants. This collaboration produced the Juvenile Delinquency and Youth Offenders Act of 1961, which provided $10 million a year for three years for technical assistance to state and local agencies. The idea was that local agencies would develop delinquency prevention programs that would stress expanding opportunities through direct community action and by coordinating the efforts of government agencies.

In May, 1962, Mobilization for Youth was funded for three years by a $12.5 million grant from the Ford Foundation, the City of New York, and the federal government. The model of community action provided by Mobilization for Youth was adopted by an even larger effort shortly thereafter. In October, 1963, the Kennedy Administration declared a War on Poverty, which was to involve $500 million of federal funds in its first year. President Kennedy was assassinated the following month, but the new president, Lyndon Johnson, expanded the War on Poverty and appointed the senior staff of the President's Committee on Juvenile Delinquency and Youth Crime to lead it.

Billions of federal dollars were spent on expanding legitimate opportunities for delinquents and the poor between 1965 and 1970. Mobilization for Youth alone received more than $30 million in government and private foundation grants. Many years later, the administration and consequences of these anti-poverty and delinquency prevention programs remain controversial.

Mobilization for Youth stressed community-level organization, bypassing city officials, who traditionally controlled access to federal funds spent within their cities. They commonly used these funds at least partially to reward political supporters. City officials accused Mobilization for Youth officials of having "subversive" (in other words, communist) leanings and of stealing program funds. Though there was some evidence of mismanagement of funds, such attacks on the programs were largely politically motivated.

Assessing the impact of Mobilization for Youth on delinquency prevention proved difficult. The program operated in a geographical area where about twenty thousand people lived. This area, composed mostly of apartment houses, had high tenant turnover, so the "subjects" were exposed to the "treatment" for widely varying periods. Juvenile arrests did decrease during the project period, but arrests in adjoining areas increased, suggesting the likelihood of a displacement effect (some juveniles residing in the project area may have gone out of their neighborhood to commit their offenses).

The War on Poverty created a set of large new programs for poor people: Head Start, a preschool cultural enrichment program; the Job Corps, a job training program; Volunteers in Service to America (VISTA), a domestic Peace Corps; Neighborhood Legal Services, a program that provided free legal assistance; and the Community Action Program, a program to bring together community members to solve their own problems. Some of these programs, while providing useful direct services to poor people, adopted adversarial strategies that soon antagonized powerful political interests. For example, lawyers employed by Neighborhood Legal Services sometimes sued the government on behalf of poor clients. The Community Action Program organized protests to inform political leaders of the "demands" of the poor: better jobs, housing, education, and social services. Confronted with increasingly threatening activities by these federally funded programs, both local officials and Congress withdrew support.

Though they functioned for only a brief period, the War on Poverty and Mobilization for Youth produced some enduring benefits unrelated to the focus and impact on delinquency prevention. The proportion of poor people in the United States was reduced for a time through antipoverty programs. Ethnic minority group leaders were identified and trained in community organizing. These leaders subsequently organized members of their own groups into enduring and powerful political forces. Government-sponsored preschool programs for poor children became a permanent fixture in American education.

Context

The historical background of the development of structural-strain theory helps explain why the theory emerged and evolved. Durkheim wrote *Suicide* at the end of the nineteenth century, after the world had seen 150 years of great social upheaval, including the end of absolute monarchy, elimination of most caste societies, reduction in the power of organized religion, success of several national revolutions, and emergence of the world's first democracies. Durkheim shared with many other people a concern for the future of humankind. His fear of the implications of the end of traditional authorities and his search for new sources of authority seem perfectly understandable.

The theme of structural strain was adopted by Merton in the 1930's, during the Great Depression. The widespread intense suffering caused by poverty provided the back-drop for the evolution of this theory, which emphasized the importance of economic deprivation. Without any explicit reference to structural-strain theory, but with a concern for the revolutionary potential of a huge group of disenchanted, unemployed citizens, the federal government introduced a variety of social reforms designed to protect people from the worst effects of poverty, disability, and unemployment.

Structural-strain theory was revived by Richard Cloward and Lloyd Ohlin around 1960, at the beginning of a period of growing restlessness among the United States ethnic minorities and poor. Again, the emphasis of structural-strain theory on social and economic inequality fit in well with the social conditions and liberal philosophical movement of the time.

On a superficial level, structural-strain theory appears to offer an accurate explanation for deviance: The inmates and patients of the institutions and programs established to manage, punish, and treat social deviants are overwhelmingly poor. It would be easy to conclude, therefore, that either poverty itself or the "strain" associated with poverty causes people to become deviant. Evidence gathered by sociologists since the 1960's, however, seriously challenges the assumed causal links between poverty, strain, and deviance. For example, a major assumption of structural-strain theory is that deviance is a phenomenon found largely in the lower class. Yet self-report studies have demonstrated conclusively that deviance exists in all social classes. Though serious violent crimes are committed overwhelmingly by members of the lower class, studies of white-collar crime routinely conclude that high-status offenders defraud the public of far more money than low-status offenders steal. Structural-strain theory is ill-suited to explain the serious, widespread deviance among people who have already attained material success.

Similarly, structural-strain theory assumes a high level of frustration among lower-class people who are unable to attain success by middle-class standards. In studying the relationship between aspirations and delinquency, sociologist Travis Hirschi (*Causes of Delinquency*, 1969), found lower rates of delinquency among lower-class youths who had high occupational aspirations. This finding challenges the assumption that delinquency is produced by frustrated ambitions.

The psychological strain that supposedly results from frustrated ambitions has seldom been studied directly. The few studies of strain among juveniles have found that it is related to relationships with parents and success in school but only weakly related to social class.

The popularity of structural-strain theory is largely a product of its philosophical attractiveness and intuitive logic. The available evidence suggests that it is not an accurate model of the cause of deviant behavior. Nevertheless, reducing poverty is a worthy goal in its own right. It would also almost certainly produce a diminution in serious, violent crimes, which are committed largely by poor people. The available evidence, however, does not lead to a prediction that reducing poverty alone would reduce other forms of deviance.

Bibliography

Agnew, Robert. "A Revised Strain Theory of Delinquency." *Social Forces* 64 (September, 1985): 151-167. One of the few studies involving directly measuring psychological strain. Agnew found, in a national sample of tenth-grade boys, that strain was unrelated to social class, undermining a central assumption of structural-strain theory.

Cloward, Richard A., and Lloyd E. Ohlin. *Delinquency and Opportunity*. New York: Free Press, 1960. One of the most important books describing the social arrangements that produce deviance. The authors introduced the idea that people choose deviant or conforming roles based on their perception of their relative positions in both legitimate and illegitimate opportunity structures.

Cohen, Albert K. *Delinquent Boys*. New York: Free Press, 1955. Cohen examined the condition of lower-class boys who accept middle-class values of material success but lack the skills and resources to compete in the middle-class world. The strain they experience, Cohen argued, caused them to engage in destructive forms of delinquency as a way to demonstrate their rejection of middle-class materialism.

Durkheim, Émile. *Suicide: A Study in Sociology*. Translated by John Spaulding and

George Simpson. Edited by George Simpson. New York: Free Press, 1951. First published in 1897. This is the first and, arguably, most interesting, work on strain theory; it tackles important and enduring questions about the human condition. A true classic of sociological theory and method. Though not easy to read, it is worth the effort.

Lemann, Nicholas. "The Unfinished War." *Atlantic Monthly* 262 (December, 1988): 37-56. A journalistic account of the War on Poverty based on interviews with the political leaders who guided it. Reveals that Attorney General Robert Kennedy was far more interested in the Cloward and Ohlin theory and Mobilization for Youth than was President John Kennedy. Describes in detail the complex politics and personal relationships surrounding this important federal initiative.

Merton, Robert K. "Social Structure and Anomie." *American Sociological Review* 3 (October, 1938): 672-682. This is the most frequently cited work in all sociology. Merton applies Émile Durkheim's concept of *anomie* to American society, spelling out the consequences of the extreme cultural emphasis on financial success, in the context of limited legitimate opportunities to achieve that success.

Joseph E. Jacoby

Cross-References

Anomie and Deviance, 100; Conflict Perspectives on Deviance, 334; Cultural Norms and Sanctions, 411; Cultural Transmission Theory of Deviance, 424; Delinquency Prevention and Treatment, 476; Deviance: Analysis and Overview, 525; Deviance: Biological and Psychological Explanations, 532; Labeling and Deviance, 1049; The Medicalization of Deviance, 1178.

THE STRUCTURAL-STRAIN THEORY
OF SOCIAL MOVEMENTS

Type of sociology: Collective behavior and social movements
Fields of study: Sources of social change; Theories of social change

Structural-strain theory describes the way a form of collective behavior known as a social movement emerges from the traditional structure of a complex industrial society. This theory explains the development of social movements by means of an economic model called the value-added process.

Principal terms

COLLECTIVE BEHAVIOR: coordinated behavior involving two or more persons that emerges from traditional culture

COMPLAINING GROUP: a group that organizes into a norm-oriented or value-oriented social movement

EMERGING BEHAVIOR: coordinated behavior involving two or more persons that is new, untried, and responsive to stimuli external to the group

MORAL PANIC: a condition in which members of a society define a condition, episode, person, or group as a threat to societal values

NORM-ORIENTED SOCIAL MOVEMENT: a complaining group's attempt to protect or change social norms

SOCIAL MOVEMENT: a movement that demands some change in the social order

SOCIAL STRAIN THEORY: an explanation of the emergence of social movements using the idea that social tensions and/or disequilibrium stimulate the actions of a complaining group

TRADITIONAL CULTURE: established and understood social patterns that are the sources of collective behavior

VALUE-ADDED PROCESS: a process in which each step in the development of the social movement adds value to the final outcome of the movement

VALUE-ORIENTED MOVEMENT: a complaining group's attempt to protect or change social values

Overview

The study of collective behavior involves the description and explanation of emerging social structures in society. The study of social movements is linked to collective behavior because of its focus on emerging social movements. The study of social movements has moved away from collective behavior research on emerging structures, however, by taking an organizational approach to social movements. A social movement is, in the words of Joseph Gusfield, a "socially shared demand for change in some aspect of the social order."

Neil J. Smelser's value-added model, first presented in his *Theory of Collective Behavior* (1963), is based on economics. It argues that determinants can be described as combining in various ways to encourage social movements. The theory is divided into six determinants, each with a set of sub-determinants. The determinants are structural conduciveness, structural strain, growth of a generalized belief, precipitating event, mobilization for action, and social control.

Structural conduciveness refers to conditions that allow a social movement to develop, conditions or social possibilities that are necessary but not sufficient for social movements to emerge in industrial society. Structural conduciveness sets the parameters and constraints for the other components of the model, particularly structural strain. Smelser describes two types of movements. Those that are norm-oriented seek to protect or change social norms, and those that are value-oriented seek to do the same thing for the core values of society. Structural strain describes conditions of tension at the level of norms and values. The sociologist views strain in terms of uncertainty.

Smelser's model instructs the researcher to look for beliefs that guide action. The notion of generalized beliefs suggests that the analyst can identify beliefs that are shared by members of complaining groups. These beliefs identify a problem and propose a solution or solutions for it. Beliefs are rooted in uncertainty. Smelser's model instructs the analyst to look for beliefs that guide action. Norm-oriented and value-oriented beliefs are rooted in conditions of strain. These beliefs become motivators of social action only if they become shared (generalized).

The precipitating event serves to focus the generalized belief on specific events or issues. In a sense, the precipitating event combines with the belief to propose solutions for the ambiguity and anxiety found under strain conditions.

Mobilization for action is movement activity. Regarding mobilization for action, the Smelser model encourages the investigator to look at the initial and derived phases of a social movement.

Regarding social control, Smelser's model directs one to investigate several dimensions that shape the development of a social movement. In the general category of social control, formal control comes from traditional sources, such as the police, while informal social control might come from the activities of the clergy or the press.

Applications

The scope of Smelser's structural-strain theory allows it to be applied in a variety of social movement contexts, including the student protest, labor, women's, civil rights, peace, and other popular culture movements.

Jon M. Shepard (1993) analyzed college student protests of the Vietnam War and suggested that structural conduciveness had to do with the opportunities for and locations of protests. Students had easy access to areas such as plazas where rallies could be held. Regarding strain, students felt the impact of the war because they did not believe the federal government's statements about the war. The generalized belief was that the federal government was not telling the truth. The bombing of North Vietnam served as a precipitating event that focused the generalized belief. The beliefs and the precipitating event encouraged mobilization for action, which included a range of activities from letter writing to mass demonstrations. Social activities moved in to deflect, minimize, or prevent the activities of the movement. Sometimes, the social control activities became the focus of the protest as they did after the national Guard shot and killed four protesters at Kent State University in 1970. Usually, anti-Vietnam War movements were norm-oriented.

The Civil Rights movement can also be interpreted using Smelser's value-added model. In this case the analyst looks at the structurally conducive conditions that cause different ethnic or racial groups to come into close contact. The structural strain is usually economic, with one group existing at a disadvantage in relation to the other. The generalized belief in a civil rights movement is typically that the inequality, whether in jobs, home buying or schooling opportunities, can be eliminated. The precipitating event can range from a simple act of discrimination to the exclusion of a significant portion of the complaining group from access to some part of society. The generalized belief and the precipitating event combine in the value-added model to encourage the political protest, or mobilization. Social control comes into play as authorities respond to the demands of the complaining groups.

The value-added model can also be used to analyze popular social movements. In 1948, Ingrid Bergman was a Hollywood film star. Bergman was popularly believed to have the qualities of the characters she played on film and stage, such as the saintly Joan of Arc, the faithful, pure Sister Benedict in *The Bells of St. Mary*, or the vulnerable Ilsa in *Casablanca*.

Bergman and director Roberto Rossellini—and a film crew—were isolated on the island of Stromboli, which had no outside access except by boat. In April, the first items appeared in the Hollywood gossip columns informing the public that Bergman and Rossellini had had an affair. Bergman was advised to deny the rumors of her affair. She did not deny them outright, but she did state that she and Rossellini were going to complete the filming of *Stromboli*, after which she would meet her husband. In February, 1950, however, Robertino Rossellini was born out of wedlock, because Bergman was unable to have her marriage annulled before her son's birth. The public was horrified that Ingrid Bergman had not only abandoned her husband and child to have a highly publicized illicit affair but also had the indecency to bear her lover an illegitimate child. *Stromboli* was released in the United States in February, 1950, and was a complete failure at the box office. Ingrid Bergman would not return to the United States until 1957—eight years after her affair with Roberto Rossellini.

The case can be analyzed using Smelser's strain model of social movements. Beginning with structural conduciveness, the analyst looks for individuals or groups that might respond to a Hollywood scandal, such as the press, ministers, women's groups, and theater owners. The press was very active in tracking the events of the Rossellini-Bergman scandal, and international coverage was very intense. Ministers and women's groups were certainly involved. Bergman may have mitigated the complaining groups' rage by announcing that she had obtained a divorce and was married to Rossellini shortly after the baby was born.

A federal politician appeared who opposed Bergman: Senator Edwin Carl "Big Ed" Johnson from Colorado. Johnson, responding to RKO's publicity for *Stromboli*, introduced a bill that would have licensed actors, actresses, producers, and film distributors to work in the film industry. The bill gave the federal government the power to revoke a license whenever the license holder was found guilty of moral turpitude. The bill also attacked film content, suggesting that a license could be taken away if the film showed "contempt for public or private morality." The bill never got out of the committee, but it does show Johnson's thinking. Thus, the structural conduciveness necessary for a social movement to happen existed.

The next determinant is structural strain. This determinant causes the analyst to look at either values or norms. Is the complaining group trying to change societal values or norms? The focus in this case was on Bergman, the actress, not Hollywood per se. The strain was the fact that Bergman had an affair and bore a child out of wedlock. In the minds of some people, such as Senator Johnson, Bergman's actions disqualified her from being a screen actress.

Ironically, many of Bergman's screen roles involved fallen or loose women. For example, in *Dr. Jekyll and Mr. Hyde* she played a barmaid prostitute, while in *Casablanca* she was Humphrey Bogart's lover. Thus, the attack on Bergman was caused by her off-screen behavior, based on the idea that audiences should not be exposed to evil-doers. The movement resisting Bergman was norm-oriented rather than value-oriented because it attacked her behavior, not the movie industry. The complaining groups and individuals were not trying to change the values of the film industry. They were attempting to prevent an actress who had not followed the rules from working. Thus, a norm-oriented movement developed.

In the Smelser model, a belief is based on something that becomes shared (generalized). The belief identifies the problem and proposes a solution or solutions. In the Bergman case, the problem underlying the belief was the "immoral" behavior of a major international film star. The solution? She should be barred from making any more films—at least in the United States. Johnson referred to Bergman as a "powerful influence for evil" and as the "common mistress" of Rossellini. The precipitating event was the anticipated release of *Stromboli* in the United States.

Mobilization for action is the actual behavior of individuals and groups. The groups involved in the movement against Bergman included church groups, women's groups, and theater associations. One film association urged its members not to book *Stromboli* in its theaters.

In the analysis of social movements, the social control determinant refers to how the social control agencies respond to the complaining groups. In the Bergman case, the response was mixed. Although there were many groups and individuals arrayed against her, she did have some supporters. The groups that supported Bergman or attacked her opponents included The Motion Picture Council, The Johnston Office, and the American Civil Liberties Union (ACLU). Ironically, the Roman Catholic Legion of Decency also supported *Stromboli*. It said, "It is our job to judge the picture itself, not the actors in it."

Context

The study of social movements is a subspecialty of the study of collective behavior. Structural-strain theory is a structural-functional approach to the analysis of social movements. Scholars of social movements have used strain theory to study two basic types of social movements. First, there are those activities that involve political activity, such as the labor, student, civil rights, peace, women's, and popular culture movements. The second topic studied by scholars of social movements is that of spiritual activities, ranging from narrowly focused cults to broad-based religious movements.

Scholars of social movements have used social strain theory to explain the emergence of movements in both categories. The best-known structural-strain theory is Neil J. Smelser's value-added model. It is a structural-functional theory because of its focus on strain and social equilibrium as well as on the importance of norms and values. Smelser was a student of and a collaborator with the famous Harvard sociologist Talcott Parsons. It is possible to link the value-added model to other strain theories, including the theory of relative deprivation and moral panic theory. These theoretical perspectives give the student of social movements insight into why members of a movement act with such intensity.

One way to analyze the intensity of social movement members is to interpret their responses as moral panics. Thus, the generalized belief is an intense belief that can be likened to panic in fire or earthquake. Stanley Cohen, an English sociologist who studies deviance, developed the idea of moral panic in his research on English youth gangs. He describes a moral panic as a situation in which members of a society define a "condition, episode, person or group, as a threat to societal values and interests." He gives particular power to the media's role in spreading the moral panic through a process that he calls deviance amplification. The media set the agenda for discourses by identifying who the "folk devils" are in any particular time or place in society. For example, the Ingrid Bergman case was a clear example of a moral panic. Why was there such a strong reaction against Bergman that she did not work in a Hollywood film for almost five years? There are several reasons why the moral panic developed. First, although Bergman played fallen women on screen, her off-screen persona was that of a healthy, vibrant girl next door. If she had not been Swedish, she might have been called an "All-American woman." Second, the baby was born to a director who was foreign, and that fact evoked great hostility. Senator Johnson called Rossellini "vile and unspeakable" and a "common love thief." No doubt considerable xenophobia was present in the reaction to Bergman's involvement with Rossellini. Third, many people linked Bergman with Rita Hayworth, who had a baby outside marriage with Prince Aly Khan. Johnson called Bergman and Hayworth "Hollywood's two current apostles of degradation." Fourth, Bergman and Rossellini made a mistake in denying what was obviously true—that Bergman was pregnant by Rossellini. Fifth, *Stromboli* was not very good. It received terrible reviews.

Another strain theory is that of relative deprivation. This theory states that people do not form a complaining group unless they believe that they are not getting their fair share of resources when compared to other groups or categories of people within the society. Thus, the feeling of disgruntlement is relative, not absolute.

Bibliography

Bergman, Ingrid, and Alan Burgess. *Ingrid Bergman, My Story*. New York: Delacorte Press, 1980. An autobiography that provides insight into Ingrid Bergman's film career.

Cohen, Stanley. *Folk Devils and Moral Panics*. London: MacGibbon & Kee, 1972. The theoretical presentation of moral panic model.

Damico, James. "Ingrid from *Lorraine* to *Stromboli*: Analyzing the Public's Perception of a Film Star." *Journal of Popular Film* 4, No. 1 (1975): 3-19. A factual account of the Bergman-Rossellini affair.

Gusfield, Joseph. "The Study of Social Movements." In *International Encyclopedia of Social Sciences*, edited by David L. Sills. New York: Macmillan, 1968. An overview of the field by a leading authority.

Shepard, Jon M. *Sociology*. 5th ed. St. Paul, Minn.: West, 1993. An introductory sociology textbook that offers an excellent treatment of the value-added model.

Smelser, Neil J. *Theory of Collective Behavior*. New York: Free Press, 1963. This volume presents the Smelser model in detail, showing its roots in the structural-functional social theory of Talcott Parsons.

Jerry M. Lewis

Cross-References

SUBCULTURES AND COUNTERCULTURES

Type of sociology: Culture
Field of study: Cultural variation and change

Subcultures are groups of people who have cultural characteristics that differ in some significant way from the dominant culture. Countercultures, besides being different in their ways, are also consciously in opposition to the widely accepted norms and values of the dominant culture. Subcultures and countercultures are examples of ways in which cultural diversity exists in a single society.

Principal terms
  BELIEFS: shared ideas about the meaning of life and other significant issues
  COMMUNE: a group of people who live together for the purpose of attaining some ideological goal
  COUNTERCULTURE: a group that is consciously in opposition to the norms and values of the dominant culture
  CULTURE: the beliefs, values, behavior, and material objects shared by a group; a system of normative guidelines
  GROUP: a small number of people who interact over time and establish patterns of interaction, identity, and norms governing behavior
  NORMS: rules and expectations by which a society guides the behavior of its members
  SOCIAL MOVEMENTS: collective efforts to resist or bring about social change
  SOCIETY: a grouping of people who share a culture and social structure
  SUBCULTURES: variations in values, beliefs, norms, and behavior of societal subgroups
  VALUES: central beliefs that provide a standard by which norms are judged

Overview

Subcultures and countercultures are aberrations of mainstream culture. Social scientists disagree on the exact definition of these concepts. Most social scientists would admit that the majority of groups considered to be either subcultures or countercultures could possibly fall into either category. For example, sociologist Donald Kraybill refers to the Amish as both a counterculture and subculture, whereas William Kephart and William Zellner consider the Amish a subculture. Sociologist J. Milton Yinger postulates that subcultures cannot be subsumed under the concept counterculture, but he is undecided whether countercultures can be subsets of subcultures.

Subcultures are shared systems of norms, values, and behaviors that distinguish some individuals and groups from others in the dominant culture. Neither membership in a particular group nor behavior alone is sufficient to define a subculture. The most important elements in defining a subculture are the degree to which norms, values, and behaviors are shared and the nature of the relationships between those who share these norms, values, and behaviors and those who do not. Subcultures can be identified by a variety of factors, including language, ethnicity, race, religion, region, social class, lifestyle, age, and occupation. Examples of subcultures therefore include juvenile gangs, homosexuals, Mormons, Hasidic Jews, Hispanics, and the Amish.

Countercultures are also shared systems of norms, values, and behaviors that distinguish some individuals and groups from others in the dominant culture. The significant difference between subcultures and countercultures is that countercultures are much more critical of society and the social order. The normative characteristics of members of subcultures are the product of socialization and interaction within the subculture rather than the result of conflict with the larger society. Countercultures are not rooted in small, tightly knit homogeneous groups such as ethnic groups, and they are much more affected by social forces. Subcultures evolve slowly, whereas counter-cultures are emergent phenomena that are much more susceptible to changes in the mainstream culture and that react based on the thrust of those changes.

According to Yinger, countercultural norms and values sharply contradict those of mainstream culture. Countercultures are generally opposed to the power structure (organization) of a society as well as to social relationships and behaviors that support and empower the dominant values of the society. Their norms and values tend to be known only by other group members, and their behavior is nonconformist. Some counterculturists drop out of society, while others remain hoping to bring about change in the social order.

Countercultures can be identified by their epistemologies (theories of knowledge and truth), ethics (theories of moral values and goodness), and aesthetics (theories of the nature and expression of beauty). Yinger suggests that countercultures can adopt a variety of forms including mixtures of prophetic activism (criticizing the status quo in order to transform it), communal or utopian withdrawal (an ascetic, isolated lifestyle based on a code of new values different from those of the mainstream culture), and mystical insight (search for spiritual insight and new consciousness-raising experiences).

In his book *Alienation and Charisma: A Study of Contemporary American Communes* (1980), sociologist Benjamin Zablocki constructs a typology (classification) of eight commune ideologies (Eastern, Christian, psychological, rehabilitational, cooperative, alternative family, countercultural, and political) that incorporates and broadens the discussion and application of Yinger's three varieties of countercultures. The one most pertinent to this discussion is the seventh commune type, countercultural.

According to Zablocki, countercultural communes are primarily concerned with bringing about change in society by first raising one's consciousness. Counterculturists view social or direct action as futile and unproductive. A typical counterculturist is concerned with an individualistic search for meaning in life. Political communes are more oriented toward direct action to bring about change in the social order even if it takes a revolution to accomplish that task. Political activists envision large-scale social change at the societal level rather than change at the individual level as sought by counterculturists.

In his book *Countercultural Communes: A Sociological Perspective* (1983), sociologist Gilbert Zicklin indicates that the communal movement of the 1960's and 1970's had its roots in a social movement that began in the late 1950's and early 1960's. This social movement became known as the countercultural movement of the 1960's. Young people turned to rural and urban communes as places of shelter and renewal. The majority of communalists were not trying to transform society and the social order but were attempting to find a meaningful system of belief.

According to Zicklin, the countercultural movement of the 1960's and early 1970's was based on four major themes: the new naturalism (focused primarily on getting back to nature), the spiritual quest (uncovering the fundamental meanings and purposes of life), the expressive mode (becoming less competitive, aggressive, emotionally restricted, and conformist), and a renewed American society (a political dimension supporting optimism, peace, equality, and freedom). Although these four themes were present throughout the 1960's and early 1970's, they were not woven into a unified, coherent system of belief. The counterculture movement of the 1960's and early 1970's included a mixture of agendas and outcomes.

Yinger postulates that social, cultural, and personality factors create the context in which countercultures emerge. For example, common structural and interactional sources of countercultures include: economic factors, demographic factors, relative deprivation (when people feel unfairly treated in comparison with others), and isolation.

Applications

The study of subcultures and countercultures can contribute to an understanding of social order and social change. Yinger believes that the task for social scientists is to measure the range of variation of culture, power, and reciprocity that exists in these groups. The knowledge and understanding gained can provide insight into the functioning of mainstream society and culture. People who are members of subcultures and countercultures usually believe that the social order of the larger society has failed them in some way. They believe that they have been cheated, exploited, neglected, or abandoned, or that the system is inadequate and lacking key values. They therefore seek alternative meaning systems and lifestyles. Countercultures, in particular, are barometers that point to weaknesses and inadequacies in mainstream culture.

Scholars have gleaned a number of significant insights from studying the Amish. Most social scientists would agree that the Old Order Amish are a subculture and that they have dealt with the issues of social order and social change in unique and relatively successful ways. In his book *The Riddle of Amish Culture* (1989), sociologist Donald Kraybill identifies the following five defensive tactics used by the Amish to resist modernity and encroachment by the dominant society: symbolization of core values, centralized leadership, social sanctions, comprehensive socialization, and controlled interaction with outsiders. These tactics are characteristic not only of the Amish but also of most subcultures. Adoption of these tactics contributes to the subculture's ability to maintain tradition and negotiate with the processes of modernity that challenge the social order of the group.

The paramount value guiding Amish culture is the concept of *Gelassenheit*, a German word meaning submission, humility, obedience, and simplicity. Gelassenheit works to control the destructive tendencies of the aggressive individualism that is the hallmark of the modern value system and the dominant American culture. The Amish have not allowed modernity and aggressive individualism to control their decision-making process. They have survived and multiplied because of their uncanny ability to use boundary maintenance (maintaining physical, social, and behavioral boundaries that set groups off from their environment) to their advantage. The Amish realize that boundaries are important for maintaining social organization and preserving their way of life. When necessary, therefore, they move boundaries (or, as Kraybill describes them, "fences") rather than discard them. The majority of the "riddles" of Amish life are actually practical solutions, or boundary-movings, used by the Amish to retain their distinctive traditional identity.

For example, the Amish of Lancaster County, Pennsylvania, can use modern hay balers and gasoline engines on farm equipment as long as the equipment itself is pulled by horses. This compromise has smoothed the conflict between modernity and tradition; it was reached so that modern harvesters, combines, and other self-propelled equipment would not challenge the productivity and economic vaibility of the Amish farm. This compromise kept the horse in the field, a strong traditional symbol for the Amish, and it allowed the family to maintain its farm while accepting limited amounts of technology. Controlled and limited social change in small doses has enhanced Amish survival and their ability to control and maintain social order.

An example of a counterculture is the countercultural movement of the 1960's and early 1970's. Predominantly, but not universally, this movement was a middle-class youth phenomenon. Zablocki has skillfully captured, in his study of 120 communes, the essence of this widely diverse counterculture. Although the communal movement was only a part of the overall countercultural phenomenon, it was the most visible and radical component of the movement. The movement's strong focus on social change and its assault on the social order shocked mainstream society. Communes are recurring historical phenomena that respond to perceived weaknesses in a society's meaning systems and point to problems concerning social order and social change.

Zablocki's most general overall finding about communes and their struggle to create new societies was that, in their search for consensus, they created intense interpersonal networks. If these personal relationships were not nurtured through charismatic renewal, the commune would become unstable and fail. (Charisma here refers to personal magnetism or charm that arouses popular devotion and enthusiasm.) When comparing communes, Zablocki found that the greater the number of love relation-ships experienced within the commune, the higher the probability that the commune would be unstable. Comparing individuals within the same commune, he noted that those who were involved in many relationships tended to be more committed to the commune.

Another major finding concerns the association between charismatic authority and the search for consensus. Those members who invest themselves in the group (are highly committed to the group) are most amenable to charismatic authority. Zablocki concludes that there is an urgent need for more study on the influence of charismatic authority and its role in the question of social order. Two tragic occurrences involving countercultural communes with charismatic leaders highlight this need. Members of the People's Temple, a group located in Guyana and led by Jim Jones, committed mass suicide in 1978. In 1993, the Branch Davidians in Waco, Texas, a group led by David Koresh, purportedly committed suicide rather than surrender to law enforcement agencies after a deadly shoot-out.

Context

Social scientists have always been interested in subcultures and countercultures. Yet since sociology is a relatively new field—the first department of sociology was not established in the United States until 1892 at the University of Chicago—the formal sociological study of subcultures is fairly recent.

Increased immigration as well as the urbanization of the American population in the late nineteenth and early twentieth centuries spawned the development and recognition of subcultures. Much of the early sociological study of subcultures was conducted by sociologists at the University of Chicago. Working throughout the city, they studied juvenile gangs and ethnic communities. This tradition continues today.

In the early 1960's, J. Milton Yinger proposed that there is a clear difference between subcultures and what he identified as "contracultures." Contracultures, he said, are subsets of subcultures. Most social scientists and commentators preferred to use the term "countercultures." Many people found this concept appealing because of the ongoing social development and sentiment tied to the student movement of the early 1960's. One of these thinkers was Theodore Roszak, who popularized the term and the concept in his book *The Making of a Counter Culture* (1969).

In his presidential address to the American Sociological Association in 1977, Yinger asserted that the fundamental reason for studying countercultures is to gain insight into the social order of mainstream culture as well as of the countercultures. The most important lessons that can be learned from the study of countercultures is what they say about the human condition. Countercultures, according to Yinger, are "calls for help in stressful times," and any society must be responsive to the messages and actions that emanate from its subcultures and countercultures.

Bibliography

Berger, Bennett M. *The Survival of a Counterculture: Ideological Work and Everyday Life Among Rural Communards.* Berkeley: University of California Press, 1981. This book describes some of the beliefs and practices of a commune known as "the Ranch" in rural California. Much of the book is devoted to the author's reflections on the research he conducted at the Ranch. Contains a useful appendix and bibliography.

Hostetler, John A. *Amish Society*. 3d ed. Baltimore: The Johns Hopkins University Press, 1980. This book is perhaps the most important volume written about the Amish. The scope of the volume is comprehensive, and Hostetler's purpose is to communicate a knowledge of Amish life. See also Hostetler's *Hutterite Society* (The Johns Hopkins University Press, 1977) and Donald Kraybill's *The Riddle of Amish Culture* (The Johns Hopkins University Press, 1989).

Kanter, Rosabeth Moss. *Commitment and Community: Communes and Utopias in Sociological Perspective*. Cambridge, Mass.: Harvard University Press, 1972. An important and creative work that investigates the ideas and values underlying utopian communities and communal living. This book is known for its discussion of Kanter's theory of commitment. Highly recommended. Excellent bibliography.

Kephart, William M., and William M. Zellner. *Extraordinary Groups: An Examination of Unconventional Life-Styles*. 4th ed. New York: St. Martin's Press, 1991. A well-written text that examines a variety of subcultures (the Old Order Amish, the Oneida Community, the Shakers, the Hasidim) from a sociological perspective.

Poll, Solomon. *The Hasidic Community of Williamsburg*. New York: Schocken Books, 1969. An interesting and readable volume about a traditional religious sect of Judaism. The author discusses the implicit and explicit characteristics of this particular subculture.

Rochford, E. Burke, Jr. *Hare Krishna in America*. New Brunswick, N.J.: Rutgers University Press, 1985. Burke spent six years (1975-1981) studying the Hare Krishna. He observed and participated in nine Krishna communities around the country, but the majority of the research was done in Los Angeles. Extensive notes and a good bibliography.

Roszak, Theodore. *The Making of a Counter Culture*. Garden City, N.Y.: Doubleday, 1969. Roszak examines some of the leading influences on the youth counterculture that questioned the conventional scientific worldview and foundation of technocracy (a government or social system controlled by scientists and technicians).

Yinger, J. Milton. *Countercultures: The Promise and the Peril of a World Turned Upside Down*. New York: Free Press, 1982. Focuses on the role countercultures play in regard to social change. Yinger relies on an interdisciplinary approach to study countercultures. Probably one of the best sources for an introduction to countercultures. Excellent bibliography.

Zablocki, Benjamin. *Alienation and Charisma: A Study of Contemporary American Communes*. New York: Free Press, 1980. A definitive study of sixty urban and sixty rural American communes during the period between 1965 and 1978. Zablocki studies how consensus is gained or lost among groups striving for similar ideological goals. He is concerned primarily with studying communes as decision-making arenas. The author developed a useful classification system of communes. Excellent bibliography.

William L. Smith

Cross-References

Churches, Denominations, and Sects, 246; Cults, 399; Cultural Norms and Sanctions, 411; Ethnic Enclaves, 682; High Culture versus Popular Culture, 870; Social Change: Sources of Change, 1786; Social Movements, 1826; Values and Value Systems, 2143.

SUBURBANIZATION AND DECENTRALIZATION

Type of sociology: Urban and rural life

As accompaniments of twentieth century urban growth, the suburbanization and decentralization of populations and economic organizations have altered urban and rural ecologies, affected social structure and stratification, and redefined many aspects of social interactions and social change.

Principal terms

COMPOSITIONAL THEORY: the theory that urbanites experience as many warm and direct interactions with family, friends, and neighbors as do people in small towns and rural environments

CONCENTRIC ZONE THEORY: the theory that urban expansion takes the form of concentric circles, in each of which land use is devoted to specific types of activity

GENTRIFICATION: the movement of affluent people into poor urban neighborhoods that they hope to upgrade, though in the process they often displace poorer residents

MEGALOPOLIS: a vast urban area composed of many metropolitan areas

METROPOLIS: a large city, usually at least a million in population, and its adjacent suburbs

SECTOR THEORY: the theory that cities grow outward from their centers in wedge-shaped sectors

URBAN ECOLOGY: the study of the interrelationships between city dwellers and their environment

Overview

Suburbanization is the process of creating, populating, and developing identifiable communities on the outskirts of cities. The process has resulted from the interplay of many factors, three of which have been evident.

One has been the settlement on urban fringes of people and organizations that are drawn toward cities—but not into them. Economic concerns about higher urban taxes, rents, and the adequacy of business locations; generally held opinions about schools, crime, racial and ethnic tensions; and anxieties about lessening the overall quality of their lives have all played roles in keeping individuals, families, and other groups on urban peripheries. Suburban living has seemed to offer many advantages of urban life, but without its presumed social costs.

A second factor underlying suburbanization has been the decentralization of urban populations and urban economic institutions. Urban crowding, shortages of satisfactory housing, high taxes and rents, a sparsity of desirable business locations, the unavailability of an adequate labor force, urban bankruptcy, hostile political climates, crime, poor schools, and racial problems have all spurred urban decentralization. Many individuals and families, however, have simply explained the suburbanization that resulted from decentralization—their moves out of the city—as part of their search for a safer, healthier, environment and a better way of life.

In some cases, a third factor, which, politically, has more imperial overtones, has helped account for suburbanization; namely, the absorption of surrounding rural towns and villages by expanding metropolises. As the modern world's first "million-peopled city," for example, nineteenth century London expanded so rapidly over the rural communities of southeastern England that it was described as "a province covered with houses." The same phenomenon has been observed in many other places. In the United States since the 1880's, and more often since the 1950's, cities such as Los Angeles, New York City, Boston, Houston, Dallas, San Francisco, Chicago, Washington, D.C., and Miami, officially or functionally, have overrun the towns and villages of their rural hinterlands.

In some cases, people drawn toward the vital life and perceived opportunities of great cities have created "bedroom" communities—suburbs from which they traveled to work into the major city during the day, only to return for rest and recreation. Brooklyn, Garden City, and Levittown, all in new York, developed along those lines, as did scores of communities that once enjoyed independent existences outside Los Angeles or New York City—indeed, outside most American cities. Eventually, the exodus of people from within the major cities provided such suburban communities with the bulk of their populations.

Suburbanization and decentralization have represented demographic changes of immense magnitude. From the noticeable beginnings of urbanization in the United States during the 1830's until the 1940's, the cities themselves were the vortices into which rural and immigrant populations alike were drawn. By the 1950's, however, these demographics were dramatically changing; The major cities began losing population to the suburbs, a process that continued throughout the twentieth century. By the 1970's, for example, New York City, Buffalo, Cleveland, St. Louis, and Pittsburgh had already lost roughly one-fifth of their residents to established or developing suburban communities. Similarly, between 1948 and 1978, a dozen of the largest northern cities lost more than two million jobs, while their suburbs added almost four million private sector jobs to their communities. By the 1990's, many of these suburbs, which had once been economically dependent upon major cities, had become largely self-sustaining.

Profound political changes went along with changing demographic and economic patterns. Before the 1950's, for example, most major cities were strongholds of liberalism and of the Democratic Party. Often, politically, such cities stood in hostile juxtaposition to conservative forces, or to the Republican Party, along upstate versus downstate or east versus west geographical cleavages. Afterward, liberal-Democratic cities were apt literally to be ringed by conservative-Republican or politically "Independent" suburbs. Moreover, suburban votes reflected markedly different socioeconomic status, age, religious, racial, and financial perspectives from those in the city—

that is, different lifestyles, the quality of which has provoked sociological debate.

These realignments of urban-suburban relationships required new definitions of "urban." Accordingly, in 1983, the U.S. Bureau of the Census replaced its older concepts, such as the Standard Metropolitan Statistical Area (SMSA), with the Metropolitan Statistical Area (MSA)—a large nucleus city together with suburban communities that are closely integrated with it—in effect, the Bureau's definition of a metropolis. In addition, the Census Bureau created a broader Consolidated Metro-politan Statistical Area (CMSA), a metropolitan complex that includes within it several large cities (center or primary cities) and their suburban communities. The Census Bureau's CMSA, in short, went beyond defining a metropolis (MSA) to define a megalopolis.

Not surprisingly, sociological theories concerning the nature of urban development and the character of suburban life—the concentric zone theory, the sector theory, and the compositional theory, among others—have all been subjected, as suburbanization and decentralization have continued, to ongoing controversies and revisions.

Applications

A measure of suburbanization has always accompanied modern urbanization. As transportation improved—when adequate roads and water transport outside late eighteenth century London, Paris, New York, Boston, Philadelphia, and Baltimore became available, for example, or when, after the mid-nineteenth century, railroads and trolleys became increasingly available—small numbers of relatively wealthy families found that they were able to pursue business and enjoy urban living while retaining seasonal, or even daily, retreats or residences outside the cities. To that extent, "ribbon-development"—that is, settlements along transportation routes—occurred outside cities nearly everywhere. Those suburban settlements reached more signifi-cant, if still modest, proportions by the 1920's with the creation of "commuter lines" to planned or developed suburban communities: outside New York City, for example, to mention only a few, Garden City, Yonkers, and Scarsdale.

In the United States, however, massive suburbanization and urban decentralization began in the 1950's, facilitated by widespread affluence, by the almost universal family automobile, by vastly improved highway networks, and by the generation of many jobs within suburban communities themselves as they became economically independent of center cities. According to the census of 1990, more Americans were living in suburban communities (within metropolitan areas or CMSAs) than were living in such areas as the 301 square miles encompassing New York City's five boroughs, the 47 square miles that was officially Boston, the 80 square miles known as Baltimore, or the 228 square miles accurately designated as Chicago. If by 1925 the United States had become a predominantly urban nation, by the end of the twentieth century it had become a predominantly suburban nation.

While increases in America's population accounted for some suburban growth, much, if not most, of that growth came at the expense of central cities. Thus, by 1990, suburbs surrounding many cities had larger populations than did their contiguous central or primary cities. For example, Boston contained only 30.4 percent and New York City only 48 percent of the population of the MSAs in which they were included. Similar figures for Chicago were 49 percent, for Cincinnati 25.6 percent, for Newark 22.2 percent, for Philadelphia 35.8 percent, for Pittsburgh 19.2 percent, and for Detroit 28.9 percent. Overall, the Census Bureau's *Statistical Abstract of the United States, 1990*, in a citation of seventy-one primary metropolitan statistical areas, noted only eighteen central cities with populations equal to those of their suburbs. Moreover, while the pre-1960 pattern was one of suburbanites commuting into central cities to work, the subsequent pattern has been for suburbanites to work either in their own or in nearby suburban communities.

Suburbs, like central cities, have characters of their own. They are far from being homogeneous. There are extremely wealthy, if not exclusive, suburbs such as Grosse Point and Bloomfield Hills, outside of Detroit; Silver Spring, Rockville, and Wheaton, outside of Washington, D.C.; and Pikesville, outside Baltimore. Although they are less wealthy than communities such as these, most suburbs are nevertheless substantially more affluent than are the populations of their nearby central cities. Furthermore, they tend to be principally white, although there are exceptions to this in parts of the West and Southwest, where some suburbs are composed chiefly of Hispanics. Moreover, politically, suburbs have tended to be markedly more independent and more conservative than the populations of central cities. For sociologists, these are only parts of the immense social, behavioral, and cultural changes that they believe to be the results of suburbanization.

Partly because suburban life has tended to be a white, middle-class phenomenon, many social scientists, novelists, government officials, leaders of minority groups, and journalists have been critical of the lifestyles and values that seem to accompany it. Some aspects of suburban living thus have been denounced for several reasons. Many critics have viewed the growth of the suburbs as a partial result of "white flight" from the racial problems of inner cities. Indeed, in 1988, while only 25 percent of the nation's European Americans were residents of inner cities, 73 percent of the nation's African Americans resided in them. In addition, suburban life has been decried as conformist, tasteless, antisocial, and sterile.

To counter continuing suburbanization, private enterprises, along with state and federal governments, have sought since the 1960's to reconstruct and revitalize central cities. Detroit's Renaissance Center, Baltimore's Inner Harbor, San Francisco's Ghirardelli Square, Boston's Quincy Market, and Buffalo's and Pittsburgh's downtown stadium complexes are examples of such revitalization projects, most of which included new, affordable housing as well. Affluent individuals and groups of professionals also have contributed modestly to this process by gentrifying older central city neighborhoods; that is, converting and updating old housing into town houses, art colonies, and professional offices. These efforts, while beneficial in terms of retaining businesses, encouraging tourism, and partially improving the appearances of central cities, have not significantly counteracted suburbanization or dramatically improved the lives and economic opportunities of inner city residents.

Context

Suburbanization and the decentralization of both the public and private institutions of central cities have increasingly captured the attention of urban sociologists since the 1950's, the period during which these phenomena assumed unprecedented proportions. In this regard, urban sociologists were following the lead of other social scientists. Among historians, for example, Stephen Thernstrom, Joel Tarr, Sam Bass Warner, and Kenneth Jackson examined the evolution of differing suburban-urban lifestyles, the influence of streetcar and rail transportation on suburban growth, and the emergence of the new, controversial havens that Americans were constructing for themselves on the "crabgrass frontier." Urban geographers and demographers such as Ronald Boyce, Noel Gist, and Dlilp K. Pal concentrated on changing urban densities and patterns of urban decentralization. In sum, sociologists shared the general curiosities that suburbanization encouraged among academics, novelists (John Updike comes immediately to mind), and journalists.

Urban sociologists such as Claude Fischer, John Logan, and Mark Schneider have examined aspects of "white flight," as well as the lure of new, low-mortgage single-family dwellings, clean air, quality schools, and reduced crime rates. M. Gottdeiner and Joe Feagin concentrated their studies on the influence of post-1950 interrelationships between private interests and government policies that quickened suburbanization; for example, the federal interstate highway system, the construction of urban expressways, and incentives for new housing developments. John Kasarda has studied the decentralization of urban jobs, the shift to service and information enterprises within the cities, and the emergence of economically "independent" suburbs. He has also considered the varied impacts of such transitions on urban "underclasses." Changing spatial adjustments attendant on suburbanization and changes within cities have been examined by W. Parker Frisbee, while Neil Smith, Peter Williams, Richard LeGates, Kathryn Nelson, and Sharon Zukin have focused on various facets of gentrification as responses to suburbanization. Not least, Leo F. Schnore, among others, has attempted to analyze "city-suburban status differences," as well as the socioeconomic status of cities and suburbs.

Studies of suburbanization, in the 1990's, generally continued to be highly specialized, but efforts to incorporate conclusions from these works into broader syntheses and cross-cultural comparisons have been made. In 1981, Peter Muller published a broad, interdisciplinary study of contemporary suburban America that drew partially on his earlier analysis of suburban Washington, D.C., while for more general audiences, including sociologists whose fields were not urban, Robin J. Pryor, Chauncy D. Harris, and John R. Stigloe tried better to define and synthesize whatever discoveries could be gleaned from special studies.

Cross-cultural comparisons, which are themselves syntheses of a kind, have also been forthcoming. David Popenoe, in the late 1970's, closely compared the famed American suburb of Levittown, Pennsylvania, with Vallingby, a Swedish suburb, and his study was complemented by David Goldfield's comparisons of a Stockholm suburb with suburban experience in the United States. By the mid-1990's, historical, sociological, and interdisciplinary studies of specific suburbs, in the United States and elsewhere, had appeared in substantial numbers. Harold Dyos's work on Victorian suburbs, Peter Goheen's study of Victorian Toronto, Herbert J. Gans's work on Levittown, Sam B. Warner's study of Philadelphia and its fringes, Mary B. Riley's chronicle of Edgefield, a Nashville suburb, and Zane Miller's work on Cincinnati's suburban development are excellent examples of this genre.

Bibliography

Donaldson, Scott. *The Suburban Myth*. New York: Columbia University Press, 1969. An experienced journalist's popularly written rebuttal of early attacks on then-prevalent concepts of the suburbs as wastelands of middle-class conformity and tastelessness. Intelligent and effective, though for some readers Donaldson's impressionism will seem to lack scholarly substance. Includes annotated bibliography that needs updating and a useful index.

Gans, Herbert J. *The Levittowners*. New York: Pantheon Books, 1967. A classic study of one of private enterprise's most famous, or infamous, post-World War II suburban tract housing developments, a Long Island suburb of New York. (Later, there were two other Levittowns). The author is a noted Columbia University sociologist. Eminently readable. Includes scholarly notes, a bibliography, and an index.

——————. *The Urban Villagers*. New York: Free Press, 1982. One of the earliest studies embodying the compositional theory, showing that urbanites, contrary to popular scholarly opinion, also had intensive social interactions that importantly modified the instrumentalism and impersonality of the society around them. The book's notes, bibliography, and index are all useful. An important, readable study.

Gottman, Jean. *Megalopolis*. Cambridge, Mass.: MIT Press, 1964. A classic interdisciplinary study by an urban geographer on the development of "Main Street, U.S.A." along the Washington-to-Boston East Coast corridor. Contains much material on suburbanization as an integral part of megalopolitan development. Includes many notes, charts, graphs, maps, a bibliography, and an index. Outstanding and essential reading.

Hatt, Paul K., and Albert J. Reiss, Jr., eds. *Cities and Society*. 2d ed. Glencoe, Ill.: Free Press, 1968. Old and in need of updating in some particulars, this book still has not been replaced as a useful reader on most aspects of urban sociology. An excellent introduction for novices, as well as for sociology students concentrating in other fields of the discipline. The book's format makes it easy to select subject matter for special purposes. Has page notes, chapter notes, graphs, charts, tables, and an extensive bibliography by subject, but no index.

Jackson, Kenneth T. *The Crabgrass Frontier*. New York: Oxford University Press, 1985. A careful, well-researched, readable historical analysis of American suburban development from the eighteenth century through the 1960's with future projections. Excellent for those who require a jargon-free introduction to the subject. Includes ample annotated chapter notes, tables, charts, an appendix, and an extensive index. Justifiably, a winner of both the Bancroft and the Parkman prizes.

Peterson, Paul E., ed. *The New Urban Reality*. Washington, D.C.: Brookings Institution, 1985. Includes significant materials on suburbanization and decentralization. Sociologists such as John D. Kasarda, whose studies covered many aspects of the effects of decentralization, are well-represented. Contains notes and a useful index.

Warner, Sam Bass. *Streetcar Suburbs: The Process of Growth in Boston, 1870-1900*. Cambridge, Mass.: Harvard University Press, 1962. An outstanding historical and multidisciplinary study of the development of Boston suburbs, thanks in part to innovations in transportation during the nineteenth century. Beautifully researched and written. Ample notes, bibliography, and a useful index are included.

Clifton K. Yearley

Cross-References

Cities: Preindustrial, Industrial, and Postindustrial, 253; The Concentric Zone Model of Urban Growth, 322; New Towns and Planned Communities, 1296; Postindustrial Societies, 1446; Urban Planning: Major Issues, 2109; Urban Renewal and Gentrification, 2116; Urbanization, 2129.

SUICIDE

Type of sociology: Deviance and social control
Field of study: Forms of deviance

Suicide refers to death that results from a person purposely attempting to end his or her life. No social, cultural, or religious group is immune from the risk of suicide. Each year in the United States more than twenty-eight thousand persons commit suicide. Knowledge of the factors associated with increased suicide risk can be used in the design of interventions formulated to prevent suicide.

Principal terms

ALTRUISTIC SUICIDE: suicide that is related to a high degree of social regulation; suicides that are prescribed by cultural norms and suicides committed so that others may live

ANOMIC SUICIDE: suicide attributed to a breakdown in social regulation or a loss of a sense of belonging

DEMOGRAPHIC CHARACTERISTICS: vital and social characteristics such as age, gender, marital status, ethnicity, income, and location of residence

EGOISTIC SUICIDE: suicide related to a lack of integration of the individual into society

INCIDENCE RATE: the number of new cases of a disease or behavior, typically expressed in cases per 100,000 population, occurring in a one-year period

INDIRECT SELF-DESTRUCTIVE BEHAVIORS: behaviors not typically classified as suicidal that are self-injurious, self-defeating, or self-destructive or that place a person's safety at risk

SOCIAL STRUCTURE: a framework that includes both the shared values of a society and the degree to which people act in accord with social values

STATUS INTEGRATION: a measure of role conflicts, incompatible status assignments, and demands based on status

Overview

Suicide is a self-initiated, intentional act directed toward, and resulting in, the ending of a person's life. While there may be an aspect of chance in the circumstances that result in the suicidal death, the events set in motion are a reflection of either psychotic thought processes or an intentional and conscious effort on the part of the suicidal individual to terminate his or her life.

It is not always easy to differentiate between suicide and indirect self-destructive behaviors. Persons who refuse to follow life-sustaining medical advice, persons who drive carelessly while under the influence of mind-altering substances, and individuals who knowingly ingest toxic substances such as tobacco products may be engaging in behaviors that will prove lethal; however, it would be a rare instance for their behavior to be classified officially as suicide. Even disregarding the preceding complications, suicide statistics are grossly underreported because of a reluctance of medical examiners, coroners, magistrates or other responsible parties to classify questionable accidents (hunting, home, or automobile) or even fairly obvious events (in the absence of a suicide note) as suicide. This tendency to underreport is further exaggerated in countries or cultures where there is extreme outrage or adverse sanctions against people who commit suicide or against their surviving family members. While the preceding factors mitigate the validity of suicide statistics, they do not negate their value for prediction and sociological analysis.

Suicide occurs in all countries and among all peoples. Suicide has been variously treated as an abomination, a sin, a crime, an act of supreme sacrifice, or a cultural requirement. Although suicide occurs throughout the world, rates are higher in developed countries than in less-developed nations. Generally, persons who are more tied to traditional values and have supporting social ties are less prone to suicide than individuals who are isolated from or are not part of a sociocultural network. Worldwide, it is estimated that more than 400,000 persons end their lives by suicide each year. While suicide is a major problem in the United States (with 28,620 officially documented suicides in 1985), the suicide rate of the United States is notably lower than that of many developed countries. According to the World Health Organization, many countries have suicide rates that are more than double that of the United States (Hungary, Denmark, Finland, and Austria among them), and many others have rates that, while not double, are substantially higher (Japan, Sweden, Germany, France, and others). Of particular concern in the United States was the rapid rise in suicide rates of adolescents and young adults between the 1950's and the 1980's. During this period there was a near tripling of the youth suicide rates. In 1988, official suicide statistics reported that 2,059 teens (ages fifteen to nineteen) and 243 children (through age fourteen) committed suicide. As of 1990, suicide was the second leading cause of death of adolescents and the third leading cause of death among young adults between the ages of twenty and twenty-four.

In nearly all societies, suicide has long been considered an unnatural, even abominable, practice. Saint Augustine, a fifth-century Christian theologian, referred to suicide as a "detestable and damnable wickedness." In the 1662 edition of the dictionary *A New World of Words*, lexicographer Edward Phillips wrote the following: "One barbarous word I shall produce, which is suicide . . . it is derived from 'a sow' . . . since it is a swinish part for a man to kill himself." Judaism and Christianity both condemn suicide. The Roman Catholic church continues to view suicide as a mortal sin and refuses burial in consecrated ground to persons who commit suicide. Islam damns the person who commits suicide, with an exception being offered for the suicide which is in direct pursuit of the causes of a holy war.

Through the eighteenth century in England, it was not uncommon for the "crime of suicide" to result in burying the body after midnight at a crossroad with a stake driven through the heart and a stone placed over the face. Suicide continued to be listed as a felony and attempted suicide as a misdemeanor in England until 1961. While suicide was never as universally or harshly condemned as a crime in the United States, many states have laws that designate aiding suicide as a crime, and several states still have laws that make attempted suicide a crime.

During times of war or religious conflict, certain suicides may be viewed as acts of supreme sacrifice. The soldier who covers a live grenade with his body so that his comrades will not be injured by the explosion or the driver who dies as his truck filled with explosives crashes the gate of a U.S. Marine barracks as part of an Islamic Jihad, for example, are held in the highest of esteem by their respective social groups. Under certain circumstances suicide can even be deemed a cultural requirement. In Japan, until the early twentieth century, the penalty for failure or shaming one's family could entail an obligation to commit *hara-kiri*. *Hara-kiri*, which the Japanese more often refer to as *seppuku*, required the disgraced individual to open his abdomen via a long, deep cut that exposed his intestines; this was followed by decapitation with a single blow from an aide's samurai sword. In India, the illegal Hindu rite of *Suttee* continues to be practiced in remote villages. *Suttee* is the voluntary self-immolation of a widow following her husband's death.

Applications

A major problem that complicates the prediction of risk and the development of interventions is that suicide has a low incidence rate. The incidence rate for suicide for the general population of the United States in 1990 was approximately 12 per 100,000. This means that in order to predict suicide accurately, a method that can separate the 9,999 people who will not commit suicide from the one who will must be devised. If one based suicide predictions on demographic characteristics, one would find that an overwhelmingly large number of people who are not at risk would be identified as being at risk. For example, it is known that in the United States, white males over the age of sixty-five are at relatively high suicide risk—there was an incidence of approximately 50 per 100,000 in 1988. If an intervention designed to lower suicide risk in this group were to be initiated, 9,995 people who would not have committed suicide would have to go through the program in order for the five who are at risk to be reached. Depending on how time consuming, costly, and invasive an intervention is, it may not be appropriate to initiate, given the low probability that it will actually reach the individuals who are at risk for completing suicide.

While low incidence rates complicate prediction, they do not negate the fact that an appreciation for the cultural, social, demographic, environmental, experiential, behavioral, biological, and psychological factors can aid persons interested in suicide prediction and prevention. Suicide is greatly affected by culture. Not only do different national groups have different suicide rates, but also persons who share certain cultural practices manifest similarities in methods and distribution of suicides. For example, in the United States young adult males are most likely to commit suicide by firearms, and they are three times more likely to complete suicide as young adult females are. In Japan and India and among the Chinese of Singapore, the suicide rates for young adult males and females are approximately equal, and both groups are more likely to commit suicide by hanging or overdose than by firearms.

A variety of social factors affect suicide risk. In the preceding example of young adult suicides, it is quite likely that the low social status of women influences the rates of female suicide in Asia. Social status has also been associated with *shinju* (the double suicide of lovers) in Japan. In *shinju*, the lovers of different social statuses whose marriage would not be approved may choose double suicide as an option. Other social factors that have been shown to have an association with suicide include economic dislocation, loss of social cohesion, a constricted social support network, poor status integration, social disorganization, subculture memberships, and social deviance.

In examining the association between various social demographic factors and suicide risk, it must be kept in mind that relationships that hold for one national or cultural group may not hold for another. A few examples of social demographic factors associated with suicide risk in the United States include findings that males are more likely to commit suicide than females across all age groups; divorced men are three times more likely to commit suicide than married men; and whites are twice as likely to commit suicide as blacks. For white males suicide increases with age, whereas for black males suicide peaks in young adulthood. Some American Indian groups have suicide rates that are five times the national average.

Environmental factors associated with increased suicide risk include temporal associations, availability of method, and milieu. Regarding temporal associations, suicides peak in the spring, are highest on Mondays, and do not increase on holidays. (There is no association between lunar phases and suicide, and data fail to show a consistent relationship to weather changes.) Availability of method has been consistently associated with increased risk. For example, police officers both have increased risk compared with the general population and are more likely to use a handgun to end their lives. Milieu can also be associated with increased risk. For example, youths who are held in adult jails are at notably higher risk for suicide than are youths held in juvenile detention facilities.

Experiential, behavioral, biological, and psychological influences are also associated with suicide risk. Experiential factors associated with increased suicide include having a family member who committed suicide, a history of childhood physical or sexual abuse, widowhood, and being under stress. Behavioral factors associated with increased suicide include previous suicide attempts, drug or alcohol abuse, withdrawal from social relationships, and impulsivity. There have been a number of hereditary, dietary, neurotransmitter, hormonal, and other physiological factors purported to be related to suicide risk; however, because of failures to replicate findings or flaws in research design, it is not possible to confirm that these biological factors influence suicide risk. Still, certain biological conditions such as terminal disease, substantial recent weight loss, and dementia have a known relationship with suicide risk. Psychological factors associated with increased suicide risk include any of several psychological disorders, feelings of helplessness and hopelessness, an inability to experience pleasure, loneliness, and a preoccupation with death.

Context

In the late nineteenth century, Émile Durkheim, a French sociologist, published a groundbreaking work entitled *Le Suicide: Étude de sociologie* (1897; *Suicide: A Study in Sociology*, 1951). Durkheim's work is of more than mere antiquarian interest. Many current theories of suicide prediction are simply re-examinations and reinterpretations of the processes and correlates that Durkheim initially identified. Whether the more recent theories based on Durkheim's work have validity that transcends the original is not yet proved.

Durkheim identified three primary types of suicide: egoistic suicide, altruistic suicide, and anomic suicide. Egoistic suicide, he wrote, stems from a lack of integration of the individual into society—from an excess of individualism. In support of the concept of egoistic suicide, Durkheim noted that there was a relatively high reported rate among Protestants compared with Catholics; that the suicide rate was lower among families with greater density; and that suicide rates declined during times of war and other national crises. Altruistic suicide was seen in many ways to be the opposite of egoistic suicide. Altruistic suicide was described as related to a high degree of social regulation. While some authors discuss Durkheim's work, as segregating altruistic suicides into fatalistic and altruistic types, Durkheim identified three types of altruistic suicide: obligatory altruistic suicide, optional altruistic suicide, and acute altruistic suicide. Durkheim discussed suicides that are prescribed by, or not opposed by, cultural norms as well as suicides committed so that others may live as prototypical of altruistic suicide. Anomic suicide was attributed to a breakdown in social regulation. Increases in suicides during times of economic crisis and the differential effect of divorce on suicide rates for men and women were discussed in regard to anomic suicide.

In 1930 Maurice Halbwachs, a student of Durkheim's, expanded on Durkheim's findings. A notable contribution of Halbwachs was the support he provided for the concept that sociological and psychopathological explanations of suicide should be treated as complementary. Sociologists Andrew Henry and James Short, Jr., in their 1954 book *Suicide and Homicide* provided a theory concerning suicide that combined sociological and psychological thinking. While their theory was provocative and stimulated considerable follow-up research, their statistical analyses were often inappropriate and improperly applied, thus making their conclusions speculative and of unknown validity.

In their 1964 book *Status Integration and Suicide*, sociologists Jack Gibbs and Walter Martin argue that suicide is inversely related to status integration. Their theory shares some commonalties with Durkheim's theory but reduces suicide to a single type. Given their tendency to redefine status categories, critics have argued, it is difficult to ascertain whether Gibbs and Martin use the theory to make predictions or whether categories are created in a manner that allows the theory to fit the idea. More recent sociological writings include labeling, critical mass, subculture, social deviance, opportunity, and role conflict theories of suicide. David Lester, in his 1989 book *Suicide from a Sociological Perspective*, provides a description of each of the theories listed except labeling theory.

Bibliography

Durkheim, Émile. *Suicide: A Study in Sociology*. Translated by John A. Spaulding and George Simpson. Edited by George Simpson. New York: Free Press, 1966. This book is based on a 1951 translation by John Spaulding and George Simpson of Durkheim's 1897 classic study. Durkheim shows how suicide can be explained through sociological events and processes. His explication of egoistic, anomic, and altruistic suicide serves as a foundation upon which many current sociological theories of suicide continue to be based.

Farberow, Norman L., ed. *The Many Faces of Suicide: Indirect Self-Destructive Behavior*. New York: McGraw-Hill, 1980. The classification, causes, and meaning of indirect self-destructive behaviors are discussed. Noncompliance with medical treatment, substance abuse, hyperobesity, self-mutilation, prostitution, and a variety of other acts that can lead to self-injury or death are included.

Gibbs, Jack P., and Walter T. Martin. *Status Integration and Suicide*. Eugene: University of Oregon Books, 1964. Status integration, operationalized as proportional to the percentage of individuals in a status or role grouping, is hypothesized to vary inversely with suicide rates. While the authors fail to reflect the broad connotation that status integration normally implies (role conflicts, incompatible status assignments, and demands based on status), their work is a significant update of Durkheim's hypotheses.

Lester, David. *Suicide from a Sociological Perspective*. Springfield, Ill.: Charles C Thomas, 1989. This relatively brief (131-page) book provides a readable review of the major sociological theories concerning suicide. Subject and author indexes are provided. The case study that the author chooses to provide as an example of sociological analysis, however, is somewhat weak.

_____ . *Why People Kill Themselves: A 1990's Summary of Research Findings on Suicidal Behavior*. 3d ed. Springfield, Ill.: Charles C Thomas, 1992. Presents a comprehensive summary of information concerning biological, sociological, and psychological factors, based on material available in 1990. The fact that it is an integrated text rather than edited readings is a positive feature. The book is hindered by a failure to provide name or subject indexes.

Taylor, Steve. *Durkheim and the Study of Suicide*. New York: St. Martin's Press, 1982. Four of the most positive aspects of this book are the consideration given to what the author refers to as microsocial forces, the integration of explanatory mechanisms that relate suicide to risk-taking behavior, the critique of official suicide rates, and an explication of problems associated with proving suicide.

Bruce E. Bailey

Cross-References

Anomie and Deviance, 100; Child Abuse and Neglect, 218; Euthanasia, 709; The Hippocratic Theory of Medicine, 890; The Medicalization of Deviance, 1178; Role Conflict and Role Strain, 1655.

TYPES OF SUPERNATURALISM

Type of sociology: Major social institutions
Field of study: Religion

A complete understanding of any given social group is not possible without knowledge of the nature and role of that society's religious sense. Supernaturalism and its subtypes theism, animism, totemism, and transcendent idealism name and define ways in which humans think and act in the religious mode.

> *Principal terms*
> ANIMISM: the belief in nature spirits that inhabit objects or living beings (such as an animal, a forest, or a river)
> EMPIRICAL REALITY: that which is able to be experienced and known through the senses
> REVELATION: a phenomenon by which a supernatural being makes its existence, truth, power, or will manifest; vehicles of revelation include visions, miracles, and doctrine
> SIMPLE SUPERNATURALISM: a belief in the existence of a power (or powers) of a divine, "otherworldly" nature
> SUPEREMPIRICAL REALITY: that which is beyond the human senses; the spiritual
> THEISM: the belief in a god or gods, powerful supernatural beings that are involved with events on earth
> TOTEMISM: the belief in the power of a sacred plant, animal, or object that symbolizes a particular clan or social group
> TRANSCENDENT IDEALISM (TRANSCENDENTALISM): the philosophical conviction that the cosmos and humanity share the same divine life principle

Overview

Religion is a rich, diverse, and pervasive feature of human life. As a subject of study, religion more readily lends itself to description than to definition. The contemporary sociologist Rowland Robertson describes religious culture as that set of beliefs and symbols which pertains to a distinction between an empirical reality and a superempirical, transcendent reality. The distinction between empirical and superempirical orders of existence supports the commonsense use of the word "religion" as the belief in gods, spirits, and other powers that occupy a world beyond that of the natural world; this distinction is also the hallmark of simple supernaturalism, defined as the belief in reality of the "realm of the spirit." In his work *Reason and Religion: An Introduction to the Philosophy of Religion* (1972), philosopher R. B. Edwards offers some family traits of simple supernaturalism: positive conviction concerning the existence of "another world" that somehow conditions the existence of the natural world; the denial of the necessity and self-sufficiency of this natural world; the conviction that some natural events have supernatural causes; the affirmation that there are other avenues of truth besides the scientific method (either "reason" broadly conceived or revelation); and a rejection of the notion that philosophies of humanness and ethics that do not take into account the supernatural are adequate unto themselves.

Within the large extended family of supernaturalism, there is a significant grouping of specific religious traditions that identify themselves by the term "theistic." These include the religions that are most familiar to Western civilization; examples are Christianity, Judaism, and Islam. The philosopher Frederick Ferré, in his work *Basic Modern Philosophy of Religion* (1967), states the three ways in which theism conceptualizes the object of worship: God as being, God as thinking, and God as willing. "God" as used in theism refers to what is most actual—that is, to the reality ultimately responsible for the being of the entire universe. God is held to be the creator of all things, both in the sense of being their primary initial condition and in the sense of being constantly involved in their continuation. The God in theism also possesses a perfect knowledge or omniscience, such that nothing that can be known remains outside the mind of God. Finally, theism ascribes to God purposive, valuing capacities that are reflected in what are believed to be God's preferences. This being so, the God of theism is both a moral agent and an appropriate subject for absolute moral adjectives such as "supremely good," "supremely loving" or "supremely just."

The question of how the supernaturalistic worldview (and, in particular, the theistic worldview) originated, commanded the attention and study of many anthropologists, classical scholars, philologists, psychologists, and philosophers of religion of the late nineteenth century. The anthropologist Edward Tylor speculated that religious ideas had their origin in a belief in immaterial souls that might inhabit individual entities in creation such as trees, streams, animals, stones, or human bodies, but which could exist independently of them. He coined the word "animism" (derived from the Greek word *anima*, "soul") to refer to the belief in the existence of such superempirical souls or spirits. According to this theory, primal people formed their notion of souls from their own experience of dreams (in which people appear in a mysterious and immaterial fashion), visions, and ecstasies (in which one seems to be temporarily transported out of the body). Having developed the notion of a soul distinct from the body, primal people then projected the idea of the soul onto the animals and objects in their environment. Through time, the powers of the many gods were ascribed to a single deity.

Not everyone was satisfied to think of the origin of supernaturalism as an intellectual mistake, as did Tylor. Sociologist Émile Durkheim believed, on the contrary, that a sense of the supernatural had as its original object something very real and empirical: human society. According to his theory, society confronts the individual as a force that requires one to behave in ways that often go against personal inclinations; nevertheless, humans are social creatures, and integration of personal life into the larger life of the community is imperative. Durkheim argued that religion is one of the ways in which individuals accomplish the socialization process. Religion scholar W. Richard Comstock, in his work *Religion and Man*, (1971), offers a summary of this view.

Durkheim, Comstock notes, tied his social theory of religion to a theory of the origin of religion and used totemism to exemplify this idea:

> Durkheim was intrigued by the phenomenon of totemism, that is, the practice of taking a particular natural object or animal and making it into a symbol (or totem) of a particular social group called a clan. Durkheim believed that in totemism the social nature of religion as well as its social origin was clearly demonstrated. The totem figures clearly represented social groups and at the same time led to the belief in distinctive gods and spirits ruling over men.

People of primal cultures are not the only ones to possess a refined sense of the supposed close relation between the spiritual and the natural: In the mid-nineteenth century, members of an intellectual and artistic tradition called transcendent idealism or Transcendentalism sought to reflect their awareness of a unified divine principle in nature through their philosophy, paintings, music, and poetry.

Applications

In a small Midwestern town, a Christian congregation gathers on an Easter dawn to celebrate the resurrection of Jesus and its implication of a new and larger life for themselves. In India a holy man seeks to use the power of "soul force" to change traditional social patterns that have caused unnecessary misery for his people. In Africa a tribal medicine man whirls a hyena's tail in the air in an effort to induce a rain-bearing wind to quench the parched landscape around him; in another part of the continent, a pygmy warrior emerges from his shelter and hymns thanksgiving to the rainbow for ending a terrible storm and deluge. In the Middle East tens of thousands of Muslim pilgrims prepare for the sacred journey to Mecca. A Jewish rabbi ponders the moral gravity of the sacred texts he is diligently studying in order to ascertain God's will. All of these accounts exemplify supernaturalism in action.

The experiential, social, economic, ecological, psychological, and artistic dimensions of supernaturalism should not be overlooked. The Dutch religion scholar Gerardus van der Leeuw points to the "preconceptual" experience of supernatural power as the root of all religion. The power of the supernatural awakens a profound feeling of awe which manifests itself both as fear and attraction. Physical shuddering, ghostly horror, sudden terror, reverence, humility, adoration, profound apprehension, enthusiasm all may be present within the awe experienced in the presence of the supernatural power. In his classic and influential study *The Idea of the Holy* (1917), Rudolf Otto stated that a person's encounter with the sacred supernatural evokes in the subject a sense of "creature consciousness" or "creature feeling." This is the emotion of a creature submerged and overwhelmed by its own nothingness in contrast to that which is supreme. Otto pointed to the universal character of the experience of the supernatural by citing examples from a wide variety of religious traditions as well as from art, music, poetry, and literature. An example is the prophet Isaiah's awesome vision of God in the Temple of Jerusalem (Isaiah VI). A similar encounter with the supernatural is recounted in the second chapter of Hinduism's sacred text, the *Bha-*

gavad Gita, in which the young warrior-hero Arjuna is granted his request to behold the Supreme Being Vishnu. Religion scholar James C. Livingston states that as the human religious consciousness is filled out more and more with rational and moral elements, the nonrational experience of the sacred supernatural may appear to be eclipsed, but it is never lost.

Comparative religions scholar Ninian Smart has pointed to certain sociological and economic ramifications. Among the Australian aboriginals, for example, marriage must be exogamous—that is, a partner must be taken from outside the totem group. It is also forbidden for members of a clan to kill or to eat the particular animal or plant to which the clan is related, except on special ritual occasions. Where food supply is poor, as in the Australian bush, these arrangements have a sort of economic function: By preserving a species from pursuit by all members of the totem group, the danger of overhunting leading to extinction is reduced. Totemism thus coordinates ritual, social custom, and the gathering of the food supply.

Suggested as a modern "echo" of totemism is a group's propensity to invest its identity in a particular nature spirit. Examples are the use of mascots for school and professional sports teams (wildcats, eagles, lions, and rams), lodge names (elk and moose), political parties (donkey and elephant), and street-gang identification tattoos (sharks, cobras).

In totemistic and animistic societies such as those of American Indians or the traditional Alaskan Inuits, nature is respected as the bearer of helpful spirits; there is no needless killing, waste, or pollution in such societies. The "vision quest" is a strong tradition in some American Indian societies. Among the Plains Indians, for example, an individual may embark upon an intense and exhausting search for spiritual knowledge that indicates a proper vocation, a source of healing, or protection for the searcher. The supernatural provider of this knowledge or protection may appear in the form of an animal—buffalo, elk, hawk, eagle, bear, rabbit, or even mice or insects.

Nature provided a rich source of inspiration for the Transcendentalists, who saw the cosmos as an interrelated whole and viewed humanity as illuminated from within by the divine mind. The historian of literature Norman Foerster proposed the "flashes of divinity" in the early American poems of Edward Taylor as one example of the religious sensitivity of the transcendent idealists.

Ninian Smart concluded his work *The Religious Experience* (4th ed., 1991) by noting that the religious experience of the human race suggests important values that should be promoted and protected: the brotherhood and sisterhood of humanity, care for living beings, dispassion in the face of negativity, concern for other forms of life and for nature, the defense of spiritual freedom, and ceremonious respect for all individuals so that each person is treated with dignity. Although the religious history of the human race has been marked by both bitterness and nobility, goodness and cruelty, the beautiful and the ugly, it can all teach lessons to those willing to learn. Whether people feel themselves surrounded by a spirit-laden world of nature or guided by one supreme being, responses to questions addressed to the world beyond the senses continue to be ardently sought.

Context

The terms "simple supernaturalism," "theism," "animism," and "totemism" are the products of the clinical and objective viewpoint assumed by the social scientists of the late nineteenth century. In that period there was a great flowering of interest in religion among sociologists who came to be regarded as the theoretical geniuses of the discipline. These include Durkheim, Max Weber, Georg Simmel, and Ernst Troeltsch. Weber reversed Karl Marx's analysis by demonstrating that certain forms of social life and behavior reflect the religious belief and practice of a society, and not vice versa. The period of Durkheim and Weber arguably remains, in terms of theoretical genius, the high-water mark in the sociology of religion.

From 1915 to World War II, there was a general decline in interest in religion as a serious subject of study among sociologists. In the decades that followed World War II, however, the sociology of religion experienced a resurgence in interest, energy, and quality of scholarship. Anthropologists William A. Lessa and Evon Z. Vogt point out that while social scientists in the nineteenth century were focused on the fundamental question of how various forms of religion originated in human history, the emphasis shifted in the late twentieth century to the basic question of what function religion has in human society. In other words, scholars came to be less concerned with the question of how religions and practices arose and more concerned with the study of what the beliefs and practices of religious systems such as animism and totemism do for individuals and societies, whatever their origin. Certain subjects emerge as important areas for continued investigation. There is a call for cross-cultural research and theoretical thinking that will lead both to a clear specification of those aspects of the human situation which require religious patterns and to a precise delineation of the functions religion performs. The social and psychological problems that are solved by religious beliefs and practices need to be known. Further inquiry is necessary in determining to what extent and in what manner a religious system helps to express, codify, and reaffirm the central values of a society in such a way as to maintain the social fabric of that society.

Bibliography

Carmody, Denis L., and John T. Carmody. *Ways to the Center: An Introduction to the World of Religions.* 3d ed. Belmont, Calif.: Wadsworth, 1989. The basic design of this book is a twofold exposition of world religions in terms of historical and structural (philosophical) analyses. The text demands fairly high linguistic and conceptual levels. An annotated bibliography and tables of historical dates make this an excellent resource.

Comstock, W. Richard, ed. *Religion and Man: An Introduction.* New York: Harper & Row, 1971. A substantial and lucid entry-level text for the study of religion in general and culture-specific religions in particular. The text is occasionally some- what dated; for example, in more recent books, the expression "primal religious system" is preferred over the possibly pejorative "primitive religious system."

Ellwood, Robert S., Jr. *Introducing Religion: From Inside and Outside.* 2d ed. Englewood Cliffs, N.J.: Prentice-Hall, 1983. Without reducing the subject of religion to something that can be explained away as simply the product of history, psychology, or sociology, the author provides a good demonstration of the process of translation back and forth between religion as it is lived and religion as it is studied by academic disciplines.

Foerster, Norman. *American Poetry and Prose*. Boston, Mass.: Houghton Mifflin, 1957. Contains a very able framing of Transcendentalism within its proper context of the Romantic movement. One obtains a clear sense of the dramatic contrast between the Transcendentalist worldview and the prevailing rationalistic thought of the late nineteenth century. Overall, it is a very informed and readable work.

Lessa, William A., and Evon Z. Vogt, eds. *Reader in Comparative Religion: An Anthropological Approach*. New York: Harper & Row, 1979. This reader offers an overview of anthropological findings about religion that spans one hundred years of work. The sections "The Origin and Development of Religion" and "Religion in Human Society" contain significant contributions to the field in their original form. The concluding abstracts of selected monographs on non-Western religious systems is a definite feature of this work.

Livingston, James C. *Anatomy of the Sacred: An Introduction to Religion*. 2d ed. New York: Macmillan, 1992. A comprehensive introduction to the nature and variety of religious belief and practice. By employing a comparative analysis across a range of ancient and modern religious traditions, Livingston exposes the reader to the ways in which certain classic forms of religious life appear in different societies over time. Includes a helpful bibliography.

Needleman, Jacob, ed. *Religion for a New Generation*. 2d ed. New York: Macmillan, 1977. A compilation of readings that constitute the intellectual community's mature response to the questions inherent in what was described at the time as a "spiritual revolution." To the extent that the nature of the questions is timeless, this work is virtually exempt from dating itself.

Smart, Ninian. *The Religious Experience*. 4th ed. New York: Macmillan, 1991. This is the fourth edition of a work by a world-renowned scholar. The introductory material includes a presentation on the dimensions of religion that provides a particularly helpful systematic guide to a complex topic.

Joseph A. Loya

Cross-References

Christianity, 231; Islam and Islamic Fundamentalism, 1022; Judaism, 1029; Millenarian Religious Movements, 1213; Religion: Beliefs, Symbols, and Rituals, 1598; Religion: Functionalist Analyses, 1603; Religion: Marxist and Conflict Theory Views, 1610; Religion versus Magic, 1617; Religious Miracles and Visions, 1623; The Sociology of Religion, 1952.

SURVEYS

Type of sociology: Sociological research
Fields of study: Basic concepts; Data collection and analysis

The survey is the most frequently used research technique in sociology. Surveys are used to examine behavior which cannot be directly observed and represent a valuable research method for gaining insights into important sociological issues.

Principal terms

CLOSED-ENDED QUESTIONS: questions that require survey subjects to respond by selecting one of several answers provided by the researcher

DEMOGRAPHICS: information that describes certain characteristics of research subjects; for example, age, gender, marital status, and education level

NONRESPONSE BIAS: an effect that may occur when a significant proportion of a research sample does not return surveys; this nonresponse results in inaccurate survey results if the nonresponders differ from those who responded

OPEN-ENDED QUESTIONS: questions that permit survey subjects to respond in their own words

PARTIALLY OPEN-ENDED QUESTIONS: questions that both provide fixed answers that the subject can select and allow subjects the option of responding in their own words

SAMPLE: a group of people chosen to represent a larger population; researchers usually attempt to choose a random sample

Overview

Surveys are used to ask people about their behavior, attitudes, beliefs, and intentions. Several steps must be considered in designing a survey. First, the topic of the survey must be clearly defined. Perhaps the biggest pitfall is that researchers sometimes try to do too much with a single survey. Surveys should be kept relatively brief. That is, they should have enough breadth to assess the behavior of interest thoroughly but not be so extensive that they lose focus and confuse the participant.

The type of information to be gathered in a survey depends on the survey's purpose. Typically, information on age, marital status, occupation, income, and education is collected; such information is known as demographics. Demographics are often used as predictor variables. That is, demographic information can be used to determine whether certain subject characteristics predict responses to other questions in the survey. For example, in a survey examining moral attitudes, it might be found that older people show more conservative responses than younger people or that males differ systematically from females.

Questions must be designed to examine the behavior of interest. For example, if the behavior of interest involves attitudes about marriage, questions will be specifically designed to measure these attitudes. There are several types of questions that can be included in a survey. Two of the more popular types are the open-ended item and closed-ended item. With an open-ended question, subjects are permitted to provide an answer in their own words. Although this type of question elicits information that is more complete and accurate, it is also possible that the subject may misunderstand the question and consequently fail to provide key information. Another problem with the open-ended question is that responses are difficult to summarize. That is, subjective decisions are required regarding how to classify and interpret open-ended responses, so there is a significant risk of incorrect classification.

A closed-ended or restricted item asks people to respond by selecting an answer from a fixed set of alternatives. D. A. Dillman, in his book *Mail and Telephone Surveys: The Total Design Method* (1978), distinguishes among three types of restricted items: closed-ended with ordered alternatives, closed-ended with unordered alternatives, and partially open-ended. The first type provides logically ordered alternatives. For example, respondents could be asked how many times they have been married, and the survey would provide the following alternatives: never, once, twice, more than twice. When alternatives do not lend themselves to this format, closed-ended questions with unordered alternatives are used. To illustrate, people could be asked which brand of soda they liked best, and the survey could list the following alternatives: Pepsi, Coke, Seven-Up. Note that when employing restricted items, rating scales are often used. Rating scales allow subjects to provide a graded response to a question. For example, if a question asked, "How well do you think the president is dealing with the economy?" the survey could provide graded responses ranging from "very poorly" to "very well." Rating scales can be constructed in several ways. Kenneth Bordens and Bruce Abbott, in their book *Research Design and Methods: A Process Approach* (1991), provide an excellent discussion of scale construction.

In making a decision on item format, a trade-off between restricted and open-ended formats must be considered. Restricted items permit control over response range. Hence, responses are easier to analyze than responses to open-ended questions. The drawback is that the information obtained is not as rich as that obtained with open-ended questions. For example, if an appropriate alternative response is not provided, the subject may select an inaccurate response. For this reason, the two types of questions are sometimes combined to produce a partially open-ended question. The strategy is to provide fixed alternatives along with an "other" category. Subjects have the opportunity to respond in their own words if alternatives are inappropriate.

Once item format is selected, the questions must be written. First and foremost, they must be kept simple. If a word being considered has more than seven letters, a simpler word should be selected if at all possible. Second, questions should be framed so that they ask only one thing. Third, questions should be precise. Fourth, they should not contain any biased or possibly objectionable wording; it is very important that no opinion be communicated from researcher to subject. Finally, the order in which questions are presented is important. It is suggested that socially important questions

Sociology

come first, that related questions should be presented together, that sensitive questions should come after less sensitive questions, and that specific questions should come before more general questions.

Once developed, the survey must be administered. The administration of a survey can be done by mail, telephone, personal interviews, or group administration. Each approach has special advantages and disadvantages. For example, when using the mail, the biggest concern is nonresponse bias. That is, subjects who do not complete the survey may differ in some important way from those who do. With interviews, whether using the telephone or a face-to-face format, the skills of the interviewer are very important. Finally, with group administration, people may not respond accurately if they believe that someone is watching them.

Applications

If appropriately constructed and administered, surveys can provide valuable insights into behavior, attitudes, and beliefs. If surveys are done incorrectly, however, results can be worse than useless; they may be misleading and potentially harmful. To illustrate, some issues involved with developing a survey to assess high school students' attitudes toward higher education will be examined.

First, the area of interest must be defined: What is meant by "attitudes toward higher education"? For example, the focus could be on whether high school students believe that college will lead to increased self-fulfillment, opportunities for social interactions, understanding of the world, or income in adulthood. Conversely, the survey may be directed at exploring whether high school students believe they have adequate access to higher education or whether they have been prepared adequately for success in college. One or all of these attitudinal domains could be examined, but a decision defining the domain must be made. The domain of whether students believe they have been adequately prepared for college might be selected as the focus of the survey. After such a decision is made, the domain of interest must be further explored to determine exactly which questions should be asked.

Once the area of interest has been defined, one must decide upon the appropriate demographic information to obtain. The best approach is to examine the literature on the selected topic and identify relevant demographics. Regarding the present example, certainly subjects would be asked about their age, gender, income, occupation of parents, marital status, and whether they have any children of their own. It may well be found, for example, that the occupation of the students' parents permits prediction regarding perception of higher education. Next, a decision must be made about the item format. Recall that closed-ended questions are less ambiguous to interpret than open-ended questions but may not produce all the information desired. To settle this dilemma, a partially open-ended response format could be selected. In this way, subjective interpretation can be kept to a minimum without losing the richness and precision of the open-ended question.

With a decision about item format made, the development of the actual questions can begin. First, questions must be simply worded. For example, a researcher might want to ask, "Do you think your high school experience has prepared you for matriculation at the university level?" (The following alternatives could then be provided: Strongly Agree, Agree, Strongly Disagree, Other.) The question, although a good one, is far too complex for most high school students. One can obtain the same information with a more simply worded question: "Do you feel high school has prepared you to succeed in college?" By using simpler terms, it is more likely that answers will be accurate. Another aspects to consider is precision. Questions should be precise but not overly precise. The question, "What should be done in high school to better prepare students for success in college?" is too vague; subjects could say nearly anything in response. The examiner might instead ask, "What changes in high school English classes should be made to prepare students better for success in college?" This question, however, is too precise. It asks subjects to tell exactly how the curriculum should be changed, and this may not be what is desired. Finally, the examiner could ask, "Do you feel you would be more likely to succeed in college if you were given more training in how to write?" This question asks subjects to respond to a specific issue but does not overly restrict their answers.

In writing the questions, great effort must be used to ensure they are unbiased. For example, if the examiners' opinion is that high school does not prepare students well for college, they might be tempted to ask, "Do you feel that high school is a joke?" This question conveys the researchers' attitude and may therefore bias responses. Objectionable or implicitly judgmental questions should also be avoided. For example, the examiner may ask, "How many times a week did you skip high school classes?" This question puts the subject on the spot. Instead it could be asked, "Which of the following best describes how often you missed classes in high school each week?" This question does not force the issue yet permits the subject to provide fairly accurate information. Care must also be used not to ask for too much information in a question or to ask two questions with one item. Regarding the first point, it would not be appropriate to ask students to rank the fifty most important issues that should be addressed to increase preparation for college. This is too much to ask. Nor does the examiner want to ask, "To be better prepared for college, do you think you should get more training in mathematics or English?" Items should ask only one question at a time, especially when using restricted items.

Once developed, questions must be properly arranged. It is unwise to place demographic information at the beginning, as this signals that the survey is going to be boring. Instead, more specific questions should be placed at the beginning. For example, a good first question might be, "Do you feel that high school prepares males for college better than females?" Such a question is likely to catch respondents' interest and get them immediately involved with the survey. One should start with specific questions and then move to more general questions; one should also cluster related questions together. A survey that is too long leads to boredom and fatigue, which in turn leads to careless responding.

With the survey finally developed, a decision regarding administration must be made. Given the susceptibility of high school students to peer pressure, it would be unwise to use the group administrative procedure. With a mailed questionnaire, it is likely that only students with an interest in going to college would respond. This same problem may influence telephone surveys as well. The best approach here, assuming that the administrator has the necessary skills and time, is the face-to-face interview. In this way students could respond to the questions freely, and the accuracy of the answers obtained would be maximized.

Context

According to Alex Thio, in his textbook *Sociology* (1992), the survey is the most frequently used research technique in sociology. Unstructured surveys seem to have been around since the beginning of written history. That is, public opinion regarding various social issues has always been solicited. Structured surveys began to be employed in Europe in the latter part of the nineteenth century. The German sociologist Max Weber, for example, used surveys to attempt to understand how people interpreted their own thoughts and feelings.

Surveys began to be used in the United States around 1900. Early American sociologists used surveys in attempts to understand problems such as crime, broken homes, and racial unrest. Shortly thereafter, surveys began to be used for predictive purposes. Early attempts were far less structured and less accurate than are contemporary efforts. Consequently, they often produced distorted or simply incorrect information. One often-cited example was the prediction made by a magazine called the *Literary Digest* as to the outcome of the 1936 presidential campaign between Franklin D. Roosevelt and Alfred M. Landon. The magazine drew its sample from automobile registration lists and telephone books. In 1936, those people with automobiles and telephones tended to be well-to-do and Republican. The survey showed that Landon would win by a landslide; the results of the election, however, were just the opposite. The magazine's survey was wrong because its designers used a poor sampling strategy.

Following such dramatic errors, investigators began to realize the importance of appropriate survey construction, administration, and sampling. For survey results to produce valuable information, it must be ensured that neither the questions nor the administrative procedure lead the responses of subjects and that the subjects sampled are representative of the population of interest. Surveys are now one of the better ways to gather information about unobservable variables of interest. Because people's attitudes, beliefs, and feelings about a wide spectrum of issues cannot be directly observed, the survey represents an avenue by which insights into such issues can be gained.

A central problem with surveys, however, is that no matter how well designed and administered they are or how carefully the sample is selected, scientists cannot draw causal inference through their use. In other words, they cannot conclude, based upon the results of a survey, that a particular belief or attitude causes a person to behave in a particular fashion. The reason for this is that no independent variable is employed in survey research, as it is in experimental research. In other words, in a survey, a situation is never directly manipulated so that researchers can observe how the change affects behavior. Research in which such systematic manipulation takes place is called a controlled experiment and is considered to be the cornerstone of science. Because sociology seeks to understand human attitudes and behavior, however, there is a wide range of important issues that can never be studied through controlled experimentation. For example, sociologists could never force married couples to get a divorce to understand how broken homes affect adult and child adjustment. Hence, the survey represents an excellent compromise method of gathering such important information.

Bibliography

Bordens, Kenneth S., and Bruce B. Abbott. *Research Design and Methods: A Process Approach.* 2d ed. Mountain View, Calif.: Mayfield, 1991. This book contains an excellent chapter on the construction and administration of surveys as well as techniques for appropriate sampling. It is very comprehensible and well written and is appropriate for both high school and college students.

Dillman, D. A. *Mail and Telephone Surveys: The Total Design Method.* New York: John Wiley & Sons, 1978. Dillman's book is a comprehensive treatment of the most important issues in survey research and represents a classic in the field. Information related to item construction and to administrative techniques pertaining to mail and telephone surveys is emphasized. Suited for high school and college students.

Kanuk, L., and C. Berenson. "Mail Surveys and Response Rates: A Literature Review." *Journal of Marketing Research* 12 (November, 1975): 440-453. This paper reviews the literature on how to maximize return rates while minimizing response bias. Incentives for improving response rates are discussed. Best suited for college students or readers with some background in research methods.

Moser, C. A., and G. Kalton. *Survey Methods in Social Investigation.* 2d ed. New York: Basic Books, 1972. This book is particularly useful for the inexperienced researcher. A thorough discussion of how to ask appropriate research questions and how to refine them so the survey can be kept both manageable and meaningful is presented. Appropriate for both high school and college students.

Singer, Eleanor, et al. "Effect of Interviewer Characteristics and Expectations on Response." *Public Opinion Quarterly* 47 (Spring, 1983): 68-83. This paper discusses how the behaviors of an interviewer can affect responses obtained. Very valuable for anyone considering using the interview approach to survey administration, whether face-to-face or via telephone. It is well written and is appropriate for both high school and college students.

Alan J. Beauchamp

Cross-References

SYMBOLIC INTERACTION

Type of sociology: Socialization and social interaction
Field of study: Interactionist approach to social interaction

Symbolic interactionism is the perspective that mind and self are not innate parts of the human body but are created in the social process of interaction among people in intimate, personal communication with one another. Linguistic communication is seen as a central aspect of symbolic interaction; it constitutes the process that makes human society possible.

Principal terms
GENERALIZED OTHER: the social groups or organized communities which give people their unity or disunity of self
MIND: a process which manifests itself whenever an individual is interacting with himself or herself by using significant symbols
ROLE: behavior evidenced by an individual and sanctioned by others
ROLE-MAKING: the process wherein a person's activity is constructed to fit the definition of a given situation while remaining consonant with the person's own role
ROLE-TAKING: the process wherein a person imaginatively occupies the role of another, looking at self and situation from that position in order to engage in role-making
SELF: a person's representation of himself or herself as an object in the world of experience
SIGNIFICANT OTHER: anyone who has or has had an important influence on a person's thoughts about self and the world
SIGNIFICANT SYMBOL: a gesture that has a shared, common meaning
SITUATION: an organization of perceptions in which people assemble objects, meanings, and others and act toward them in a coherent, organized manner
SYMBOLS: arbitrary signs of objects or concepts that can stand in place of the objects or concepts themselves

Overview

The symbolic interactionist perspective in social psychology is usually traced to the works of social philosopher George Herbert Mead. Much of Mead's influence on symbolic interactionists came through his students at the University of Chicago, who organized and published his lectures and notes in *Mind, Self, and Society* (1934) after his death in 1931. One of these students, Herbert Blumer, is responsible for originating the term "symbolic interactionism" to describe this perspective.

In their book *Symbolic Interaction: A Reader in Social Psychology* (3d ed., 1978), social psychologists Jerome Manis and Bernard Meltzer describe seven basic propositions that summarize the main features of modern symbolic interactionism. The first proposition, and the central idea in symbolic interactionism, is that distinctively human behavior and interaction are carried on through the medium of symbols and their meanings. Human beings do not typically respond directly to stimuli; instead, they assign meanings to the stimuli and act on the basis of these meanings. The meanings of the stimuli are socially derived through interaction with others rather than being inherent in the stimuli themselves or idiosyncratically assigned by the individual. Meanings exist in people, not in objects, and when meaning has been constructed, people act toward the object or event based on the meaning that has been ascribed. For example, the U.S. flag does not have intrinsic meaning; it consists of cloth and dye. Americans attribute meaning to the flag, and when that occurs, they may hold it in reverence or use it symbolically to show disapproval.

The second aspect of symbolic interactionism is that human beings become capable of distinctively human conduct only through association with other human beings. By "distinctively human conduct," Mead and his colleagues meant the ability to imagine how other people feel in given situations, the ability to use symbols, and the ability to behave toward oneself as toward others. This last ability is essential in creating the concept of "self." The roles of the generalized and significant others is especially important. This proposition expands the previously existing view of socialization from the individual's social learning of culture, statuses, and roles, to the symbolic interactionist conception of socialization as comprising humanization, enculturation, and personality formation. Human interaction becomes of paramount importance because it makes possible the acquisition of human nature, thinking, self-direction, and all other attributes that distinguish the behavior of humans from that of other forms of life.

Third, human society consists of people in interaction; therefore, the features of society are maintained and changed by the actions of individuals. Symbolic interactionists recognize that the organization of any society is a framework within which social action takes place, not a set of complete determinants of the action. Social roles and social classes set conditions for human behavior and interaction, but they do not cause or fully determine the behavior and interaction.

This idea sets the stage for the fourth proposition, which is that human beings are active in shaping their own behavior. This view is in direct opposition to the view of behaviorists, who believe that humans passively react to the dictates of specific internal and external stimuli or impersonal forces. Symbolic interactionists believe that humans have the ability to select and interpret stimuli and the ability to interact with themselves by thinking; therefore, humans are capable of forming new meanings and new lines of action. Symbolic interactionists do not believe that humans transcend all influences, but they do believe that humans can modify these influences and in so doing create and change their own behavior.

The fifth proposition is that consciousness, or thinking, involves interaction with oneself. Symbolic interactionists believe that when one thinks, one necessarily carries on an internal conversation. This conversation involves two components of the self: the "I," that part of the individual that is impulsive, spontaneous, and unsocialized by society, and the "Me," which is the social self. The Me is that object which arises in interaction and the one which the individual communicates toward, directs, judges, identifies, and analyzes in interaction with others. This proposition is crucial to understanding symbolic interactionism, for it is only through the use of socially derived symbols in intrapersonal activity that the individual can perform such uniquely human functions as abstract and reflective thinking. These kinds of thinking allow the individual to designate objects and events remote in time and space, to create imaginary phenomena and other abstractions, and thereby to learn without having direct experience of the things to be learned.

The sixth proposition states that human beings construct their behavior in the course of its execution. Symbolic interactionists believe that the individual is not necessarily a product of past events and experience, although he or she is influenced by them.

The seventh proposition states the chief methodological implication of symbolic interactionism. This proposition states that an understanding of human conduct requires study of the individual's covert behavior as well as overt behavior. Symbolic interactionists believe that human beings act on the basis of their interpretations or meanings; therefore, it becomes essential to understand the individual's meanings in order to understand and explain their conduct. Consequently, the use of procedures allowing sympathetic introspection is part of the methodology of most symbolic interactionists.

In summary, symbolic interactionism focuses on interaction rather than personality or social structure, definition rather than response, the present rather than the past, and the human as an active rather than passive participant in the world.

Applications

The concept of symbolic interaction can be applied to any human experience and can describe and explain everyday situations as well as complex social problems. Because symbolic interactionists believe that human beings are not easily manipulated, altered, or predictable, the goal in using this perspective is to understand human complexity, not to suggest how to predict behavior or change people. Among many other uses, the perspective is regularly applied in sociology to understanding social deviance and the problem of racism and racial conflict.

In his book *Violent Criminal Acts and Actors: A Symbolic Interactionist Study* (1980), sociologist Lonnie Athens investigated violent offenders to find out why some people choose violence in their life situations. His subjects described in detail what happened in situations where they committed violent acts and what they were thinking. The data show that violent actors construct violent plans of action before they commit violent criminal acts and that they take the role of a violent generalized other that approves of this type of action in this situation. View of self, type of generalized other, and length of violent career are all factors that contribute to the definition of the situation as one calling for violence. Actions by the other are interpreted; in turn, they influence whether the actor maintains a violent definition or alters the definition.

Violence is not the only kind of deviance that has been examined using this perspective. In *Sexual Stigma* (1975), sociologist Kenneth Plummer examines sexual deviance from a symbolic interactionist perspective and concludes that sexuality is a social construction learned in interaction with others. Therefore, sexual practices that are defined by certain societies as deviant, such as homosexuality, are deviant only because of the prevailing definition, and the reasons an individual chooses a particular sexual orientation rather than another are contained in a process of definitions and interactions. People learn to be sexual; therefore, the question of why some individuals are led to certain kinds of sexual experiences and not others requires an understanding of their interaction with significant others. Like all other human action, sexuality must be understood as consisting of a stream of action involving decisions influenced by interaction with others and with self.

Sociologist Joel M. Charon presents a symbolic interactionist explanation of racial conflict in his book *Symbolic Interactionism: An Introduction, an Interpretation, an Integration* (1992). According to Charon, people who interact with one another form society. They take one another into account, they communicate, role-take, and cooperate. They share an understanding of reality, and they develop a set of rules to live by. The development of society through cooperative symbolic interaction will, by its very nature, cut off interaction with those outside that interaction. This is the basis for racial problems in society. When interaction creates separate societies, as it has in the United States, each will develop its own culture, and individuals will be governed by different sets of rules and will share a different perspective. Without continuous interaction between the societies, members of each will fail to communicate and to understand the other, and role-taking between them will be minimized. If one of the separate societies has more political power than the other, its members will be able to define the other as having a culture that is unacceptable and even threatening to the dominant society. Through interaction, people in the dominant society develop a perspective that is useful for their understanding of reality. Included in this perspective is their definition of those in the other society and the reasons for their differences, as well as a justification for the inequality that exists between the dominant society and the other society. Through this definition of those who are different (as heathens, infidels, savages, slaves, or enemies), one society develops a justification for taking land from, enslaving, discriminating against, or segregating the other society.

Where interaction is segregated, and all people are therefore unable to develop a shared culture, the others will continue to be seen as different; these differences will be exaggerated and condemned. To the extent that people see their own culture as right and true, others who are different will be perceived and defined as threats. This perception of the other makes destructive actions against them appear justifiable. Destructive action against others also seems justifiable if they can be made into objects instead of people. When people do not regularly interact, communicate, and cooperate with others, it is easy to see others as objects instead of people. This viewpoint not only encourages destructive action but also works against efforts to help the other. Finally, without interaction, which includes communication, role-taking, and recognizing the mutual identities of actors who are necessary for cooperative action, no shared culture is likely to develop, and the conflict is likely to continue. In the symbolic interactionist view, social problems such as racism and racial conflict can be understood through focusing on interaction, cooperation, communication, culture, and definition. When interaction is cut off between societies, perspectives cannot be easily shared, the acts of each cannot be understood by the other, problem solving becomes impossible, and emotion and habitual response replace cooperative symbolic interaction between the groups.

Context

Symbolic interactionism is a distinctively American sociological perspective that arose in the early part of the twentieth century and whose roots lie in the philosophy of pragmatism. This philosophical tradition, identified with such scholars as Charles Peirce, William James, John Dewey, and George Herbert Mead, the principal founder of symbolic interactionism, takes the view that living things attempt to make practical adjustments to their environment, actively intervening in order to create reality. Two other theories that influenced the formation of symbolic interactionism are Charles Darwin's theory of evolution and psychologist John Watson's theory of behaviorism. Darwin was influential on Mead in his emphasis on an evolutionary, dynamic universe rather than a static one, which set the stage for conceptualizing humans as dynamic, changing actors always in the process of being socialized. Watson's theory of behaviorism influenced Mead in a negative way. Watson was a student of Mead's who rejected pragmatism in favor of behaviorism, which ignores all aspects of thought and behavior except those which can be observed directly. Mead reacted vigorously to this theory, believing that without an understanding of mind, symbols, and self, human behavior cannot be understood for what it is. Mead believed that as scientists observe overt action they must always consider what is occurring in terms of definition, interpretation, and meaning.

Symbolic interactionism is considered the largest and most influential field in modern American sociology, with a separate society and several journals dedicated to it. It adds to the understanding of the sociology of knowledge, describes the social nature of reality, and explains the power available to those who control symbols, perspectives, and definitions. As sociologist Joel M. Charon points out, symbolic interactionism can be applied to understanding other sociological theories such as the "collective consciousness" in Émile Durkheim's works, the "class consciousness" and "false consciousness" in Karl Marx's, and the religious perspectives in Max Weber's. Symbolic interactionism has also been instrumental in the development of two related theoretical approaches: dramaturgy and ethnomethodology. Dramaturgy, as developed by sociologist Erving Goffman, is based on the premise that when human beings interact, each desires to manage the impressions the other receives of him or her. Ethnomethodology is concerned with the methods people use to produce meaning.

In the 1980's, symbolic interactionism experienced a resurgence within the field of sociology as sociologists used the concept of symbolic interaction in their analysis of socialization, culture, society, and social structure. Several other disciplines, including communication studies and philosophy, realized that the perspective could have valuable applications; this trend is expected to continue in the future, because the nature of reality, the meaning of self, the emergence and importance of society, the nature of symbols, and the importance of human communication are all topics that symbolic interactionists share with these disciplines.

Bibliography

Blumer, Herbert. *Symbolic Interactionism: Perspective and Method.* Englewood Cliffs, N.J.: Prentice-Hall, 1969. Blumer was a student of Mead's at the University of Chicago, and he is largely responsible for continuing the symbolic interactionist tradition. In this book, he integrates Mead's ideas with those of John Dewey, William James, Charles Peirce, William Thomas, and Charles Horton Cooley. He provides a valuable overview of the perspective.

Charon, Joel M. *Symbolic Interactionism: An Introduction, an Interpretation, an Integration.* 4th ed. Englewood Cliffs, N.J.: Prentice-Hall, 1992. This book presents a clear, organized, and interesting introduction to symbolic interactionism. The last chapter is particularly useful because it presents specific examples of applications as well as examples of representative studies using symbolic interactionism.

Deegan, Mary, and Michael Hill, eds. *Women and Symbolic Interaction.* Boston: Allen & Unwin, 1987. This series of articles describes how social customs, institutions, and patterns of interaction create gender differences. The editors take a strong feminist perspective as they try to show the potential of symbolic interaction to link the everyday, public actions of people with the hidden rules of social life.

Denzin, Norman. *Symbolic Interactionism and Cultural Studies.* Cambridge, Mass.: Blackwell, 1992. Denzin's book offers a historical overview of symbolic interactionism, complete with several useful charts, and then examines the perspective as it relates to poststructural and postmodern theory. Although the ideas offered are valuable and thought provoking, the prose is dense and difficult to read; it may not be easily accessible to an audience which does not have an understanding of deconstructionist theory.

Fernandez, Ronald. *The I, the Me, and You.* New York: Praeger, 1977. A lively, thorough book that covers socialization, human development, personality, roles, dramaturgy, reference groups, and collective behavior from the perspective of symbolic interactionism. Contains a complete glossary of useful terms.

Hewitt, John. *Self and Society: A Symbolic Interactionist Social Psychology.* 5th ed. Boston: Allyn & Bacon, 1991. Provides an excellent discussion of the basic tenets and concepts of symbolic interactionism. Although there is no glossary, the terms are defined clearly in the text, and the writing is easy to understand. The last chapter is particularly valuable because it discusses the value of symbolic interactionism and the use of participation and observation as a specific methodology.

Manis, Jerome, and Bernard Meltzer, eds. *Symbolic Interaction: A Reader in Social Psychology.* 3d ed. Boston: Allyn & Bacon, 1978. This remains one of the best and most readable books about symbolic interactionism. Its coverage is thorough and far reaching, encompassing theory and methods, research implications and applications, and appraisals of symbolic interactionism by various sociologists.

Mead, George Herbert. *Mind, Self, and Society.* Chicago: University of Chicago Press, 1934. After Mead's death in 1931, his students gathered their notes from his lectures, together with material from his unpublished manuscripts, and published them in the form of this book. The result is a surprisingly well-organized and readable treatment of Mead's ideas concerning social behaviorism, the mind, the self, and society. An extensive bibliography of Mead's writings is included.

Karen Anding Fontenot

Cross-References

Dramaturgy, 566; Ethnomethodology, 702; Exchange in Social Interaction, 715; Interactionism, 1009; The Looking-Glass Self, 1099; Microsociology, 1192; Significant and Generalized Others, 1748.

TECHNOLOGY AND SOCIAL CHANGE

Type of sociology: Social change
Fields of study: Sources of social change; Theories of social change

Social change refers to the transformation of culture and social institutions over time, as reflected in the living patterns of individuals. Technology refers to the application of cultural knowledge to tasks of living in the environment. As technological advances occur, changes in culture naturally occur. The study of the relationship between technology and the changes it brings about is crucial as sociologists seek to understand today's increasingly technological society.

Principal terms
    CHANGE AGENT: something that provides a bridge between the source of an item to be diffused and the potential recipients
    CULTURAL LAG: a term coined by William Ogburn to describe the situation that occurs when a technological invention, device, or process is developed but the social setting cannot keep pace with changes and thus lags behind
    CULTURE: the beliefs, norms, values, language, behavior, and material objects shared by a particular set of people
    CYBERNETICS: the study of complex, self-regulating, probabilistic systems, both human and technological
    DIFFUSION OF INNOVATION: the process whereby innovative ideas and traits are communicated and presented to people not previously familiar with them
    INVENTION: a novel design that has meaning and a useful function
    MATERIAL CULTURE: the tangible products of human society
    NONMATERIAL CULTURE: the intangible creations of society, such as ideas and beliefs
    SOCIETY: a group of people who interact with one another within a limited territory and who share a culture

Overview

Norbert Weiner, an expert on cybernetics, made a startling pronouncement in 1954: "We are the slaves of our technical improvement. . . . We have modified an environment so radically that we must now modify ourselves in order to exist in this new environment." Others, however, such as Robert Nisbet, a historical sociologist, have argued that "even the most massive pieces of technology can in themselves exert no influence upon human behavior except insofar as they are caught up in sets of human purposes." Social change is brought about by many forces; technology is only one of them. Theorists have dealt with the issue of social change from the time of the ancient Greeks. Many causes have been postulated for change, including geographic and climate factors, the development of certain types of material culture, and the existence of some "essence" of humankind that makes change inevitable.

Technological changes that have had an impact on social change include sources of power, such as nuclear energy; cybernetics and automation (as in the "computer revolution"); changes in transportation including space travel; and the growth of the mass media as forms of communication. Technological advances in the field of medicine, such as birth control and extension of life expectancy, also influence social change, as do other medical issues such as organ transplants, artificial body parts, and genetic manipulation. The mechanisms whereby technology influences social change are of interest to some sociologists; others are interested in the "chicken or egg" question regarding whether social change brings about technological change or vice versa.

A major concern in the area of technology and social change is society's ability or inability to place controls on technology. In other words, is technological change inevitable, or should society exercise controls to ensure that unwanted changes do not "just happen"? William F. Ogburn's idea of "cultural lag" is perhaps one of the most important concepts influencing this facet of the discussion regarding technology and social change. Ogburn posited that material culture changes by a process which is different in pace from changes in nonmaterial culture. The larger the technical knowledge of a society, the greater the possibility of new combinations and innovations. Thus, material culture tends to grow exponentially. Because society cannot develop methods of controlling and utilizing new technology before the technology is accepted and used, there exists a "cultural lag" in creating controls and altering social relationships related to the new conditions brought about by the new technology. Many examples of this phenomenon have occurred in recent history.

Everett Rogers, in *Social Change in Rural Society* (1960), did much groundbreaking work on the issue of adoption of new technologies and the accompanying social changes that might occur. Rogers pointed out that for an innovation to be adopted, it must have relative advantage over whatever it is going to replace (a mechanized potato peeler, for example, should be easier and faster to use than a knife and one's hand). It should have compatibility with the existing values and experiences of the adopters, be fairly simple, and be able to be tried on a limited basis. It should also be easy for people to observe the innovation in use and communicate about it. Rogers also pointed out that, in a group of individuals, there are usually about 2.5 percent who are very willing to try an innovation (they are called "innovators"). Another 13.5 percent are fairly willing to try something new and can be called "early adopters." About 34 percent adopt just before the normative "average" person would adopt a new idea; another 34 percent adopt just after this average person; and finally, some 16 percent ("laggards") tend to resist any change. Early adopters tend to be the most influential in terms of helping others adopt a technological change. They also tend to have relatively high incomes and high social status, and they tend to be younger and more educated than the average person.

Neil J. Smelser, in his history of social change, *Social Change in the Industrial*

Revolution: An Application of Theory to the British Cotton Industry (1959), laid out a pattern of stages for social change vis-à-vis technology which has provided a paradigm for examining social change. These stages, based on his study of the Industrial Revolution, include "dissatisfaction," described as a general feeling that "all is not as it should be." A stage of "manifest unrest" follows, in which people make (in Smelser's terms) "unjustified" and "unrealistic" movements against the current situation; most of these activities are misdirected (when one takes a historical view of them). A third stage involves the search for and assessment of solutions. In this stage there are many innovations and "trial balloons" in a frantic search for improvements that will solve the unrest. The next stage involves formalization of patterns. Testing of various solutions occurs, and some with potential benefit are instituted. Surviving patterns are not always the "best," but rather appear to be those which can achieve public acceptance. Next comes the stage of legitimization and institutionalization. In this stage, innovations become accepted and become a part of "day to day" activities.

Applications

The relationship between technology and social change can perhaps best be illustrated through examples from modern industrial society; among those that readily come to mind are changes related to medical technology, computer technology, and the technology of mass communications. Medical technology, for example, has far-reaching impacts on social issues. Among the issues with relevance to social change are definitions of life and death; how to provide equal access to life-giving technologies to all individuals rather than to an elite few; controlling the costs of medical care; the costs of increasing the life span, with the attendant issues of housing and medical care of the aged; and population problems caused by such medically influenced changes as decreases in infant mortality. The list could continue, making it very obvious that efforts to improve medical technology are not changes which occur in a vacuum; they affect humans in all spheres of their lives.

In addition to the changes mentioned above, advances in medical technology have caused other social changes that might go unnoticed unless attention was called to them. For example, increased medical knowledge has caused increased medical specialization. This has changed the type of training that medical students receive, creating a nation of specialist physicians and a move away from the general practitioner, which was the historic social mechanism for the delivery of medical care. Specialization also has increased the cost of medical care, as specialists can charge more for their services. In addition, specialists tend to congregate in urban centers, creating hospitals which seek to obtain a reputation for medical excellence in a certain field. All these social changes contribute to changes in the accessibility of medical care for the average individual and to changes in how persons obtain routine care.

The computer revolution has changed and is changing the way individuals communicate, do business, and spend their work and leisure time. The rapid changes in computer technology from the mainframe era to the present has affected most people in the United States in the workplace, the school, and, for many, the home. For some people, the computer has become an extension of themselves, allowing electronic communication with the world, as well as a device with which to work, play, and learn. Computerized databases in banks, lending agencies, insurance companies, and law enforcement have profound implications in the area of individual privacy. One's medical records, records of conviction, telephone calls, credit history, and much more are stored permanently in various banks of computer memory, accessible to those who can tap into them.

Telephone networks and computerized access numbers allow many transactions to be made without physical exchange of currency, leading to a day when individuals may not need to carry coins or paper money at all in order to purchase goods and services. Automation of routine assembly, guided by computerized systems, has altered the routine of the factory worker markedly. Secretarial and managerial staff alike also find the computer changing the way they handle work. In fact, there is hardly anyone in the work world whose job descriptions have not changed because of the computer revolution.

The technology of mass communication has changed so rapidly that it is possible for a person born in the early twentieth century to have lived through an age in which there were hardly any telephones to an era of telephones, fax machines, picture phones, fiberoptics, and satellite dishes. Television has brought the world (at least the world pictured by television cameras) into many homes. Interactive television devices, televised shopping networks, and other alterations have made television much more than it was at its beginning.

Given the ability of television to transmit culture to the masses, the widespread adoption of this invention creates a primary example of technology as an influence on social change. There are those who approve of television's mass distribution of culture and others who strongly oppose its potential. Those opposing such mass distribution point out that, since few broadcasting companies exist, the net effect is to maintain an ideological hegemony and legitimize the status quo. These critics warn that mass-mediated culture emphasizes quantity over quality, encourages mediocrity, causes a loss of individuality, reduces creativity, and creates a public addiction. Those supporting mass culture via television say that it gives people what they want, increases potential access to cultural riches, may encourage creativity, and opens new technological horizons.

Some observers (Alvin Toffler, for one) see technology bringing about a reversal of the trend toward mass culture distributed by television. His book *The Third Wave* (1980) foresaw a "de-massifying of the media." Major network television stations are threatened in viewership by such "individualized" media delivery systems as cable and satellite television, video games, rented videotapes, and computer information services. As Toffler pointed out, "All these different developments have one thing in common: they slice the mass television public into segments, and each slice not only increases our cultural diversity, it cuts deeply into the power of the networks that have until now so completely dominated our imagery."

Transportation is another area in which rapid technological changes have occurred.

Changes have shrunk the world so that a traveler can go around the world in a few days instead of a few years. Changes in transportation appear to change people's sense of time and to thereby affect many related issues of how they do business and even plan leisure travel. Speedier transportation implies the accessibility of perishable products from other geographical areas, making (at least for those with the funds to purchase them) fruits and vegetables always "in season." In addition, a day in the tropical sunshine is rarely more than half a day away from any traveler tiring of winter's cold.

Jacques Ellul, one of the most prolific and frequently quoted writers on technological change, set forth four propositions (in *The Technological Bluff*, 1990) which relate to applications of technology and their effects on social change: "First, all technical progress has its price. Second, at each stage, it raises more and greater problems than it solves. Third, its harmful effects are inseparable from its beneficial effects. Fourth, it has a great number of unforeseen effects." In examining any of the technological applications mentioned above, the veracity of these propositions can be seen.

Context

Early sociologists, including Auguste Compte, dealt with the issue of social change as they attempted to explain the growth and evolution of societies with a large-scale conception of the history of social change. Compte saw societies progressing from superstition through a metaphysical stage, in which all things are explained via abstract conceptions and principles, to a positivistic society in which explanations would be "truly scientific." Herbert Spencer laid out a formula for progressive evolutionary change in his works in the late nineteenth century. Most of the individuals trying to produce one evolutionary model of social change eventually were replaced by sociologists who dealt with more small-scale aspects of social change.

William F. Ogburn was one of the most influential sociologists working in the area of technology and social change in the early twentieth century. His concept of cultural lag, previously discussed, has influenced work in social change from the 1920's to the present. Ogburn and S. C. Gilfillan (Gilfillan published *The Sociology of Invention* in 1935) held the view that social change arises as a result of technological innovations and that, if the time is ripe, the appropriate technological invention will arise. In other words, technological ideas combine and recombine to form new inventions, which cause social change when material culture has accumulated sufficiently to make this happen.

Numerous scholars (sociologists, anthropologists, and others) point to specific technological changes which they feel have been the major force in terms of social change. These scholars include historian Louis Mumford, who cites the clock as a key machine of the modern age. In the 1950's, Fred Cottrell proposed that technological advances in the area of energy were the prime movers in terms of social change. Other scholars who have studied technology as a major force in social change include S. McKee Rosen and Laura Rosen (*Technological and Social Change*, 1941), Meyer Nimkoff (*Technology and the Changing Family*, 1955), and Gerhard Lenski and Jean

Lenski. Such popular works as Toffler's *Future Shock* (1970) and *The Third Wave* have highlighted the effects of mass communications, the "knowledge explosion," and the computer revolution on individuals and societies. These books have also pointed out the social effects of increasingly rapid change experienced by those living in current decades.

Critical theorists point out that any "technological revolution" affects the haves and have-nots in society inequitably. The tensions and conflicts generated between these groups also lead to social change, which is sometimes gradual, sometimes revolutionary. Access to the benefits of technology is not equally available to all, thus leading to other sources of social change and unrest.

Bibliography

Ellul, Jacques. *The Technological Bluff.* Translated by Geoffrey W. Bromiley. Grand Rapids, Mich.: Eerdmans, 1990. Somewhat more optimistic than his earlier book, this details the events of the thirty years since Ellul wrote *The Technological Society*, pointing out his correct predictions and raising issues regarding social change vis-à-vis technology.

_____ . *The Technological Society.* Translated by John Wilkinson. New York: Alfred A. Knopf, 1964. A somewhat pessimistic work, warning of the problems of subordinating science to technology and interpolating the potential risks and dangers of such a scenario.

Haferkamp, Hans, and Neil J. Smelser, eds. *Social Change and Modernity.* Berkeley: University of California Press, 1992. Contains chapters by influential individuals such as Alain Touraine and Neil Smelser. Especially relevant to this topic are sections on information technology, external and internal factors in theories of social change, and critical appraisals of theories of social change as technology is involved.

Ogburn, William F. *Social Change with Respect to Culture and Original Nature.* New York: B. W. Huebsch, 1922. Ogburn's classic work outlining his theory and the concept of cultural lag.

Ryan, Bryce F. *Social and Cultural Change.* New York: Ronald Press, 1969. A readable text in the general area of social change. The chapter "Technological Change in Contemporary Society" is most useful to this particular topic; however, the chapters on theories of causation, innovation, and diffusion are also extremely helpful. Includes a very good bibliography up to the time of its publication.

Scott, William G., Terence R. Mitchell, and Philip H. Birnbarum. "Technology and Organization Structure." In *Organizational Theory: A Structural and Behavioral Analysis.* Homewood, Ill.: Richard D. Irwin, 1981. This chapter provides an excellent view of technology and social change, discussing how technology affects management, the worker, and all aspects of the business world. Readable and illustrated with many charts and diagrams. Good bibliography.

M. C. Ware

Cross-References

The Agricultural Revolution, 67; Culture: Material and Expressive Culture, 430; Culture and Technology, 443; The Industrial Revolution and Mass Production, 946; Postindustrial Societies, 1446; Social Change: Evolutionary and Cyclical Theories, 1773; Social Change: Functionalism versus Historical Materialism, 1779; Social Change: Sources of Change, 1786.

TERRORISM AND POLITICS

Type of sociology: Major social institutions
Field of study: Politics and the state

Terrorism is a political tactic intended to produce intimidation through the use or threatened use of violence. It has become an increasingly common feature of political disputes at both the domestic and international levels.

Principal terms
COUNTERTERRORISM: government efforts to defeat terrorist activities; terrorist actions by governments against individuals, groups, or sympathizers identified as terrorists
HOSTAGE-TAKING: holding a person captive for publicity purposes or for ransom; release may be linked to some political objective
LOW-INTENSITY WARFARE: conflicts that are limited in scope; particularly in terms of the weaponry involved; examples are terrorism, guerrilla warfare, and insurgencies
NARCOTERRORISM: the use of terrorist tactics by those involved in international narcotics traffic
SKYJACKING: holding aircraft and/or their passengers hostage
STATE-SPONSORED TERRORISM: the supporting of terrorists in one country by the government of another country
STOCKHOLM SYNDROME: a condition in which hostages begin to identify with or sympathize with their captors
TERRORISM FROM ABOVE: the use of terrorism by official organs of the state against their own people
TERRORISM FROM BELOW: the use of terrorism by individuals or groups against official organs of the state

Overview

There are nearly as many definitions of terrorism as there are commentaries on the subject. In his book *Political Terrorism: A Research Guide to Concepts, Theories, Data Bases, and Literature* (1984), Alex P. Schmid counted more than one hundred definitions produced between 1936 and 1983. Most have at least one thing in common: Violence or the threat of violence is employed in order to frighten or intimidate people as a means of achieving a goal that is usually unrelated to the violence itself. Terrorists do not attack governments directly with the object of seizing power, although that may be their ultimate goal. Terrorists are too weak to confront directly the instruments of state security, such as the police and the military. Instead, they attack citizens in order to create anxiety and weaken public support for the government or its policies. Victims serve as examples to others.

The appeal of terrorism as a political tactic derives from the simple fact that it is based on a distinctive, normal aspect of human psychology and behavior. Every child learns early in the process of socialization that it is possible to influence the behavior of others by using or threatening to use violence. Terrorism differs from crimes such as robbery and extortion only in terms of the character of the goals that are sought. Crimes are committed for tangible monetary rewards; terrorism is tied to political goals that may be intangible. As a political tactic, terrorism is as old as society. People individually and in groups have sought, through intimidation, to gain or retain influence over one another in pursuit of their respective ends.

The core word "terror" is itself of fairly recent origin. It derives from the French Revolution and the period known as the Reign of Terror. Despite this link, terrorism has a narrower meaning than that conveyed by the Reign of Terror, which was a widespread campaign of violence against the class enemies of the revolutionaries. The Reign of Terror was an end in itself; terrorism is a means to an end.

The issue of defining terrorism is further clouded by the fact that the subject carries a heavy load of moral baggage. There is a pronounced tendency among practitioners, governments, and analysts alike to differentiate between good and bad terrorism (legitimate and illegitimate uses of violence, for example). Those using tactics of violence and intimidation (terrorism) in pursuit of causes deemed worthy by observers or by terrorists themselves are frequently called "freedom fighters" or "guerrillas." The term "terrorism," which nowadays carries with it a strong negative connotation, is reserved for those whose goals are considered illegitimate.

In its most common usage, terrorism refers to acts committed by individuals or groups against the state or other forms of authority such as economic institutions. This is sometimes referred to as "terrorism from below." In this sense, terrorism has received its most detailed treatment at the historical and theoretical levels. An extensive literature is contained in the writings of Marxist revolutionaries and others of similar beliefs. Another group that attempted to develop systematic arguments justifying the use of violence to achieve political ends was that of the anarchists, who were represented by such advocates as Michael Bakunin and Peter Kropotkin.

A form of terrorism that has received far less attention than terrorism from below but is much more common and considerably more effective is official or state terrorism, or "terrorism from above." This is the use or threatened use of violence by agents of the state or other authoritative institutions (businesses or landlords, for example), which is intended to produce changes in or to maintain established patterns of behavior. There are many historical examples of this kind of terrorism, and few societies have failed to experience it. Given its near monopoly of coercive power, it is relatively easy for the state to intimidate citizens by means of incarceration, corporal punishment, or execution. Nonstate groups or institutions use terrorism in the form of beatings, lynchings, or property destruction. Given their disorganization and general political and economic weakness, targets of this type of terrorism are highly vulnerable.

Terrorism attracted attention during the nineteenth century, when civil violence associated with revolutionary movements increased in frequency and visibility. The incidence of terrorism and other forms of political violence increased dramatically during the first half of the twentieth century. Terrorism has become even more commonplace in recent times, and at one point, president Ronald Reagan declared international terrorism to be the most serious threat to international peace and stability.

Most terrorism is associated with domestic political processes in individual countries. The foundations of such activities include ethnic, religious, tribal, and linguistic rivalries as well as other kinds of social differentiation. The purpose of such terrorism is to gain or retain political or economic status. A newer form of terrorism is international in scope. This is the involvement in terrorist activities by a group of people or government in one country in the internal affairs of a group of people or government in another country. One example is the support provided by American Irish Catholics for the Irish Republican Army. International terrorism attracts considerable attention, although it is not as important as the domestic form.

The growing significance of terrorism is attributable to three factors that are characteristic of the modern world: urbanization, technological change, and expanded communications. In large cities, terrorists have many targets to choose from; government offices, businesses, and industrial facilities are usually located in urban areas. The people who work in these facilities are extremely vulnerable, especially as they travel between their homes and their places of work. Terrorists are also less likely to be caught in cities, where there are more places to hide and social linkages are weaker, than in rural areas. The terrorist's weapon of choice—explosives—has become easily obtainable, reliable to use, and hard to detect. Bombs are favored by terrorists because they affect many people at the same time, do extensive damage, and promote the shadowy, ominous image that terrorists prefer. Perhaps most important, modern communications, and especially television, vastly expand the terrorist's potential audience. Viewing the results of terrorist incidents on television promotes public fear and anxiety and publicizes terrorists' demands.

Despite the frequency of its occurrence and the attention it attracts, terrorism (other than official terrorism) is not particularly effective. Few examples can be cited in which terrorism alone has achieved its intended political goals. (The *goals* of terrorism—that is, its long-term strategic ends—should be carefully distinguished from its *tactical objectives*. The latter are limited to only the immediate targets of violence.) In fact, the use of terrorism against the state or other institutions is an indication that its practitioners are weak, lacking more effective sources of attaining political objectives such as money, organization, military power, or electoral strength.

Applications

Analysis of terrorism as a political phenomenon and of the psychological characteristics of those who practice it has yielded insights into its causes and has suggested countermeasures. Among those who view the subject negatively, terrorism is pathological; it is at worst a cancer threatening the survival of civilization and at best the activity of misguided zealots. Its apologists and advocates see terrorism as the self-sacrificing efforts of those seeking to achieve liberation from oppression or to right some profound injustice. Terrorists see themselves as fighting evil. A less partisan interpretation considers terrorism as one type of unconventional, extralegal political action that is frequently associated with social, economic, or ideological frustration. As the probability of total war, particularly at the nuclear level, declines, more attention is being paid to forms of "low-intensity warfare," including terrorism.

Approaches to terrorism are closely associated with the way in which the subject is defined and structured. Probably the most common approach is the conceptualization of terrorism in terms of ideology. Ideology provides the motivation and justification for those employing terrorism and also serves to explain why such events occur. In this regard, radical ideologies of the left (which are invariably attacks on the established order) have often supported terrorism and have endured for the longest time. In these ideologies, the state is perceived as the source of oppression, which can only be relieved by radically restructuring the state or destroying it altogether. Advocates of right-wing ideologies have also employed terrorism for the sake of such diverse points of view as those of Japanese monarchists and American anti-abortion groups. In all cases, the target of terrorism is perceived to be so evil as to justify the use of violence against it.

Explanations of terrorism as a behavioral phenomenon draw heavily upon psychology. There have been efforts, for example, to identify and describe a "personality type" that is generally descriptive of terrorists or others who engage in forms of civil violence. In this connection, Freudian theories of personality development have been popular. Terrorists usually come from middle-class backgrounds, although they profess to represent the interests of the downtrodden. Psychological approaches are potentially rewarding but extremely difficult to implement because of the lack of detailed information about individual subjects. There is, however, little likelihood of defining a "terrorist personality." As Walter Laqueur observed in *Terrorism* (1977), about the only thing terrorists have in common is the fact that they are young.

Socioeconomic approaches explaining political violence have probably produced the greatest volume of literature. Among the more popular of these are variations on deprivation theories. These explanations are based on the proposition that terrorism and other violent behaviors arise because of the real or perceived denial of some goal or reward. Those who engage in violence are thus "frustrated" and lash out at what they consider to be the source of their frustration. The remedy would thus appear to be the removal of these sources.

Increased concern about terrorism has prompted governments to develop counterterror strategies and acquire the capabilities of dealing with terrorist incidents. Understanding the psychology of terrorists and developing effective negotiating tactics are among the more important approaches. Many countries, particularly in the West, have developed antiterrorist strike units in their military or police organizations. These are specially trained forces intended for rapid intervention in terrorist situations, for such purposes as rescuing hostages.

Concerns over the threat of terrorism have produced a substantial commerce in methods and techniques of countering it. These include consulting operations that advise businesses and other organizations on the best methods of providing physical security for personnel and facilities. These are also conferences, workshops, and publications dealing with various aspects of terrorism, from the practical to the theoretical.

Despite the attention given to "international terrorism" and terrorism against the citizens and governments of Western countries, the fact is that most terrorist violence occurs in the Third World and is part of domestic political, economic, and social disputes. Terrorism in and against Western countries or involving Israel in some way is most visible because it attracts the most media attention. In fact, terrorist violence of this kind is neither the most common nor the most significant in terms of its social and political impact.

Context

Prior to World War II, most of the literature on terrorism fell into two categories. Scholarly studies included historical descriptions of terrorism and revolutionary activities, mostly in Europe, and analyses of their causes and consequences. The second category consisted of philosophical statements that criticized the political and economic status quo and justified the use of violence against it. Marxist-inspired movements that ultimately led to the Russian Revolution were the focal points of both categories.

Following World War II, worldwide political developments became not only increasingly complex but also were conducted at a higher level of intensity. The use of violent means, including terrorism, became more common. Areas that had formerly been parts of European colonial empires experienced elevated levels of violence associated with independence and secessionist movements and ongoing struggles for political control. Particularly in the Middle East, terrorism became a regular feature of the political landscape.

In the postwar period, the attention of social scientists, especially in the United States, was directly toward unconventional forms of political activity such as terrorism and to the political development of the non-Western world in general. Much of this attention became associated with the Cold War concerns of the United States and its allies. Accordingly, terrorism became closely identified with U.S. opponents such as the Soviet bloc, Arab countries actively opposed to Israel, and leftist movements in Africa and Latin America. Right-wing terrorism and state terrorism, however, received little attention, as did terrorist activities in non-Western parts of the world.

Despite the attention drawn to terrorism and the substantial literature that has grown out of it, there has been very little effort devoted to identifying its underlying causes. Richard E. Rubenstein notes in *Alchemists of Revolution: Terrorism in the Modern World* (1987) that there is a tendency to dismiss the link between social grievances, especially economic deprivation, and terrorism because to acknowledge the connection would lend credibility to the terrorist cause. Since terrorism is seen by most analysts as pathological, it must be continually delegitimized.

The significance of ideological constraints on approaches to terrorism is rapidly diminishing. The end of the Cold War means not only that support for terrorists as part of Cold War strategies is over but also that it is now increasingly difficult to differentiate "friends" from "enemies." These developments are bringing about a less biased approach to the study of terrorism and, presumably, to ways of dealing with it.

Bibliography

Herman, Edward, and Gerry O'Sullivan. *The "Terrorism" Industry: The Experts and Institutions That Shape Our View of Terror*. New York: Pantheon Books, 1989. Shows how academic and government experts have perpetuated views on the subject of terrorism that are frequently erroneous and exaggerated.

Kegley, Charles W., Jr. *International Terrorism: Characteristics, Causes, and Controls*. New York: St. Martin's Press, 1990. A collection of essays that reflect the views of those who comment on and analyze terrorism most frequently. A good source for determining the "conventional wisdom" regarding the subject.

Laqueur, Walter. *Terrorism*. Boston: Little, Brown, 1977. A landmark comprehensive analysis of terrorism as a political phenomenon. Reflects the view characteristic of much of the literature, which substantially limits terrorism to the Western political-revolutionary experience although its existence elsewhere is acknowledged.

Long, David E. *The Anatomy of Terrorism*. New York: Free Press, 1990. This book reflects the official or government perspective based on the author's long experience in the State Department's Office of Counter Terrorism. Despite this fact, the analysis is balanced and weighs the possibilities and limits of government efforts to deal with terrorism.

Rule, James B. *Theories of Civil Violence*. Berkeley: University of California Press, 1988. A comprehensive analytical review of major theories of the origins and characteristics of collective violence within politics. The author evaluates the virtues and flaws of social theories from the time of Thomas Hobbes to the present. Recommended for the serious student of the subject.

Vetter, Harold J., and Gary R. Perlstein. *Perspectives on Terrorism*. Pacific Grove, Calif.: Brooks/Cole, 1991. A comprehensive treatment of the subject which combines perspectives from a variety of social science disciplines. Historical and theoretical material is combined with extensive references to actual cases. Includes coverage of the role of the media, narcoterrorism, and the involvement of women in terrorism.

Wardlaw, Grant. *Political Terrorism: Theory, Tactics, and Counter-measures*. 2d ed. Cambridge, England: Cambridge University Press, 1989. A comprehensive review of terrorism from a strictly political point of view. The author attempts to address the problem of terrorism from the perspective of public policy in the democratic state.

Weimann, Gabriel, and Conrad Winn. *The Theatre of Terror: Mass Media and International Terrorism*. New York: Longman, 1994. One of the few analyses of terrorism that provides detailed coverage of the role of the media. Victims of terrorism are not themselves the targets; a larger audience is. Without publicity, terrorist acts would have little, if any, impact.

Wolfenstein, E. Victor. *The Revolutionary Personality: Lenin, Trotsky, Gandhi*. Princeton, N.J.: Princeton University Press, 1967. This is one of the best attempts to employ psychoanalytic techniques to explain the causes of revolutionary behavior, including terrorism. The approach employed here draws heavily upon the theories of Sigmund Freud, which stress early child development and father-son relationships.

Louis D. Hayes

Cross-References

Authoritarian and Totalitarian Governments, 153; Deprivation Theory of Social Movements, 512; Legitimacy and Authority, 1055; Mobs, Riots, and Panics, 1226; Revolutions, 1641; Traditional, Charismatic, and Rational-Legal Authority, 2064; War and Revolution, 2164.

TRACKING AND INEQUALITY IN EDUCATION

Type of sociology: Major social institutions
Field of study: Education

Tracking is a practice used by schools to place individual students in educational programs based on test scores, ability, social class, and various other categories. Dividing students into instructional groups is a widespread practice. Educational inequality exists when schooling produces different results for lower-class and minority children than it does for other children.

Principal terms

ABILITY GROUP: one type of grouping used in the separation of students within a single classroom, usually based on test scores, ability, or social characteristics, for purposes of instructing students with similar capacities for learning

LIFE CHANCES: the probability an individual has of obtaining society's economic and cultural goods, such as housing, education, good health, and food

MERITOCRACY: a society in which success is based on merit in terms of universal criteria of achievement, not on ascribed statuses such as sex, race, or inherited wealth

SEGREGATION: the act, process, or state of being set apart; for example, stringent separation between racial or ethnic groups

SOCIAL CLASS: a part of a society whose members have a similar share of wealth and who share attitudes, values, and an identifiable lifestyle

SOCIAL MOBILITY: the movement of individuals from one social status to another, usually defined occupationally

SOCIAL STRATIFICATION: the separation of society into levels based on wealth, age, race, or other characteristics that is maintained by the educational, economic, religious, and familial institutions of society

SOCIOECONOMIC STATUS: an individual's socially defined position in society, determined by a combination of factors such as income, occupation, and education

Overview

Schools in the United States have placed individual students in educational programs based on their test scores, social class, and various other categories for more than fifty years. This process, known as tracking, often involves testing students to identify ability and aptitude levels. Scores on intelligence and achievement tests are sometimes used as a means of grouping children by ability. The practice of tracking is based on the assumption that it is most effective to teach students of similar ability. The United States Supreme Court decision of 1967 in *Hobson v. Hansen* ruled that separation of students into fast and slow tracks results in the unconstitutional segregation of poor and minority students. Despite this decision, most school districts continue to use tracking in one guise or another. Advocates argue that placement by ability enables instruction to be directed at students' capacity for learning.

The practice of dividing students into instructional groups ranges from assigning them temporarily to separate groups within a single classroom to creating classes of students presumed to possess similar ability. Tracks or ability groups are usually based on reading and math and assume different competence within the same grade level. Ability grouping typically produces about three groups of equal size in a classroom. Placements are based on a student's ability compared with the abilities of others in the classroom.

Students in different tracks or ability groups have quite different school experiences. Jeannie Oakes in *Keeping Track* (1985) found that students placed in low academic tracks received an inferior education. There were clear differences concerning the content and quality of instruction, teacher-student and student-student relationships, the expectations of teachers for their students, and several other aspects of the educational experience. Moreover, the quality of the education provided varied substantially from track level to track level within schools.

Ability is not a perfect predictor of track placement. Characteristics such as the percentage of minority students in the school are also influential in placement. Variability is also expressed in differences between public and private schools. Tracking is not irreversible, but it is affected by many factors beyond individual control; socioeconomic status, race, and sex. Poor and minority students are especially at risk of being placed in "slower" tracks. Such placement affects students' self-concepts, motivations, achievement levels, and other aspects of school and life chances.

Tracking begins as early as first grade, when students may be assigned to "fast," "average," and "slow" categories. It is often difficult for students to move out of an assigned group because teachers come to expect a certain level of performance from them. Sensing this expectation, the student will frequently perform at this level. Consequently, tracking becomes a self-fulfilling prophecy—the process through which an expectation leads to behavior that causes the expectation to become a reality. The consequences of tracking extend beyond academic achievement; tracking affects future life chances. Schools often track students based on socioeconomic status rather than on measured aptitude or ability. In this way, educational equality is denied to many students who are placed in low academic tracks. This is particularly apparent for minority students, who often come from economically disadvantaged backgrounds.

A meritocratic society gives everyone an equal chance to succeed. In a meritocracy, social status is based on ability and achievement (merit) rather than on background characteristics such as race, sex, or socioeconomic status. The meritocratic principle implies that all individuals have an equal chance to develop their abilities for the benefit of themselves and society. Many Americans believe that their educational system is meritocratic. From its beginning, public education proclaimed equality of educational opportunity. This meant that all children, regardless of their social and economic backgrounds, must be provided a free public education, and that all schools must be equitably financed by local tax revenues. There are, however, a number of recurring problems which suggest that the system is far from meritocratic.

School segregation was ruled illegal by the Supreme Court in the 1954 case *Brown v. Board of Education*. In his book *Savage Inequalities* (1991), Jonathan Kozol comments on education nearly forty years after the Supreme Court ordered the integration of public schools. Kozol examined schools throughout the country and found children attending schools in deplorable conditions a short distance away from beautiful, well-equipped school campuses. He concludes that two separate and unequal school systems, divided by race and class, exist in the United States. Kozol describes rich schools that spend more than twice per pupil as poor schools can in the same metropolitan area. These gaps in school funding appear to be consistent from one metropolitan area to another. Students in suburban communities attend wealthier schools because of higher property tax bases and because of federal deductions for property taxes and mortgage payments.

According to the meritocratic model, as a society becomes more efficient and modern, the nonmeritocratic barriers to equal opportunity for all people disappear. The educational system is supposed to be free of the barriers that prevent individuals from developing their talents. Educational inequality exists when schooling produces different results for lower-class and minority children than it does for other children. Many educational sociologists engage in research designed to establish the existence of barriers to achievement based on merit.

Applications

Equality of opportunity means that all people have an equal chance of achieving a high socioeconomic status in society, regardless of sex, race, or social class. Related to schools, this concept typically refers to equal facilities, financing, and programs. Students who obtain the best educations are more likely to be selected for the best jobs. Sociological research on tracking and inequality in education is extensive. Two particularly relevant topics are teacher expectations and school quality. An examination of these areas demonstrates how inequality in education is characteristic of both individuals and schools.

Teacher expectations are displayed in behavior toward and treatment of students in classroom situations and in teachers' groupings of children. In research published in 1968, Robert Rosenthal and Lenore Jacobson evaluated the effects of teacher expectations on intelligence levels of students in an elementary school. After intelligence tests were administered to 650 lower-class elementary school students, teachers were told by researchers that the test would predict which of the pupils would "bloom" intellectually during the next year.

The teachers were led to believe that the tests would identify the superior students in the class. This was not, in fact, the case: Twenty percent of the students were randomly selected to be designated as "bloomers" even though there was no measured difference between them and the other 80 percent of the student population. The purpose of the study was to determine whether the teachers' expectations would have any effect on the bloomer students.

At the end of the school year, all the students were retested. The bloomer group was found to have made significantly greater gains than the control group. Rosenthal and Jacobson concluded that teacher expectations toward the students subtly influenced students' performance.

The gain on test scores was greatest for first and second graders. The following year, however, when these students were promoted to another class and assigned to teachers who had not been told that they would be instructing bloomers, the students no longer displayed the types of gains evidenced during the previous year. On the other hand, the bloomer students in the upper grades did continue to gain during their second year, showing long-term advantages from positive teacher expectations. Apparently younger students need continuous input to benefit from teacher expectations, whereas older students need less.

Attempts to replicate Rosenthal's and Jacobson's study have produced mixed results. Although not all researchers have confirmed the operation of the self-fulfilling prophecy in the classroom, some have. In her book *Teaching and Learning in City Schools* (1969), Eleanor Burke Leacock reports the self-fulfilling prophecy at work in a study of second and fifth graders in predominantly African American and white lower and middle socioeconomic status schools.

Educational equality exists when students in different schools perform at the same overall levels of academic achievement. This assumes that the resources available at each of the schools are equal. Moreover, educational inequality exists even if lower-class and upper-class students attend schools with equal resources as long as the academic performance of one group exceeds the other.

The 1966 Coleman Report is the most widely known study of educational inequality in the United States. Sociologist James S. Coleman and associates were authorized by Congress to conduct an investigation of the effect of discrimination on educational inequality. The study sought to assess the educational opportunities and performance of minority children compared with those of white children. Beginning in 1964, information was collected on approximately 600,000 students, 60,000 teachers, and 4,000 schools.

The results of Coleman's study were published in 1966 as *Equality of Educational Opportunity*. The authors reported consistent differences between predominantly African American and white schools. Overall, African American students attended schools with fewer laboratories and other instructional facilities, and they were supplied with fewer textbooks. Inequities in school financing account for these differences. Using data from the Coleman report, sociologist Christopher Jencks in *Inequality: A Reassessment of the Effect of Family and Schooling in America* (1972) concluded that approximately 15 to 20 percent less money per year was spent for the average African American school pupil than for the average white pupil.

The Coleman Report quickly became controversial. Although it revealed differences in resources allocated to white and African American schools, the authors also found that the differences in resources accounted for only a small part of the differences in student performance on standardized achievement tests. It was the social class background of the students themselves that explained the differences between African American and white achievement. Coleman's crucial finding was that minority students underachieved principally because they came from economically disadvantaged backgrounds.

The Coleman Report suggested that it was not enough to provide minority children with equal educational resources, because it was the socioeconomic background of the students in the school that had the greatest impact on academic achievement. This finding led Coleman to suggest that the academic achievement of poor and minority children would improve if the schools were truly desegregated. Integrating disadvantaged children with children from predominantly middle-class backgrounds would produce an atmosphere conducive to high academic achievement. Consequently, the Coleman study had a major effect on educational policy and provided the empirical basis for the desegregation of the nation's public schools.

Context

A concern with the relationship between education and social stratification—the status hierarchy in society—was established early among sociologists in the United States. In *Social Mobility* (1927), sociologist Pitirim A. Sorokin described the way social institutions provide channels for social mobility—the movement from one status to another. Schools are among these mobility channels.

Interest in education and mobility increased in response to post-World War II liberal political programs in Great Britain, Europe, and the United States. After World War II, as part of the analysis of status attainment, sociologists concentrated on measuring the connection between schooling and economic achievement. Building on the 1960's work of sociologists Peter M. Blau and Otis D. Duncan, researchers have repeatedly documented that education has by far the largest independent impact on adult attainment.

Once educational achievement was established as a crucial component of social mobility, sociologists sought to identify the characteristics of schools that affect achievement. The Coleman Report concluded that the relationship between crude measures of school quality (such as expenditures per pupil) was weak. The study did not measure within-school differences in educational resources and learning environments, however, and consequently was unable to analyze specific school practices such as tracking and ability grouping. Therefore, the actual educational experiences of students in individual classrooms became a central topic of study. Research in this area directs attention to the impact of tracking.

Studies continue to demonstrate that when students are tracked into separate programs according to test scores or grades, those in the lower-level groups are likely to encounter serious barriers to their educational progress. A school's social class and racial composition also influence individual achievement. Minorities and socio-economically disadvantaged students are much more likely to be assigned to lower-level programs and courses than are other children. Tracking is seen by many social scientists as a major barrier to educational equality.

Sociologists seek to understand how students' educational achievements result from decisions about what schools to attend and what programs and courses to take. Some of these decisions are made by the students themselves; however, many decisions are made by other persons—parents, teachers, counselors, or principals. Among the most critical of these decisions are placement in an academic program and how far to continue once placed in the program. These decisions have important consequences for achievement, because they establish the educational opportunities and ultimately future life chances available for the student. Sociological research on tracking and inequality in education is continuing its efforts to identify the sources of educational achievements and the contribution of these achievements to social mobility.

Bibliography

Blau, Peter M., and Otis D. Duncan. *The American Occupational Structure.* New York: John Wiley & Sons, 1967. A classic work in the study of mobility in the United States. While dated in important areas (for example, the study includes only males), it remains informative in its analysis of the relationship between family background and education, occupational achievement, and mobility. Contains footnotes and separate name and subject indexes.

Coleman, James S., et al. *Equality of Educational Opportunity.* Washington, D.C.: U.S. Government Printing Office, 1966. The best-known study of educational inequality in United States schools. The report (the "Coleman Report") remains controversial and important because of its impact on national educational policy, such as school desegregation. Most accessible to a college student audience.

Jencks, Christopher, et al. *Inequality: A Reassessment of the Effect of Family and Schooling in America.* New York: Basic Books, 1972. A reanalysis of the data used by James S. Coleman et al., while also including additional information. The book is more accessible to both high school and college audiences than is the Coleman Report itself. Contains footnotes, subject indexes, appendices, and a bibliography.

Kozol, Jonathan. *Savage Inequalities: Children in America's Schools.* New York: Crown, 1991. A description of urban education forty years after the Supreme Court ordered the desegregation of United States schools. The author concludes that there are still two separate and unequal school systems, divided by race and class. Written for a general audience. Contains footnotes and a combined name and subject index.

Leacock, Eleanor Burke. *Teaching and Learning in City Schools.* New York: Basic Books, 1969. A well-written description of research demonstrating that negative self-impressions are transmitted by teachers to students through the self-fulfilling prophecy. Readable and useful for both high school and college students.

Oakes, Jeannie. *Keeping Track.* New Haven, Conn.: Yale University Press, 1985. A superbly written discussion of tracking in junior and senior high school classrooms.

The author uncovers differences between upper and lower tracks in the quality of instruction, the expectations of teachers for their students, and several other aspects of the educational experience. Contains footnotes, a combined name and subject index, but no bibliography.

Rosenthal, Robert, and Lenore Jacobson. *Pygmalion in the Classroom.* New York: Holt, Rinehart and Winston, 1968. A report on an experiment in a public elementary school designed to test the self-fulfilling prophecy. While the study remains controversial, it highlights the importance of teacher expectations on the performance of schoolchildren in the classroom. Suitable for both high school and college students.

Sorokin, Pitirim A. *Social Mobility.* New York: Harper, 1927. A pioneering work considered by many to have opened the field of mobility to the social sciences. Although dated, the main concepts and terminology continue to be used, and many of Sorokin's conclusions regarding education and social mobility have been confirmed by subsequent studies. Contains footnotes and a subject index.

Michael Delucchi

Cross-References

Education: Conflict Theory Views, 579; Education: Functionalist Perspectives, 586; Education: Manifest and Latent Functions, 593; Educational Credentials and Social Mobility, 600; Educational Inequality: The Coleman Report, 607; Equal Educational Opportunity, 661; School Desegregation, 1686; Standardized Testing and IQ Testing Controversies, 1966.

TRADITIONAL, CHARISMATIC, AND RATIONAL-LEGAL AUTHORITY

Type of sociology: Major social institutions
Field of study: Politics and the state

Traditional, charismatic, and rational-legal authority are the three kinds of legitimate authority—power that is willingly obeyed and sanctioned by those who are subordinate to it—that have existed throughout history. Legitimate authority is an essential aspect of political, economic, social, and religious institutions, and understanding it is necessary in order to understand human actions.

Principal terms

AUTHORITY: the acknowledged right of those who occupy certain positions to exercise their will over others

BUREAUCRACY: a formal organization that emphasizes the rational and efficient pursuit of goals through a highly structured network of statuses and roles

CHARISMATIC AUTHORITY: authority derived from a person's unique vision, inspiration, or sense of destiny

IDEAL TYPE: a composite of a set of general characteristics showing the essence of a social phenomenon

PATRIARCHALISM: the traditional authority held by the male over his family and his servants; upon his death, this authority passed to his oldest son

POWER: the ability to impose one's will upon another, even if that person does not wish to comply

RATIONAL-LEGAL AUTHORITY: authority based on the formally defined rights and obligations of people who possess official status

ROUTINIZATION OF CHARISMA: the process whereby the leadership of a charismatic figure is institutionalized in an organization

TRADITIONAL AUTHORITY: authority that is based on customs and long-standing practice

Overview

According to the German sociologist Max Weber, a fundamental feature of all complex systems of human relationships is the fact that a minority of people have the ability to control the actions of the great majority. This fact forms the basis for Weber's theory of legitimate authority. He defines legitimate authority not merely as a structure of command that elicits obedience, but as obedience that is willingly given. Authority depends upon the willing, unconditional compliance of a group of people who have a shared belief that it is legitimate for the superior (whether it is a person or an agency) to impose his will upon them and that it is illegitimate for them to refuse obedience.

Weber classified the claims to legitimate authority into three broad types—traditional, charismatic, and rational-legal.

Traditional authority is based on the belief in the legitimacy of an authority that "has always existed." In this view, people have authority by virtue of their inherited status. Their commands are legitimate in the sense that they are in accord with custom, but they also possess the prerogative of free personal decision making, so that conformity with custom and personal arbitrariness are both characteristic of such rule. The most important form of traditional authority is patriarchalism, from which patrimonialism and feudalism developed. Weber says that the origins of patriarchalism are to be found in the master's authority over his household. The patriarch wields his power without legal restraints and is unencumbered by formal rules. All that really circumscribes his authority over his subjects is respect for sacred custom.

Patrimonial domination, regarded by Weber as the commonest form of traditional authority, is an extension of patriarchy. The basis of legitimacy is again the loyalty and fidelity of subjects for their master. The major difference between the two is that patrimonial rulers foster the same relationship with their political subjects that they enjoy with members of their households. If patrimonial rulers use their power to excess, and in defiance of custom, they risk losing their legitimacy. Under traditional authority, obedience is based not on compliance with stated norms and codified procedures but on unquestioning personal loyalty, exemplified above all in the notion of filial piety. The patrimonial ruler depends greatly on the goodwill of his subjects, because the loss of their goodwill would result in the end of his authority. The patrimonial ruler thus allows subjects a share of his own booty, tax revenues, and spoils of war.

Feudalism differs from patrimonialism in that the relationship between the lord and his vassals is a freely contracted one. The vassal identifies his fortune with that of his lord, and his claim to legitimacy with his own subjects comes directly from the legitimacy of the feudal lord.

Charismatic authority is different from both traditional and rational-legal authority because it lacks all forms of established organization. It relies upon no hierarchy of office, salaried employees, technical administration, or procedural rules of any kind. Weber defined charisma as the quality of a person that creates a willingness in his or her followers to subject themselves unconditionally to his leadership. The authority of the leader depends entirely upon the ability to convince followers and disciples that he or she possesses charisma by virtue of magical powers, revelations, heroism, or other extraordinary gifts. The charismatic leader must perform miracles and heroic deeds, continually proving his or her divine mission in the eyes of his or her followers. Unlike the bureaucrat, he or she cannot rest on the security of office; unlike the patriarch or patrimonial leader, he or she cannot take refuge in the sanctity of custom. The charismatic leader has no sway over his or her followers other than the faith that they voluntarily invest in him or her. When they cease to believe in the leader, the leader's authority is immediately annulled. Under a charismatic leader, officials are chosen on the basis of their own charisma and personal devotion, rather than on the basis of their special qualifications, status, or personal dependence. Charismatic authority is relatively unstable and temporary because it exists within the leader, and upon his or her death the charismatic authority must become routinized.

Rational-legal authority is the form of authority that is most characteristic of the Western world. The typical form of this type of authority is bureaucracy. Under the other two types of domination, the authority resides in persons—patriarch, lord, or charismatic leader. Under bureaucracy alone is authority vested in rules. The rules themselves are legitimized by having been enacted by an agency that has legitimate authority to do so, such as a legislature, when this has been done by the legally correct procedure. The rules are generalized, impersonal, and apply impartially to all persons without regard to personal loyalties or privileges. The persons who exercise the power of command are typically superiors who are elected or appointed by legally sanctioned procedures and are themselves oriented toward the maintenance of the legal order. The people subject to the commands are legal equals who obey "the law" rather than the persons implementing it.

In summary, Weber said that the major difference between the three types of legitimate authority is the grounds upon which the demands for obedience are based. In traditional authority, the ruler must be obeyed because this is the way it has always been. In charismatic authority, the ruler must be obeyed because he or she has exceptional powers or qualities. In rational-legal authority, the ruler must be obeyed because the law sanctions this obedience.

Applications

Because the role of authority and its basic structure occur in all fields of human relationships, Weber's theory of legitimate authority can be applied to economic, social, religious, and political activities. Before describing how this theory applies to real-life situations, two issues must be clarified. First, Weber made it very clear that the three types of authority do not necessarily follow one another. His theory was not intended to be a linear perspective of world history leading from charismatic forms of government at the beginning to bureaucratic forms of government at the end.

Second, Weber pointed out that none of these types was ever to be found in historical or social reality in a pure form. All forms of legitimate authority that are found in empirical reality are mixtures of these pure types, although in greatly varying combinations. For example, Weber says that charisma is the source of all creative individual leadership, and for that very reason no other type of political domination, either traditional or rational-legal, can ever work without at least an element of charisma. Neither can systems of charismatic rule achieve even a minimum of stability without elements of traditional and bureaucratic legitimacy. Authority can remain purely charismatic only so long as the number of followers is small, because the creation of an administrative machine and the acquisition of funds make it possible to command people by providing financial inducements. Once such creation and acquisition occur, an element of traditional authority has been introduced. Moreover, the duration of a hierarchy instills the habit of obedience to the office, which soon acquires a force of inertia independent of the personal qualities of the holder. When this inertia develops, elements of rational-legal authority appear. Weber developed the theory of the pure types because he maintained that using clear-cut ideal type constructs was necessary if the social scientist wished to examine reality. His theory is particularly useful in examining political and religious movements.

For example, at different points in its history, the former Soviet Union exemplified all three types of legitimate authority. For more than one thousand years, Russia was ruled by a traditional form of authority. This traditional authority was rooted in feudalism and patrimonialism and was based on the belief that the czar, a hereditary ruler, had been preordained to rule over the country. The czar's subjects were bound to him by personal loyalty and economic dependence, because social prestige and opportunities for financial gain through political manipulation depended upon having the proper connections at the czar's court. As Weber pointed out, however, the traditional ruler depends on the goodwill of his or her subjects, and the loss of that goodwill results in the end of his or her authority. This loss of goodwill occurred in 1917, when Russia's traditional form of authority was replaced by that of a charismatic authority, the revolutionary leader Vladimir Lenin. It is no coincidence that charismatic authority often is connected to revolutions. Weber noted that charisma is probably the greatest revolutionary power in periods of established tradition, because the followers of a charismatic leader believe in the leader's extraordinary qualities rather than in stipulated rules or in the dignity of a position sanctified by tradition. Under Lenin's charismatic authority, a revolution was fought and Russia became the Soviet Union. Weber stated, however, that charismatic authority is inherently unstable and temporary. Because charisma is a quality that is innate in the individual, it cannot be passed on, and after the death of the leader there is a crisis of succession that results in the charismatic authority reverting either to a more traditional type of authority or to a legal-rational authority, depending upon how the charisma is routinized. If a successor to the charismatic leader is chosen, then the emerging authority will be traditional. If the charismatic leader's beliefs and opinions are put in the form of law, then the new authority will be rational-legal. In the case of the Soviet Union, Lenin's charismatic authority was transformed into rational-legal authority. After Lenin's death, the new head of the country, Joseph Stalin, started the process of turning the Soviet Union into a bureaucracy. Russia remained under rational-legal authority even after the breakup of the Soviet Union in 1991.

When examining religious movements, the routinization of charisma becomes especially important, because most religions are founded by charismatic leaders. In many cases, the leadership of the charismatic founder is institutionalized by the establishment of worship rituals and the emergence of a clergy that preaches the principles enunciated by the leader. This process of routinization of charisma takes the emotional and personal aspects of the charismatic authority and transforms them into an organization that has established rules and patterns of authority. One example of the way in which charisma is routinized can be found in Islam.

Weber used Muhammad, the founder of Islam, as an example of a charismatic leader who gathered followers through his powers of persuasion and leadership, becoming the founder of a new religion. The routinization of Muhammad's charisma was possible because his principles and beliefs were written down for his followers and achieved a rational-legal authority of their own. In countries such as Saudi Arabia and Iran, these laws provide the main basis of political government, and any demarcation between civil law and religious law is very difficult to make. Islam can therefore be said to have changed from operating under a charismatic authority when Muhammad was alive to operating under a rational-legal authority today.

Context

Weber's theory of legitimate authority developed out of his earliest work as a social scientist, which dealt with status groups and the influence of ideas on behavior. This interest led him to write about the sociology of religion, which dealt with, among other things, the power of individual religious leaders or of status groups such as priests in their relations with the masses. The phenomenon of power became a dominant theme in all of Weber's later work. Unfortunately, many of these works were not readily available to the public. When Weber died in 1920 at the age of fifty-six, he left behind a series of incomplete works that had to be edited and published posthumously. Among these works was the essay in which he put forth his theory of traditional, charismatic, and rational-legal authority. This essay did not become available in the United States until thirty-seven years after Weber's death, when it was translated and edited by sociologist Talcott Parsons and published as *The Theory of Social and Economic Organizations* (1947).

The roots of Weber's theory of the three pure types of legitimate authority can be traced back as far as the Greek philosopher Aristotle's theory of three forms of government circulating: from monarchy to oligarchy to democracy, then back to monarchy. Weber extended the concept of legitimate authority to encompass not only government but also all human social activity, including religious and economic actions.

Issues of power, domination, and legitimate authority were of primary concern to Weber. He believed that societies and subcultures were held together not so much through contractual relations or moral consensus as through the exercise of power. Even where harmony and peace apparently prevail, the threatened use of force is never altogether absent. Weber's theory of the three types of legitimate authority is an important contribution to sociology because the individual's social actions constitute the basic building blocks of larger social structures. An understanding of what motivates people to accept authority from others is necessary in order to analyze economic, political, and religious institutions and how these institutions change. For example, the growth of modern urban-industrial society can be seen in terms of a shift from traditional authority structures to rational-legal structures, especially in the growth of large-scale bureaucratic organizations. Weber's strategy of using ideal-type analysis was an important contribution to sociological methodology. Ideal-type analysis enables the theorist to transcend particular events and to engage in comparative analysis using general theoretical categories.

Several of the issues that Weber introduced in his theory of legitimate authority remain of interest to sociologists. For example, sociologists of religion are concerned with the theoretical questions Weber raised concerning the dynamics of social processes in religious institutions, such as the routinization of charisma. Sociologists who specialize in complex organizations frequently trace the beginnings of their field to Weber's analysis of the bureaucratic organization. Weber's theory of traditional, charismatic, and rational-legal authority is likely to be useful to anyone studying power, leadership, and organizations for years to come.

Bibliography

Albrow, Martin. *Max Weber's Construction of Social Theory*. New York: St. Martin's Press, 1990. This is a useful book that puts Weber's ideas into context with those of other sociologists. Albrow gives a thorough review of Weber's ideas. Very readable prose, with many definitions. Provides an index of names and an index of subjects.

Andreski, Stanislav. *Max Weber's Insights and Errors*. London: Routledge & Kegan Paul, 1984. Andreski describes the personal and political background that helped to form Weber's theory; this information is both interesting and useful. He also provides a thorough description of how feudalism and patrimonialism developed through traditional authority.

Bendix, Reinhard. *Max Weber: An Intellectual Portrait*. Garden City, N.Y.: Doubleday, 1960. This is the most thorough book about Weber's theory of authority that is available. It is long (461 pages) but very well-written, and it uses many examples to clarify the main points. Provides good background information about Weber's personal life. Has an index.

Freund, Julien. *The Sociology of Max Weber*. New York: Random House, 1968. Freund is one of the leading authorities on Max Weber, and his book is considered the most comprehensive account of Weber's sociology. Uses extensive quotations from Weber, which is useful because many of Weber's works are not easily available.

Hamilton, Peter, ed. *Max Weber: Critical Assessments*. London: Routledge, 1991. Provides critiques from noted sociologists on various aspects of Weber's theories. One of the best is Talcott Parsons' discussion of power and authority structures. The writing in this book is fairly pedantic and may be difficult for some readers.

Mommsen, Wolfgang. *The Age of Bureaucracy: Perspectives on the Political Sociology of Max Weber*. Oxford: Basil Blackwell, 1974. Provides a good, clear description of the three types of legitimate authority. One of the best features of this book is a very detailed chart that compares the three systems in terms of the sources of authority, forms of legitimacy, and type of legal system that apply to each one. The book also has a good bibliography.

Parkin, Frank. *Max Weber*. London: Tavistock, 1982. A very readable and interesting description of Weber's ideas. Provides a bibliographic sketch of Weber that helps to put his ideas into the context of the times. Gives many clear examples and definitions of Weber's terms. Provides an index.

Wrong, Dennis, ed. *Max Weber*. Englewood Cliffs, N.J.: Prentice-Hall, 1970. Provides a very thorough analysis and critique of Weber's methodology, theory, and philosophy. The chapter on charismatic leadership is especially interesting because it describes four actual political leaders and analyzes their respective charismatic authority according to Weber's criteria.

Karen Anding Fontenot

Cross-References

Authoritarian and Totalitarian Governments, 153; Bureaucracies, 172; Conflict Theory, 340; Legitimacy and Authority, 1055; Power: The Pluralistic Model, 1484; The Power Elite, 1491; Social Stratification: Analysis and Overview, 1839; Social Stratification: Weberian Perspectives, 1866.

TRIANGULATION

Type of sociology: Sociological research
Fields of study: Basic concepts; Data collection and analysis

Triangulation is the use of a variety of research techniques, such as surveys, experimentation, and observation, within a research project. Some sociologists have argued that traditional, tightly focused scientific techniques are not well-suited to sociology; the goal of triangulation is to increase the validity of research exploring the many complex dimensions of social life.

Principal terms

GROUNDED THEORY: a theory that is generated and modified during field research; different from a conventional theory in that theory and data gathering perpetually interact

METHODOLOGICAL TRIANGULATION: a technique in which either diverse sources of data are generated and compared using the same research approach, or data are generated and compared using different research approaches

MULTIPLE TRIANGULATION: a technique in which the same inquiry uses multiple investigative strategies—that is, some combination of research methods, types of data, observers, and theories

THEORETICAL SAMPLING: a technique in which data collection is controlled by the demands of an emerging theory rather than by an existing theoretical framework

VALIDITY: the extent to which the data gathered about a social phenomenon in the empirical world adequately reflect the reality of the phenomenon

Overview

Triangulation, the use of more than one strategy for collecting and analyzing data, is an attempt to come to grips with the complexity of social life. Triangulation is multidimensional; that is, the approach uses different combinations of data, methods, and theory to explore what is happening in a research field.

Triangulation applies a flexible approach to the scientific process of observation. The approach is critical of the rigidity of the procedures used in the conventional approach to scientific knowledge, the scientific method. The scientific method provides a linear approach to research. The step-by-step procedures of the scientific method include selecting a topic, performing a literature review on previous research, defining the research variables for measurement purposes, selecting a sample to represent the population, and gathering the data. Finally, conclusions are drawn based on the findings. Theory (that is, the scientific interpretation of the findings) enters the picture only at the beginning or at the end of the process.

Interest in the triangulation approach to social research stems from a foremost scientific goal, attaining validity. Validity refers to enhancing the likelihood that accurate conclusions are being drawn about information extracted from the social world. Validity is concerned with the one question which is continually raised about research findings: Did the sociologist have all the necessary data for inferring the conclusions that he or she reached?

Barney G. Glaser and Anselm L. Strauss, in their insightful book on the interconnection between theory and research, *The Discovery of Grounded Theory* (1967), develop an alternative to the conventional method of scientific research. Validity is established through the intellectual movement back and forth between theoretical conclusions and the empirical data. "Grounded theory" results from this process. The sampling procedures used in this approach differ from traditional sampling procedures. Whereas random sampling may be used to meet the requirements of a specific research design, theoretical sampling is used when there are multiple sources of data. Theoretical sampling involves identifying the groups that are pivotal for theory development. All the data pertinent to these groups are gathered and analyzed.

Triangulation of data seeks to alleviate several opposing pressures confronting sociologists. Often these pressures present themselves as research dilemmas. Sociologists are pressed to adhere to the scientific method as they conduct their research in order to eliminate potential biases. Often it is presumed that if one is faithful to the scientific method from start to finish, objectivity will be an automatic outcome. Glaser and Strauss, however, mention several ways that the paramount goal of scientific knowledge can be violated if a researcher rigidly follows the conventional procedures of scientific research. In a tightly focused study, many channels that might lead to a scientific discovery are closed off. Also, the likelihood of misinterpreting the data increases, because influential factors are dismissed as side issues that do not fit into the study.

Another aspect of the dilemma stems from the nature of the subject of sociological research, which involves studying human relations and social interaction. The linear procedures of the scientific method make it unreceptive to the dynamic quality of social life. Social life is not a "thing" but a process. Human beings are certainly important units in the analysis of the process, but the process cannot be reduced to individual experiences.

Herbert Blumer addressed the issue of the inadequacy of a purely scientific approach to the study of social life in the book *Symbolic Interactionism: Perspective and Method* (1969). Blumer argued that social scientists deceive themselves when they assume that society has an objective reality, which can be studied by simply defining, isolating, and testing variables. Furthermore, the deception does science a disfavor because a false notion of stability is imposed on social reality. Social reality is not fixed, but flexible and ever changing. Thus, in order to study social life the sociologist must make sense of the entire context of the research scene.

Sociologist Norman K. Denzin extended the notions of Glaser and Strauss and of

Blumer to sociological research in general in his groundbreaking approach to theory and methods, described in *The Research Act: A Theoretical Introduction to Sociological Methods* (1970). Other introductory texts on research methods have incorporated parts of Denzin's approach into their discussions of research procedures. For example, Earl R. Babbie, in the third edition of the text *The Practice of Social Research* (1983), maintains a high regard for triangulation.

Babbie overviews the research techniques of social surveys, experiments, observations in the field, and unobtrusive research. All these approaches contain strengths and weaknesses, but the strengths and weaknesses of each design vary. Thus, a project can be designed that taps the strengths of each while offsetting weaknesses.

Applications

Two methods of triangulation are detailed below. Both examples illustrate what Denzin calls "methodological triangulation." The first example depicts the "within-method" technique of triangulation: One mode of observation is used for data collection and analysis, but data sources vary. Unobtrusive research is the mode of observation in this example. The data include a diverse assortment of archaic materials. The second example illustrates the "across-method" technique: Different modes of observation provide different vantage points for investigation. Survey, experimental, and observational techniques are used in this hypothetical example to explore the topic of changing community attitudes toward health care.

A sociologist wanted to analyze the phenomenon of power as it was revealed in the implementation of governmental reforms demanded by citizens in North Dakota in the early decades of the twentieth century. She relied heavily on historical data generated during those years. The research topic scrutinized the intertwining factors of citizen appeals for change and private capitalism; the first permitted, and the other constrained, the economic activities of the state.

Grounded theory provided an overall framework for the study, while theoretical sampling presented a scheme for data collection. The investigator was aware of the historical limits to sampling. Triangulating the data from diverse sources surmounted this difficulty. The researcher selected two specific, timely issues that cross-cut the fabric of the state: the creation of a state-operated system for wheat marketing and the confiscation of state mines during a winter coal strike. The use of multiple sources of data provided assorted viewpoints that minimized bias. The data included letters from archival collections, legal publications, transcripts from legislative hearings, and newspapers. Newspapers provided a chronology of events from diverse, timely viewpoints, which in turn allowed the researcher to place archival materials in a broader context. Finally, census data furnished the study with a descriptive summary on the demographic characteristics of the state's population in 1910 and 1920.

A second example of triangulation demonstrates the across-method approach (triangulation of research modes). This approach is vital for the study of complex contemporary issues. For example, a researcher has designed a study to examine ways of changing community attitudes regarding health care. The study uses three techniques: surveys, experimentation, and observation.

The survey portion of this study consists of two phases. The same random sample of households is used in both. Research subjects respond twice to a structured questionnaire with a long lapse of time between each contact. In the meantime, the public is exposed to a series of ten-minute media announcements broadcast twice daily by a local television station. Information is provided on the personal savings of preventive health care, guidelines for a healthy lifestyle, and the availability of support groups and social services in the local community.

Survey research has assorted strengths and weaknesses. The ability to provide descriptive snapshots of a population that can be quantified and statistically manipulated is a pivotal strength for this study. The shallow quality of the findings is the major weakness. The research topic involves the complex process of attitudinal change, and face-to-face interactions as well as other interpersonal relations are essential concerns for understanding this process. Other research techniques may be used to alleviate the shallow quality of questionnaire research.

The second technique in this research project is experimentation. A social experiment is designed to examine more precisely the impact of health care professionals on attitudes toward preventive health care. Liberal arts students enrolled in a required course are randomly assigned to one of two groups: an experimental group or a control group. Students in both groups are administered a questionnaire on attitudes toward health care. Students in the experimental group are exposed to a series of lectures and films presented by health care professionals. All students are questioned again on their attitudes. Finally, the two groups are compared for attitudinal change.

By incorporating a social experiment into the project, the affect of a communicated message (the independent variable) can be closely scrutinized. Social experiments, however, contain several major weaknesses. The experimental findings are created in an artificial setting over a brief span of time. It is hard to extend research conclusions beyond the participants in the study (college students). It is also difficult to infer that any measured attitudinal change is permanent.

Both experimental and survey techniques ignore the face-to-face interaction patterns that generally reinforce or change attitudes. Field observations, a third technique, focus on this research weakness. Health care professionals are recruited for this phase of the study. Using observational techniques, these professionals scrutinize attitudinal changes of clients attending workshops on preventive medicine. During the duration of the study, they explore changes occurring in the workshop settings. Diaries are kept, documenting the characteristics of clients seeking information on health care and participating in the workshops. Conclusions reached by these investigators are documented with observations.

While this hypothetical example demonstrates techniques of multiple triangulation, it should be noted that there are still large gaps in the data pool. For example, the private lives of clients remain unexplored. Both examples presented demonstrate the value of using triangulation in empirical research. Triangulation is essential for uncovering the full texture of social phenomena.

Context

During the 1960's, strong criticisms arose over both the theory and the methods being used in sociological research. The political and social upheavals of the 1960's and early 1970's led to charges that the then-dominant viewpoint in sociology could not adequately explain contemporary social phenomena. The "conventional" sociology of the Cold War era was under attack, and the development of research that employed triangulation was one outgrowth of this criticism.

Critics leveled their attack on the dominant theoretical perspective of the era, structural-functionalism (or, simply, functionalism). The functionalist perspective asserts that consensus exists on fundamental values and norms, making social order possible. A number of academics charged that functionalism ignored conflict within society; soon other criticisms were also made. Sociologists with a theoretical focus attacked functionalists for supposing that human actions are guided by an overarching scheme of norms, values, statuses, and roles. Under this model, human beings assume the characteristics of mere objects with little input into the creation or interpretation of their social world.

Renowned sociological theorist Herbert Blumer noted that sociologists should use the techniques of exploration and inspection in their research endeavors. Exploration involves becoming acquainted and increasingly familiar with a sphere of social life that is unknown to research. It is a flexible approach to social research. If the process continues, research proceeds to a more structured and focused examination of the subject matter under investigation. Blumer refers to this as inspection. During inspection, a researcher defines the characteristics of the social units analyzed and specifies the relationships between these units. This phase of the research process is more focused than the earlier one.

Under this new framework, theory and methods exist in an interactive relationship. According to Barney G. Glaser and Anselm L. Strauss (1967), the outcome is grounded theories. Grounded theories are continually generated, modified, and reformulated, with the researcher moving back and forth between theory and data. Another link in the historical process that began with the criticisms of functionalism was the development of a research approach to intertwine theory and methods. Norman K. Denzin accomplished this union by publishing the techniques of such research in 1970. The "research act," Denzin wrote, focuses on the human decision-making process in conducting research. First, a topic with theoretical relevance is selected. Next, guided by the research topic, the researcher examines a theory in the field. Finally, the theory is reshaped according to the new information supplied by the data.

Bibliography

Babbie, Earl R. *The Practice of Social Research.* 3d ed. Belmont, Calif.: Wadsworth, 1983. Beginning with this edition, Babbie's texts have used the same format for introducing students to research methods. The advantages derived from incorporating diverse observational strategies into a research project (triangulation) is the common thread running throughout his texts.

Blumer, Herbert. *Symbolic Interactionism: Perspective and Method*. Englewood Cliffs, N.J.: Prentice-Hall, 1969. This is a key theoretical piece in sociology. Blumer pinpoints the methodological limitations of surveys and experiments when used to explore and interpret social life. According to Blumer, these approaches distort the social world.

Denzin, Norman K. *The Research Act: A Theoretical Introduction to Sociological Methods*. Englewood Cliffs, N.J.: Prentice-Hall, 1970. This text intertwines theory and methods, arguing that theory and methods exist in a flexible relationship. In contrast, conventional modes of scientific inquiry provide only two options: induction to theory or deduction from theory. Concludes with a discussion of triangulation techniques.

_____ , ed. *Sociological Methods: A Sourcebook*. Chicago, Aldine, 1970. Part 7, "Triangulation," provides readings that are particularly insightful. Hovland examines discrepancies in the findings of experimental and survey studies on attitude change. Vidich and Bensman stress the value of using several measures of prestige in community studies. Zelditch reviews the strengths and weaknesses of three research strategies.

Glaser, Barney G., and Anselm L. Strauss. *The Discovery of Grounded Theory*. Chicago: Aldine, 1967. Presents a groundbreaking discussion on developing theory from field research. The notions of comparative analysis and theoretical sampling are leveled at the hidden biases of research efforts that test theories created by academics.

Williams, Chancellor. *The Destruction of Black Civilization: Great Issues of a Race*. Rev. ed. Chicago: Third World Press, 1987. This abridged version of a lengthy study splendidly exemplifies data triangulation. Williams, a historian, challenges the "conventional" interpretation of African history as lacking a sophisticated cultural heritage. He weaves together numerous data sources, including historical materials housed in European museums and oral histories that have been cross-checked for accuracy.

Nancy Balazadeh

Cross-References

Experimentation in Sociological Research, 721; Paradigms and Theories, 1328; Qualitative Research, 1540; Quantitative Research, 1546; Sociological Research: Description, Exploration, and Explanation, 1920; Surveys, 2030; Unobtrusive Research, 2103; Validity and Reliability in Measurement, 2136.

TWO-CAREER FAMILIES

Type of sociology: Major social institutions
Field of study: The family

Two-career families are families in which both husband and wife are employed in professions and/or managerial occupations and have at least one child. Individuals in two-career families are employed in positions that require a greater degree of commitment than do those of members of other types of families. This topic provides insight into families who have achieved a measure of gender equality.

Principal terms

DUAL-EARNER FAMILIES: families in which both husband and wife are employed in the labor market

GENDER ROLES: the socially determined sets of rights and obligations that are associated with being male and female

ROLE: the expected behaviors that accompany a social status

ROLE CONFLICT: a condition that occurs when two or more of a person's roles contain incompatible expectations

ROLE STRAIN: a condition that occurs when the expectations found within a single role are incompatible

Overview

Two-career families are those families in which both husband and wife are employed in highly paid, prestigious occupations. Their occupations demand commitments of time and energy beyond those required in other types of work. The concept of two-career families was first introduced by sociologists Rhona Rapoport and Robert N. Rapoport in the late 1960's and was further explored in their book *Dual-Career Families Re-examined: New Integrations of Work and Family* (1976). This family type is less common than that of the dual-earner family (in which both the husband and wife are employed but at least one of them does not have a career) but has attracted considerable research attention because of its unique pattern of gender roles.

As sociologist Rosabeth Moss Kantor found in *Men and Women of the Corporation* (1977), traditional couples, those in which the husband had a career and the wife was a full-time homemaker, required the input of both partners for the husband's career to be successful. For example, in the early years of his career, the husband was expected to work long hours or to take frequent business trips. A wife sometimes adapted to the resulting loneliness by becoming her husband's informal helper. Also, at this stage in his career, the husband was expected to be geographically mobile, and having a wife who was a full-time housewife minimized problems in flexibility. In the second stage of a traditional man's career, a wife contributed to her husband's success by making important social connections in the community as a result of her involvement in civic affairs. In all cases, the man's career was of primary importance and his wife played a helper role, but his wife's input was essential to his ascent up the career ladder.

In their essay "The Dualities of Careers and Families: New Integrations or New Polarizations?" (1990), sociologists Janet G. Hunt and Larry L. Hunt suggested that in the 1950's a woman with a career was a relatively rare person. There was an implied bargain that stated that a woman who had a career could do so only if her family came first. A woman who did not do so was considered deviant (someone who violates important social rules and/or expectations). Therefore, a woman was likely to choose work that made fewer demands upon her time and resources. It was also believed by employers, as well as by the woman herself, that less should be expected of her in her work because of her family obligations. As a consequence, a woman rarely reached a high position in her work organization. Her husband's attitude was often that he was "letting" his wife work for her own fulfillment rather than for her contribution to the family income. Therefore, there was little expectation that the husband should expand his role in the household as a result of his wife's employment.

The dual-career family type has become more common in the last few decades as a result of changes that have accompanied the women's movement of the 1970's. Many more young women expect to have a career as well as a family and expect to compete equally with men in the workplace. This situation, however, places special demands on women and their families. According to sociologist Rosanna Hertz's *More Equal Than Others: Women and Men in Dual-Career Marriages* (1987), women must satisfy the expectations of two careers without the assistance provided by the traditional stay-at-home wife of the 1950's. Dual-career couples face the problem of family and work roles that are not structured to meet the needs of dual-career families. Most corporate careers are designed for males who can turn over family responsibilities to wives. These careers often demand long hours, frequent travel, and geographic mobility. In dual-career families, both spouses value achievement and desire a measure of self-sufficiency but do not have the benefit of a traditional wife to provide the necessary support that makes this possible.

Most of the burden of juggling family and career falls to the wife. The family is still considered the woman's responsibility even when she has a demanding career. Although husbands may take more of a responsibility in the home to make up for their wives' involvement in careers, their contributions are usually not equal to those of their wives. As a result, dual-career families use the hired labor of women to provide the household work formerly done by the wife. It is still the wife's responsibility, however, to see that the family's needs are provided, and if they are not, she is the one who usually interrupts her work to remedy the situation.

Women's family obligations are reflected in different career paths for women, as was found in *Dual-Career Marriage: A System in Transition* (1992) by psychologist Lisa R. Silberstein. Many of the husbands in her study had a clear career path with few interruptions. Women's career paths, however, were more circuitous. For example, many of the women in the study only developed a desire to move up the career ladder later in life. Other women started careers only after they had helped put their husbands through school. Also, the women in her study were less likely to view their careers as a central aspect of their identity than were men.

Applications

The problems of dual-career families are shared to some degree by most American families today. According to the Population Reference Bureau, in 1988, 65 percent of mothers with children under eighteen and more than 53 percent of mothers with children under three were in the labor force. Even though these mothers may not be juggling the unique demands of a career, they still have to meet the challenge of combining paid employment and family responsibilities. Because women are more likely to have double responsibilities, they are more vulnerable to the problems of role conflict and role strain. For example, working mothers have to spend several hours each day at their place of employment providing for the economic well-being of their families and still find time in the evening to cook dinner, do laundry, and perform other household tasks as well as to meet the emotional needs of husbands and children.

This double day, in which women work all day in paid employment and all evening at home, has been called the second shift by sociologist Arlie Hochschild in her book *The Second Shift* (1989). Hochschild interviewed both dual-career and dual-earner families and found that an important source of tension in working families was the husband's unwillingness to do work at home. For example, all of the couples who considered divorce in her study had husbands who did not share work at home.

The women she interviewed had various strategies for dealing with problems of the second shift. Women's strategies included directly working to change the division of labor in the family through negotiation as well as through other indirect strategies. For example, one wife persuaded her husband to cook because she claimed that he was better at preparing rice than she. Another woman used illness as a way of getting her husband to share in housework. Other women tried to be supermoms and fulfill the demands of both roles without help from their husbands. Others cut back work responsibilities by working part-time, quitting work, or cutting ties with friends from work. Other women cut back on family life, lowering their standards of housecleaning and spending less time with the husband and children. Those who could afford to do so hired household help. Many of these women also cut back on time for themselves, such as time for hobbies or friends.

Some of the husbands in Hochschild's study had a genuine desire to help their wives, although they were sometimes discouraged by wives who did not want to give up their sphere of influence in the home. Other men offered resistance to sharing roles. Some would resist indirectly by waiting to be asked rather than taking responsibility for certain tasks. This created stress for their wives, who had to see that things got done.

In *Two Careers/One Family* (1993), psychologist Lucia Albino Gilbert describes the way in which society has responded to the needs of dual-career families. Federal legislation includes the Pregnancy Discrimination Act of 1978, which requires employers to include pregnancy as a disability. As a result, pregnancy must be included as a condition for receiving such disability benefits as sick leave. It should also be noted that this law did not require maternity leave of employers. Five states, however, require employers to provide maternity leave, and thirteen states require employers to hold a woman's job when she is on maternity leave. Another bill designed to support families was the Act for Better Family Care of 1990, which provided grants for the development of quality day-care services and tax credits for families who use day care.

According to Gilbert, some employers are responding to the needs of dual-earner families by developing policies that make it easier to combine work and family roles. These programs can be expensive but can work to the advantage of employers because they provide a means of recruiting and retaining high-quality employees. These programs also help to reduce employee stress and therefore improve worker productivity.

There are types of work arrangements that can provide the flexibility that workers need to accommodate family demands. Companies can provide flexibility in many ways, such as allowing a person to work part-time temporarily (such as for a year after the birth of a child) and then return to full-time work. Flextime allows an employee to adjust work hours to meet family needs. For example, with flextime, a woman may choose to work from seven o'clock until four o'clock instead of the usual eight o'clock to five o'clock because that allows her to be home when her children return from school. With the advent of sophisticated technology, women can work at home and communicate with the office and with clients through their home computers. Job sharing is another innovation in flexibility. In job sharing, a husband and wife who have expertise in the same field can share one job, thus reducing work obligations. Corporations have also developed programs to assist with child care. This assistance ranges from providing information and referral services to providing day care on the premises.

Context

The dual-career family is a phenomenon that is relatively recent and occurs within the context of the changing role of women in society and the family. Beginning in Victorian times, gender roles in American society were represented by the doctrine of separate spheres, in which the women's domain was the home and men's was the world. There was an interdependence between husband and wife in which each would provide for the needs of the other, each in his or her separate domain. In this arrangement, the husband was the breadwinner and the wife took care of the needs of the husband and children at home.

The functionalist perspective in sociology, as found in the works of Talcott Parsons, reflected this view of the family. According to Parsons, the family has a natural division of labor in which women's reproductive functions make them most suitable to stay home and raise children. Men, who are not restricted by childbearing functions, are freer to contribute to the family through their roles in the broader community. Husbands provided for their families as breadwinners as well as by providing a link between the family and the rest of the community. In this system, husband and wife are interdependent and contribute to the survival of the family by performing the functions most suitable to their situations.

Critics of the functionalist perspective point out that this view of the family neglects the role of male dominance, in which men's work is more highly valued than women's, in determining family arrangements. Men's roles in the community give them more resources and therefore more power, whereas women's isolation in the home makes them more dependent and less able to exercise power and influence.

Over the course of the last century, women have steadily increased their participation in the paid labor force; now, most women work outside the home. Although most women work in female-dominated occupations, many women have made inroads into male domains as well. For example, the number of women graduates from professional schools such as law and medical schools has increased steadily since the 1970's.

Accompanying women's labor force participation is a breakdown of the doctrine of separate spheres and a resulting renegotiation of gender roles to accompany the new realities. As women enter the world of work, they expect that their husbands will contribute in the home. The dual-career couple represents people who are at the forefront of this renegotiation.

Bibliography

Gilbert, Lucia Albino. *Two Careers, One Family*. Newbury Park, Calif.: Sage Publications, 1993. Part of the Sage Series on Close Relationships edited by Clyde and Susan Hendricks, this book reviews relevant research findings on the dual-career family, discusses implications for public policy, and gives predictions for the family form.

Hertz, Rosanna. *More Equal than Others: Women and Men in Dual Career Marriages*. Berkeley: University of California Press, 1986. A study of Chicago area corporate families with an emphasis on the interconnection of couples' careers and the family as a third career. Appendices include research methods and interview schedule.

Hochschild, Arlie, with Anne Machung. *The Second Shift*. New York: Viking, 1989. A study of dual-earner and dual-career families in the San Francisco Bay Area. Gives examples of types of couples and their responses to the demands of dual-career family life. Appendices include a description of methods and an interview schedule.

Hunt, Janet G., and Larry L. Hunt. "The Dualities of Careers and Families: New Integrations or New Polarization?" In *Perspectives on the Family*, edited by Christopher Carlson. Belmont, Calif.: Wadsworth, 1990. Views the dual-career family in historical perspective.

Kanter, Rosabeth Moss. *Men and Women of the Corporation*. New York: Basic Books, 1977. Reports the findings of a study of families in which the husband was employed by a large corporation. Although this family type may have changed, this study provides insight into the relationship between family life and work life.

Rapoport, Rhona, and Robert N. Rapoport. *Dual Career Families Re-examined: New Integrations of Work and Family*. London: M. Robertson, 1976. An update of the first study of dual-career families conducted in Great Britain in the 1970's. Includes case studies of five dual-career couples.

Silberstein, Lisa R. *Dual-Career Marriage: A System in Transition*. Hillsdale, N.J.: Lawrence Erlbaum, 1992. Reports findings from a study of dual-career families in the Boston and New York City areas. Also includes information on how individuals developed career aspirations. Appendices include study methods and an interview schedule.

Charlotte Chorn Dunham

Cross-References

The Family: Functionalist versus Conflict Theory Views, 739; Gender Inequality: Analysis and Overview, 820; Gender Socialization, 833; Women in the Labor Force, 2185; Women in the Medical Profession, 2191; The Women's Movement, 2196.

UNEMPLOYMENT AND POVERTY

Type of sociology: Social stratification
Field of study: Poverty

Unemployment and poverty are two related problems that defy easy solutions. Understanding public policies meant to alleviate them necessitates an appreciation for the government's concerns about inflation and the nature of modern economies.

Principal terms
CYCLICAL UNEMPLOYMENT: unemployment associated with cyclical downturns in aggregate economic activity
MACROECONOMICS: the branch of economics that concentrates on the overall level of economic activity, such as output, employment, and the general level of prices
POVERTY LINE: the income measure of poverty based on a federal formula that accounts for insufficiency in food, housing, clothing, medical care, and other items required to maintain a decent standard of living for families of varying sizes
PUBLIC SECTOR: the portion of the economy that is under the direct control of the government
STRUCTURAL UNEMPLOYMENT: unemployment that remains even after cyclical unemployment recoveries

Overview

The 1992 presidential election revolved primarily around an economy that had seen many people become unemployed and poor in preceding years. An eighteen-month recession, one of the longest in U.S. history, produced numbers of people in poverty unequaled in three decades and an unemployment rate that hovered slightly under 7 percent in 1991 and near 7.5 percent throughout 1992. On the positive side, however, the double-digit inflation of the late 1970's, as measured by changes in the consumer price index (CPI), was very low throughout the latter 1980's and early 1990's. Rather than wage war against unemployment and poverty, the Reagan and Bush administrations had sustained a successful fight against inflation. Any discussion of the relationship between unemployment and poverty, and government responses to them, necessitates consideration of inflation.

By and large, there are two major types of unemployment: cyclical and structural. Cyclical unemployment refers to unemployment associated with recessions—that is, with cyclical downturns in aggregate economic activity. Structural unemployment refers to unemployment that remains even after economic recoveries. About 90 percent of cyclical unemployment involves increases in job losses and layoffs. More than half (60 percent) of structural unemployment is composed of voluntary job leavers, labor force entrants, and re-entrants. The remainder are job losers.

Sociologist Greg J. Duncan, in *Years of Poverty, Years of Plenty* (1984), has noted that many poor people move in and out of the labor force with far more frequency than had been thought in the 1960's when the Johnson Administration launched its War on Poverty. Relatively short-term spells of unemployment (lasting less than twenty-six weeks) and intermittent poverty (lasting two years or less) are quite common. During recessions, the incidence of long-term unemployment increases sharply, but many of the unemployed nevertheless find jobs or withdraw from the labor force relatively quickly. Acknowledging the high rate of labor-force participation among many of the nation's poor, policy analyst David T. Ellwood in *Poor Support: Poverty in the American Family* (1988) and social worker and policy analyst Richard K. Caputo in "Patterns of Work and Poverty" (*Families in Society*, 1991) offer a range of program and policy prescriptions that stress the need for rewarding work more and penalizing welfare receipt less. The single best attack on cyclical unemployment, however, is to maintain a sound economy.

In 1990, 5.5 percent of the civilian work force was unemployed. This was a slightly lower rate than in 1985 (7.2 percent) and a somewhat higher rate than in 1970 (4.9 percent). In 1990, 13.5 percent of the population fell below the official federal poverty level. This was a slightly lower rate than in 1985 (14.0 percent) and somewhat higher than in 1970 (12.6). By and large, unemployment and poverty rates are positively correlated: In general, as unemployment rises and falls, so does poverty. The official federal poverty line is an income measure of deprivation based on a formula that accounts for insufficiency in food, housing, clothing, medical care, and other items required to maintain a decent standard of living.

This relationship varies somewhat across racial and ethnic groups. In 1990, 15.1 percent of the white population fell below the poverty line, as did 44.2 percent of African Americans and 39.7 percent of Latinos. These rates were slightly lower than in 1985 for whites (15.6 percent) but slightly higher for African Americans (43.1 percent) and Latinos (39.6 percent). They were higher than in 1970 (10.5 percent for whites and 41.5 percent for African Americans. Comparable data were unavailable for Latinos). These data suggest that whites benefited to a greater extent than black Americans and Latinos from the economic gains of the 1980's. They underscore the differential impact that an expanding economy, one that simultaneously increases the Gross Domestic Product (GDP) and creates jobs, has on diverse populations in America.

High rates of unemployment tend to increase the numbers of individuals who become poor, particularly people of color, and they tend to breed more persistent poverty. Hence, the availability of jobs in general, and of higher paying jobs in particular, plays a key role in social solidarity in the United States. If young people can routinely expect to get jobs on leaving school and to remain, for the most part, gainfully employed throughout their adult lives, a mindset exists that is quite different from one in which work is a privilege unavailable to many. For the most part, the young and long-term unemployed adults can benefit from policies and programs aimed at structural unemployment.

Since unemployment has such adverse consequences as increased and more persistent poverty, one might ask why the United States tolerates unemployment rates in the vicinity of 5 percent, instead of targeting a lower percentage, such as Sweden's relatively stable 3 percent or Japan's 2 percent, which would add millions of jobs. What prevents the federal government from adopting a "full employment" economic policy, one that guarantees every citizen the right to a job? In a nutshell, a big part of the problem is determining how to generate a sufficient number of jobs for a growing population while also controlling the rate of inflation. One of the principal constraints on reducing unemployment, notes economist Paul Krugman in *The Age of Diminished Expectations* (1990), is the fear that too low an unemployment rate will lead to accelerating inflation. At all costs, it seems, the federal government is determined to prevent the double-digit inflation characteristic of the late 1970's, when for a time both inflation and unemployment exceeded 10 percent.

The government has at its disposal a range of both macroeconomic policies and micro-level programs designed in part to encourage the private sector to create jobs, to educate and train economically disadvantaged workers, and to buffer the economic impact of temporary unemployment. For the most part, macroeconomic policies are set by the Federal Reserve, which is a relatively freestanding body unencumbered by the day-to-day politics and public accountability of the office of the president and both chambers of Congress. The president and Congress, however, can and do use fiscal policy and structural measures as means to influence the rates of unemployment and poverty. Tax incentives are made available for businesses to create jobs. Job training and employment programs are initiated to assist economically disadvantaged or dislocated workers. Area redevelopment plans and economic enterprise zones target low-income neighborhoods. Authorized public works often put many would-be poor and economically disadvantaged people to work.

Applications

Since the early 1970's, federal financing and services regarding employment and job training have fluctuated drastically. In the 1960's and early 1970's, the greatest share of such federal outlays (that is, money actually spent) went into training programs. By 1978, however, outlays for public service jobs exceeded training. Thereafter, outlays for jobs declined as a significant portion of federal outlays. Although the overall level of federal outlays for employment and training financing and services decreased throughout the 1980's and early 1990's, job training regained its lion's share by 1986, nearly $4 billion of a total $5.3 billion. In 1982 Congress passed and President Reagan signed the Job Training Partnership Act (JTPA).

JTPA encompassed several separate programs. Its centerpiece was Title II, which provided for training grants to states, a summer jobs program for youth, and funds for education and older worker programs. Title III addressed the needs of workers dislocated because of foreign competition or technological change, while Title IV continued a variety of already existing programs such as the Job Corps (and others designed for migrant and seasonal farmworkers, American Indians, and veterans), whose administrative responsibility remained the direct responsibility of the federal government. On the whole, as economist Sar A. Levitan and his research associate Frank Gallo note in *A Second Chance: Training for Jobs* (1988), JTPA stressed state and business leadership for job training efforts; prohibited the use of public service jobs, in sharp contrast to its 1973 legislative predecessor, the Comprehensive Employment and Training Act (CETA); and reduced the income support payments.

In addition to job training efforts, the federal government has from time to time used public service employment as a mechanism to reduce unemployment and thereby to enable individuals and their families to escape poverty. Public service ventures, however, take time to implement and are far more costly than job training efforts. Such was the case in the 1970's with the CETA program. CETA called for locally managed but federally funded training and job creation programs in the public sector. It authorized a standby public service employment program, to be implemented whenever national and local unemployment rates rose too high. The Carter Administration subsequently greatly expanded the public service component under CETA from 300,000 to 750,000 job slots in nine months. This short time frame resulted in isolated, but nevertheless highly publicized, cases of mismanagement and enrollment of ineligible applicants that in turn eventuated CETA's replacement by JTPA.

"Safety net" programs, such as Unemployment Insurance (UI) and Workers' Compensation and Disability Insurance (WCDI), are designed to cushion the adverse economic effects of unemployment from recession, illness, and disability. In reviewing research on these programs, however, sociologist Kay Young McChesney notes that minorities are underrepresented in the UI program and that low-income workers are the least likely to receive unemployment compensation, primarily because of unstable work histories and low wages. About three-fourths of those who receive workers' compensation, however, are pushed above the poverty line. Many workers who are nevertheless unemployed because of illness or disability are not injured on the job and hence fall outside of the "safety net" programs, unless they are totally and permanently disabled. This is why they make up a majority of the involuntarily unemployed family householders living below the poverty line.

Context

The contemporary mix of fiscal policies and structural measures meant to reduce unemployment and poverty dates back to the Great Depression of the 1930's. At that time the Roosevelt Administration and New Deal legislation tied economic objectives to social welfare initiatives by using spending to create deficits. Fears of massive unemployment in the aftermath of World War II precipitated congressional discussion of a full-employment economy. Passage of the Employment Act of 1946 acknowledged the role of the federal government to monitor economic affairs. It created the Council of Economic Advisors (CEA), which annually reports on the state of the economy to the president. This act, however, rejected the idea that it was a proper role of government to act as employer of last resort. It reaffirmed the United States' commitment to market forces and the private sector as the best means of accelerating productivity, increasing wages and employment, and reducing poverty. For the most part, the act relied on the tools of Keynesian economic policy—that is, on variations in government income and spending that occur automatically with the business cycle.

In the early and mid-1960's, the federal government made its first effort to stimulate the economy, not in the form of government spending, but in tax cuts. The Kennedy and Johnson administrations advanced tax-cutting legislation but retained active use of Keynesian principles to combat unemployment. Each decision to raise or lower taxes in accordance with these principles, however, provoked controversy and opposition in Congress; calls for balanced budgets threatened the use of automatic stabilizers. At the same time, the Johnson Administration's War on Poverty, as sociologist Margaret Weir notes in *Politics and Jobs* (1992), incorporated two decisions about the federal government's labor market policies: They should be remedial measures targeted at the lower end of the labor market, and they should aim to alter labor supply by modifying workers' characteristics rather than seeking to change the demand for labor. These decisions reflected the "structural interpretation" of unemployment, which, in contrast to Keynesian analysis, argued that labor markets would not by themselves adequately adjust to industrial change.

A range of measures was needed to increase the efficiency of the labor market, provide an adequately skilled labor force, and reduce unemployment. Unlike the 1930's, unemployment and poverty in the 1950's and 1960's were seen as concentrated in particular groups and geographical locations: the rural poor of Appalachia, unemployed miners, laid-off automobile workers and aircraft workers. Socialist Michael Harrington's *The Other America* (1962) portrayed the stark relationship between structural unemployment and the poverty of the period. The revelation of these conditions spurred such legislation as the Manpower Development and Training Act (MDTA) of 1962; the Economic Development Act of 1964, more commonly referred to as the War on Poverty, which contained the concentrated Employment Program and Job Corps; and the Public Works and Economic Development Act of 1965. In 1968, the Johnson Administration moved away from public employment strategies per se and introduced legislation to encourage private-sector jobs, known as the Job Opportunities in the Business Sector (JOBS) program.

Until the 1970's, employment policy was in part premised on the notion of a stable trade-off between unemployment and inflation, graphically represented by the Phillips curve. Based on empirical observation, the Phillips curve allegedly allowed policy makers to choose a point along the curve for a politically desired mix of unemployment and inflation. Discretionary actions by the federal government, such as tightening or loosening fiscal and monetary policy, were used to correct deviations from the desired position. After 1969, however, both inflation and unemployment increased. Throughout the 1970's, policy makers debated the merits of public service employment, which relied on Keynesian ideas and briefly found favor in the CETA program, and the "monetarist" and market-oriented policies of economists Milton Friedman and Martin Feldstein. These economists argued that government policies and other factors such as labor unions, minimum wage laws, and the Healy and Davis-Bacon acts (which guaranteed union wages on government construction projects) discouraged employment and that the federal government should remove them. The Nixon Administration borrowed ideas from both camps to improve the economy and reduce unemployment and poverty. Nixon's proposed Family Assistance Plan, for example, would have necessitated greater government spending but also would have provided cash assistance and work incentives for the nation's eleven million working and nine million nonworking poor.

In 1978, Congress passed the Full Employment and Balanced Growth Act, also known as the Humphrey-Hawkins Act (for its congressional sponsors, Senator Hubert H. Humphrey and Representative Augustus F. Hawkins). The act neither enhanced the planning capabilities of the federal government nor guaranteed full employment. In effect, Congress and the Carter Administration abandoned the idea that the struggle against unemployment should guide economic policy, a central tenet of the Democratic Party since the New Deal. Instead, fighting inflation, a tenet of the Republican Party, assumed ascendancy and dominated the supply-side, tax-cutting economic policies of the Reagan and Bush administrations throughout the 1980's and early 1990's.

Bibliography

Caputo, Richard K. "Patterns of Work and Poverty: Exploratory Profiles of Working-Poor Households." *Families in Society* 72 (October, 1991): 451-460. This article explores the dynamic relation between durations of employment and poverty. It uses data from the Survey of Income and Program Participation (SIPP).

Danziger, Sheldon H., and Daniel H. Weinberg, eds. *Fighting Poverty: What Works and What Doesn't.* Cambridge, Mass.: Harvard University Press, 1986. This book contains an excellent collection of scholarly articles. Includes notes at the end of the book, as well as an extensive reference section and an index.

Ellwood, David T. *Poor Support: Poverty in the American Family.* New York: Basic Books, 1988. Offers employment strategies and other approaches for economically disadvantaged families. Some have suggested that it may provide the backdrop to the government's job training, welfare reform, and antipoverty efforts in the 1990's. Contains detailed footnotes and an index.

Levitan, Sar A., and Frank Gallo. *A Second Chance: Training for Jobs.* Kalamazoo, Mich.: W. E. Upjohn Institute for Employment Research, 1988. This book compares the merits of CETA and JTPA in fairly straightforward language. Extensive notes are gathered at the back, and the volume has an index.

McChesney, Kay Young. "Macroeconomic Issues in Poverty: Implications for Child and Youth Homeless." In *Homeless Children and Youth: A New American Dilemma*, edited by Julee H. Kryder-Coe, Lester M. Salamon, and Janice M. Molnar. New Brunswick, N.J.: Transaction Publishers, 1991. This article highlights how macroeconomic factors influence poverty and homelessness. It reviews the merits of several "safety net" programs. The article reads well and includes notes and references.

Sundquist, James. *Politics and Policy: The Eisenhower, Kennedy, and Johnson Years.* Washington, D.C.: Brookings Institution, 1968. This book is a classic work on the formative years of government policies intended to address unemployment and poverty among other issues. It has extensive footnotes and an index.

Weir, Margaret. *Politics and Jobs: The Boundaries of Employment Policy in the United States.* Princeton, N.J.: Princeton University Press, 1992. An excellent single volume that traces the development of job-related policies that address unemployment and poverty. Detailed notes are gathered in the back. Includes an index.

Richard K. Caputo

Cross-References

Antipoverty Programs, 107; The Feminization of Poverty, 754; Poverty: Analysis and Overview, 1453; The Culture of Poverty, 1460; Poverty: Women and Children, 1466; Poverty and Race, 1472; The Poverty Line and Counting the Poor, 1478; Racial and Ethnic Stratification, 1579; The Urban Underclass and the Rural Poor, 2122; Welfare and Workfare, 2172.

UNIFORM CRIME REPORTS AND CRIME DATA

Type of sociology: Deviance and social control
Field of study: Controlling deviance

The Uniform Crime Reports (UCR) refers to a government program for collecting and reporting statistics supplied by police; UCR is also used to refer to the reports themselves. It was the first and is still the best known of the major data sources on the amount of crime in the United States. The UCR and other sources of crime data provide some measure of the effectiveness of social control of crime.

Principal terms

CRIME: behavior identified by society as a violation of criminal laws

CRIME RATE: a comparative tool for reporting crime; it allows population differences and different times to be compared when crime is measured

DARK FIGURE OF CRIME: a widely used term that refers to crime that is not reported in official data sources

DESCRIPTIVE STATISTICS: data that are presented without any attempt to infer causation or to infer other amounts of data

INCIDENCE: the number of incidents or events (such as crimes), as opposed to the number of people involved (prevalence)

INDEX: in research, a measure using a few selected kinds of cases in a category from which an indication can be obtained of the total quantities in the category

POLICE STATISTICS: a term that, along with "official crime statistics" and "FBI statistics," usually means UCR data

PREVALENCE: a research term which refers to the number of people (such as criminals) rather than to incidence

SELF-REPORT STUDIES: research that relies on the research subjects anonymously completing questionnaires in which they report deviance they have committed

VICTIMIZATION SURVEYS: research using interviews or questionnaires in which people tell researchers of the times they have been victims of crimes

Overview

In order to know whether criminal law and the criminal justice system are effective (or can be made more effective) as formal social controls of criminal behavior, it is necessary to know how much crime there is, how the amount of crime changes over time, and how crime changes in response to changes in criminal justice. The first effort to gather ongoing information on the amount of crime in the United States was initiated in the 1920's by the International Association of Chiefs of Police (IACP). In 1930 Congress authorized the U.S. attorney general to require the agency now known as the Federal Bureau of Investigation (FBI) to use the IACP methodology to gather and distribute the information. Thus was born the National Uniform Crime Reporting Program, commonly referred to as the UCR or, more appropriately, the UCR Program.

Rather than use a sample of police departments and infer the total amounts of various kinds of crimes, the methodology required the FBI to gather the data from all police departments. The U.S. Bureau of the Census has estimated coverage to be 97 percent, even though the cooperation of the police agencies is voluntary. To make it easier to handle the huge amount of data, the IACP carefully developed the Crime Index. This was to be used instead of trying to gather data on all kinds of crime. The index crimes were homicide, aggravated assault (life-threatening assaults), forcible rape, robbery, burglary, larceny-theft, and motor vehicle theft. In 1979, Congress added arson. Because every state's laws differ from those of every other state, the definitions of the index crimes do not completely correspond to any statutory definitions. Each police organization was given responsibility for summarizing its data for the UCR. To help them, the IACP had developed a manual, which has been updated and is called the *Uniform Crime Reporting Handbook*. The data gathered by the UCR is published in its annual report, *Crime in the United States*, which is often referred to as the UCR.

Crime in the United States data are descriptive statistics reported in the form of raw numbers, rates, and trends. The crime rate is determined by dividing the number of crimes by population and multiplying the result by 100,000. Trends are given by showing (through percentage changes in the rates) how much crime has increased or decreased over a period of time, such as the previous year or the previous ten years. Data are given by the month and for the nation, geographic regions, rural and suburban counties, and cities of various size categories. Graphics of several kinds are used. Data on crimes reported to police, arrests, cases cleared (solved), and other aspects are given. Data on arrested offenders' age, sex, race, and other characteristics, as well as data on police, including those assaulted and killed, are reported. Other reports are issued, and electronic data banks are available.

Most states now collect UCR-type data from police agencies and issue their own reports. The UCR then collects the data from those state agencies instead of from the individual police departments. As the sophistication of the states and police departments grew, the UCR included its index crimes in a category identified as Part I offenses. Part II offenses data included twenty-one more categories but no record of incidents reported to the police. Arrest data and other criminal justice processes data were collected for both parts. Criminal career data were later included.

In a huge undertaking that lasted eight years in the 1980's, a "Blueprint for the Future of the Uniform Crime Reporting Program" was created, tested, and debated by UCR and Bureau of Justice Statistics (BJS) researchers, independent researchers, a private research consultancy, and major police organizations. The changes have been largely agreed upon, but they are so profound that the UCR will continue to be in a transitional stage until after the year 2000.

Several index crimes were changed by this process; for example, the index crime rape became "sexual battery," with a broadened definition. Additional crimes were identified so that they could be reported. The most important change was to stop making the individual police departments responsible for summarization. Although many changes have been made in the UCR over the decades, three characteristics had been constant: the use of the Crime Index, the dependency on the voluntary coopera-tion of all police agencies in the United States, and the reliance on police agencies to summarize the data for either the national or their state UCR program. By shifting to a system in which data on each incident (crime) are reported directly to the UCR, called the National Incident-Based Reporting System (NIBRS), much more data on more crimes, as well as more accurate data, can be gathered, coding errors can be minimized, and better interfacing with other data banks can be established.

Applications

Does the UCR measure the amount of crime in the United State? The answer is both yes and no. Yes, it measures the amount of selected crimes reported to police, although there have been serious problems even with this data. No, it does not measure the total amount of crime in the United States. The amount that is not measured is important, for it is huge.

In 1965 the first national survey of households was conducted to find out how many people would report being a victim of various crimes in the previous twelve months. The results showed that many crimes were not reported to the police and therefore were not counted in the UCR. The BJS (which, like the FBI, is within the Department of Justice) now publishes the National Crime Victimization Survey (NCVS) under the title *Criminal Victimization in the United States*. From when it became an annual report in 1975, the NCVS has shown that, of the same kinds of crimes, there are more crimes than reported in the UCR.

Comparisons of NCVS and UCR trends, though difficult because of methodological differences, have been made. The NCVS showed a decline in total crime victimization from 1975 through 1991, while the UCR showed a decline in Index Crimes reported to police from 1979 through 1991. The fact that both data sources showed a decline, which was contrary to popular opinion, reinforces the finding that there was indeed a decline and emphasizes the value of having more than one source of data.

The fact remains that police statistics cannot ever be an accurate measure of all the crime that occurs, because not all crime is reported. Victimization surveys are themselves conservative measures of the "dark figure of crime." In 1947 the first major study in which people were asked to report whether they had committed any of a large number of specified crimes found that 99 percent admitted to committing crimes. Self-report studies have become popular among criminologists, and they indicate that a staggering amount of crime goes unreported to police. For example, James Inciardi did a study of 699 Miami crack and cocaine users. They reported that between 1988 and 1991 they had committed 1,766,630 crimes but that less than 1 percent resulted in arrest. Most of these crimes were victimless crimes and could be expected to go unreported, but the figure also included more than 25,000 index crimes. Major ongoing self-report sources of crime data include the National Household Survey of Drug Abuse (which misses the incarcerated and street people) and the High School Senior Survey of Drug Use (which misses dropouts), conducted by the National Institute of Drug Abuse, and the Drug Use Forecasting Program, conducted by BJS, which obtains voluntary reports from arrested persons and checks their reports against urinalysis.

The self-report studies, too, are fraught with conceptual and methodological problems, and care should be used in relying on them. On the basis of their self-report studies, criminologists have claimed that, because of discriminatory police practices in handling calls and making arrests, the UCR greatly overemphasizes crime in inner cities while greatly underestimating it in other areas. This argument has been challenged by Delbert Elliot, whose self-report studies indicate that more serious crime does occur in areas generally recognized as high-crime areas. Even self-report studies do not identify the total amounts of organized crime, crime in which there is no victim in the sense of a complainant (consensual or victimless crime), or crime committed by legitimate organizations (white-collar crime).

Some of the potential uses of the UCR can be gleaned from early abuses of it. A police chief would report more index crime than warranted and then would say that the FBI crime statistics supported his case that crime was increasing rapidly in his city and that he needed more resources to fight it. To show that he or his mayor were successful in fighting crime, particularly around election time, he would report lower figures. At a time when Chicago and New York were rivals, they would have their police departments submit false figures to the FBI, resulting in one city appearing to have lower crime than the other one year, and the other city lower crime the next. Gross manipulation of UCR data has long been precluded by UCR techniques, but the earlier the UCR data the less trustworthy it is.

The UCR reports contain cautions against misinterpreting such striking graphics as its crime clocks, drawing comparisons using trends, or using the Crime Index as though it included all crime reported to police. The media and others nevertheless continue to misuse the data. UCR data always makes headline news, suggesting the importance of this kind of information to the general public.

Criminologists have criticized the methodology used by the UCR from the early years, particularly the Crime Index, which is an arbitrary index from a research methodology perspective. The limits and use of the UCR have been summarized by Victoria Schneider and Brian Wiersema in an article in *Measuring Crime: Large-Scale, Long-Range Efforts* (1990). Many of the criticisms have been well taken and are being addressed through the changes taking place. The UCR will never be perfect, however, and some serious flaws do remain. Criminologists have often made use of UCR data, and as the data improve in quantity and quality, this use will increase, particularly for studies involving data on arrests.

Context

The police administrators and researchers who have created and shaped the UCR have probably never heard of Adolphe Quetelet, but the UCR is predated and foreshadowed by his work. In the 1820's this natural scientist looked at the figures on crime in France, Holland, and Belgium and concluded, to his surprise, that despite the varied circumstances of individual crimes he could predict crimes: the amount, the kinds, the seasons, and certain characteristics of offenders, such as age, sex, and murder weapon. He was the first to apply the newly described bell curve to social phenomena. He coined the term "social physics" to describe his approach, a term that inspired Auguste Comte's word "sociology," which Comte used to identify a potential new science.

Quetelet's findings bear an uncanny resemblance to those reported in the UCR, despite the fact that the United States is a different culture—separated from the one he studied by an ocean and more than 150 years. Both sources, for example, show that age and sex have very strong relationships to criminality and that the ratio of female to male offenders is low, especially for violent crimes (the first four index crimes). Both show that women are more likely than men to use poison to kill. Both show that poverty alone cannot be associated with higher rates of crime but that it appears to be related. Both show that violent crime is more likely to occur in hotter months. Many of his findings go beyond the UCR but are supported by other contemporary sources of crime data. For example, the incidence of homicides in which alcohol is involved was found to be about the same by Quetelet and by Marvin Wolfgang, who examined homicides in Philadelphia.

Karl Marx was impressed by Quetelet's findings. In later years, however, neither the conflict theorists nor the social control theorists (who have gathered their own data on crime) have made extensive use of UCR data in trying to determine the causes of crime. The future of the UCR, with its NIBRS, will lead to greatly increased data and to closer, more detailed comparisons with NCVS data. It will make possible more accurate comparisons with crime data from other countries, which have always presented a thorny problem. It will also dovetail with a data system created around 1970 but never fully developed called Offender Based Transaction Statistics (OBTS). This system could be expanded to trace any offender, any group of offenders, and all offenders through each of the many steps ("transactions," in OBTS terms) they take in being processed through the criminal justice system. It could also give much more accurate statistics on how many enter the system again (recidivism). Many state and local governments already maintain computerized records of this depth of detail. Such information will allow fine-tuning of the criminal justice system to make it more efficient and effective. It will also lead to the kind of statistical base needed for studies of patterns or types of crimes. This massive, coordinated database could lead to new research-supported theories of crime causation. For example, labeling theorists would have a powerful tool to use in defining the conditions that help lead to a "criminal career."

Yet while the promise is real, so are the dangers. File information on individuals has always been abused by the unscrupulous and by the mistaken but well-intentioned. No totalitarian country will have every had such detailed dossier information as this database represents.

Members of the BJS Princeton Project, as reported by John DiIulio, Jr., in *Rethinking the Criminal Justice System* (1992), propose that in addition to using crime rates and recidivism rates, the criminal justice system develop new performance measures that would reflect a new emphasis on the civic ideals inherent in a democracy. If the UCR and other data sources that focus on crime and criminality are matched in importance by as yet undeveloped measures focusing on civic ideals, the dangers can perhaps be minimized, at least within the criminal justice system.

Bibliography

DiIulio, John, Jr. *Rethinking the Criminal Justice System: Toward a New Paradigm.* Washington, D.C.: U.S. Department of Justice, Office of Justice Programs, Bureau of Justice Statistics, 1992. This is a thoughtful and succinct discussion paper that is a report of the Bureau of Justice Statistics Princeton Project, which included ten well-known social scientists and practitioners.

Federal Bureau of Investigation. *Crime in the United States.* Washington, D.C.: United States National Criminal Justice Information and Statistics Service. This is the annual report often referred to as the UCR. It contains a history of the UCR Program and explanations of terms and data as well as easy-to-comprehend crime data.

MacKenzie, Doris, et al., eds. *Measuring Crime: Large-Scale, Long-Range Efforts.* Albany: State University of New York Press, 1990. This book contains eleven chapters, two of them dealing directly with the UCR, by different authors. These are summary articles that contain much useful information.

United States. National Criminal Justice Information and Statistics Service. *Criminal Victimization in the United States.* Washington, D.C.: Author. This annual publication is the principal report of the National Crime Victimization Survey. It is used as a companion work to the UCR. It includes the questionnaire the research interviewers use. Available from the U.S. Government Printing Office.

_____ . *Sourcebook of Criminal Justice Statistics.* Washington, D.C.: Author. Most university and large public libraries will have this annual work among their government documents even if they do not have the UCR. It contains most of the UCR and NCVS material and much more. It is the best single work providing crime and criminal justice related statistics. Available from the U.S. Government Printing Office.

Hill Harper

Cross-References

The Courts, 367; Crime: Analysis and Overview, 373; The Criminal Justice System, 380; Descriptive Statistics, 519; Deviance: Analysis and Overview, 525; Drug Use and Addiction, 572; Organized Crime, 1322; Surveys, 2030; Victimless Crime, 2150.

UNIONIZATION AND INDUSTRIAL LABOR RELATIONS

Type of sociology: Major social institutions
Field of study: The economy

As the excesses of the Industrial Revolution created an impoverished working class in late nineteenth century Europe and the United States, workers organized collectively to deal with big business effectively. Since these workers formed labor unions to express their collective will, sociologists call this process unionization. In the United States, the New Deal viewed unionization as the preferred method of organizing industrial labor relations.

Principal terms

AMERICAN FEDERATION OF LABOR-CONGRESS OF INDUSTRIAL
  ORGANIZATIONS (AFL-CIO): a national federation of labor unions
  formed in 1955

BARGAINING UNIT: a clearly defined group of employees whose shared
  common interests warrant their bargaining as a group

CLOSED SHOP: this form of labor organization, which the Taft-Hartley
  Act made illegal, required employees to be union members before
  they were hired

COLLECTIVE BARGAINING: in the process of collective bargaining, a
  company and a union negotiate wages, hours, and conditions of
  employment and seek a collective bargaining agreement

CONTRACT BAR: the period of time during a valid collective bargaining
  agreement during which no representation questions can be asked

IMPASSE: a stalemate in collective bargaining negotiations which occurs
  when the union and the employer are unable to reach agreement

NATIONAL LABOR RELATIONS ACT (NLRA): this 1935 act, more
  commonly known as the Wagner Act, created public policy to
  encourage unionization and created the National Labor Relations
  Board

UNION SHOP: a shop in which membership in a union is mandatory for
  employees thirty days after employment or thirty days after the
  signing of the union shop's contract, whichever comes later

WILDCAT STRIKE: a work stoppage not authorized by the union which
  holds collective bargaining rights

Overview

The middle and late nineteenth century in western Europe and the United States saw an Industrial Revolution. Improved technology led to the development of a more mechanized industry, and huge firms arose that dominated whole industries and often intimidated governments.

As a result of the Industrial Revolution, agriculture ceased to be the dominant form of employment, first in Great Britain, then in the United States and elsewhere. Small independent craftsmen were less and less able to compete, and many craftsmen experienced downward social mobility.

Farmers and immigrants swelled the ranks of the wage-earning poor in large American cities. Large corporations kept wages low, and employment was uncertain because of business cycles.

In these unpleasant circumstances, working men and women increasingly formed labor unions such as the American Federation of Labor (AFL) to protect wage levels and increase their employment security. The economically secure viewed unionization with alarm, since collective action through unionization often had socialist and communist undertones. The Industrial Workers of the World (IWW), also known as the "Wobblies," was founded in 1905, and this union gained significant support among American unskilled workers in the early decades of the twentieth century by advocating an end to capitalism and a complete restructuring of society.

Labor unions were not legal in Great Britain until 1871, and American law was also painfully slow to recognize unions as a legitimate form of social organization. Even as late as 1896, Justice Oliver Wendell Holmes wrote as a dissenter in *Vegelahn v. Gunter* when he approved of worker-organized picketing of a business.

As long as the philosophy of individualism and laissez-faire dominated the courts, unionization was hindered by charges of criminal conspiracy against workers acting as a group against their employers and by injunctions against striking workers. In addition, employers used "yellow dog contracts," in which workers had to pledge not to join unions as a condition of employment.

When the Sherman Act was passed in 1890, courts used it to forbid strikes that affected interstate commerce on antitrust grounds. Employers could sue for treble damages under the Sherman Act.

In 1914, Congress passed the Clayton Act, which provided unions with some relief from their Sherman Act problems. Section 6 declared that Labor was not a commodity, and section 20 provided that courts should not issue injunctions against strikes and information picketing.

The Clayton Act provided limited help to unions. Probusiness courts continued to find legal rationales for anti-union decisions. *Duplex Printing Press Co. v. Deering* (1921) provides an example of probusiness interpretation of the Clayton Act, since the Supreme Court found a union boycott of an employer's customers and sympathetic strikes illegal in this case.

Unions found little legal relief until the New Deal. The Railway Labor Act of 1926 provided an exception to the bleak legal position of unions in the 1920's, since it secured the right of railroad employees to organize and to bargain collectively.

With the election of President Franklin Delano Roosevelt and the coming of the New Deal in 1933, public policy began to favor unions. On the eve of the New Deal in 1932, Congress passed the Norris-La Guardia Act, which has been popularly known as the Anti-Injunction Act, and established a policy of government and judicial neutrality in labor disputes. When Roosevelt took office in 1933, he appointed a pro-union Secretary of Labor, Frances Perkins, whose social work background had given her a desire to relieve the economic misery she saw in Depression America. In 1935, Congress passed the National Labor Relations Act (NLRA), which is sometimes called the Wagner Act. The express purpose of the NLRA was to encourage unionization and collective bargaining, and public policy has remained essentially pro-union ever since the NLRA established the National Labor Relations Board as an administrative agency to govern industrial labor relations.

Under the NLRA, five employer practices became illegal. Employers could no longer refuse to bargain in good faith with a properly certified union; interfere with employees in their right to form or assist unions; dominate a union or interfere with its operation, a provision that banned "company unions"; discriminate against or discharge union affiliated employees; or retaliate against employees assisting the NLRB. All employers involved in interstate commerce are covered by the act in dealing with nonsupervisory employees outside agriculture.

Passage of the NLRA helped stimulate aggressive union action. The militant Congress of Industrial Organizations (CIO) was formally organized in 1937. Soon increasing numbers of unskilled workers joined the CIO, which was more broadly representative of all segments of American society than was the craft-dominated AFL. The CIO contained groups such as the United Automobile Workers of America, the United Steelworkers of America, and the Textile Workers of America, which sought to organize entire industries.

The separation between the AFL and the CIO, which arose in the New Deal era, did not prove permanent. The two organizations merged in 1955 after CIO successes had made most of its members middle class.

Republican control of Congress between 1946 and 1948 resulted in curbs on union rights, when the Taft-Hartley Act was passed in 1947. Although this act retained the five employer unfair labor practices specified in the NLRA, the Taft-Hartley Act created five unfair labor practices restrictions on union activity. Union unfair labor practices under the Taft-Hartley Act include refusing to bargain in good faith with an employer, attempting to coerce employer selection of management representatives in collective bargaining, featherbedding, requiring excessive or discriminatory dues from employees in a union shop, and securing the discharge of an employee or securing discriminatory action against an employee for reasons other than the failure to pay union dues in a union shop.

In 1959, Congress placed further restrictions on union activity in the Labor-Management Reporting and Disclosure Act, which is also known popularly as the Landrum-Griffin Act. Title I of the act is a bill of rights for union members. In addition, the Landrum-Griffin Act limits secondary boycotts and imposes reporting requirements on union officials.

While unionization of American workers received significant official sanction in the 1930's, unions have never represented a majority of the American workforce. Union membership as a percentage of the total workforce has declined since 1970, since union-dominated manufacturing jobs in the automobile, steel, rubber, and other heavy industry jobs now represent a decreasing percentage of the American economy.

Applications

Although union members are a declining percentage of the total American workforce, they still exert disproportionate economic and political influence. Labor political action committees (PACs) are a major source of funding for Democratic Party campaigns, and union members provide significant grassroots support for Democratic candidates. The AFL-CIO has made a notable contribution to American foreign policy by supporting democratic trade unions overseas, including the Solidarity Movement in Poland led by Lech Walesa.

Whereas union membership in the private sector of the American economy will probably continue to decline as a percentage of the total workforce, union membership among public employees is increasing. Although many state, county, and municipal employees still lack the right to strike, most may now select a collective bargaining agent, and the American Federation of State, County, and Municipal Employees (AFSCME) should continue to grow. Teacher organizations such as the National Education Association (NEA) are now de facto unions, and many local branches of the NEA are collective bargaining agents.

Federal employees have enjoyed statutory collective bargaining rights since 1978, when the Federal Service Labor Management and Employee Relations Law was passed as part of Title VII of the Civil Service Reform Act. Federal employee relations are governed by the Federal Labor Relations Authority, which is modeled after the NLRB. Strikes by federal employees are still illegal, and federal employees are still unable to bargain on key topics such as agency mission, budget, compulsory payment of union dues, and wages and salaries.

Union wages tend to exceed the wages paid nonunion workers in comparable jobs, and these high wages exert an upward pressure on the salaries of all workers. In addition, unions have consistently sought to protect worker health and safety, and union efforts were crucial in obtaining passage of the Occupational Health and Safety Act (OSHA) in 1970.

Although unions have enabled relatively unskilled industrial workers to bargain on an equal basis with large corporations and have exerted upward pressure on wages and benefits throughout the economy, the impact of unionization has not been uniformly positive. High union wages and inflexible work rules have had a negative impact on the competitiveness of American products in an increasingly interconnected world economy. Some unions, such as the Teamsters under President James R. Hoffa, have caused national scandals as a result of their corrupt, gangster-influenced leadership.

Unions encourage a collective mind-set in the workplace, since employees covered under union contracts lose the right to seek individual accommodations of their specific needs from employers; instead, detailed collective bargaining agreements spell out who gets what and when. Disabled individuals seeking accommodations under the Americans with Disabilities Act (ADA) may find that collective bargaining principles make it difficult to accommodate their needs. Unions dominated by white males may use the principle of their rights as an exclusive bargaining agent to ignore the gender- and race-specific needs of minority and female workers, and unless unions can be shown to have violated the duty of fair representation (DFR) imposed by the courts, minorities and women may find themselves second-class union members. Elizabeth Iglesias (1993) makes a cogent argument that union power under the NLRA still effectively curtails gender and race discrimination claims based on Title VII of the Civil Rights Act of 1964.

Context

Even during the European Middle Ages, workers acted collectively to control wages, hours, and working conditions through the guild system. In most major trades, medieval guilds allowed workers to exercise control over the entry into and practice of most major trades. They also performed significant social welfare functions for guild members and their families.

The modern study of unionization and industrial labor relations dates at least back to Karl Marx, who viewed collective action by workers as the key to overthrowing capitalism and creating a new form of proletarian classless society. Whereas Marx saw proletarian triumph as inevitable, however, most working men and women in late nineteenth and early twentieth century Europe sought reform within existing political and economic structures rather than revolution. Samuel Gompers, the first leader of the American Federation of Labor (AFL), which was founded in 1886, recognized that union members would gain more by humanizing the existing political and economic order than they would by overthrowing it.

Contemporary American sociologists study the impact of unions in several subdisciplines. These disciplines are conflict theory, the examination of collective behavior and social movements, the study of industrial sociology and the culture of the workplace, and the sociological study of economic systems such as capitalism, communism, and socialism.

Although unions are not likely ever to represent the same percentage of the American workforce that they did in 1970, union labor is still a significant force in American politics, as the 1993 debate over the North American Free Trade Agreement (NAFTA) revealed. Fearful of continued losses of manufacturing jobs, union members will almost certainly remain protectionist in their attitudes toward international trade even after their defeat in their attempt to stop NAFTA. In addition, many union members may resist calls to gain the added education and training necessary to keep U.S. productivity up and U.S. products competitive in world trade unless they can be convinced that realistic efforts are being made to provide them with secure and meaningful jobs.

Increased labor-management cooperation in the unionized segment of the American economy is an issue of national concern in the late twentieth century. Many union members see calls for labor-management cooperation as a strategy that is being used to justify wage and benefit givebacks in a declining manufacturing sector. David A. Dilts expresses skepticism over labor-management cooperation that reflects labor fears of employer-dominated unions and loss of hard-won rights. The American economy is not without shining examples of labor-management cooperation, however, such as General Motors' cooperation with the United Auto Workers in its successful Saturn Project at Spring Hill, Tennessee, and more such success stories are needed.

Bibliography

Brenner, David B. "The Effect of ERISA Preemption on Prevailing Wages and Collective Bargaining in the Construction Industry." *Detroit College of Law Review* 1993 (Fall, 1993): 1123. Brenner advocates limiting ERISA preemption of state laws dealing with prevailing wage, apprenticeship programs, and mechanics' liens. ERISA is the Employee Retirement Income Security Act, which was enacted in 1988.

Cox, Archibald, et al. *Cases and Materials on Labor Law.* 11th ed. Westbury, N.Y.: Foundation Press, 1991. The growth of labor unions is effectively documented in this law school text, which includes both historical and contemporary sources. Although it is intended for law students, general readers will find it easy to use and helpful.

_____. *Cases and Materials on Labor Law, 1993 Statutory Supplement.* 11th ed. Westbury, N.Y.: Foundation Press, 1993. This supplement updates the 1988 casebook. It includes the text of the National Labor Relations Act.

Dilts, David A. "Labor-Management Cooperation: Real or Nominal Changes in Collective Bargaining." *Labor Law Journal* 44 (February, 1993): 124-128. Dilts supports labor-management cooperation programs but has reservations about them. He clearly fears management attempts to dominate employee organization and to achieve goals that management is unable to secure through collective bargaining.

Hill, Myron G., Jr., Howard M. Rosen, and Wilton S. Hogg. *Labor Law and Employment Discrimination.* 3d ed. Larchmont, N.Y.: Emmanuel Law Outlines, 1988. This review covers basic labor law for law students. The rights and obligations of both unions and employers under the National Labor Relations Act receive detailed treatment, as do collective bargaining, the collective bargaining agreement, and picketing and boycotts by unions and union members.

Hunter, Jerry M. "Potential Conflicts Between Obligations Imposed on Employers and Unions by the National Labor Relations Act and the Americans with Disabilities Act." *Northern Illinois University Law Review* 13 (Spring, 1993): 207. Hunter analyzes the potential for conflict between the individual rights orientation of the NLRA and the collective orientation of the ADA. He is, however, optimistic that employers and unions can resolve these problems unless underlying, unrelated problems interfere.

Iglesias, Elizabeth M. "Structures of Subordination: Women of Color at the Intersection of Title VII and the NLRA. Not!" *Harvard Civil Rights-Civil Liberties Law Review* 28 (Summer, 1993): 395. Iglesias contends that union governance structures are designed to keep women of color in a subordinate position and that Title VII has not afforded these women adequate protection against white male union leadership. She posits a need for substantial modification of the current system of exclusive representation under the NLRA.

Katz, Harold A. "Filling the Court-Created Gap in the Protection of Concerted Activities: The Need for Striker Replacement Collective Bargaining." *Northern Illinois University Law Review* 13 (Spring, 1993): 247. Katz, a prominent union lawyer, advocates striker replacement legislation to prevent employers from permanently replacing strikers and breaking unions.

Pike, Cynthia Lynne. "*Lechmere, Inc. v. NLRB*: Its History and Its Ramifications." *Detroit College of Law Review* 1993 (Fall, 1993): 1103. *Lechmere, Inc. v. NLRB* is a crucial 1992 case that puts severe limits on the rights of nonemployee union organizers to obtain access to company property. Pike regards this decision, written by Justice Clarence Thomas, as a major blow to the union movement.

St. Louis, Glen. "Keeping the Playing Field Level: The Implications, Effects, and Application of the Nonstatutory Labor Exemption on the 1994 National Basketball Association Collective Bargaining Process." *Detroit College of Law Review* 1993 (Fall, 1993): 1221. St. Louis traces the antitrust limitations on the free agency of both basketball and football players, covering the dramatically different legal positions of players' unions in these sports.

Susan A. Stussy

Cross-References

Class Consciousness and Class Conflict, 271; Corporations and Economic Concentration, 360; Deindustrialization in the United States, 462; Industrial and Postindustrial Economies, 940; The Industrial Revolution and Mass Production, 946; Industrial Societies, 953; Industrial Sociology, 960; Monopolies and Oligopolies, 1248; Organizations: Formal and Informal, 1316; Workplace Socialization, 2202.

UNOBTRUSIVE RESEARCH

Type of sociology: Sociological research
Field of study: Data collection and analysis

Unobtrusive research refers to a variety of techniques in which the information collected (the data) is undisturbed by the presence of the investigator. Methods of unobtrusive research include such techniques as interpreting written documents and analyzing statistical data.

Principal terms
ANALYSIS OF EXISTING STATISTICS: unobtrusive research in which existing statistical files, such as the annual *Statistical Abstract of the United States*, are used as data
CONTENT ANALYSIS: unobtrusive research in which human communications, such as written materials, are used as data
HISTORICAL/COMPARATIVE METHOD: unobtrusive research in which historical records and published materials are used as data; typically more than one data source are analyzed
NONREACTIVE RESEARCH: research in which the process of measurement has no effect on the data gathered by researchers
PHYSICAL TRACES: physical evidence in the form of accretions (deposited materials) or erosion (wear on materials) which are used as data
RELIABILITY: consideration of the extent to which the same data are collected when using an unobtrusive measure in repeated observations
VALIDITY: consideration of the extent to which an unobtrusive measure produces the information intended or necessary for an unbiased analysis of the data

Overview
Unobtrusive research includes a wide range of techniques that have one characteristic in common: All use measurement strategies that disengage the researcher from the subject under investigation. The social scientist has no effect on the environment from which information (that is, data) is collected. For this reason, unobtrusive measures are also nonreactive measures.

Nonreactive techniques can be devised to measure a wide range of social phenomena. Techniques can be designed, for example, to probe individual responses to stimuli in the environment. Other procedures can be contrived to examine large-scale social patterns. Unobtrusive research includes methods of qualitative measurement (examining and interpreting objects and patterns) and quantitative measurement (statistically manipulating the numbers representing social phenomena and patterns). Three specific techniques, explained by Earl Babbie in *The Practice of Social Research* (1983), are content analysis, analysis of existing statistics, and historical/comparative analysis.

Unobtrusive research has a long history in sociology. Many early sociologists in Europe and the United States used unobtrusive measures to provide substantive support for their theories. In the middle decades of the twentieth century, interest in unobtrusive measurement waned. Interest in this type of research experienced a revival with the publication of the classic volume by Eugene Webb, Donald Campbell, Richard Schwartz, and Lee Sechrest, *Unobtrusive Measures: Nonreactive Research in the Social Sciences* (1966). Trace measures can be used as an example of unobtrusive research. The trace measures of accretion and erosion are of particular utility to sociologists. The shortcomings of trace measures noted also apply to other unobtrusive techniques.

Erosion refers to the deterioration of physical objects from repeated use. Examining the wear on reference books in the library to infer which ones are used most often is an example of erosion research. Investigating records on the replacement of floor tiles to detect which exhibits are most popular in a museum is another. Social scientists conclude from the evidence that they have identified, respectively, the most essential reference materials in the library and the most popular exhibits in a museum.

Measures of accretion refer to the buildup or deposit of some form of physical evidence. For example, a research topic on the association between lifestyles and chronic illness might include examining the household garbage of selected participants. Items such as cigarette butts, empty cans of soda and beer, and discarded packaging materials from chips and frozen pizzas could be designated evidence for risky behavior for chronic illness. Researchers compare the medical records of these households with others lacking these trace indicators, and then draw conclusions. Graffiti in the high school restrooms of male and female students can be examined as trace measures of gender differences in conduct and attitudes. Also, differences can be noted in the amount and the content of graffiti in the restrooms of high schools located in different income areas of a city. Conclusions can then be drawn about gender and class differences based on this evidence.

Trace measures may create problems for the social scientist when these measures are used alone. In such cases, research findings can be attacked as simplistic and as unsubstantiated by means other than physical evidence. Perhaps, in the first example given, stress underlies the actions that are damaging to a person's health. This factor must be discounted before a researcher can convincingly state that he or she has discovered that lifestyle as measured by food preference is a principal cause for chronic illnesses. In the second example, graffiti are used to indicate the long-run and short-run interests, opinions, conflicts, and expectations of the writers, who in turn represent the views of high school youth. Situational factors and other beliefs of the writers remain concealed; also unknown are the opinions and attitudes of the writers' peers.

The illustrations above demonstrate a major weakness of trace measures as a research strategy for sociologists. In all cases, individual behaviors are inferred from the physical evidence. This behavioristic approach has been criticized sharply. First, psychologists have said that it oversimplifies the mental processes of human beings; second, sociologists have noted that it ignores the complex influence of the social environment on individual beliefs and conduct. The detachment of the researcher from the empirical world is a weakness that permeates all unobtrusive measures. It is mentioned here because it is a glaring limitation of trace measures. Closely related to this weakness, however, is a source of strength. A major limitation of other types of research, such as surveys, experiments, and field observations, is the possibility of the social scientist having a detrimental effect on the data. Unobtrusive research by definition excludes this possibility.

Applications

Three examples may be used to illustrate three types of unobtrusive research: content analysis, analysis of existing statistics, and historical/comparative methods. First, however, the concepts of validity and reliability need a brief introduction. In unobtrusive research it is essential that researchers (who are detached from the field) remain vigilant about the issues of validity and reliability throughout their research. Validity involves the extent that a measure produces the information intended or necessary for an unbiased analysis of a research question. Reliability considers the extent to which the same data will be collected if a research procedure is repeated.

Content analysis involves research on the artifacts of human communications. Artifacts include a diverse range of materials, such as letters, documents, and mass media items. The two-volume work by William I. Thomas and Florian Znaniecki, *The Polish Peasant in Europe and America* (1927) is an exemplary study of content analysis. Thomas and Znaniecki investigated the process whereby Polish immigrants interpreted and reinterpreted the environments of Poland and the United States through kinship ties. The first volume of the work pieces together private letters into family files. The second volume joins the family files with the public records of adjustment found in popular newspapers, court proceedings, the files of social service agencies, and an immigrant's life history.

The unobtrusive research of this study withstands the criticisms leveled against trace measures noted earlier. The study appears to have high levels of both validity and reliability. Thomas and Znaniecki gathered varied sources of information and used assorted angles of inquiry to study their research topic. The study's reliability is assessed according to the points noted above. In qualitative research, reliability results from familiarity with a data pool. Increased familiarity leads to greater reliability.

Analysis of existing statistics is another form of unobtrusive research. Here the focus is on using numbers to represent social phenomena and patterns. Émile Durkheim is a renowned figure in sociological theory for assorted publications including *Le Suicide: Étude de sociologie* (1897; *Suicide: A Study in Sociology*, 1951). In this study, Durkheim proposed that social bonds are key influences predisposing certain groups toward suicide and restraining others. Social bonds can be either too weak (leading to egoistic suicide), or too strong (altruistic suicide), or nonexistent (anomic suicide).

"Official statistical publications" of various countries supplied Durkheim with the data for his theory. The official data encompassed only yearly numerical figures including population size, gender, age, marital status, occupation, military status, civilian and military deaths, and civilian and military causes of death. These raw data were inadequate for the needs of the study, forcing Durkheim to compensate for assorted weaknesses and omissions. For example, religious affiliation was a central consideration in Durkheim's study. Durkheim inferred this relationship by, first, comparing the suicide data from predominantly Protestant and Catholic regions within the countries for differences in suicide rates.

When existing statistics are used for analysis, researchers are forced to design their studies around an existing data pool. Certain interesting research concerns must be dropped, while other decisive issues must be revised. Durkheim demonstrated a remarkable ability to discount factors that were not social as causes of suicide and to compensate for missing data in his research. To a great extent these actions enhanced the validity of his study. The reliability issue remained beyond the investigator's control, however, since others were responsible for gathering the data. Durkheim could only presume that he was using reliable information.

Another form of unobtrusive research is historical/comparative analysis. This type of inquiry involves such things as analyzing historical processes. Max Weber's study of the influence of Protestant beliefs on the development of capitalism, *Die Protestantische Ethik und der Geist des Kapitalismus* (1904; *The Protestant Ethic and the Spirit of Capitalism*, 1930), exemplifies historical/comparative analysis. Weber contends that values are pivotal in social change. To convince a scholarly audience that he was on the right track, Weber compared and contrasted the beliefs of Protestant denominations with those of the Catholic church. Then he examined varied Protestant teachings. He held John Calvin's beliefs as pivotal in explaining the origins of Western capitalism. Calvin's teachings, he argued, transformed the pursuit of profit from a sin into a morally justified activity. Two ideas were central in the transformation: First, one's earthly existence should glorify God, and second, one's material success provides a "sign" of salvation. The pieces of the puzzle fell into place when he examined the entrepreneurial values expounded by prominent secular figures such as Benjamin Franklin.

Again, Weber's research can be scrutinized to ascertain its validity and reliability. Weber addressed the possibility of weaknesses in his research in a manner similar to Durkheim's, using qualitative data instead. Weber compared and contrasted the ideas and beliefs presented in the writings of varied religious and nonreligious figureheads. While Weber remained uninvolved in the field, his immersion in diverse data pools undoubtedly made him familiar with the research topic. For the most part, the study's findings can be judged as reliable and valid. One weakness in his study stems from Weber's reliance on the writings of a German contemporary in his overview of religion and stratification. Another stems from his Eurocentric view of religious values and the development of capitalism. Weber tends to deny preconditions other than Calvinism for capitalism's development in Europe and the United States.

Context

A number of factors have helped create a renewed appreciation of unobtrusive research since the 1960's. One is simply that the use of a single research approach has been criticized as creating too narrow a focus. Another is that the human element in social research has received increased emphasis. For example, research subjects' awareness of their roles affects data quality and depth. Moreover, ethical qualms about exposing subjects to possible harm (and the related possibility of lawsuits) have made researchers increasingly careful not to violate subjects' right to privacy.

Social researchers are increasingly receptive to a multifaceted approach to social inquiry. In their overview of nonreactive measures, Webb and associates note the value of unobtrusive measurement when used in conjunction with other research approaches. A number of characteristics of survey, experimental, and field research make each inadequate when used alone. The findings of surveys and social experiments are limited to the specific attributes of research subjects which are checked against a contrived trait—for example, age, sex, ethnicity, and income differences in opinions concerning taxes. Interviews and field observations provide a deeper understanding of the human subjects being researched. The data available to the investigator, however, include only what he or she directly observes or observes through the eyes of informants. Also, the data gathered by surveys, experiments, and field observations tend to be embedded in the present and subject to all the attitudes, opinions, and concerns which are associated with a narrow slice of time.

Second, sociologists are increasingly aware of the effect of role-playing on the quality and depth of data. The roles of investigator and research subject are immediately activated when participants become aware that they are being studied. Research participants are likely to assume the "proper" role in order to meet the demands of the situation. Personal attitudes toward the subject matter and toward the researcher affect the unfolding communication process. The researcher can hide his or her identity, which is considered unethical (and is often illegal), or use artifacts—that is, unobtrusive measures—to uncover more information about a process or event.

Third, ethical controversies have prompted an interest in unobtrusive measurement. Noteworthy is one involving a participant observer who deliberately concealed his identity. In the late 1960's, Laud Humphreys conducted a study on homosexual encounters in public restrooms for his dissertation, which was later published as *Tearoom Trade: Impersonal Sex in Public Places* (1970). Humphreys told the men he was observing that he would serve as their lookout for intruders. Later Humphreys tracked down these men for home interviews by noting the numbers on their license plates to determine their home addresses. This scenario created major concerns within sociology on the professional limits to social inquiry. The American Sociological Association (ASA) now publishes and automatically distributes a handbook to all ASA members specifying a code of ethics in professional conduct. Creative use of unobtrusive measurement is increasingly recognized as both a viable alternative and a complementary device to other forms of research.

Bibliography

Babbie, Earl R. "Unobtrusive Research." In *The Practice of Social Research*. 3d ed. Belmont, Calif.: Wadsworth, 1983. Babbie's book presents a thorough overview of the varied forms of research methods. Every few years this text is updated, but the format has remained unchanged since the third edition. The chapter on unobtrusive measures provides a lengthy discussion of content analysis, analysis of existing data, and comparative/historical analysis.

Sechrest, Lee, ed. *Unobtrusive Measurement Today*. San Francisco: Jossey-Bass, 1979. This book, the initial publication in the series New Directions in the Methodology of Behavioral Sciences, begins with an overview. Other selections discuss unobtrusive measures in evaluating treatments, designing field experiments, developing measures for cross-cultural research, studying nonverbal behaviors, and using garbage for detecting behaviors.

Thomas, William I., and Florian Znaniecki. *The Polish Peasant in Europe and America*. Abridged by Eli Zaretsky. Champaign: University of Illinois Press, 1984. This is a short version of a two-volume work published in 1927. It is a classic study tracing industrialization's impact on the social life of local communities and families in Poland and later in the United States. Personal letters provided a major source of data for the study.

Webb, Eugene J., Donald D. Campbell, Richard Schwartz, and Lee Sechrest. *Unobtrusive Measures: Nonreactive Research in the Social Sciences*. Chicago: Rand McNally, 1966. This book stimulated interest in the use of unobtrusive measures by social researchers. The text presents a strong case for incorporating such measures into research projects. The limitations of relying exclusively on nonreactive measures are noted as well. The bibliography is extensive, nearly thirty pages.

Webb, Eugene J., Donald T. Campbell, Richard D. Schwartz, Lee Sechrest, and Janet Belew Grove. *Nonreactive Measures in the Social Sciences*. 2d ed. Boston: Houghton Mifflin, 1981. This is the second edition of the descriptive text noted above. There are many updated examples of research projects using unobtrusive measurement. This volume includes a longer discussion of ethical considerations, and a longer bibliography than the earlier edition.

Nancy Balazadeh

Cross-References

URBAN PLANNING: MAJOR ISSUES

Type of sociology: Urban and rural life

Urban planning is knowledge-based planned change intended to improve the quality of life in urban areas and the regions of which they are a part. Sociological concerns include the group interests of planners and other stakeholders and the social consequences of change.

Principal terms

CHANGE AGENT: a person who plays a significant, intentional role in the social change process

PLANNING: a process that includes identifying problems, clarifying goals, recommending courses of action, planning implementation, and evaluating outcomes

PUBLIC INTEREST: interests of the larger community, as contrasted with narrower interests such as those of social classes, ethnic groups, or private sector stakeholders

SOCIAL CHANGE: an observed difference in a sector of the social system, or in its entirety, between two points in time

URBAN AREA: characteristics of the classic "urban" ideal type, developed by sociologist Louis Wirth, are large size, high density, and considerable social heterogeneity

Overview

Urban areas in the United States and throughout most of the world face severe problems such as crime, insufficient affordable housing, pollution, unemployment, and extreme inequality. These problems are a consequence of such powerful socio-economic and technological changes as the mobility of capital in a global economy, increased national and international migration, and the shift of employment from manufacturing to service and from low to high technology. They are also caused by counterurbanization, involving the relocation of a significant portion of capital invest-ment, residence, recreation, and employment to what sociologist Manuel Castells has termed enclaves on the city's periphery. As a result, urban areas have to some extent become "dual cities" of inequality. Most national and local leaders want to ameliorate or contain these problems.

Urban planning, intertwined with unplanned cultural, economic, political, and social change, helps to shape the future of urban areas as a whole as well as their regions and neighborhoods. Planning, guided by personal or collective visions of the better community and drawing upon various domains of knowledge, is often designed to enhance stability and social control—or perhaps, as sociologists John Logan and Harvey Molotch have put it, to smooth the functioning of the marketplace. Planning may also promote redistribution and democratization.

The argument for planning is twofold: First, planners assume that the future can in part be shaped by rational human thought and action. This view of planning has its roots in the scientific revolution. Second, many planners believe that private market forces and individual or group self-interests often fail to take into account the larger public interest. Promoting the public interest is often seen by citizens as the responsibility of a locality's government, and this view is the basis of the legitimacy of professional urban planning in the public sector.

In a sense, any urban official or active community member tries to plan urban change. Various actions of people with power, including corporate executives and even mob bosses, have effects on urban areas and may be based on rationality. Professional urban planners, however, often have significant responsibility for public sector urban planning. This profession, which usually requires a specialized graduate degree, is multidisciplinary, drawing upon and contributing to sociology as well as anthropology, architecture, economics, engineering, geography, psychology, and political science. Since planners, like most professionals in the United States, do not constitute a representative sample of the population, they face the challenge of understanding the larger community interest. Indeed, it is concern for the urban community that draws many people into the profession.

Many urban planners are politically subordinate technicians who provide "objective"—often quantitative—information to policy makers by identifying housing, social services, and other needs or opportunities, diagnosing problems, specifying and assessing alternative courses of action, formulating implementation plans, and evaluating outcomes. Planners often employ computer analyses and mapping. Other urban planners, however, have a major impact on the policy-making agenda and process; they are effective "politicians" who know what is possible and can convince officials and citizens to accept or at least seriously consider their ideas. The central importance of political action in determining the future of an urban area is why some planners are activists working to achieve their own visions or serving as advocates for less powerful citizens.

Whether technicians or advocates, planners find the public interest easy to invoke but difficult to validate, given the diversity of cultures and interests in urban communities. Defining the public interest is complex; it is not simply determined by counting votes and siding with the majority. Minority rights, cultural interplay, and tradeoffs are important to consider in planned change. Furthermore, as sociologist Herbert Gans notes, people view the public interest in different ways; there may, for example, be differences of opinion and understanding based on education, gender, sexual orientation, race, and so forth. Different cultures in part account for disputes over the intended and unintended consequences of proposed actions. Developing a consensual public interest is made even more complex because, as sociologist Martin L. Needleman points out, American culture supports both capitalism and democracy.

When plans evoke conflict, political economist Stephen Elkin observes, the victors are often members of the local business-political elite attempting to further their locality's economic future by intensifying land use. Most urban planners are employed by members of this elite. To illustrate, urbanist Mike Davis points out that growth-control building restrictions and environmental regulations in California are claimed to be in the public's interest in preventing the overurbanization or population of suburbs. In reality this strategy has the consequence of defending the socioeconomic privileges of those already living in the suburbs. Robert M. Fogelson's study of Los Angeles indicates that zoning essentially sanctions the preferences of private enterprise. Davis reports that the committee formed to produce a strategic plan for Los Angeles was dominated by one set of stakeholders: corporate executives.

The scope of urban planning varies from city to city. Planners may try to realize various visions or goals by focusing on a particular urban function such as housing or the environment; or, for purposes of integration and coordination, they may consolidate a wide range of functions into what is called a "comprehensive" urban plan. Similarly, the geographic unit of planning may vary from a single neighborhood or municipality to a larger entity.

Applications

In many urban areas, planners are involved in virtually every aspect of the community's life; the range might include the site of a new power plant or road, the assessment of the health of homeless people, and even the location of tolerated prostitution. Two examples of the types of problems faced by urban planners are issues concerning housing and accessibility. Houses are typically designed by architects and built by contractors and their workers. Groups of houses (tracts or subdivisions) are often the result of investments by real estate developers. Urban planning both creates opportunities for and places constraints on development, and it thereby has a significant impact on community life. Most planners and citizens alike, for example, agree that large high-rise structures should not be located in the middle of residential low-rise neighborhoods.

The case of Parma, Ohio, a white working-class and lower-middle-class suburb bordering Cleveland, Ohio, exemplifies planning at the national/regional and community levels as well as conflicting views of the public interest. Working within the terms of the antisegregation 1968 Fair Housing Act, planners in Cuyahoga County decided in the early 1970's that, to relieve overcrowding in Cleveland's poor neighborhoods, the surrounding suburbs should provide their "fair share" of housing. A developer proposed for Parma a 201-unit, low- and moderate-income residential complex with twin ten-story towers. Planners and politicians of Parma fiercely resisted this attempt to change their community demographically and physically. For example, the city council enacted building height and parking space restrictions. In the court battles that followed, planners from around the country became deeply involved. Some of them suggested that racial prejudice was a factor in the resistance; others, including advocate-planner Paul Davidoff, proposed solutions. Another view was that community concern about a change in the built environment and demand for social services was legitimate.

Federal courts decided in favor of fair-share housing and against exclusionary zoning—that is, in favor of what they saw to be the national and regional public interest. In 1980 a federal district judge appointed a "master" to direct change in Parma. The changes that eventually came to Parma were moderate, however, representing an implicit compromise between competing views of the public and its varying interests. A small apartment complex was built, and not all its residents came from Cleveland's poor neighborhoods.

Next, planning to make a community accessible can be considered. Urban residents with physical disabilities often find that they are prevented from full community participation: Buildings, paths, and other physical components of their locality are not accessible to them. For example, a wheelchair user may be unable to use a town's public transportation system because of the restrictive elevation and width of entry doors. In this case a majoritarian view of the public interest might not suggest change; after all, people with disabilities constitute a minority. Change, however, would be in the interest of people with disabilities as well as in the spirit of community equity.

Encouraged by the Rehabilitation Act of 1973 and more forcefully guided by the Americans with Disabilities Act of 1992, local governments in the United States have tried to improve accessibility. The first phase has been to develop and enforce published accessibility guidelines that call for some buildings being ramped, for toilet doors to be widened and grab-bars installed, for infrared communication systems and sign-language interpretations to be used at public activities, and so forth. Yet meeting the formal guidelines may not accomplish the goal of access, because a modification that seems appropriate to an outsider might not create manageable and expected access from the perspective of the person with the disability.

Understanding the needs of people with disabilities usually requires information from people with disabilities—that is, it requires meaningful citizen participation. In one planning study of community access, residents with disabilities reported that information about access was so inaccurate that it could not be trusted and that some facilities for access were broken, hard to find, or demeaning to use. Even access to the local Red Cross headquarters was through an obscure lower-level side door. Based upon citizen input, planners were able to develop a frequently updated information system, a better training program for information providers, and a more effective schedule for facility inspection and maintenance.

Context

Urban agglomerations have undoubtedly been shaped by some form of planning since the dawn of civilization. Until the modern era, a primary purpose was to arrange the use of space for religious and military or political advantage. Modern urban planning, which emerged in the United States in the late nineteenth and early twentieth centuries as an outgrowth of efforts at civic reform, has by contrast been dedicated to improving the efficiency and quality of urban life—often for the politically and economically advantaged—in the face of the increasingly undesirable aspects of cities. In this sense, urban planning is a form of applied sociology.

By the 1920's, a number of U.S. municipalities had appointed reformist planning commissions charged to develop master plans designed to guide development toward the commissioners' vision of a more beautiful, healthier, and less dangerous city. Early urban plans emphasized land use control, often employing the tool of zoning based upon the police power as a legal means to divide a locality into limited-use districts by regulating the purpose, size, and sometimes aesthetics of buildings on privately owned land. Economic planning was added to the repertoire as local governments sought to create growth machines that would increase jobs and revenues by attracting and retaining business establishments, industrial plants, and office complexes.

Initially in the 1930's, and especially after World War II, utopian visions of the good community led to some "garden" new-town development and, more frequently, to large-scale "urban renewal" that cleared entire blocks of "undesirable" urban neighborhoods. (These neighborhoods were nevertheless often deemed satisfactory by their residents.) Huge projects were built in attempts to revitalize inner-city areas, including new residential, commercial, and monumental construction. Projects ranged from giant public housing projects to arts centers. Unfortunately, as T. J. Kent stated in his 1964 urban planning text, it was not understood in the planning stages what the true impact of these immense physical changes upon economic and social life would be. Ultimately, communities were destroyed and cultural patterns were disrupted. Poor people were often dislocated and removed rather than relocated in improved or even acceptable housing. Rather than seeing life improve, area residents saw an increase in crime and social disorganization.

In 1961, social commentator Jane Jacobs issued a scathing attack on this kind of urban change. "Whole communities are torn apart and sown to the winds," she wrote. Her view was that planners should work to preserve the mixed-use, small-scale complex fabric of historically rooted urban neighborhoods. Eventually, her voice and the voices of others, plus the influence of the social unrest of the 1960's, led to a critical reevaluation of planning strategy, including its dependence on the "one-best-way" rational model and the assumption that there is a single public interest.

On important outcome of this rethinking has been greater interest in understanding what impact the built environment has on human behavior. Environmental psychology and environmental sociology are now active fields of intellectual activity for a growing number of planners; physical determinism is yielding to the view that the impact is significantly mediated by values, cognitions, and other factors. Thus, neither the big housing project nor the mixed-use older neighborhood provides a universal solution. A second outcome has been the gradual decline of physical planning. Indeed, planning historian M. Christine Boyer has written about "the eclipse of physical planning as it abandons once and for all its traditional focus on the physical order of the American city." A third outcome of the rethinking is greater concern for the relationship between planning and democracy. The emergence of citizen participation as a planning issue, which dramatically surfaced in the 1960's, calls for the integration of rational and democratic processes respecting a plurality of perspectives on the public interest. The work of activist Saul Alinsky and advocacy planner Paul Davidoff helped to bring neighborhood interests and citizen participation to the planning forefront. More recently, equity planning, designed to create greater equality in the allocation of benefits and burdens, has found favor within the planning profession.

Since the 1980's, planners have begun to enlarge their geographic unit of analysis. The beginning of cooperation among jurisdictions has led to the formation of inter-governmental planning councils among the many home-rule jurisdictions of typical U.S. metropolitan areas. More dramatically, the "L.A. school" of planning, led by John Friedmann and others, has focused on global conditions and change in order to explain local conditions and to improve the outcomes of planned change at the local level. These developments have begun to forge stronger links between sociologists and planners as theory and practice are joined in an effort to shape social change into the twenty-first century.

Bibliography

Davis, Mike. *City of Quartz: Excavating the Future in Los Angeles.* New York: Verso, 1990. A lecturer in urban theory, Davis reveals a keen understanding of interests favoring and opposing change. The book focuses on change in Los Angeles.

Friedmann, John. *Planning in the Public Domain.* Princeton, N.J.: Princeton University Press, 1987. Friedmann is a leader of the school of planning that emphasizes theoretical foundations and international perspectives.

Gans, Herbert J. *People and Plans: Essays on Urban Problems and Solutions.* New York: Basic Books, 1968. These sociological essays on planning explore such topics as environment versus culture and the potential for planning to ameliorate the crisis of urban poverty. He thinks planners should be user oriented and equity promoting.

Hall, Peter. *Cities of Tomorrow.* Oxford, England: Blackwell, 1988. This history of the ideologies and practices of planners over the past century traces the humanistic and self-protective concerns that led national and local elites to support urban planning.

Jacobs, Jane. *The Death and Life of Great American Cities.* New York: Random House, 1961. This influential work's accurate first sentence reads: "This book is an attack on current city planning and rebuilding." Jacobs argues for an emphasis on preserving neighborhoods.

Logan, John R., and Harvey L. Molotch. *Urban Fortunes: The Political Economy of Place.* Berkeley: University of California Press, 1987. A sociological analysis focusing on who gains, loses, and is legitimized by virtue of urban planning.

Needleman, Martin L., and Carolyn Emerson Needleman. *Guerrillas in the Bureau-cracy: The Community Planning Experiment in the United States.* New York: John Wiley & Sons, 1974. This sociological study of the experiment to provide planning expertise to communities within larger urban jurisdictions focuses on the competing interests of central city government and community groups.

So, Frank S., and Judith Getzels, eds. *The Practice of Local Government Planning.* 2d ed. Washington, D.C.: International City Management Association, 1988. A broad compilation of essays by experts in the field, this encyclopedic work is often used to prepare practicing planners for the profession's certification examination.

William John Hanna

Cross-References

Cities: Preindustrial, Industrial, and Postindustrial, 253; The Concentric Zone Model of Urban Growth, 322; Industrial Societies, 953; New Towns and Planned Communities, 1296; Suburbanization and Decentralization, 2010; Urban Renewal and Gentrification, 2116; Urbanization, 2129.

URBAN RENEWAL AND GENTRIFICATION

Type of sociology: Urban and rural life

Urban renewal was a federal program designed to eliminate substandard housing and replace it with better housing and commercial endeavors. Gentrification is a phenomenon in which decayed homes in decayed neighborhoods are privately renovated. Both have had major impacts on American cities and their residents.

Principal terms

COOPERATIVE FEDERALISM: the working together of different levels of government; in urban renewal, the coordination of federal and local governments

DISPLACEMENT: the phenomenon in which people are forced to move from their homes by urban renewal, gentrification, highway construction, and the like

EMINENT DOMAIN: the right of the government to take private land for public use as long as it compensates the owners

INFRASTRUCTURE: roads, sewers, water supply systems, and other structures essential for a municipality to operate

SITE CLEARANCE: in urban renewal, the clearing of land, usually covered by decayed homes and businesses, to make way for new buildings

Overview

The problem of inadequate housing did not begin with the Great Depression, but like so many other facets of American life and politics, it was affected by it, and programs were then first begun to attempt to deal with the problem. The first major housing legislation was the National Housing Act of 1934, which recognized housing as an important concern. It created the Federal Housing Administration (FHA), with the purpose of guaranteeing home mortgages; the FHA was primarily beneficial to people with middle-class incomes rather than poor people. The Housing Act of 1937 laid the foundation for slum clearance, public housing, and, later, urban renewal. This act created the U.S. Housing Agency, which aided local housing authorities in clearing slum land and in providing public housing.

The passage of the Housing Act of 1949 began a more intensive effort to provide adequate and decent housing for millions of Americans who lacked it. This legislation authorized the use of federal money to build new housing units in the areas in which dilapidated units had been destroyed and to refurbish less decayed units. This was the beginning of large-scale site clearance, a "bulldozer approach" to urban renewal in which physically deteriorated housing units were razed and new housing was built. The program known as urban renewal grew out of this 1949 act and its subsequent amendments. It authorized the purchase of slum land by local public authorities and then sold it to private developers who were to build and then sell primarily residential units. Local housing authorities used the power of eminent domain to acquire land at market value, often improving the infrastructure surrounding the land, and then sell it at relatively low prices. The difference was made up by federal grants. Developers understandably liked the program, and it became popular. Between 1949 and 1969, site clearance eliminated an estimated 450,000 units of substandard housing. Even though urban renewal in its early years was tied to the creation of new housing, more units were destroyed than were built.

The 1954 amendments to the 1949 Housing Act changed the character of the original act, moving it away somewhat from the provision of housing to a new emphasis on urban renewal. The 1954 amendments emphasized renewing or rehabilitating old structures rather than razing and rebuilding them. They also allowed 10 percent (changed to 20 percent in 1959 and 30 percent in 1967) of the funds to be used for nonresidential construction, thus further removing the program from its original emphasis on providing decent housing for the poor.

Urban renewal was a good example of cooperative federalism, or the sharing of costs and administrative responsibilities by federal and local agencies. In order to qualify for urban renewal funds, a city had to create a local public agency (which was often the same as their local housing authority). This agency designated land to be cleared with urban renewal funds and submitted to the federal urban renewal agency its plans for a workable development. Upon approval of the plan, the federal agency provided funds to the local agency to acquire land, clear it, and reinstall water and sewer lines, as well as to improve roads, streetlights, and any other necessary infrastructure. After this had been done, the local authority offered the cleared and improved land for sale to developers at a price that was often much less than what it had paid for it, minus costs of clearance and improvements. The federal government usually paid two-thirds of the local authority's net costs (for acquisition, clearance, and improvements, minus the price paid by the developer); the remainder was provided by the local government in the form of bonds, cash, or other funds.

Unlike urban renewal, a federally sponsored and largely federally funded attempt to make cities more habitable, gentrification is an unorchestrated, privately driven event in which older, often seriously decayed, homes in the cities are renovated. Gentrification typically occurs when a once gracious but now decayed home in a blighted neighborhood is bought, renovated, and occupied by its new middle-class or upper-middle-class owners for their own housing needs. In the earliest stage of gentrification, people move into their renovated home in the midst of the urban decay all around them. Later, as word spreads of the area's rebirth, others buy property, renovate, and move in.

In the 1970's, much was made of the discovery of gentrifying neighborhoods in several central cities. It was stated that this was a new and significant trend that would greatly improve the cities, all without direct governmental intervention. While it did spread to most large cities, gentrification generally proved to be limited to the few neighborhoods with the most potential to be transformed from decay into splendor, usually areas containing large old Victorian houses or townhomes.

Applications

A typical example of urban renewal and gentrification in action is the case of Philadelphia, Pennsylvania. Begun in the late 1940's, the urban renewal process and subsequent gentrification totally changed the character of the central business district. Prior to these changes, the central city was dominated by old industrial buildings, aging warehouses, and crumbling infrastructure. The land adjacent to city hall was occupied by a huge terminal of the Pennsylvania Railroad. Surrounding the central business district in old, rundown tenements and aging homes lived poor minority and white working-class residents. Philadelphia's urban renewal transformed this area, and subsequent gentrification furthered the process.

Urban renewal projects replaced much of this old gritty Philadelphia with expensive new hotels and restaurants, upscale specialty shops, university campus facilities, and gleaming office towers. Land values in the central business district skyrocketed, as did the city's revenue in the form of property and sales taxes. Old, narrow streets were widened; parking lots were built and parks planted where once homes and warehouses had stood. The focus of the renewal of Philadelphia was the new Penn Station, created from the old Philadelphia Railroad terminal. This new Penn Station, developed by the railroad, included banks, offices, and retail facilities.

Urban renewal also severely affected the inner-city population of Philadelphia. The largely poor and minority residents and small businesses in the neighborhoods that were displaced to make room for the many urban renewal projects found themselves without places to which they could relocate. While the urban renewal of Philadelphia did create a large number of new dwelling units, the majority were designed for upper-middle-class professionals. While some public housing was constructed on urban renewal land, twice as much land was developed for the housing of affluent groups. This creation of new upscale housing in the central city stimulated a gentrification boom in neighboring areas, successfully returning many older, once-beautiful homes to their former splendor. This uprooted still more people who were dependent on low-cost housing.

Gentrification in central Philadelphia lasted much longer than the process of urban renewal, which had largely ended by the late 1960's. As the gentrifying areas grew and spread, working-class areas also became affected. Many cities with ambitious urban renewal programs had results similar to those of Philadelphia. Old industrial and commercial buildings, old dwelling units, and old infrastructure were ripped out, and new, largely upscale businesses, offices, and dwellings were built. Gentrification often followed as private individuals and later developers sought to capitalize on the "rebirth" of the city. While this had many positive effects, it also had many negative ones.

The implications and impact of urban renewal can best be seen in two broad categories: the economic impacts and the human impacts. In economic terms, the effect of urban renewal was to increase the value of the improved land and thus increase the city's property tax revenues from those parcels which had been renewed or rebuilt. Additionally, the improved parcels often generated a multiplying effect, with improvements spilling over to neighboring property, again increasing tax revenues to the municipality. Some critics of urban renewal discount these tax revenue increases, arguing that much of the new development would have occurred even without urban renewal. Some critics argue that cities actually lost a considerable amount of tax revenue because much land remained vacant for years after it was cleared, creating an absence of tax revenue for those years. Additionally, they argue, land increases in value over time anyway, so that some of the gains attributed to urban renewal projects are really attributable to the natural increase in the value of land. Despite these criticisms, most observers feel that urban renewal has led to greater tax revenues and economic growth in those cities with urban renewal projects.

Because urban renewal projects needed to be profitable to the city and to the developer, certain types of projects were favored over others. The city needed increased tax receipts as well as spinoff economic growth in the neighboring area in order for the city to invest its time and money into the project. Additionally, and perhaps more important, the projects chosen had to be ones in which private developers believed that they could make a profit. Thus, the development of privately owned low-income housing and public housing projects, the original goal of the 1949 Housing Act, was least profitable both for developers and for the city. It was less profitable for the city because public housing generates no property tax revenues, and even though privately owned low-income housing generates modest property taxes, it by definition attracts low-income people—those with little money to spend on neighboring businesses. Developers can make larger profits building more expensive residential units, office buildings, or other commercial spaces. Thus, one important effect of urban renewal was gradually to shift land use from lower- to higher-cost enterprises. Urban renewal exacerbated a trend toward the creation of luxury housing and commercial or industrial enterprises where once existed functional, if unattractive, low-income communities.

Another result of the need to create profit was that the very worst slums were rarely razed or renovated; the local housing authorities and developers picked the best site that could be called decayed or dilapidated enough to merit urban renewal. The result was that well-located decent, although run-down, neighborhoods were destroyed, while the worst of the slums remained.

An additional impact was the creation of jobs in the central cities. The clearing of the sites, the rebuilding of infrastructure, and the new building on the site all required labor. Additionally, when renewal sites were complete, permanent jobs would often be created in the businesses newly located on that spot.

In addition to economic impacts, urban renewal had human impacts. These effects centered on the displacement and relocation of the people originally living at the urban renewal site. It is estimated (no one really knows exactly how many people were dislocated) that approximately two million people and 136,000 small businesses were forced to move to make way for urban renewal projects. Most of those affected were the poor, especially ethnic and racial minorities. This led to the somewhat bitter quip in the 1960's that urban renewal was really "Negro removal." Although roughly 50 percent of the displaced families qualified for public housing, only about 20 percent of them actually moved into public housing, largely because of its unavailability or stigma. While the legislation creating urban renewal required that assistance be given to the displaced in finding suitable housing, in most cases this entailed token amounts (sometimes $100) to be used primarily for moving expenses. The displacement of persons is seen by many as the largest of the problems associated with urban renewal.

Additionally, the displacement of small businesses by urban renewal projects often resulted in their demise. Few of the small businesses affected, usually of the "mom and pop" variety, actually moved and reopened in a new location. Most shut their doors forever; urban renewal caused the destruction of many once-viable small businesses.

Gentrification was not without impact, either. On a positive note, gentrification helped decrease the vacancy rate in the central cities. Older, rundown, vacant homes were renovated and occupied. This helped a city in several ways. In addition to providing residents for once-vacant homes, the upgrading of the homes returned them to the tax rolls—and at a much higher rate. Thus, gentrification helped the city increase its property tax base. An additional positive impact of gentrification was that the addition of homeowners to an area added new stability to transient neighborhoods of renters and squatters. This in turn rekindled interest in the city among the upper-middle-class as a viable place to live. All these positive aspects of gentrification were welcomed by the city, by developers and business interests, and by established and prospective city residents. They were lauded by the media.

Gentrification also had its down side, however; displacement of the original population, as with urban renewal, was a major negative aspect of the phenomenon. Additionally, the new, more affluent residents made increased economic demands on the city for services such as increased fire and police protection, better roads, and improved streetlights and sidewalks.

Context

Urban renewal developed from the perceived need to provide decent housing for the many Americans living in decayed housing, and it evolved into a program that attempted to clean up and reinvigorate many of the older cities of the United States by means of razing dilapidated structures and building new ones. Unfortunately for the poor, the original goal of providing decent housing for the less advantaged was lost in the desire to create more affluent and more desirable cities, resulting in a greater creation of office buildings, specialty shops, and upscale housing than low-income housing. Urban renewal displaced more poor people than it helped house.

Gentrification, following urban renewal efforts in many cities, first affected a few people, then spread to cover larger (though still relatively small) parts of the city. As a privately generated phenomenon, it did not rely on governmental funding. As a renovation-centered phenomenon, it did not seek to raze structures and rebuild. Yet although gentrification focused on renovation rather than the more drastic actions of urban renewal, it sometimes changed the character of neighborhoods as dramatically as did many urban renewal projects.

Another impact of urban renewal and gentrification was perhaps the increased number of homeless individuals living in these "renewed" cities. Urban renewal took place largely from the late 1940's through the late 1960's, and gentrification occurred most widely from the late 1960's through the early 1980's; the number of homeless individuals greatly increased during this same time. While a number of reasons are often cited for the increase in homelessness, it is not a debated point that urban renewal and gentrification played some role in the increase in the homeless population. The extent of its effects, however, remains unknown.

Bibliography

Caputo, David. *Urban America: The Policy Alternatives*. San Francisco: W. H. Freeman, 1976. Although an older book, this is one of the best overall discussions of urban renewal and the federal policies which created massive urban change. The book is thorough and easily read.

Downs, Anthony. *Neighborhoods and Urban Development*. Washington, D.C.: Brookings Institution, 1981. Downs argues that urban policies are designed to (and do) benefit the middle and upper classes, not the poor. Includes a good discussion of displacement.

Fainstein, Susan, Norman Fainstein, et al. *Restructuring the City: The Political Economy of Urban Redevelopment*. New York: Longman, 1986. A comprehensive empirical analysis of urban renewal, gentrification, and subsequent policies, based on case studies of five cities.

Friedman, Lawrence M. *Government and Slum Housing*. Chicago: Rand McNally, 1968. A history of American housing policy. The last third of the book examines urban renewal in detail. Interesting and readable.

Peterson, Paul, ed. *The New Urban Reality*. Washington, D.C.: Brookings Institution, 1985. Chapter 3, "Islands of Renewal in Seas of Decay," by Brian Berry, is concerned with gentrification. A very thorough and informative analytical article.

Lisa Langenbach

Cross-References

THE URBAN UNDERCLASS AND THE RURAL POOR

Type of sociology: Social stratification
Field of study: Poverty

"Urban underclass" has come to refer to a segment of the population that resides in urban or central-city areas and experiences high and persistent poverty, social isolation, anomie, and a sense of hopelessness. The "rural poor" consist of poverty-stricken persons living in small or sparsely populated communities. Examination of these groups may help to establish policies to alleviate poverty.

Principal terms
ABSOLUTE POVERTY: condition of people who fail to receive sufficient resources to support physical health and well-being
ANOMIE: social condition characterized by the breakdown of norms and values governing social interaction
CULTURE OF POVERTY: the notion that the poverty-stricken have different values from the rest of society
DEVIANT BEHAVIOR: behavior contrary to or in violation of accepted group norms
NORMS: societal guidelines that dictate how people should behave in various situations
POVERTY TRAP: situation in which people find it difficult to escape poverty because if they increase their earnings through employment they lose welfare benefits
RELATIVE POVERTY: determines poverty based on the standards of living in a given society, rather than on some absolute level
VALUES: ideas shared between people regarding what is desirable or undesirable, good or bad

Overview

The use of the terms "urban underclass" and "rural poor" is controversial, and there seems to be no consensus regarding how best to define them. It is estimated that 33 million poor people live in the United States (1990). Journalist Ken Auletta, in *The Underclass* (1983), estimates the number of American underclass to be anywhere from 2 to 18 million, while Joel A. Devine and James D. Wright, in *The Greatest of Evils: Urban Poverty and the American Underclass* (1993), cite figures of 3 to 3.5 million. The number of rural poor in the United States is more than 9 million. These dramatically different figures and discrepancies in the totals are indicative of continued debate in defining both rural and urban poverty.

Swedish sociologist Gunnar Myrdal was the first to use the term "underclass" in his book *Challenge to Affluence* (1962). In the early 1960's, he began referring to the underclass as unemployed, unemployable, and underemployed. Myrdal noted also their lack of opportunity for upward mobility, since upward mobility requires highly trained, skilled, and educated workers. Those who are not sufficiently trained—the unskilled and uneducated—will be displaced. Myrdal furthermore linked chronic unemployment and persistent poverty both directly and indirectly to crime, prostitution, and other forms of deviant behavior.

In 1993, sociologists Devine and Wright proposed that the underclass includes

persons living in urban, central city neighborhoods or communities with high and increasing rates of poverty, especially chronic poverty, high and increasing levels of social isolation, hopelessness, and anomie, and high levels of characteristically antisocial or dysfunctional behavior patterns.

This explanation, in combination with Myrdal's earlier work, involves structural and socioeconomic factors, social-psychological elements, behavioral elements, and spatial or ecological aspects of the underclass.

A number of subgroups are more likely to be among the urban underclass than others, including children, the elderly, women, nonwhites, and members of female-headed households. Of these, racial affiliation is perhaps the most noted in research. Sociologist William Julius Wilson points out that underclass neighborhoods "are populated almost exclusively by the most disadvantaged segments of the black urban community." This has not changed significantly since Myrdal wrote in 1962: "The largest and still most handicapped minority group in America is that of the Negroes."

Increased crime and deviant behavior are two of the most disturbing characteristics of the urban underclass. The entrenched hopelessness found on inner-city streets provides little motivation for members of the underclass to adhere to the norms and values of mainstream society. Consequently, drug dealing, use of drugs and alcohol, prostitution, theft, and other forms of crime are prevalent among members of the urban underclass.

Turning now to an examination of the rural poor, it is necessary first to clarify the term "rural." As defined by the U.S. Bureau of the Census, "rural" generally applies to settlements with concentrated populations of less than 2,500. Demographic studies show that the rural poor are concentrated heavily in the southern region of the United States. For example, the 1987 rural poverty rate in the South was 21.2 percent, 7.6 percent higher than the rest of the country. Moreover, in excess of half the rural poor in the United States lived in the South in 1987.

The majority of the rural poor are white (although this predominance in the rural poor reflects the overall population makeup of rural America). This is not to say that rural blacks, Hispanics, and American Indians do not experience high poverty rates. Statistics show that these subgroups have poverty rates of 44 percent, 35 percent, and at least 35 percent, respectively. These figures represent poverty rates several times higher than those of their white counterparts. Those suffering from persistent rural poverty are more likely to be elderly, black, female, or members of a female-headed household.

There are a number of reasons that many members of the rural population are unable to work. Most noteworthy is the fact that many are children too young to work. Illness and disability are additional reasons that many of the rural poor are not among the work force. Overriding all this, a large percentage of the rural poor are simply unable to find work because of factory closings or manufacturing cutbacks.

On the surface it might appear that the only difference between the urban underclass and the rural poor is their geographic location and concentration of population. A closer look at the population subgroups (such as elderly, female-headed households, and nonwhites) reveals that this is not the case. In 1987, for example, the rural elderly had a higher poverty rate than the urban elderly. Also, a significantly smaller number of impoverished rural families live in female-headed households than in urban areas.

It appears that behavior is the key to distinguishing the urban underclass from the rural poor. In his provocative book *The Truly Disadvantaged: The Inner City, the Underclass, and Public Policy* (1987), William Julius Wilson maintains that "there is a heterogeneous grouping of inner-city families and individuals whose behavior contrasts sharply with that of mainstream America." The anomie or normlessness displayed among the urban underclass manifests itself through high rates of out-of-wedlock births, welfare, unemployment or underemployment, low educational attainment, drug and alcohol abuse, and crime.

According to numerous studies, the rural poor exhibit attitudes toward work that are different from the attitudes of the urban underclass. For example, U.S. census data from 1973 and 1987 indicate that the percentage of rural poor who worked was a full 10 percent higher than the working urban poor.

Applications

Just as it is difficult to determine the exact number of poor in the United States, it is also difficult to assess the annual cost of poverty. In 1990, the total annual federal budget was $1.5 trillion. Of this amount, antipoverty programs totaled $200 billion dollars, roughly 15 percent. A breakdown of the $200 billion antipoverty budget indicates the following expenditures: Medicaid, $50 billion; Aid to Families with Dependent Children (AFDC), $20-30 billion; food stamps, $20-25 billion; Housing and Urban Development (HUD), $20 billion; and an additional $10 billion in state funds spent on general welfare and relief programs. Not included in these funds are costs which are the direct or indirect result of poverty, such as crime, loss of property as a result of crime, protection measures to reduce crime rates, alcohol and drug abuse rehabilitation, and health care expenses paid out for poverty-related illness and disease. Some experts say that hundreds of billions of dollars are spent annually on poverty and its consequences.

Those who seek to reform the welfare system recommend a number of general policies. Among these are revisions to national income and welfare policies, national employment policies, national education policies, national family and health care programs, and national drug policy.

One of the most widely proposed initiatives focuses on the implementation of a nationwide guaranteed annual income (GAI). This policy would ensure a minimal standard of living for all citizens by paying individuals enough to raise their income levels above the poverty line. While some suggest that a GAI would provide the poor with incentives not to work, any viable GAI program would incorporate a negative income taxation (NIT). The NIT would provide the necessary incentive to work by allowing those in the program to keep part of their earnings without sacrificing their base guaranteed level. Many welfare programs now provide little incentive for individuals to work and in fact penalize those who do work. For example, if AFDC recipients work, the amount they earn is deducted from their monthly AFDC checks.

There are a number of additional positive aspects of a nationally implemented guaranteed annual income. First, a GAI would encourage people to work and still assist those who cannot work. Second, it would allow for national equity by omitting state-to-state differences in welfare. Third, a federal GAI would simplify the current welfare system by utilizing the existing structure of the Internal Revenue System. Finally, a GAI would help not only the elderly, children, and disabled, but anyone in the United States who falls below a minimum standard of living.

As critics point out, a guaranteed annual income would cost a lot of money. Defenders of the concept argue that the total amount of cash transfers (AFDC, Supplemental Security Income, and veterans' payments), combined with noncash payouts (food stamps; Women, Infants, and Children), would at least equal the funds required for GAI.

Another policy to alleviate poverty in the United States addresses nationwide unemployment. A national employment policy would identify the types of work needed across the country and provide individuals with the adequate training to do it. Proponents of this type of plan note the shortages of day care professionals, teachers, teachers' aides, and nurses, all greatly needed in low-income areas. Others suggest that homeless and unemployed men and women could help physically rebuild the run-down inner cities, thus providing jobs and housing at the same time.

The general problem of poverty is made worse from generation to generation as parents and children receive less and less education. Experts insist that education should be "life preparation," enabling graduates to find work. Included in this definition should be increased math and reading skills, as well as combined efforts with local businesses to determine required job skills for better chances of placement. Finally, national education policy should expand the existing Head Start program and introduce adult literacy programs throughout the nation.

In looking at the possibilities for alleviating the problems of the poor in the United States, the majority of recommended programs target the urban poor, particularly single mothers and their dependents. This in itself is a dilemma for advocates for the rural poor, who argue that their needs are not being met. One of the major obstacles in assisting the rural poor is their location. Manufacturers simply do not want to locate in areas outside suburbia, which lack the infrastructure they desire for maximum productivity. Moreover, the national economy is such that corporations are having difficulty competing in the international market. In short, the problem of unemployment in rural areas is lack of employment. Perhaps the rural poor should be given tax incentives to relocate and find work in suburban areas.

Context

From the end of World War II until the late 1960's, the United States experienced an economic boom. There was virtually no urban poverty, and rural poverty declined as a result of migration to cities. During this period of general prosperity, the eyes of the country turned to the less fortunate. When President Lyndon B. Johnson declared unconditional "war on poverty" in 1964, the federal government established an official poverty line and assistance programs. Not all elements of the poor population were helped by federal programs; the focus was mainly on the Appalachia area and poor children and mothers. Sociological research on poverty increased in the 1960's and flourished until the mid-1970's.

Following national economic restructuring beginning in 1979, rural areas experienced economic growth; manufacturers built factories and brought new jobs to small towns. Prices for farm products increased, domestic energy industries expanded, and retirees began moving to rural areas. As Duncan notes, however, this "rural turnaround" was short-lived. Rural poverty has been on the rise since the late 1970's, mainly because the national economy has been hit hard by high inflation, recessions, low wages, unemployment, and slow job growth—the results of international competition, factory closings, and layoffs.

The formation of the urban underclass from the 1960's to the 1990's is generally attributed to the mass exodus of the middle- and working-class residents from cities to the suburbs, and to the simultaneous decline in semiskilled and unskilled employment opportunities in the inner cities. In the early 1980's, many middle-class African Americans left the urban areas to take advantage of educational and employment opportunities in the suburbs.

With the absence of middle-class families and their incomes came a substantial decrease in the tax base available to support public schools and other government-run programs. The quality of education declined and urban youths found opportunities slipping even further out of reach and thus became caught in the poverty trap. The departure of the middle class eventually destroyed other stabilizing social institutions, including black churches and local businesses.

During President Ronald Reagan's administration in the 1980's, the situation worsened. Republican constituents were not, in general, poor or black, but rather middle- and working-class people who were tired of their tax dollars supporting the welfare state. This attitude led to the further neglect of the inner-city poor, which brought with it an increase in underclass violence. Incidents such as the Los Angeles riots in 1992 are evidence of the dysfunctional behavior and anomie characteristic of the underclass. These behaviors and sociological phenomena have drawn considerable attention from the media and sociologists alike, and will continue to do so until the problems of the poor are alleviated.

Bibliography

Devine, Joel A., and James D. Wright. *The Greatest of Evils: Urban Poverty and the American Underclass.* New York: Aldine de Gruyter, 1993. This work discusses several principles of urban poverty. First, poverty is not monolithic. Second, Devine and Wright consider the underclass and potential problems associated with it. Finally, they claim that poverty policies need to be bolder. A thorough study, at the same time nontechnical and interesting.

Duncan, Cynthia M., ed. *Rural Poverty in America.* New York: Auburn House, 1992. Duncan focuses on the rural poor as they sit in the shadow of the more visible urban problems. She contends that rural poverty is different from urban poverty, that there is no "single" rural poverty, and that social, economic, and political barriers keep the rural poor economically disadvantaged. A detailed review of the issues.

Ellwood, David T. *Poor Support: Poverty in the American Family.* New York: Basic Books, 1988. This book focuses on poor American families, addressing various forms of poverty and possible relief for them. Ellwood suggests specific steps to eradicating poverty in logical yet general terms. Good introductory reading.

Harrington, Michael. *The New American Poverty.* New York: Penguin Books, 1985. Harrington provides readers with a provocative and insightful look at the social and political roots of poverty. His in-depth examination of the state of the country indicates, as did his groundbreaking *The Other America* (1962), that the dilemma of the poor has not been remedied.

Jencks, Christopher. *Rethinking Social Policy: Race, Poverty, and the Underclass.* Cambridge, Mass.: Harvard University Press, 1992. An analytical look at social policy as it relates to the poor in the United States. Jencks deals with affirmative action, intergenerational poverty, urban ghettos, and the size and extent of the urban underclass, making recommendations for welfare reform. A good theoretical approach to defining the underclass.

Jencks, Christopher, and Paul E. Peterson, eds. *The Urban Underclass.* Washington, D.C.: Brookings Institution, 1991. In this series of essays, the authors confront virtually all aspects of the underclass, including a generational overview, economic conditions, causes and consequences of the urban poor, inner-city life, and policy reform. Case studies with solid data, tables, and charts. Recommended for the advanced student of poverty.

Myrdal, Gunnar. "Challenge to Affluence: The Emergence of an 'Under-class.'" In *Structured Social Inequality: A Reader in Comparative Social Stratification,* edited by Celia S. Heller. 2d ed. New York: Macmillan, 1987. This excerpt, taken from *Challenge to Affluence* (Penguin Books, 1962) by Myrdal, affords readers one of the earliest definitions of the underclass. This concise essay assesses the characteristics and sources of the underclass. Especially recommended for those desiring a fundamental understanding of the theoretical development of this segment of society.

Wilson, William Julius. *The Truly Disadvantaged: The Inner City, the Underclass, and Public Policy.* Chicago: University of Chicago Press, 1987. This controversial work highlights the debate on race, poverty, and the underclass. Wilson concentrates on the deteriorating conditions of the black underclass, from which he then turns to relate these issues to policy implications. Readers may wish to look also at his earlier book, *The Declining Significance of Race* (University of Chicago Press, 1978).

Liesel A. Miller

Cross-References
Antipoverty Programs, 107; The Feminization of Poverty, 754; Homelessness, 897; Poverty: Analysis and Overview, 1453; The Culture of Poverty, 1460; Poverty: Women and Children, 1466; Poverty and Race, 1472; The Poverty Line and Counting the Poor, 1478; Unemployment and Poverty, 2083; Welfare and Workfare, 2172.

URBANIZATION

Type of sociology: Urban and rural life

Urbanization is the complex process by which large numbers of people form, settle in, work in, and live in cities. Although urbanization occurred in ancient and preindustrial times, it is most dramatically associated with the development of industrial and postindustrial societies, in both of which it has acted as an important agency of social change.

Principal terms
CITY: a relatively large, densely populated, and diverse human settlement
INVASION-SUCCESSION: the replacement of one group by a different group when the first group moves to a different area
MEGALOPOLIS: a complex of overlapping metropolises that form a continuous sprawl, as is the case with the extended urban area from Washington, D.C., to Boston, Massachusetts
METROPOLIS: a large urban area containing a central city and adjacent communities that are in many ways linked to it, such as that of Los Angeles
URBAN AREA: generally, a densely populated area; officially, any place with a population above 2,500, according to the U.S. Bureau of the Census
URBAN DIFFERENTIATION: the process whereby cities develop distinct business districts, industrial areas, cultural centers, recreational areas, and residential sectors
URBANISM: refers to the lifestyles characterizing city dwellers, usually in contradistinction to the lifestyles of rural folk

Overview

Through prehistory as well as throughout most of historical times, human existence has been spent in small groups of nomads, hunter-gatherers, or agriculturalists. The precise beginnings of urban settlements are unknown, although legends, myths, archaeological evidence, and inferences drawn from the known origins of cities that have developed in recorded time have minimized some obscurities. Roughly ten thousand years ago, during the Neolithic period, villages of between two hundred and four hundred residents appeared, indicating that food production and associated technologies, along with increases in population and the specializations of labor, had made relatively permanent settlements feasible. For perhaps another five thousand years, this was as close to "urban" life as humans came.

About five thousand years ago (c. 3000 B.C.E.), what have since been defined as preindustrial cities had developed along some of the world's major river valleys: the

Nile in Egypt, the Tigris-Euphrates in the Middle East, the Yellow River in China, and the Indus in Pakistan. Elsewhere, preindustrial cities emerged within Inca and Mayan civilizations in South and Central America, as well as among the peoples of ancient Greek and Roman civilizations. These cities, often more appropriately identified as city-states, generally had populations of between five thousand and ten thousand, though in rare instances (such as pre-Christian Rome or Constantinople), the population may have reached several hundred thousand.

In many ways, these preindustrial cities differed markedly from later industrial and postindustrial societies. To begin with, they seldom dominated the overwhelmingly rural cultures surrounding them. Indeed, quite the contrary was true. Consequently, in regard to family and kinship networks, urban dwellers continued to live in social contexts that remained much like those of their rural brethren. In addition, the cosmopolitanism of later cities was lacking. Despite their mergers of residential and commercial quarters—a result of traders and artisans working at home—preindustrial cities were highly segregated. They confined different trades and crafts to distinct quarters of the city, frequently even walling them off from one another. Still further separations of the urban populations—along religious, ethnic, occupational, class, and caste lines—curtailed social mobility.

Obvious limitations checked the expansion of preindustrial cities. Agricultural techniques, for one thing, remained inadequate for the support of large, nonagricultural populations. One study, for example, indicates that the labor of seventy-five farmers was required in the pre-Christian era to sustain one urban dweller. Reliance on human muscle power or that of animals, moreover, restricted the carriage of foodstuffs and other supplies—especially those needed for heavy construction—from countryside to city. Furthermore, endemic and epidemic diseases, fostered by poor sanitation, sustained high death rates, which went unmeliorated by early medicines and medical practices. Not least, the functions of preindustrial cities tended to be circumscribed. One authority notes that until the sixteenth century, urban centers tended to be court cities, cathedral cities, markets, ports, fortresses, or simply country towns that satisfied the demands of their immediate rural hinterlands and of highly stratified societies.

Sociologists and other social scientists attribute urban development before and since the appearance of preindustrial cities to the interactions of four major factors: the size of total population; control over the natural environment; technological advances; and changes in social organization.

A significant coalescence of these factors, under way in the late eighteenth century and accelerated during the nineteenth century by the Industrial Revolution, produced the industrial city, typified by boomtowns such as England's Manchester and Birmingham. A beneficiary of more efficient commercial agriculture and its surplus capital, the industrial city's rapid development was facilitated by many factors. Certainly the utilization of coal and steam power was essential, but growth of the industrial city also relied heavily on new modes of transportation and communications, the use of new materials, and new production and managerial techniques. Improved diets, sanitary conditions, and medical knowledge contributed to a population explosion that sustained increases in the size of industrial cities. At the end of the nineteenth century, Great Britain, France, the Low Countries, Germany, and, preeminently, the United States were dotted with industrial cities. By 1850, in fact, England had become the world's first urban nation, with more than half of its population living in cities.

Comparatively, industrial cities were larger and more numerous than their preindustrial counterparts. For example, by the opening of the nineteenth century, London's population had exceeded one million. New York's topped that mark by 1865, to be followed before 1925 by Tokyo, Paris, Berlin, Chicago, Buenos Aires, Osaka, Philadelphia, and eighteen others with populations ranging between 1.2 million and 7.8 million. Within their respective countries such cities evolved integrated urban networks, and major centers like New York, London, Paris, Tokyo, and Shanghai, in addition, were linked by international networks of diplomacy, trade, and ideas.

Industrial cities were also more heterogeneous in their functions and compositions than were their predecessors. Besides vast complements of skilled artisans, white-collar workers, businessmen, and managers, they included many cosmopolites: artists, journalists, professionals, and intellectuals. Because industrial cities culturally and physically dominated the rural hinterland, tending to drain the countryside of its best talents, they were filled with immigrants—those from rural areas and the farms and cities of other countries. The scale on which they incorporated various ethnic groups, socioeconomic classes, religions, customs, and political beliefs was unprecedented in world history. They were characterized, too, by their dynamism. Their denizens constantly altered their schemes of land use, devised new forms of governance, changed neighborhoods through invasion-succession, expanded into suburbs even as they grew internally, and (as some sociologists have insisted) altered human behavior by producing distinctive urban types who pursued uniquely urban ways of life.

Almost within a generation of industrial cities spilling over their original bounds to become metropolises, many of them between the 1960's and the 1990's further evolved into megalopolises. Both metropolitan and megalopolitan growth had become a hallmark not only within the world's "advanced" or highly developed nations but also with the developing nations of Asia, Africa, and Latin America. There, after the mid-twentieth century, the growth of cities and the rates of urbanization have been more rapid and dramatic than were those of their counterparts in the first industrialized countries.

Applications
Entire societies within relatively brief spans of time—between 1850 and the close of the twentieth century—have been completely transformed by urbanization. This is explained in part because urbanization, the increased size and density of urban populations, has been both a cause and a consequence of economic modernization, and with the way in which humans secure their livings. Urban populations have generated the increases in productivity, the intensive divisions of labor and specializations, and the complex forms of economic activity that have yielded the unprecedented high standards of living that characterize modern life. To state it another way,

urbanization, for all of the problems common to it, has been synonymous with expanding individual and organizational opportunity.

American experiences with urbanization have much in common with the experiences of other countries that were also early leaders in industrialization and in subsequent economic development. In 1800, the new United States conformed almost totally to a world that was overwhelmingly non-urban. Of the world's estimated population of 900 million in 1800, only about 1.7 percent lived in cities of 100,000 or more; only 2.4 percent lived in cities of 20,000 or more; and 3 percent lived in urban places of 5,000 or more: in sum, only 7.1 percent of the world's people were urban. While the United States' total population growth and urban concentration soon after 1800 were to far exceed estimates of world rates, the first U.S. census, in 1790, indicated that 95 percent of the population lived in rural places of fewer than 2,500 persons. The first census counted a mere twenty-four urban places, only two of which—Boston and New York— had populations greater than 25,000.

Thereafter, between 1800 and 1950, there were notable increases in both world population and urbanization. World population, for example, soared by more than 2.5 times, while the number of people living in places of 5,000 and over rose twenty-six times; those living in places of more than 20,000 increased twenty-three times; and those living in cities of 100,000 or more grew twenty times. By 1950, one-third of the world's population resided in urban communities of more than 5,000 people. In the meantime, by 1925 half of the U.S. population, which had grown from the 3.5 million of the 1790's census to 105 million, had become urban. By the close of the 1950's, the United States counted 5,400 urban places in which more than 70 percent of its population lived. These two trends continued. According to the census of 1990, 77.1 percent of the United States' 248.2 million people lived in the nation's 283 metropolitan areas, which accounted for about one-third of the world's 1,046 metropolitan areas.

These momentous demographic manifestations of urbanization have generated profound changes in social life that have also drawn the attention of sociologists—especially since twentieth century technologies (such as electricity and the automobile) have obliterated previous restraints on urban growth, and, as Lewis Mumford observed, allowed urban places to burst their bounds and sprawl into megalopolitan dimensions.

Accordingly, urban sociologists have proposed a number of theories about cities as physical constructs, about whether they tend, in functional terms, to grow in concentric zones, or sectors, or tend to expand from several, functionally distinctive nuclei. Urban sociologists have likewise examined effects on human behavior of the greatly increased interpersonal contacts that seemed to distinguish the daily lives of urbanites from the lives of rural dwellers. Because, in American cities in particular, these contacts include interactions among a wide variety of socioeconomic, religious, ethnic, and racial groups, urban specialists have explored the processes of "Americanization."

They have asked, too, whether urban heterogeneity has nurtured a comfortable cosmopolitanism, has strengthened the integrity of specialized groups, or, on the contrary, has eroded normative standards of conduct and increased individual disorientation and isolation—that is, whether heterogeneity has contribued to anomie. In these connections, they have studied the interdependence of personal and group relations, as well as the shift of personal relationships away from status toward utilitarian, impersonal, contractual relations.

Not least, urban sociologists have sought to explain changes in social structures that have been attributable to urbanization. They want to know how the extended family and kinship networks gave way to the nuclear family; how urban social institutions came to be "enacted" by legislative or administrative fiat rather than created spontaneously; how urban bureaucracies and other rational-legal organizations became all-pervasive. They also seek to discover how urbanization altered social stratification and to understand the roles of the middle-classes in redefining traditional schemes of social stratification. Generally, therefore, urban sociologists have found inexhaustible materials in the social changes that accompanied the creation and expansion of the mass societies that urbanization created.

Context

As an area of intellectual inquiry and a scholarly discipline, sociology has evolved simultaneously with industrial and postindustrial urbanization. The growth and proliferation of cities, and their effects upon and dominance over modern cultures, consequently engaged the interests of pioneer sociologists right from the early years of their profession. Representative of these figures were Europeans, such as Max Weber, Georg Simmel, and Oswald Spengler (the so-called German school), along with Émile Durkheim, Ferdinand Tönnies, Numa-Denis Fustel de Coulanges, and Henri Pirenne. Not all of these figures could be classified only as sociologists, of course, and none was interested solely in studying cities.

Some of their works were purely theoretical, while others, if geographically and historically wide-ranging, were more specific in focus. Weber, for example, not only theorized about humanity's collective urban experiences but also closely studied medieval cities of the Low Countries as well as those of Renaissance Italy. In general, however, these nascent urban sociologists tended to apply historical techniques to analyses of their subjects. Generally, too, they perceived industrial urbanization as a disruptive, even corrupting, process, harmful both to society-at-large and to individual personalities. Accordingly, they tended to be pessimistic, or at least dubious, about its outcomes.

On a selective basis the influences of these Europeans, particularly those of Weber and Simmel, contributed to the development of America's "Chicago school" of urban sociology. During the early 1900's, Chicago, not New York, was widely regarded as the quintessential "American" city. Economically it dominated the country's heartland, and demographically it lay close to the nation's center of population. It likewise enjoyed vital colonies of poets, novelists, journalists, and the beginnings of a brilliant academic community at the University of Chicago.

Whereas America's earliest observers of urban life had been inclined to moralize

2134 *Sociology*

about the character and impact of cities, the Chicago school of urban theorists concentrated on developing a viable ecological framework for their observations. Three men, in particular, were responsible initially for the school's national—soon international—reputation: Robert E. Park, Ernest W. Burgess, and Louis Wirth. Park and Burgess wrote and edited *The City*, a collection of insightful essays, in 1925, and subsequently all three men published numerous works dealing variously with urban spatial patterns, concentric-zone theory, cities and civilization, urbanism as a way of life, Chicago's urban immigrants and ghettos, community life and social policy, collective behavior, urban news and opinion, and measurements of urbanization. Like their European counterparts, Chicago's pioneer urban sociologists published most of their works between 1900 and 1950. All of them viewed the city, not as a mirror of the whole society (and its problems), but as a distinctive entity, as an independent variable, in which major social changes were being generated and in which new ways of life were being evolved.

By the mid-1920's, the Chicago school had helped found modern American urban studies as a distinct branch of sociology precisely at the time when demographics indicated that the United States had become a predominantly urban nation. Its inquiries, of course, were augmented by related ones conducted elsewhere. Prominent among such studies, for example, were those of Helen M. and Robert S. Lynd, Pitirim Sorokin, Otis Dudley Duncan, Horace Miner, Philip Hauser, Gideon Sjoberg, Beverly Duncan, Albert J. Reiss, Jr., E. Franklin Frazier, and Donald Bogue, along with contributions by other social scientists such as anthropologist Robert Redfield and historians Lewis Mumford, Charles Glabb, and Oscar Handlin. Building on the theories and empiricism of these works, urban sociologists during the last half of the twentieth century continued producing insightful studies of great diversity, as indicated by the publications of Theodore Roszak, Oscar Lewis, Raymond Williams, Claude Fischer, Scott Greer, William Whyte, Herbert J. Gans, S. N. Eisenstadt, and Richard Sennett.

Bibliography

Boskoff, Alvin. *The Sociology of Urban Regions*. New York: Appleton-Century-Crofts, 1962. A clear, standard introduction to the subject. Coverage ranges from analyses of human communities, demographics, and urban ecology to social organization and urban planning. Many useful tables, graphs, charts, and illustrations. Page notes, chapter references, and an extensive index.

Hatt, Paul K., and Albert J. Reiss, Jr. *Cities and Society*. 2d ed. Glencoe, Ill.: Free Press, 1968. A collection of major scholarly essays on important aspects of theoretical and empirical urban sociology. Well organized and splendidly referenced with notes and bibliography. Although it needs updating, it remains the best work of its kind. Charts, graphs, and tables, but no index.

Hauser, Philip M., and Leo F. Schnore, eds. *The Study of Urbanization*. New York: John Wiley & Sons, 1965. First-rate essays by distinguished urban scholars: sociologists, historians, anthropologists, and demographers. Hauser's introductory

"Overview" remains an outstanding one. Extensive chapter notes, but no index. Invaluable.

Sennett, Richard, comp. *Classic Essays on the Culture of Cities.* New York: Appleton-Century-Crofts, 1969. Edited by a major urban scholar, this collection lives up to its name. The ten essays, by seven distinguished sociologists, an anthropologist, and Sennett, are thought-provoking. Sennett's fine introductory essay briefly reviews the development of urban sociology. Some page notes; no bibliography or index.

Sirjamaki, John. *The Sociology of Cities.* New York: Random House, 1964. A useful work written for laypersons, the author's approach is historical, and concentration is on American cities. The book is written from the perspective of the national community and the social-cultural changes it has wrought on cities. Chapter notes; select bibliography and index.

Smith, Michael P. *The City and Social Theory.* New York: St. Martin's Press, 1979. Diagnostic and prescriptive essays by Wirth, Sigmund Freud, Simmel, Roszak, and Sennett have been chosen for critical analysis by Smith because they share the view that modern urban culture is repressive, and Smith seeks to refute them. Clearly written, convincingly argued. Chapter notes, useful index.

Weber, Max. *The City.* Translated and edited by Don Martindale and Gertrud Neuwirth. Glencoe, Ill.: Free Press, 1958. A classic, like so much of Weber's work. Indispensable reading, and better yet it is exciting, insightful, and provocative. Few notes or other aids.

Clifton K. Yearley

Cross-References

Cities: Preindustrial, Industrial, and Postindustrial, 253; The Concentric Zone Model of Urban Growth, 322; New Towns and Planned Communities, 1296; Suburbanization and Decentralization, 2010; Urban Planning: Major Issues, 2109; Urban Renewal and Gentrification, 2116.

VALIDITY AND RELIABILITY IN MEASUREMENT

Type of sociology: Sociological research
Field of study: Basic concepts

Research in the social sciences involves studying behavior. Accurately recording what subjects are doing is difficult, and research is always in danger of being influenced by the expectations of the researcher. The concepts of validity and reliability are employed to ensure the soundness and consistency of measurement techniques. Validity refers to whether research actually measures what it was intended to measure; reliability refers to whether the research produces consistent results.

Principal terms
ASSESSMENT: an estimation or measurement of some quality or event; an evaluation or judgment about a performance, behavior, or skill
CONSTRUCT: an abstract attribute or group of related ideas that cannot be observed but that is associated with observable behavior (loyalty cannot be observed, but acts of loyalty can)
CORRELATION: a statistical concept that measures how frequently two events co-occur, thereby suggesting either a relationship or a lack of relationship between the events
CRITERION: a standard to which something is compared or upon which a judgment is made
ERROR: with respect to assessment, reliability, and validity, error refers to variation in scores generated by the measurement device when measuring the same thing more than once
RELIABILITY: consistency or stability in scores generated by some method of measurement
VALIDITY: the extent to which an assessment device actually measures what it claims to measure

Overview

Science depends on accurate and systematic measurement. Because researchers must demonstrate that they are recording events accurately, scientific instruments are tested regularly for accuracy. Obviously, instruments that do not give true readings are not useful. Though dependence on instrumentation is necessary for all science, demonstrating reliability and validity in the social sciences is often more difficult than it is in the natural sciences. In the natural sciences, for example, official standards for items such as weight, temperature, or chemical purity are available for testing instruments. Social scientists do not usually have this luxury. Measuring such things as attitudes or intelligence is very difficult, because there are no universally accepted "official standards." Verifying behavioral records or surveys and determining what standard to compare data to are therefore problematic.

The credibility of field studies, naturalistic observations, and archival research (collectively known as qualitative research) depends on clear and convincing evidence that recording techniques are acceptable. Thus, investigators must demonstrate that behavioral measures are reliable and valid. Reliability and validity refer to data collection. That is, they refer to whether data recording devices are reliable and valid and to whether surveys, tests, or observational systems really address what the investigator is studying.

Reliability refers to consistency—whether the measuring device generates the same data repeatedly if measuring the same thing. If the behavior has not changed, then neither should the data. Variability means that an error has occurred, and the researcher cannot then be sure if the behavior truly occurred. There are four main types of reliability: internal consistency, test-retest, equivalent forms, and interjudge.

Internal consistency refers to the degree of agreement between various items on the measurement device. If assessing aggression among children on a playground, one could record many types of behavior. There could be acts of physical violence, vocal outbursts, angry gestures, and facial expressions. One would record many types of each and then check to see if certain behaviors correlate with others. For example, certain facial expressions might always accompany certain acts of violence. If the data show no relationships between the measures, one might wonder if one's observers are recording real behavior—in other words, whether the observers and devices are reliable.

Taking a measurement more than once is common to both the test-retest and the equivalent form types of reliability. A test-retest procedure is one in which the same device is used two or more times, as when one weighs oneself each morning on the bathroom scale. If one goes from a spring scale (as most bathroom scales are) to a balance scale (as in most doctors' offices), however, one is using an equivalent form. In either case, one expects the data to agree; the weight should be the same each time.

When measuring aggression in children, one would expect the amount to remain relatively constant if no new children are added, none leaves, and there are no new reasons for the children to get along more or less amicably. If one uses the same recording system for many days, one is employing test-retest. If, instead, one uses different definitions of aggression each day, one is using equivalent forms. Finally, recording techniques often require judgment. Observers studying aggression have to judge intent. Two boys wrestling on the ground may be playing without harmful intent. Interjudge reliability compares data collected from different observers to see if they agree about the behavior.

Though reliability is necessary, it is not sufficient. Data records may agree without being accurate. If the bathroom scale is broken, for example, one may get the same incorrect weight each time. Likewise, taking records on different days and using different techniques or observers does not guarantee that the data are really about the topic of interest. A testing device may be reliable without being valid.

The validity of a measurement device addresses whether it measures what it claims to measure. Validity is in question if a researcher intending to measure aggression actually measures frustration. Even if investigators can demonstrate reliability (because the data are stable), they are not assured that aggression is being addressed. There are six major categories of validity: criterion (with two subtypes, concurrent and predictive), content, construct, internal, ecological (also called external validity), and face validity.

A criterion is a standard used for comparison purposes. Criterion validity is comparing the data to some established or desired criterion. The standard for predictive validity is the occurrence of a future event. For example, the Scholastic Aptitude Test (SAT) is supposed to predict how students will perform in college. Though there are individual exceptions, the test performs reasonably well as a group predictor. Usually, students with high scores perform better in college than those with poor performances do. Since the test does predict future events, it is generally valid. (There has been considerable controversy, however, about whether the SAT is equally valid for males and females and for those of Asian, African, European, Hispanic, and American Indian ancestry.)

Another criterion is concurrent validity. Here, the investigator compares the data to a current, accepted standard. The criterion is whether one's data agree with the other indicators. Considering SAT scores, one might expect agreement with high school grades: Do the students with the best grades get the highest scores? If so, this concurrent criterion suggests that the SAT is valid.

A second major type of validity is content validity—whether the test measures a sufficient breadth of its intended topic. If researchers are measuring aggression, are they recording enough of the different types? If only physical violence is noted, the sample does not include a sufficient variety of aggressive acts. The researchers need to include verbal and gestural behaviors as well.

Construct validity is a difficult topic. Much of the behavioral research concerns phenomena that have no objective existence. That is, they are not things; they are ideas, abstract attributes. Yet they are related to observable events. Gravity is a good example of a construct. One cannot see gravity, but one can see its effects. Color and shape are other examples. Though squareness and blueness can be seen, they are attributes of objects and not objects themselves. In sociology, such concepts as racism, culture, and social structures are not things; though their effects are observable, they cannot be seen directly. Construct validity is concerned with the essence of a concept. Data collected must be demonstrated to correlate with other behaviors believed to be involved with the construct one is studying.

Internal validity is usually used in experimental research, and it refers to experimental design: Does the research methodology address the construct in question, or are there errors in design that make conclusions from the study impossible? Ecological validity addresses the generalizability of results (often called external validity). Experimental conditions may be so controlled that an experiment's results have no relevance to the "real world." If a study is performed in a natural setting, conditions may be so contrived that the investigator can learn nothing about normal behavior. If so, the results will be invalid for any other circumstances.

A final type is called face validity, which is often the first one employed. One simply looks at the data collection method and judges its apparent usefulness: Does it look like it will do the intended job? Investigators with considerable experience can generally make a good guess about the validity of a measuring device simply by examining it.

Although, as stated before, a measurement device can be reliable without being valid, it cannot be valid without being reliable. Since validity concerns measuring what is intended, if the device does this correctly, it will necessarily generate agreement when performed again.

Applications

Though the concepts of reliability and validity are necessary for scientific advances, they are also relevant to our everyday life in innumerable ways. Every day, decisions are made that are based on judgments concerning the validity and reliability of information. From an employer's decision regarding whom to hire to a physician's analysis of the results of a laboratory test, decisions must be made, often with very little information.

Personnel managers, for example, must determine the best prospective employees for their company from a combination of written applications and personal interviews. They have to decide what information (such as education, work experience, or letters of recommendation) best predicts who will be the most productive and trustworthy employee and must decide which factor should carry the most weight. Similarly, physicians must decide what diagnostic tests to perform, college boards must decide whether grades or test scores are better predictors of college success, and attorneys need to know which potential jurists are most likely to sympathize with their clients. In each of these cases, a decision must be made. The method of making the decision is often subjected to tests of reliability and validity.

The various types of reliability and validity can be explored through the example of how teachers create tests to check their students' acquisition of knowledge. In this example, an English teacher has assigned his class two plays by Shakespeare. The teacher will wish to evaluate how well the class understood the plays. Generally, this means that the class will take a test from which the teacher will determine a grade for each student. It is presumed that this grade will "mean something"—that it will be measuring, reasonably accurately, something truly relevant to the course content. Issues of reliability and validity are important to this procedure.

A reliable test should yield consistent results. If the teacher asks multiple choice questions about the characters in the plays and, in addition, asks students matching questions and fill-in-the-blank questions about the same characters, one would expect the students' performance on each of these sections of the test to agree. This is internal reliability. If a student takes the same test twice (without studying between times) and gets similar scores, test-retest reliability has been demonstrated. If a student takes a different test covering the same material and gets a similar grade, equivalent forms of reliability has been shown.

If the teacher scores the test more than once, students should get the same grade each time. This might not be true, however, if someone else were to grade the test. This type of checking of reliability is especially helpful regarding essay examinations, for which grading is more subjective than a multiple choice (or other "short answer") type of test. If a new grader's scores agree with those given by the first grader, then interjudge reliability has been demonstrated.

So far, the issue of what the grade means has not been addressed. Reliability refers only to consistency. A test that does not address the Shakespeare plays that were read may produce similar grades. Whether the test measures knowledge of the plays' content is a validity issue. Schools may occasionally compare class performance on in-class tests to performance on standardized tests purchased from a testing service. When this is done, the administration is checking concurrent validity, and the criterion is the standardized test. The other type of criterion validity is predictive validity. To determine this type, the teacher must wait for some future event. Perhaps, for example, the students are required to take a second English class in which other Shakespeare readings are assigned. One might expect students' performance in both classes to agree. If the first accurately predicts the second, then the criterion has been met. The test should also reflect the content of the assignments. If two plays are assigned and the test covers only one (or covers plays not assigned), the test is invalid because it does not possess content validity.

Construct validity is difficult to demonstrate. Does the test really demonstrate knowledge of the topic assigned? One would expect students who do well in related areas also to do well when studying Shakespeare. They could be expected to recognize key issues from the assigned readings if they appear in other places, even other media. If they truly understand the plays, they should be able to discuss them intelligently, write about them, and use that knowledge elsewhere. Construct validity refers to these matters.

Internal validity is a practical concern. If the grading sheet is not correct, then the grades will not reflect performance. Also important are whether the teacher calculated the grade correctly and whether the students can (and do) cheat on the test. Ecological validity refers to generalizability. Does performance in this class tell anything about the student's abilities? Students should be able to use the knowledge they have gained outside this particular class. If the test and the class are so narrowly focused that the students do not recognize the plays' characters or topics outside the class, one would question the validity of the test and the usefulness of the class.

Finally, face validity can be tested. Does the test look like it is a valid measure of the plays? It might appear to be either too easy or too difficult. Could a student who did not do the readings pass? Is the test impossible even for diligent students? An experienced teacher can usually tell these things simply by looking at the test.

Context

John J. Macionis, in his text *Sociology* (4th ed., 1993), says that sociology "may be defined as the scientific study of human society." To study human society, researchers must be able to determine general patterns of behavior while observing individual people. Whether by observation or experimentation, through standardized tests, surveys, or unobtrusive measures, researchers are hoping to discover something about the individual subjects. Through their behavior, investigators hope to form general conclusions about the group(s) to which the subjects belong. If the techniques for collecting data are not trustworthy and do not address the attributes that the researchers are studying, efforts are wasted. Issues of reliability and validity of assessment devices are among the most important in any research venture.

The most important criterion that must be met in order for any study to quality as a scientific endeavor is systematic observation. Different fields of science use different approaches to reach this end; astronomy depends on observation, chemistry on laboratory experiments, some subfields of psychology and sociology on testing or surveys, and so on. Yet all require that their methods generate consistent results and that the results actually reflect the existence and occurrence of the attributes of interest. The attributes of interest for the behavioral sciences are often invisible; they include attitudes, beliefs, emotions, or intellectual capacities. Since these cannot be observed directly, the data collection devices are especially subject to error. Demonstrating acceptable levels of reliability and validity is critical.

Bibliography

Jackson, Douglas Northrop, and Samuel Messick, eds. *Problems in Human Assessment*. New York: McGraw-Hill, 1967. The chapter "Standards for Educational and Psychological Tests and Manuals" in this work is intended for professionals in the field of behavioral research. Thus, it is rather advanced, but it is also a classic. Presents and defines virtually all concepts relevant to educational psychological testing, including reliability and validity.

McCain, Garvin, and Erwin M. Segal. *The Game of Science*. 5th ed. Pacific Grove, Calif.: Brooks/Cole, 1988. This is an immensely popular book for the beginning student or readers interested in scientific research in any field. McCain and Segal address the concepts of reliability and validity, but they do so in the context of a larger, general discussion of all scientifically relevant concepts.

Murphy, Kevin R., and Charles O. Davidshofer. *Psychological Testing: Principles and Applications*. 2d ed. Englewood Cliffs, N.J.: Prentice-Hall, 1991. Reliability and validity as applied to psychological testing are discussed in chapters 5 through 8. These chapters are clearly written and may be read independently of the rest of the text. Written for somewhat advanced readers (the book is intended as a text for upper-division college courses).

Pyke, Sandra W., and Neil McK. Agnew. *The Science Game: An Introduction to Research in the Social Sciences*. 5th ed. Englewood Cliffs, N.J.: Prentice-Hall, 1991. The authors intend this text for the layperson, but it is written at a relatively advanced level. It presents the principles of behavioral research well and includes chapters on validity (chapter 6) and qualitative methods (chapter 8).

Rosnow, Ralph L., and Robert Rosenthal. *Beginning Behavioral Research: A Concep-*

tual Primer. New York: Macmillan, 1993. This is a text for an introductory college course in research design. It is very easy to understand; most readers will have no difficulty following the text. The best feature, however, is that it collects all the relevant concepts, types, and subtypes of reliability and validity in one chapter (chapter 6).

Salvador Macias III

Cross-References

Conceptualization and Operationalization of Variables, 328; Descriptive Statistics, 519; Experimentation in Sociological Research, 721; Hypotheses and Hypothesis Testing, 915; Inferential Statistics, 983; Logical Inference: Deduction and Induction, 1093; Measures of Central Tendency, 1147; Measures of Variability, 1153; Quantitative Research, 1546; Samples and Sampling Techniques, 1680.

VALUES AND VALUE SYSTEMS

Type of sociology: Culture
Field of study: Components of culture

*Because values are a key determinant of behavior, an understanding of a group's
values makes it easier to understand the behavior of its members.*

Principal terms
   CULTURAL RELATIVISM: the view that a culture is to be judged by its
      own standards
   ETHNOCENTRISM: the attitude that one's own culture is best and that
      other cultures are to be judged by its standards
   NORMS: patterns of behavior that are generally followed in particular
      situations
   VALUE SYSTEM: a set of values held by an individual or shared by a
      group
   VALUES: general ideas of what is desirable

Overview

Values and norms are different but closely related. Values are general ideas about
what is desirable, but such general ideas do not specify how one should act in particular
situations; norms do that. Societies that value cleanliness, for example, may have
different norms about how often one should bathe. As a value, however, cleanliness
provides reason to have some norm about bathing. Because values are general ideas,
they can lead to conflicting norms. For example, the value of fairness might lead to
the norm "hire the best-qualified candidate" or to the norm "hire the candidate from
the group that has suffered from discrimination in the past." Such situations might
arise from having different ideas about the nature of the value at stake. In some cases,
the norms of a society do not reflect its professed values. When American society
claimed that segregated schools would be equal, it professed the value of equality and
proceeded to uphold the practice of inequality.

In general, values are expressed in norms and norms reflect values. The norm "one
does not chew one's food with one's mouth open" reflects the value placed on social
refinement, and the norm "one does not murder human beings" reflects the value
placed on human life. Knowing a culture's values provides some insight into how its
members are likely to behave. When members of a society share the same values, the
values let them know what to expect from one another. As a source of consensus, the
values help to hold the society together. Values and norms are an important part of a
culture's identity. Transmitting values is essential for transmitting the culture to the
next generation.

Children learn values from their parents, family members, peers, and teachers. One
function of schools is to transmit values. Beginning every school day by pledging alle-

giance to the flag of the United States tends to instill patriotism in students. Schools also aim to teach the values of self-discipline, hard work, and social adaptability. Churches teach the importance of religious faith and a caring regard for others.

A society's literature can provide insight into its values. The Hebrew Bible gives primacy to obedience to God. The *Iliad* and the *Odyssey* strongly suggest that personal glory was a major value for Homeric Greeks. Fifth century B.C.E. Athens' relish for rational discussion is embodied in the dialogues of Plato. Aeneas, the hero of the Roman epic *The Aeneid*, reflects in his behavior the values of piety and patriotism. His devotion to the gods and to Rome's greater glory prompt him to leave the woman he loves and to sacrifice his own happiness. Rama, in the Indian epic the *Ramayana*, exemplifies the virtues of a model ruler, husband, son, and brother. Architecture can reveal values as well. Classical architecture expresses the value of rational order, sober simplicity, and due proportion; medieval Gothic cathedrals express the importance of communion with the divine; and sleek twentieth century business towers embody the value of efficiency.

Sociologists can seek out values in a variety of ways. First, they can simply ask people what values they hold. Second, they can systematically study choices that people make in experimental or nonexperimental situations. For example, during an interview, they might ask, "If you could only save one person from drowning, would you save the Queen or your mother?" They might also detect values by seeing what kind of behavior tends to be encouraged and rewarded, since such behavior is valued behavior.

A society's value system is the set of values that the majority of its members tend to favor. Those who reject major elements of the predominant system constitute a counterculture. For example, nonreligious people in a very religious society make up a counterculture. Detecting a society's value system involves determining what its values are and how they are related to one another. Some values may be interdependent, such as democracy, freedom, and equality. Others may be hierarchically ordered; for example, tradition may be considered more important than individual freedom.

In *American Society: A Sociological Interpretation* (1970), sociologist Robin Williams, Jr., set out to detect important American values. He asked himself various questions: "How widespread is this value?" "How long has it been a value?" "How strongly is it held?" "Which groups within the society accept the value, and which groups do not accept it?" Guided by such questions, he cataloged such traditional American values as the following.

Achievement and success in one's occupation are key American values. Hard work and strenuous activity, as related to success, are also valued. Efficiency and practicality are valued as effective means for accomplishing tasks. Science is valued because it makes it possible to control nature, thereby leading to material comfort—that is, adequate food, shelter, and medical care. Material comfort is another key American value. Americans value a moral approach to living. They have a humanitarian regard for others, whether near or far, and try to help the victims of natural disasters. They value an equality of rights and opportunities. They consider freedom—the ability to live as they like—a major advantage of the American political system. They also value responsible, autonomous individuals and democracy, because it is a form of government that respects individual dignity.

Not surprisingly, in culturally diverse American society, Williams discovered conflicts between values. For example, the emphasis placed on nationalism, patriotism, and conformity may at times conflict with individual freedom. Traditionally, some Americans have made racial or group membership the basis of worth or privilege. Placing such a value on group membership conflicts with the values of individual worth and equality.

In such cases, whereas some members of society are confused about which value to uphold, many others are not. A systematic denial of equal rights and opportunities to African Americans led to the civil rights campaign of the 1960's. As a result, the U.S. Congress passed laws against segregation and discrimination. Subsequently, equality has become more important than racial membership. In 1944, 55 percent of American whites opposed equal employment opportunities for African Americans. In 1972, however, only 3 percent of whites opposed this kind of equality.

Applications

In *New Rules: Searching for Self-Fulfillment in a World Turned Upside Down* (1981), survey researcher Daniel Yankelovich claims that the twentieth century has seen a variety of shifts in American values. For example, the importance of marriage for women has decreased. In 1957, 80 percent of those surveyed regarded women who did not marry as "sick," "neurotic," or "immoral." In 1978, however, only 25 percent held this view.

The value of traditional gender roles has also shifted. In 1938, 75 percent disapproved of a married woman who worked outside of the home if her husband could support her. By 1978, however, only 26 percent disapproved. The percentage of those believing that child care duties should be shared by both parents increased from 33 percent in 1970 to 56 percent in 1980. Those willing to vote for a woman for president increased from 31 percent in 1937 to 77 percent in 1980. In addition, there have been important shifts in attitudes toward work. In 1970, 34 percent of those surveyed regarded work as the center of their lives. This figure decreased to 13 percent in 1978. Those agreeing that "hard work always pays off" decreased from 58 percent in 1969 to 43 percent in 1976.

Attitudes have also shifted regarding the relative importance of being financially well-off and having a meaningful philosophy of living. In 1988, nearly 75 percent of the college freshmen surveyed regarded financial well-being as very important, up from 44 percent in 1967. Only 50 percent of the 1988 freshmen, however, made "developing a meaningful philosophy of living" a major goal, down from 83 percent of the 1967 freshmen.

In some countries, shifts in values have been caused by political propaganda or the use of force. In *Pyramids of Sacrifice* (1976), sociologist Peter Berger details the techniques used by the Communist Chinese regime to undermine traditional Chinese peasant values, such as family, ancestor worship, and private land ownership. The government sent out teams of government officials whose goal was to persuade the peasants of the wisdom of government policies. The first teams executed those they considered "antirevolutionary." That made open disagreement with the teams less likely in the future. The teams preached the primacy of obedience to the party. Lyrics of propaganda songs extolled Chairman Mao as dearer to the people than their own families. Ancestor worship was declared an opiate of the masses, and private land ownership was decried as a potential source of capitalism. Open disagreement with the teams could result in execution, prison, the loss of privileges, or reeducation through manual labor. These policies, which were consistently applied, led to extremely uniform expressions of support for government policies and the values they embodied.

When the values of two different cultures come into conflict, one culture may try to impose its ways on the other. For example, British missionaries in Kenya pressured the Gikuyu tribe to abolish its practice of female circumcision, calling the custom barbarous. The missionaries and the European politicians who supported their cause were charged with ethnocentrism, which is a tendency to judge other cultures in terms of one's own culture and to assume that the ways of one's own culture are best. Besides leading to attempts to force others to be like oneself, this bias in favor of one's own culture can undermine attempts to study other societies objectively.

Hence, sociologists advocate cultural relativism regarding the study of other societies. According to this idea, other cultures should be judged on their own terms. Their practices that conflict with the practices of one's own culture are not necessarily wrong. These practices cannot be properly understood or evaluated without reference to their cultural context.

In _Facing Mount Kenya_ (1965), anthropologist Jomo Kenyatta explains female circumcision in the context of Gikuyu culture. Uncircumcised females are ineligible for full membership in the tribe. The Gikuyu regard clitoridectomy as a culminating part of the rite of passage from girlhood to womanhood. The circumcision ceremony creates a unity between the girl and her community, both living and dead. In fact, the ceremony symbolizes this unity. It also signifies that the girl has gone through an initiation that teaches her the social and moral customs of the tribe. It has taught her to face pain and to bear it with dignity. Gikuyu who continued this custom in the face of British opposition valued loyalty to tribal traditions over avoidance of pain and conformity to British demands. A cultural relativist approach to clitoridectomy demystifies this custom by focusing on the role it plays in Gikuyu culture and not on whether it is morally right.

Some sociologists have taken variations in cultural practices as a basis for drawing conclusions about the ontological status of values. In _Folkways_ (1960), sociologist William Graham Sumner notes that a custom might be regarded as good in one society and bad in another. On this basis, he concludes that good and bad are solely matters of societal opinion. In _The Elements of Moral Philosophy_ (1986), philosopher James Rachels criticizes this reasoning. He states that different tribes might have different beliefs about the shape of the earth, but points out that this does not mean that the shape of the earth is solely a matter of societal opinion.

One may say that values, unlike shapes, are subjective, but this should not merely be assumed. It may be difficult to determine what is actually desirable, but that does not mean that being desirable is nothing more than being thought desirable. Another problem with the conclusion drawn by Sumner is that if being desirable amounts to being thought desirable, societies cannot make mistakes about what is desirable. Yet such mistakes do seem possible. For example, a society might value aggressiveness as a means to happiness, yet aggressiveness may not bring happiness. It seems that societies do make moral mistakes, and this much is presupposed by the ideas of moral reform and moral progress. In studying other cultures, it seems justifiable to suspend judgment about whether their practices are good or bad, but it does not seem justifiable to claim that good and bad are solely matters of societal opinion.

Context

For most of the first half of the twentieth century, sociologists tended not to study values. Believing that social scientists, like natural scientists, should concern themselves with empirically observable matters, sociologists noted that desirability was not an empirically observable quality. Thus, they regarded values as unsuitable for scientific study.

By mid-century, however, sociologists had begun studying values. They focused their attention not on whether a particular thing was really desirable but on whether people *regarded* it as desirable. This much was empirically detectable. After determining what a group believed to be valuable, sociologists could consider how these beliefs functioned in the group's social system. Sociologists described and explained cultural values, in many cases tracing them to an ideological source. Then they used the beliefs to predict and explain social behavior. Generally, such studies were descriptive and explanatory, without being evaluative.

Accepting the scientific legitimacy of such studies, many sociologists still maintained that for sociology to be a social science, it must be value free. They took value freedom to be an essential part of the scientific attitude. Yet what does it mean to say that "sociology must be value free"?

If it means "sociologists *as* sociologists must not make value judgments," it seems false because methods of sociology such as cost-benefit analysis and risk-benefit analysis involve ranking or valuing of alternatives. Sociologists may use these methods when they work as policy analysts for the government. They also make value judgments when they choose their research projects. If "sociology must be value free" means instead "the results of sociological research must not be determined by personal preferences," it also seems false because the results of sociological research are determined by a personal preference for science over superstition, knowledge over ignorance, and rationality over intuition. Finally, if value freedom in sociology means that "for social research to be scientific, its results must not be caused by researchers' believing just what they want to believe," it is plausible because scientific thinking is not mere wishful thinking. In science, theories are tested by evidence, not by hopes.

Though there is a sense in which sociology must be value free, there are other ways that values are involved in sociology. Professional standards of conduct for sociologists are based on values. Faithful reports of one's findings are based on a concern for truth, and a respect for individual persons and their dignity is behind the concerns raised about experiments that invade privacy or betray confidentiality. The values of individual sociologists also guide them in their choice of research topics. Do they work on problems of solely theoretical interest or on problems whose solution may be of social benefit?

With the development and use of nuclear weapons, some sociologists began to believe that they should include value judgments in their sociological works. For example, in *The Causes of World War Three* (1958), sociologist C. Wright Mills charged world leaders with immorality. Other sociologists criticized Mills for preaching instead of analyzing, but he regarded it as part of his obligation to humanity to speak out against what he regarded as the moral insensibility of those in power. Many sociologists upheld ethical neutrality as a condition of social science and therefore condemned political advocacy within sociological writings.

Sociologist David Popenoe, in *Sociology* (1977), reports that more and more sociologists have become dissatisfied with this separation between politics and sociology. They reject the separation because they believe that it provides support for the political status quo. They see nothing wrong with sociological writings that make evaluative judgments of particular political ideologies. Many sociologists disagree with this approach, but as the twentieth century has progressed, increasing numbers of sociologists have written social critiques.

Bibliography

Berger, Peter L. *Pyramids of Sacrifice*. Garden City, N.Y.: Anchor Press/Doubleday, 1976. Berger's interesting book focuses on the political ethics of Third World development strategies.

Kenyatta, Jomo. *Facing Mount Kenya*. New York: Vintage Books, 1965. Kenyatta's classic work includes a chapter on Gikuyu initiation rites for boys and girls and European attempts to abolish this ancient practice.

Mills, C. Wright. *The Causes of World War Three*. New York: Simon & Schuster, 1958. This is sociology outside the value-free tradition. Mills worried that the "crackpot realism" of the world's leaders would lead to another world war.

Popenoe, David. *Sociology*. 3d ed. Englewood Cliffs, N.J.: Prentice-Hall, 1977. Popenoe's discussion of values is especially good.

Rachels, James. *The Elements of Moral Philosophy*. New York: Random House, 1986. Written by a leading moral philosopher, this introductory ethics text is well written and well argued. The chapter on cultural relativism covers the strengths as well as the weaknesses of the approach.

Sumner, William Graham. *Folkways*. New York: New American Library, 1960. In this work, originally published in 1906, Sumner initiated the important distinction between norms whose violation was not severely sanctioned (folkways) and norms whose violation was severely sanctioned (mores).

Williams, Robin M., Jr. *American Society: A Sociological Interpretation.* 3d ed. New York: Alfred A. Knopf, 1970. Williams' sixty-six-page chapter on values in American society is an agreed-upon starting point for studies of American values.

Yankelovich, Daniel. *New Rules: Searching for Self-Fulfillment in a World Turned Upside Down.* New York: Random House, 1981. Yankelovich is a psychologist and a survey researcher. This valuable resource provides survey data on major twentieth century shifts in American values.

Gregory P. Rich

Cross-References

Cultural Norms and Sanctions, 411; Cultural Relativity versus Ethnocentrism, 417; Cultural Transmission Theory of Deviance, 424; Culture and Language, 436; Culture and Technology, 443; High Culture versus Popular Culture, 870; Religion: Functionalist Analyses, 1603; Subcultures and Countercultures, 2003.

VICTIMLESS CRIME

Type of sociology: Deviance and social control
Field of study: Forms of deviance

Victimless crime includes a wide variety of illegal adult activities—such as drug use, prostitution, homosexuality, and gambling—involving human actions or social interactions that do not directly harm others. Modern trends have been toward decriminalizing some but not all such acts. Controversy persists concerning how society should regard and handle them.

Principal terms

ANOMIE: the condition of a society in which normative standards of belief and conduct are missing

BLUE LAW: a statute regulating amusement, commerce, or activity on Sundays; one type is the "Sunday closing law"

DECRIMINALIZATION: changing the law to legalize something that was formerly illegal

DEVIANCE: behavior that varies (deviates) from social norms

DISSENSUS: disagreement or lack of public consensus

JIM CROW LAWS: statutes that enforced racial segregation in the American South until the Civil Rights movement succeeded in having them overturned

LEGAL MORALISM: the view that government should prohibit what society considers immoral or evil conduct regardless of whether it harms others

LEGAL PATERNALISM: the view that government should play a supervisory role in regulating social behavior

PLURALISM: a social system combining people of diverse races and ethnic origins

PROSCRIBE: to forbid or make illegal

PUNITIVE: involving punishment

SODOMY: human sexual activity between males or with animals

STIGMA: a mark of social disapproval

Overview

The phrase "victimless crime" originated in the mid-twentieth century to describe various illegal acts that violate predominant social standards. In most cases the perpetrators do not regard the acts as harmful, and nobody complains. Most laws against victimless crime are modern remnants of the traditional social practice of enforcing morality through legal means.

The list of victimless crimes varies according to experts (and according to cultures and eras), but in the United States has usually included homosexuality and certain other atypical patterns of consensual sexual behavior; drug use; gambling; prostitution; consensual marriages to multiple partners (bigamy or polygamy); loitering and vagrancy; certain Sunday activities prohibited by blue laws; consumption or sale of illegal pornography; and such businesses as massage parlors and bath houses. An authority on crime, Eugene Doleschal, argued in 1971 that truancy, disobedience, incorrigibility, attempted suicide, abetting suicide, euthanasia, obscenity, liquor law violations, curfew violations, flag burning, and draft card burning should be added to the list.

One issue of victimless crime concerns an act's relative likelihood of harming others. Drunkenness, for example, may be considered a victimless crime, but drunk driving has the imminent potential of harming, even killing, others and therefore cannot be considered a victimless crime. Other types of acts, such as lewd exposure, are socially offensive but not directly hurtful. Concern over protecting children also complicates the issue of victimless crime. Some people, for example, would tolerate legalizing recreational adult use of marijuana but fear that legalization would set bad examples for children. "It's against the law" seems to reinforce parental warnings, while "It's legal" seems like a stamp of social approval.

As sociologist Edwin M. Schur points out, victimless crime tends to have predictable features: consensual participation; the absence of a victimized participant who complains or seeks legal protection; harmlessness, in the view of the participants; and the willing exchange of goods or services that are in demand by some citizens but of which most people socially disapprove. Participants generally believe that their actions, though illegal, are not wrong—sometimes they even believe they are worthwhile—and should be protected, especially by the constitutional guarantee of the right to privacy. As *The Oxford Companion to the Supreme Court of the United States* (1992) notes, however, the right to privacy "depends on a complex set of social interactions," and public and private matters are often hard to separate.

The removal of homosexuality from the American Psychiatric Association's list of "mental disorders" in 1973 was a milestone in the gradual social acceptance of gay sexuality as an alternative practice. The gay rights movement, which gained momentum in the 1980's and 1990's, seemed less successful than the women's rights lobby in bringing about legal change. Laws against sodomy remained on record in twenty-four states and the District of Columbia in 1986. In *Bowers v. Hardwick* (1986), the United States Supreme Court refused to protect consensual homosexual activity by adults in their own homes. Legal discrimination against homosexuals persisted into the early 1990's but was routinely being challenged in the courts. Prominent among gay issues was the debate over allowing gays legally to serve in the military. A compromise solution, the "Don't ask, don't tell" policy proposed in 1993, was controversial (opposed both by some who wished to continue a complete ban on gays and others who believed that gays should be allowed to serve openly) but was less punitive than the earlier policy had been.

Society's attitude toward victimless crime, according to Schur, is often based on stereotypes, misconceptions about the deviant behavior, and ignorance of its benign aspects. People, for example, may falsely equate homosexuality with child molestation, denying or not realizing that many gays have stable relationships and are productive citizens and that heterosexuals are as likely to be child molesters as homosexuals are.

Numerous sociologists and legal experts after 1950 have pointed out problems with making crimes out of private actions that do not harm others. Schur notes that there is dissensus about the morality of the acts proscribed and that the laws are largely unenforceable, since most such crimes go unreported. Studies in the 1970's showed that the public often regards victimless crimes as not important enough to punish. Each type of victimless crime carries its own complexities and has its own legal, psychological, sociological, ethical, and (often) medical implications. Although defining "deviant" is a difficult, ongoing process in a pluralistic society such as the United States, scholarly advocacy since 1950 for decriminalizing various victimless crimes has helped generate many social changes.

Applications
Understanding the practical reality associated with any type of victimless crime requires that one try to answer several questions. For example, how does making the act illegal affect or control behavior? To what extent is the law enforced or enforceable? Does the law deter the action or merely stigmatize people? What might happen if such an act were decriminalized? Though victimless crimes have obvious practical effects on citizens convicted of them, their illegality also has real social and psychological implications for undetected participants; they are effectively branded as deviant outcasts and may be shunted into patterns of furtive activity or associations with truly criminal types.

A main result of proscribing homosexuality has been to stigmatize a large group (estimates generally range between 5 and 10 percent of the population) as "deviant," making a minority lifestyle even more problematic. Though the crime of sodomy is usually not reported and homosexuals have infrequently been charged or convicted of it, occasional "stings" and other random prosecutions of gays have generated insecurity among the group wherever their preferred sexual activity is still illegal.

Most authorities doubt that keeping gay sex illegal has had much effect on limiting the behavior, and little apparent social change has occurred where sodomy laws have been repealed. The very illegality of homosexuality has helped keep gay life closeted to the extent that, even in the 1990's, many people thought that they did not know any gay people. Such social ignorance, in a circular fashion, has perpetuated negative stereotypes and thus maintained social support for outlawing gay behavior.

Polygamy offers a different example of victimless crime. According to the National Broadcasting Company (NBC) television show *Now*, some fifty thousand Americans lived in polygamous marriages as of November, 1993. Most were in remote locales in Western states where Mormons once practiced polygamy widely. Prosecution was rare, whether states considered polygamy a felony or a misdemeanor. Generally the participants saw polygamy as a lifestyle with positive benefits and a tradition of institutionalized religious sanction, even though the Mormon church no longer supports the practice.

In another category, Nevada is the only state that has allowed legal houses of prostitution; they must be approved by county referendum. In all other states, a "revolving door" pattern of police activity reveals the unsuccessful effort of law to control the practice: Prostitutes are arrested and booked, pay their bail, and quickly return to the streets. Policies in other countries (Panama is one) that legalize prostitution and require licensing and routine health examinations have never caught on in the United States, where a strong moralistic tradition makes society especially intolerant of sexual license.

Trying to police and prosecute all sorts of victimless crimes takes up much of the resources of the American criminal justice system. According to Doleschal, more than half of all arrests in 1970 were for such crimes. The most significant categories included drunkenness (24.23 percent of all arrests); disorderly conduct (9.78 percent); narcotics violations (3.97 percent); liquor law violations (3.63 percent); and runaways (2.72 percent). Gambling and prostitution accounted for smaller fractions. Figures for 1990 from the *Statistical Abstract of the United States* (1992) show somewhat different patterns but indicate a continuing preoccupation with victimless crime.

Context

Throughout Western history, laws have reflected morality, and church and state have been closely connected. Even in the United States, where religious freedom was constitutionally established before 1800, the religious mores of communities were often codified into law. In the American South, where whites controlled society, the Bible was routinely cited to support laws requiring racial segregation in public institutions well into the 1950's. In the twentieth century United States, especially after midcentury, the multiethnic character of the country, various counterculture constituencies such as the Beats and hippies, and the growing advocacy of women's and gay rights all led to increasing discontent over intrusive laws controlling personal and private activities.

During the 1950's and 1960's, the special kinds of victimless crimes prohibited by the "Jim Crow" laws were gradually abolished, with the federal government and courts taking the lead. In the case of such laws, the "victims" of some "victimless crimes" were really the criminalized perpetrators themselves: They were being forced against their wills to conform to the dominant social ethic of the majority, thereby losing civil liberties and being treated as second-class citizens. Collective disobedience to the unjust laws helped bring about their repeal.

Widespread recreational drug use in the late 1960's represented another instance in which many citizens routinely broke the law. The outcome was not a national consensus to decriminalize drugs. In fact, police drug busts and school antidrug programs continued into the 1990's as a part of the nation's ongoing "war on drugs" despite dissenting voices arguing that some drugs should be legalized and taxed as tobacco and liquor are. The connection between drugs and deviant behavior as well as fears that mild drugs lead users to try more dangerous ones kept decriminalization from gaining momentum during decades when a national "war on crime" became a priority. The increase of homeless people in the 1980's forced officials to give up trying to control vagrancy with arrests; other petty crimes also were ignored by default as official preoccupation with serious crime grew. Public drunkenness was decriminalized in some places even as a nationwide crackdown on drunk driving gained force. In the early 1990's, debate about decriminalizing suicide and assisting with suicide was active, but no consensus emerged; suicide can arguably be seen as a victimless crime more easily than can helping another commit suicide. Moreover, the debate over physician-assisted suicide or euthanasia involves issues of medical ethics and the Hippocratic oath never to harm a patient intentionally.

Since midcentury, scholarly and legal opinion has tended gradually to solidify in favor of decriminalizing most or all victimless crimes. England decriminalized suicide in 1961, and the *Wolfenden Report* (1957) advocated (unsuccessfully) that homosexuality be removed from the crime list in Great Britain. In 1970, the National Council on Crime voted to decriminalize all "socially disapproved acts which do not harm others" in the United States, recommending that rehabilitation programs and social services be used, instead of laws, to deal with such behaviors.

As Joel Feinberg explains in *The Moral Limits of the Criminal Law* (1984-1988), the liberal tradition in American law assumes that the only appropriate legal restriction on a citizen's liberty is to safeguard others from harm or serious offense. A conflicting view, however, is that the law should enforce moral behavior—even protecting people from themselves. Many victimless crime laws reflect this second view of laws. Conservative groups such as the Moral Majority and religious organizations such as the Catholic church have helped keep some victimless crime laws in place despite the social drift toward decriminalization.

The American legal system, operating in a republic that respects both national and local authority, is a vast complex of local, state, and federal laws that control behavior. This legal labyrinth is another factor that makes repeal of victimless crime laws difficult. This is especially true at the state and local levels, because advocates of change may be branded as supporters of deviance and perversion by their political or religious opponents. In this climate, it was left to the Supreme Court as late as the 1960's to overturn a state law that criminalized contraceptive use, even for married couples. Many laws have similarly remained on the books into the last decades of the twentieth century because no one had the time, money, courage, or motivation to push for their repeal. It has thus become a job of the federal courts—whose judges do not run for office—to take the lead in decriminalization.

After World War I, the United States outlawed alcohol nationwide, but Prohibition (the Volstead Act) had to be repealed in 1933 because too many people broke the law. That precedent suggests that a society cannot "legislate morality" in areas where public opinion is heavily divided—and should not try to do so. The rights of privacy, ethical choice, free association, free expression, and the pursuit of happiness are all supported by the Constitution, and American society has worked gradually toward discarding old laws that infringe on these privileges of citizenship.

Bibliography

Balkan, Sheila, Ronald J. Berger, and Janet Schmidt. *Crime and Deviance in America: A Critical Approach*. Belmont, Calif.: Wadsworth, 1980. A Marxist textbook that criticizes most aspects of the American criminal and penal system. Argues that law itself favors the "deviance" of the powerful (organized and corporate criminals) while penalizing the deviance of the less powerful (women, homosexuals, the mentally ill). Calls for radical reformation of society and widespread changes in law.

Bloch, Herbert Aaron, and Gilbert Geis. *Man, Crime, and Society: The Forms of Criminal Behavior*. New York: Random House, 1962. This comprehensive study of crime just after the mid-twentieth century reflects—in its treatment of homosexuality, abortion, prostitution, gambling, and vagrancy—the growing sense that some types of behavior are not well handled by punitive laws.

Doleschal, Eugene. *Victimless Crime*. Washington, D.C.: National Council on Crime and Delinquency, 1971. This slim pamphlet summarizes the recommendation in 1970 by the NCCD that victimless crime be decriminalized. Defines victimless crime; analyzes its extent; describes its legal status; shows problems with using the criminal justice system to deal with it; and offers nonlegal alternatives for handling it. A clear and authoritative first source.

Feinberg, Joel. *The Moral Limits of the Criminal Law*. 4 vols. New York: Oxford University Press, 1984-1988. In this exhaustive study—comprising volumes entitled *Harm to Others*, *Offense to Others*, *Harm to Self*, and *Harmless Wrongdoing*—a legal expert examines aspects pertinent to victimless crime. Illustrates the bewildering complexity of defining "victimless" and shows the difficulty of determining legitimate functions of law in society. Examines the claims of legal moralists that law should control evil and mold behavior.

Hills, Stuart L. *Crime, Power, and Morality: The Criminal-Law Process in the United States*. Scranton, Pa.: Chandler, 1971. A "sociologically oriented" criminologist argues against using law in a pluralistic society to control private morality. Illustrates numerous negative effects of laws punishing marijuana users as an example.

Knutson, Donald C., ed. *Homosexuality and the Law*. New York: Haworth Press, 1980. This volume consists of a special double issue of the *Journal of Homosexuality*, including essays by experts who explore the many ways that laws control gays in society. Most authors argue that such discrimination should be ended, since it unfairly invades privacy and violates constitutional liberties. The book also documents the rise of the gay liberation movement through 1980.

Schur, Edwin M. *Crimes Without Victims; Deviant Behavior and Public Policy: Abortion, Homosexuality, Drug Addiction*. Englewood Cliffs, N.J.: Prentice-Hall, 1965. A widely published sociology professor calls for better understanding of deviance and argues against using law to try to control victimless crimes.

Schur, Edwin M., and Hugo Adam Bedau. *Victimless Crimes: Two Sides of a Contro-versy*. Englewood Cliffs, N.J.: Prentice-Hall, 1974. Here a sociologist and a phi-losopher present diverse arguments from the perspectives of their disciplines, finding many areas of agreement. Both generally oppose the criminalization of vice, immorality, and victimless social deviance.

Skogan, Wesley G. *Disorder and Decline: Crime and the Spiral of Decay in American Neighborhoods*. New York: Free Press, 1990. The final chapters examine some late-twentieth century problems resulting from decriminalization of public drunk-enness and look at zoning as a means of controlling massage parlors, bath houses, and adult bookstores and theatres.

Roy Neil Graves

Cross-References

Alcoholism, 74; Crime: Analysis and Overview, 373; Decriminalization, 456; Deviance: Analysis and Overview, 525; Deviance: Functions and Dysfunctions, 540; Drug Use and Addiction, 572; The Medicalization of Deviance, 1178; Prostitution, 1526.

VIOLENCE IN THE FAMILY

Type of sociology: Major social institutions
Field of study: The family

Family violence is the maltreatment of one family member by another; in the broadest sense, it includes acts of physical abuse, emotional abuse, sexual exploitation, and neglect. Violence among family members is a serious social problem requiring multidisciplinary, multilevel remedial and preventive interventions that focus on the individual, the family, the community, and society at large.

Principal terms
> NEGLECT: the repeated failure to meet minimal standards for satisfying a dependent's basic needs for food, clothing, shelter, medical care, and safety
> PHYSICAL ABUSE: any nonaccidental injury including but not limited to fractures, burns, bruises, welts, cuts, internal injuries, and death
> POST-TRAUMATIC STRESS DISORDER (PTSD): a reaction to a traumatic experience; symptoms include anxiety, depression, emotional withdrawal, and antisocial behavior, and its onset may be delayed by months or years
> PSYCHOLOGICAL ABUSE: intentional acts of rejection, fear-induction, corruption, isolation, ridicule, scapegoating, intimidation, or harassment
> SEXUAL ABUSE: sexual contact with or exploitation of a nonconsenting individual, including exhibitionism, voyeurism, fondling, sodomy, and rape

Overview

Contrary to American culture's expectation that the family is a place of nurturance and safety, a person is more likely to be physically assaulted or emotionally injured in the home by a member of the family than she or he is anywhere else by anyone else. Each year, it is estimated that more than six million men, women, and children are the victims of severe physical attacks by a family member and that nearly one-quarter of the homicides in the United States are the result of intrafamily violence. Although public attention is often directed toward controlling political violence, community violence, and media violence, it is within the family setting that most people suffer their earliest experience with physical assault or psychological maltreatment. The existence of cultural norms that discourage outside interference in the privacy of the family tacitly sanctions the proliferation of violence in the home. Intrafamily violence is further legitimized by cultural norms that tolerate hitting and harassment among family members for the purpose of discipline or competition. Thus, the American family is allowed to be a training ground for violence and, as such, has the paradoxical distinction of being one of society's most violent institutions.

Family violence can be defined as the maltreatment of one family member by another. It involves acts of physical aggression (such as hitting, pushing, biting, or punching), psychological abuse (threats, ridicule, or harassment), sexual exploitation (voyeurism, fondling, or rape), and acts of omission or neglect. Violent families can be found within all socioeconomic classes and within all racial groups. Both perpetrators and victims are male and female, young and old. While estimates of the incidence and frequency of abuse may seem alarmingly high, family violence statistics are, at best, underestimates of the true pervasiveness of the problem both because of the large number of cases that go unreported and because of the lack of agreement as to precisely what behaviors constitute violence and abuse.

Child abuse involves acts of omission and commission by a parent or guardian that either harm or threaten the health or welfare of a child under the age of eighteen. Estimates of the extent of child abuse in the United States vary from approximately one-quarter of a million to four million cases per year. The most widely accepted incidence figure comes from the National Committee for the Prevention of Child Abuse finding that more than one million children are "severely abused" each year, a figure that includes more than two thousand abuse-related deaths. Studies also examine less severe forms of abuse. Spanking, which many experts consider abusive, is used as a means of discipline in approximately three out of every five American families with minor children. While there is no "typical" abused child or "typical" abusive parent, research suggests that premature infants, low birth weight infants, and children with problems such as hyperactivity, physical disabilities, and mental retardation are at particularly high risk for abuse. Abusive parents tend to exhibit low frustration tolerance, to have unrealistic expectations regarding age-appropriate behaviors, to utilize inconsistent parenting techniques, and to view themselves as inadequate parents.

Incidence estimates for spouse abuse suggest that in more than one out of every six American households, some kind of violence between spouses occurs each year. Marital violence includes both "one-way violence" and "mutual combat." Women are the most frequent victims. Each year in the United States, nearly two million women (approximately one out of every twenty) are beaten by their husbands, and more than one million women seek medical attention for injuries caused by battering. Approximately 30 percent of all female homicide victims are killed by their husbands or boyfriends. Husband abuse does occur, but it is rarely reported.

Violence between siblings is the most common form of family violence. Indeed, sibling aggression is so commonplace that it is often regarded as a normal part of family functioning. Parents often permit or even encourage "sibling rivalry" as a means of preparing their young for the aggressive competitiveness of the real world. As a result, sibling abuse often occurs repeatedly over long periods of time without adult intervention. Research suggests that sibling violence occurs in approximately 60 percent of all American households each year. Children of all ages and both genders engage in physical, psychological, and sexual violence against their siblings. Boys tend to be slightly more aggressive than girls, and the rate of violence decreases as children grow older. Victims of these so-called normal acts of aggression often exhibit long-term, negative psychological effects equal in severity to the deleterious effects of parental child abuse.

As can be seen in the case of sibling abuse, children are not only victims of abuse but also perpetrators. Family violence research indicates that approximately 10 percent of parents admit to being violently assaulted by their minor children each year. These child perpetrators are predominantly age ten and older. Mothers are the most frequent victims.

Elder abuse, the mistreatment of an elderly relative by a younger one, can take on many forms, including physical violence, psychological abuse, financial exploitation, overmedication, neglect, and abandonment. It is estimated that between 500,000 and 2.5 million persons over the age of sixty-five are abused by their caretakers each year. Victims are most likely to be women over the age of seventy-five who are dependent on the abuser for their basic daily care and who are suffering from a physical or mental disorder. The perpetrators are most often adult women in the caretaker role who are experiencing stress related to personal crises or financial difficulties.

Applications

Abusive families share several common characteristics. All forms of family violence are more common in families in which economic deprivation, unemployment, undereducation, and the experience of chronic or unmanageable stress are serious problems. Family abuse has also been associated with social isolation, as it is found more often in families who have few connections to stress-buffering support systems within an extended family or a local community. Given this composite of sociodemographic factors, it is not surprising that lower-class families are at especially high risk for intrafamily violence.

Family violence is rarely an isolated event. Once abuse has occurred between family members, it tends to be repeated. For example, nearly one-half of all female victims of spouse abuse experience three or more violent attacks per year. In addition, different forms of family abuse tend to coexist. Research has shown that men who abuse their wives are more likely to abuse their children and that children are more likely to attack their own parents violently in homes where spouse or child abuse also occurs. Regardless of form or frequency of abuse, however, and contrary to the media's tendency to focus upon the severest examples of abuse (serious injury, torture, abandonment, and murder), most of the violence occurring in families falls within the less severe range of pushing, slapping, and name calling.

Another central issue of family abuse is the misuse and abuse of power that characterizes family dynamics. Family violence is not only an act of simple aggression committed by one family member against another. Family violence involves a situation in which a more powerful person takes advantage of a less powerful one. Research and clinical data further suggest that the "stronger" perpetrator acts violently to compensate for a perceived lack of or loss of power, control, or esteem. For example, both child abuse and spouse abuse have been associated with job loss, financial failure, marital separation, and other personal setbacks. Contrary to the stereotypical view of abusers, research provides little substantiation for the claims that most perpetrators suffer from psychiatric illness or that alcohol or drug use causes family violence.

Violence within a family distorts the development of each individual member—victims, perpetrators, and witnesses. Victims of the various forms of family violence display similar long-term effects such as depression, suicidal feelings, low self-esteem, self-blame, and an inability to trust others and to develop intimate relationships. In severe cases, symptoms of post-traumatic stress disorder (PTSD) are common. There also appears to be a significant degree of "intergenerational transmission" of abuse. Research indicates that, when compared to the general population, children who are victims of abuse or witnesses to marital violence are more likely to abuse their own children, to abuse their spouse, or to be the victim or marital violence as adults. It is important to keep in mind, however, that being abused by a family member may not be the primary factor responsible for the psychological problems found among victims, given the host of negative sociodemographic variables that are often a part of the abusing family's larger social environment.

At the core of these negative adaptive outcomes is the fact that violence within the family system deprives each family member of the raw materials necessary for the development of a positive self-identity and feelings of self-worth. That is, family violence diminishes the type of values and experiences that contribute to a sense of personal competence and a sense of belonging to something that is "good."

Psychological exploitation is at the heart of all forms of family abuse. All acts of abuse involve a betrayal and a misuse of a relationship that is supposed to be one of an individual's primary sources of a feeling of trust, safety, and well-being. Typically, both the act of victimization and the sustainment of injury are denied or rationalized so that the "family secret" is well kept and a sense of unreality prevails. In this way, experiences in an abusive household distort the way family members construct reality—about themselves and about the world in which they live. As a result, victims often come to think, feel, and behave as if they were powerless to control any aspect of their lives.

Context

The beginnings of a national recognition of family abuse as a serious social problem can be traced to the early 1960's, when reports of the "battered child syndrome" shocked the American public. A decade later, the rising prominence of the women's movement exposed the pervasiveness of spouse abuse in American households. Violence between siblings and the mistreatment of a parent or older family member by a younger one have received relatively less public attention and systematic investigation despite their frequency and the seriousness of their medical, legal, social, and personal consequences.

Violence in the family is a complex phenomenon that has defied easy description, explanation, or amelioration. One central problem is that there is no consensus among medical, legal, and social science professionals regarding a useful and acceptable definition of "abuse." Different definitions have been based on a variety of factors including the type, intensity, and frequency of the abusive act; the degree of physical or psychological injury to the victim; the intentions of the perpetrator; the presence or absence of mitigating circumstances; and cultural standards regarding what is considered to be appropriate conduct. These differences in definition have resulted in considerable variability in estimated prevalence rates, legal practices, and intervention strategies.

Sociologists have proposed several theoretical models that look to the social context of abuse for explanation. Exchange theory states that an abuser will use violence when the benefits of being violent outweigh the costs. Differences in subcultural rules and values that legitimize violence for certain cultural subgroups are emphasized by the subculture of violence thesis. Conflict theory proposes that the family is inherently an arena of conflicting interests and that abusers use violence as a means of conflict resolution when other solutions have failed. Resource theory claims that success in getting what one wants depends on how many resources one has and that an abuser uses violence when other resources are lacking. According to social learning theory, violence is a learned behavior that is acquired by imitation or by reinforcement (the perception that abusers get what they want). General systems theory argues that family violence is the product of the entire family system rather than individual pathology and that the positive feedback for violent acts serves to escalate violence, whereas negative feedback maintains it within acceptable limits. Family violence is clearly a multiply determined phenomenon for which no one theory offers a complete explanation. The ecological model, which views family violence as the product of forces at work within a series of nested environmental systems (extending from the individual to the family to the local community to society at large) is generally considered to be the most comprehensive.

Efforts to remedy the problem of family violence have focused primarily on treatment designed to assist victims or to help perpetrators cease their abusive behavior. While several treatment approaches have proved to be successful, there are numerous obstacles blocking the effective remediation, including insufficient resources to service all affected individuals or families adequately, a lack of clear and effective law enforcement practices, a continued reluctance to disclose or report cases of abuse, and the practice of compartmentalizing the investigation and treatment of the different forms of family abuse by entirely different social institutions.

While remediation of family violence is an important goal, it is essential that efforts designed to prevent new cases of abuse also be initiated. Studies of aggression, in general, and of so-called resilient individuals (those at high risk to become abusers but who do not abuse) suggest that aggression is least likely when the individual experiences high self-esteem, has adequate problem-solving skills, and enjoys supportive social relationships. Thus, in addition to more specific abuse-related prevention efforts (such as parenting programs for adults and personal safety education for children), more general health-enhancing, community-based prevention efforts designed to increase both social competence and social support are needed.

Finally, since family violence is at least partly a symptom of deeper and more extensive problems in society, issues related to the larger social and cultural context that contributes to the existence of family violence must be addressed. Only when many of the social conditions associated with family violence—poverty, unemployment, unequal educational resources, insufficient quality care for dependent children and the elderly, and so on—are alleviated can the problem of violence in the family truly be prevented.

Bibliography

Ammerman, Robert T., and Michel Hersen, eds. *Case Studies in Family Violence*. New York: Plenum Press, 1991. A multidisciplinary presentation of individual cases representing the various forms of family violence. Each case is examined in terms of medical, social, family, and legal issues; the assessment of pathology; and a variety of treatment options.

Gelles, R. J., and C. P. Cornell. *Intimate Violence in Families*. Newbury Park, Calif.: Sage Publications, 1985. A readable, nontechnical overview of the field of family violence including child, spouse, sibling, parent, and elderly abuse. Historical information and cross-cultural issues are presented.

Hampton, R. L., T. P. Gullotta, G. R. Adams, E. H. Potter, and R. P. Weissberg, eds. *Family Violence: Prevention and Treatment*. Newbury Park, Calif.: Sage Publications, 1993. Edited chapters by experts from the fields of sociology, psychology, and social work addressing issues related to the assessment, treatment, and prevention of violence in families. Early identification of risk and early intervention are emphasized.

Hotaling, G. T., D. Finkelhor, J. T. Kirkpatrick, and M. A. Straus, eds. *Coping with Family Violence: Research and Policy Perspectives*. Newbury Park, Calif.: Sage Publications, 1988. Edited chapters discuss methodological and ethical problems in prevention work, the changing response of the criminal justice system, treatment programs for batterers, and a range of prevention efforts.

_____, eds. *Family Abuse and Its Consequences: New Directions in Research*. Newbury Park, Calif.: Sage Publications, 1988. Edited chapters discuss a wide range of issues related to the prevalence, risk factors, and consequences of physical child abuse, sexual abuse, spouse abuse, elder abuse, and dating abuse.

Straus, M. A., R. J. Gelles, and S. K. Steinmetz. *Behind Closed Doors: Violence in the American Family*. Newbury Park, Calif.: Sage Publications, 1988. Reports of the results of the first comprehensive national study of the extent, patterns, and causes of violence in American families. Based on a seven-year study of two thousand families.

Van Hasselt, V. B., R. L. Morrison, A. S. Bellack, and M. Hersen, eds. *Handbook of Family Violence*. New York: Plenum Press, 1988. An edited collection of chapters discussing the different forms of family violence and the theoretical models used to explain abuse. Special issues such as legal and cross-cultural considerations, neurological and alcohol involvement, and research and intervention strategies are presented.

Judith Primavera

Cross-References

Child Abuse and Neglect, 218; The Incest Taboo, 934; Parenthood and Child-Rearing Practices, 1336; Socialization: The Family, 1880; Spouse Battering and Violence Against Women, 1959.

WAR AND REVOLUTION

Type of sociology: Major social institutions
Field of study: Politics and the state

The study of international and internal conflict focuses on the clashes between various states, groups of states, or elements within states, which are intended to transform or preserve the international or domestic political, social, economic, and/or cultural status quo.

Principal terms

BIPOLAR INTERNATIONAL CONFIGURATION: an international system in which two powers outclass all other powers in terms of strength and importance

IDEOLOGY: a coherent system of values, beliefs, and concepts that attempts to explain social, economic, political, and/or cultural reality, change, and goals

MULTIPOLAR INTERNATIONAL CONFIGURATION: an international system composed of three or more powers that are roughly equal in strength and importance

NATIONAL INTERESTS: general goals that states pursue over a prolonged period of time

POLITICAL OBJECTIVES: specific goals whose attainment will help secure the state's national interests

Overview

In his celebrated book *Vom Kriege* (1832-1834; *On War*, 1873), the famous nineteenth century Prussian military theoretician Carl von Clausewitz defined war as "an act of force to compel our enemy to do our will." Clausewitz emphasized that wars are not merely acts of violence that are ends in themselves but are acts of violence that are designed to attain political objectives. Clausewitz further stated that the perceived value of the objectives of a war influences the degree of resolve of the belligerents and their willingness to make sacrifices in pursuing the war. Indeed, he observed, "Once the expenditure of effort exceeds the value of the political object, the object must be renounced and peace must follow." Thus, the perceived value of the objectives of the war, ranging from the total socioeconomic and political destruction of the enemy to more limited objectives, such as border adjustments, territorial exchanges, and so forth, influences the scope, intensity and duration of the war itself. Conversely, however, the longer the duration of the war and/or the greater its intensity and scope, the stronger the tendency among the belligerents to escalate their respective objectives and the less likely it is that the dispute will be resolved by compromise.

Clausewitz goes on to delineate three broad elements of enemy strength against which military power may be focused in war: the will of the enemy, the enemy country, and the enemy armed forces. He argued that, in the context of wars for unlimited objectives, the enemy's armed forces must be completely neutralized and the enemy's territory occupied. He noted, however, that even after this goal has been accomplished, the war may continue until the will of the enemy population has been completely broken. In short, wars fought for unlimited objectives usually require total victory over the enemy.

The total wars of the nineteenth and twentieth centuries are characterized by, among other things, the complete mobilization of the socioeconomic resources of the belligerents, intense popular identification with nationalistic and/or ideological beliefs, liberalization of the rules of engagement of the respective armed forces, significant effects of hostilities on both the urban and rural elements of the belligerents' populations, and massive civilian and military casualties caused by the large-scale application of the increasingly destructive firepower of modern weaponry.

Alternatively, however, if limited objectives are sought (limited war), then something less than total victory over the enemy may suffice. In limited wars, the capture of one or a group of specific geographic locations and/or the limited battlefield defeat of the enemy's armed forces may be sufficient to induce the enemy to abandon the struggle and yield to the victor's limited demands. Moreover, limited wars are often characterized by mutual restraints by the belligerents, including the degree to which the civilian population is affected by the war, the types of weapons utilized, the geographic definition of the war zone, and the definition of military targets within the war zone.

In short, the experience of the last three and a half centuries indicates that wars vary markedly in terms of their objectives, as well as in scope, intensity, and duration. Furthermore, hostilities have extended across the spectrum of conflict, ranging from guerrilla warfare pursued by small groups of soldiers who are often indistinguishable from the larger civilian population upon which the guerrillas are dependent for support, to conventional operations involving concentrated field armies utilizing a complete array of military weapons except nuclear, lethal chemical, or biological weapons, to hostilities involving all weapons systems, including weapons of mass destruction.

Since the emergence of the modern state system with the Peace of Westphalia in 1648, the character of wars has been influenced by a series of environmental factors. First, they have been influenced by the degree to which the belligerents subscribe to a common set of values and loyalties. During periods in which the leaders of the warring states subscribe to shared concepts upon which the existing political order is founded and, further, when these common loyalties are reinforced by cultural, family, and/or class bonds that transcend national boundaries, these ruling elites generally display a willingness to pursue clearly defined, limited political objectives that are susceptible to compromise and to keep the level of violence proportionate to the objectives sought. Alternatively, when the leaders of the warring powers, joined by the people of these states, do not subscribe to common values and perspectives concerning the desired character of the international order and are not united by personal bonds, but instead are sharply divided by nationalism and/or ideology, conflicts tend to assume an unlimited character in pursuit of unlimited objectives.

Second, the configuration of the international system has influenced the character of wars during the past three and a half centuries. In fluid, multipolar configurations in which the principal states are not rigidly aligned into permanent blocs but frequently realign into various coalitions as their respective interests demand, and, further, in which neutral powers play a significant role in contests between conflicting states, wars tend to remain limited in objectives, scope, intensity, and duration. Alternatively, when the multipolar international configuration rigidly solidifies into two rival coalitions, leaving little or no room for neutrals, or when the international configuration transforms from multipolar to bipolar, then wars tend to assume an unlimited character.

Third, the physical destructiveness of weaponry influences the character of warfare. In one respect, in situations in which the sheer destructiveness of the weapons quickly results in high casualties and enormous physical destruction to the respective belligerent societies, it often becomes very difficult for political leaders to prevent the escalation of wartime objectives, as well as the scope and intensity of the war itself. In this sense, military technology tends to promote war. From another perspective, however, the terrible power of the weapons of mass destruction of the mid and late twentieth century has had a mutually stabilizing deterrent effect in those situations in which neither side has an incentive to use these weapons to obtain victory in war.

Clausewitz stressed that all types of wars are waged by the people, the government, and the armed forces, all acting in concert. The government determines the objectives of the war, the armed forces provide the means for waging the conflict, and the people provide the will to pursue the war until the political objectives are attained. Each element is indispensable to the success of the war effort.

Many of these observations concerning international conflict also apply to internal conflicts involving indigenous groups of individuals within a particular state. In these internal conflicts, those in rebellion seek to displace the authorities presently in control of the central government or to dismember the state by establishing independent, or at least autonomous, control over a portion of the country. In some cases, these internal conflicts merely involve elite factionalism in which the mass of the population is only marginally involved and do not result in any fundamental socioeconomic, political, or cultural change. Alternatively, other internal conflicts involve large-scale popular support and seek to transform radically the existing political, economic, social, and/or cultural character of the state and society by displacing the entire ruling elite and the established political order with another order controlled by and embracing the values and goals of the revolutionaries. In either case, the internal conflict may range across the conflict spectrum and involve the whole of the country or may be concentrated within a particular portion of the country, leaving the remainder of the country comparatively untouched by the hostilities.

Applications

Between 1648 and the French Revolution of 1789, the international system was configured along relatively fluid, multipolar lines. In addition, the states were governed by elites who subscribed to common values and were united by common sociocultural bonds. Moreover, military technology was comparatively primitive during this preindustrial period. Hence, warfare was limited in terms of the objectives sought by the belligerents, as well as in terms of the scope, intensity, and duration of the conflicts. Typically, these wars involved disputes over issues that normal diplomatic interaction had failed to resolve, such as territorial or colonial conflicts, dynastic succession, trade patterns, and so forth. The conflicts themselves were limited in that they were often characterized by comparatively bloodless maneuvers designed to compel the enemy to surrender, as opposed to battles yielding high casualties for both belligerents. Moreover, the wars were conducted in such a way as to minimize their impact on the civilian urban and rural populations.

The French Revolution at the end of the eighteenth century represented a major turning point in the evolution of both social change and warfare. As Crane Brinton pointed out in his important study *The Anatomy of Revolution* (1938), the French Revolution bore a number of similarities to the English Revolution during the seventeenth century, the American Revolution of the 1770's and 1780's, and the Russian Revolution, which began in 1917. In these cases, prior to the actual outbreak of the revolution, each society had experienced significant economic growth. The impetus to revolt came not from society's downtrodden members but from those individuals who had prospered from that growth but had recently come to believe that they were restricted from acquiring additional socioeconomic and political benefits. Moreover, each society exhibited significant class antagonisms, with intellectuals transferring their allegiance to the forces of the revolution. All four governmental systems had failed to meet new challenges effectively, and the old ruling elite had lost confidence in its legitimacy and capacity to govern. In each case, a particular event or sequence of events triggered the actual revolution. In three of the four examples, financial pressures were central and, in the context of the crisis, the discontented organized and made revolutionary demands upon the ruling elite. Although the elite rejected these demands and attempted to use force to crush the rebellion, the instruments of coercion were applied ineptly and, indeed, elements of the military began to side with the revolutionaries. In the end, in each of the four revolutions, the revolutionaries took power. Immediately following the takeovers, however, in the cases of France, England, and Russia, the relative cohesion that had characterized the revolutionaries prior to the seizure of power broke down and extreme elements displaced the moderates. Eventually, the movement toward extremism culminated in France and Russia in reigns of terror. In the end, however, the moderates reemerged as the cycle of revolution came full circle. In short, for Brinton and other analysts, the French Revolution has served as a basis for comparison in studying revolutions.

The French Revolution was not significant only in the history of sociopolitical change; in fact, the revolution and the subsequent Napoleonic era fundamentally transformed the character of the international system and, largely as a result of that transformation, fundamentally altered the character of warfare. The overthrow of the French monarchy destroyed the common bonds and consensus concerning basic values that had united the ruling elites of the international system since 1648. Instead, the French revolutionary leaders, backed by the mass of the French people, were inspired by both nationalism and ideology to spread the revolution throughout Europe under French leadership. Consequently, the relatively fluid multipolar system of the previous period reconfigured into two confronting coalitions, one led by France and the other composed of France's enemies. As a result, the wars between these coalitions assumed an unlimited character that was much different from those of the wars of the preceding period. French society was fully mobilized, first in defense of the French Revolution and, subsequently, under Napoleon, to spread French hegemony throughout Europe. The wars were fought by armies larger than any that had been seen in Europe for centuries, and, unlike military commanders during the previous period, Napoleon focused his campaigns on the battlefield annihilation of the enemy field forces. In the broader sense, European society suffered more during the period between 1789 and 1815 than during any comparable period of time since the Thirty Years War (1618-1648).

Following the demise of Napoleon in 1815, the victors gathered at the Congress of Vienna to restore the international system to its pre-French Revolutionary character. The French monarchy was restored to power, thereby reestablishing the basis for consensus among the ruling elites concerning the values upon which the international system rested. Moreover, at least until the outset of the twentieth century, when the multipolar system ossified into two alliance systems, rigidly reinforced by the war plans of the major powers, the multipolar system established at the Congress of Vienna remained sufficiently fluid and flexible to serve as an ameliorating influence on the character of international conflict. Another factor that contributed to limiting the character of warfare during this period was that one side was rapidly able to assert battlefield superiority over the other, thereby ameliorating pressure to escalate the war as a result of high casualties and operational stalemate. Thus, notwithstanding the gradual reemergence of the forces of ideology and nationalism, and the dramatic increase in the availability and firepower of weapons as a result of the Industrial Revolution, the wars of the ninety-nine-year period between 1815 and 1914 remained limited in objectives, scope, intensity, and duration.

Indeed, the only example of total war between 1815 and 1914 was the American Civil War (1861-1865). During the course of this secessionist conflict, both the U.S. federal government and the Confederacy fully mobilized their socioeconomic resources. Eventually, however, the Confederates abandoned the cause of national independence and availed themselves of the generous peace terms offered by the federal government when they were no longer capable of sustaining concentrated field armies; the option of continuing the conflict via guerrilla warfare was rejected as being too costly. In retrospect, however, the American Civil War, more than the limited European wars of the nineteenth century, provided a glimpse of the infinitely more destructive wars that were to take place between 1914 and 1945.

By 1914, the characteristics of the international system were very conducive to total war for unlimited objectives. Thus, although World War I was a limited conflict focusing on the Balkan power balance, the conflict quickly escalated to a system-wide war, because of the dynamics of the alliance network and the war plans of the major powers. These factors, combined with the operational stalemate that rapidly developed on the western front and exacerbated by the tremendous casualties sustained by all the belligerents as a result of advances in military technology, led to a popular nationalistic response and a resultant further escalation of the war's objectives, scope, intensity, and duration. In the end, World War I led to the collapse of the Russian, German, Austro-Hungarian, and Ottoman Empires, casualties unequaled in any war for centuries, massive societal destruction, and revolution throughout many areas of Europe. Indeed, when the war finally ended in November, 1918, Europe emerged severely crippled.

During the interwar period, the nationalism that contributed to the unlimited character of World War I was intensified and exacerbated by the influence of ideology, as the principal powers divided into democratic, fascist, and communist blocs. Indeed, many historians view World Wars I and II as one continuous conflict. World War II, a composite conflict that engulfed the entire globe, brought total war for total objectives to heretofore unimagined dimensions of human death and suffering, and caused socioeconomic devastation.

Since 1945, the international power configuration has shifted from a bipolarity in which the United States and the Soviet Union dominated the immediate postwar system to a configuration that is increasingly characterized by political, military, economic, and cultural multipolarity. The lack of consensus regarding values and perceptions that has characterized the international system throughout the entire twentieth century and that sharply divided the two superpowers immediately following World War II, however, continues and, in some respects, has been further supplemented with the rise of new nationalist/ideological movements, such as militant Islam. Yet, throughout the second half of the twentieth century, the principal military powers of the international system have refrained from actively utilizing their unprecedentedly lethal weapons of mass destruction to resolve international conflicts. This has largely been the result of the nuclear deterrent balance, which has deprived the principal military powers of any incentive to use their weapons of mass destruction for anything other than to dissuade others from attacking them or challenging their vital interests.

Although the world community has thus been spared from an infinitely more devastating repetition of World War II, which destroyed Europe and much of East Asia, there have been an number of limited wars and revolutionary struggles throughout the post-World War II period. These have ranged from internal guerrilla wars born out of revolution to conventional wars, such as the Korean War, the 1967 and 1973 Arab-Israeli Wars, the Iran-Iraq War, and the Gulf War. Some wars have involved only regional powers, while others have involved powers from outside the region. All, however, have remained geographically localized and limited in character.

Context

After the states of the international system convulsed under the horrors of the two total wars of the twentieth century and stood on the brink of nuclear annihilation throughout the post-1945 period of superpower confrontation, sociopolitical analysts attempted to place the experiences of modern war and revolution into a broader context in order to understand better both these phenomena, as well as their future impact upon humankind.

Two principal perspectives have emerged concerning this issue. The "realist school" holds that, in the same way that individuals are prone to resort to violence to resolve disputes, states also periodically resort to warfare to resolve disputes when national interests clash and other means of conflict resolution fail. Hence, the realists argue that war is both an inevitable and a permanent feature of international relations. Consequently, all states should attempt to maximize their power individually and in coalitions with other states in order to defend their interests. Peace results when the balance of military power between the states and coalitions denies the members of the international system an incentive to resort to war to satisfy their ambitions.

Alternatively, the "idealist school" holds that, unlike animals, people have the capacity to resolve disputes rationally, without resorting to violence. Indeed, the idealists maintain that all people throughout the world seek common goals, including personal security for themselves and their families, reasonable prosperity, personal freedom, and so forth. If individuals keep in mind their common aspirations, they will compromise and reach a consensus in the resolution of personal disputes, rather than inflict harm upon themselves and others. Similarly, the idealists argue that when national interests conflict, the leaders of these states must keep in mind humankind's common aspirations and rationally approach the dispute in order to resolve the conflict peacefully, without resorting to violence or the threat of violence. According to the idealist school, wars are the products of bungling, power-seeking, and/or greedy elites who lead their countries into war to satisfy their own ambitions against the greater interests of the people of their respective societies. Hence, the idealists believe that wars are avoidable. They maintain that democratically elected governments of states that are based on the principle of national self-determination of peoples and are united by the bonds of economic interdependence are humankind's best guarantee that conflicts, when they occur, will be resolved peacefully. They assert that governments that are truly representative of the interests of the people who elected them will never needlessly inflict the suffering of war and economic deprivation upon their own and other societies. Indeed, for the idealists, war is a legitimate instrument of policy only when it is used to preserve the principles of national self-determination of people, the democratic process, and respect for human rights against an outlaw regime or coalition that threatens the security of the peace-loving members of the international community.

In short, for the realist, war is simply a normal, if regrettable, part of the functioning of the international system, whereas the idealist views war as a failure of the international system to function properly. Hence, while both schools provide approaches for preserving peace, the assumptions underpinning the two schools are very different. Similarly, sociopolitical analysts disagree concerning the inevitability of violent revolution and internal war as a method of social change in future societies. As technology provides humankind with an increasingly destructive array of weaponry with which to pursue violent social change and military hostilities internally and on an international level, these questions will inevitably become increasingly urgent.

Bibliography

Brinton, Crane. *The Anatomy of Revolution*. Rev. and exp. ed. New York: Vintage Books, 1965. This well-written landmark study, originally published in 1938, highlights similarities in the English, American, French, and Russian revolutions.

Clausewitz, Carl von. *On War*. Edited and translated by Michael Howard and Peter Paret. Princeton, N.J.: Princeton University Press, 1984. Clausewitz's book, which was first published in 1832, remains the point of departure for all discussions of warfare.

Johnson, Chalmers. *Revolutionary Change*. Boston: Little, Brown, 1966. Johnson's study formulates a model for the analysis of revolutions. It is particularly useful when read in conjunction with Brinton's study.

Osgood, Robert E. *Limited War*. Chicago: University of Chicago Press, 1957. This excellent study carefully examines the phenomenon of limited war.

Osgood, Robert E., and Robert W. Tucker. *Force, Order, and Justice*. Baltimore: The Johns Hopkins University Press, 1967. Osgood and Tucker examine the evolution of and rationale for the use of force in the international arena.

Wright, Quincy. *A Study of War*. Chicago: University of Chicago Press, 1942. In this classic, two-volume work, Wright examines the history of warfare and provides a framework for the analysis of war.

Howard M. Hensel

Cross-References

The Cold War, 284; Conflict Theory, 340; The Military-Industrial Complex, 1207; The Nation-State, 1282; Political Sociology, 1414; Revolutions, 1641; Social Change: Functionalism versus Historical Materialism, 1779; Social Change: Sources of Change, 1786.

WELFARE AND WORKFARE

Type of sociology: Social stratification
Field of study: Poverty

"Workfare" entails efforts to transform welfare from a means-tested entitlement into a reciprocal obligation in which getting a welfare check would carry with it a requirement to look for and accept a job or to participate in activities that prepare one for a job.

Principal terms

ENTITLEMENT PROGRAMS: government payments or services to which individuals are "entitled" because they meet certain criteria

TITLE IV: the part of the 1935 Social Security Act that established the federal-state aid program that became known as Aid to Families with Dependent Children (AFDC)

WELFARE: a general, informal term for government programs that provide payments and services to the poor, particularly Aid to Families with Dependent Children

WORK INCENTIVE PROGRAM (WIN): the first federally mandated work-related welfare program, authorized in 1967

WORKFARE: a general, informal term for welfare programs in which payments and services carry an obligation on the part of the recipient to prepare for, seek, and accept employment

Overview

Aid to Families with Dependent Children (AFDC) is the major federal-state anti-poverty program; it has essentially been in existence since it was authorized by the Social Security Act of 1935. Numerous suggestions for and attempts at reforming the program have been made, and many of them, particularly in the 1980's and early 1990's, involved the inclusion of work-incentive provisions. Will Marshall, the president of the Progressive Policy Institute (PPI), and political scientist Elaine Kamarck note in *Mandate for Change* (1993) that the United States lost its initiative in the fight against poverty. Increased poverty among children, high teenage pregnancy rates, out-of-wedlock births, higher concentrations of urban poor, and the advent of crack cocaine babies all attest the intractable nature of poverty since President Lyndon Johnson launched the War on Poverty in the mid-1960's. In 1965 a monthly average of 4.3 million persons, representing 1.1 million families and 3.3 million children, received AFDC payments. Despite periodic purges to reduce the welfare rolls in the 1970's and 1980's, by 1991 the monthly average had tripled to 12.9 million persons, representing 4.5 million families and 8.7 children. Nominal payments for the AFDC program increased more than 1200 percent, from $1.6 billion in 1965 to $20.9 billion in 1991.

Many observers see the U.S. welfare system as a failure, at best offering palliatives and at worst fostering dependency rather than self-sufficiency. The welfare system, however, harbors conflicting impulses, and social welfare policy continually attempts to balance competing objectives such as alleviating poverty and promoting self-sufficiency in a manner consistent with values regarding the primacy of the family and the importance of work. Reform efforts have sought to transform AFDC from a means-tested entitlement into a reciprocal obligation, in which getting a welfare check would carry with it a requirement to look for and accept a job or to participate in activities that prepare people for work.

In 1988, Congress passed the Family Support Act (FSA), affirming an evolving vision of the responsibilities of parents and government for the well-being of poor adults and their dependent children. The new law left intact the basic entitlement nature of AFDC and even expanded it by requiring states to extend coverage to certain two-parent families. In addition, FSA sought to shift the balance between permanent income maintenance and temporary support toward the latter. The anchoring principle of FSA is that parents should be the primary supports of their children and that, for many people, public assistance should be coupled with encouragement, supports, and requirements to aid them in moving from welfare to self-support. FSA placed a responsibility both on welfare recipients to take jobs and participate in employment services and on government to provide the incentives and services necessary to help welfare recipients find employment. For the noncustodial parent, usually absent fathers, this is reflected in greater enforcement of child support collections. For the custodial parent, usually mothers, this means new obligations to cooperate in child support collection efforts, as well as new opportunities for publicly supported child care, education, training, and employment services, coupled with obligations to take a job or cooperate with the program.

Applications

FSA established the Job Opportunities and the Basic Skills (JOBS) Training Program to ensure that needy families with children will obtain education, training, and employment necessary to help avoid long-term welfare dependency. The JOBS program replaced several other work-incentive programs, such as the Work Incentive Program (WIN) demonstration projects of the 1980's. Child care and supportive services must be provided to enable individuals to accept employment or receive training. State JOBS programs must include appropriate educational activities, including high school or equivalent education (combined with training as needed), basic and remedial education to achieve functional literacy, and education for individuals with limited English proficiency. They must also include job skills training, job readiness activities, and job development and placement. State programs must also include, but need not be limited to, two of the following four services: group and individual job search; on-the-job training, during which the recipient is placed in a paid job for which the employer provides training and wages and in return is paid a supplement for the employee's wages by the state Title IV-A (AFDC) agency; work supplementation in which the employed recipient's AFDC grant may be diverted to an employer to cover part of the cost of the wages paid to the recipient; and community work experience programs or other Department of Health and Human Services-approved work programs that generally provide short-term work experience in public projects.

The JOBS program also amended the "unemployed parent" component of AFDC to provide that at least one parent in a family must participate for a minimum of sixteen hours a week in a work program specified by the state. If a parent is under the age of twenty-five and has not completed high school, the state may require the parent to participate in educational activities directed at attaining a high school diploma or in another basic education program. The second parent may be required to participate at state option unless he or she meets another exemption criterion.

Retired social work professor Catherine S. Chilman is critical of many aspects of the FSA legislation, not the least of which is JOBS. She notes that many requirements do not apply to recipients in two-parent families. Where they do, fathers are placed mainly in on-the-job training or "workplace" programs and are provided with far fewer services than those available to mothers. A possible reason for this differential treatment is that work training and placement experiments with AFDC men have resulted at best in only marginal, if at all measurable, gains when experimental groups are compared with control groups. Another criticism is that the funding for JOBS is a "capped" entitlement. That is, the federal government matches expenditures by each state up to a fixed amount. Congressional appropriations for this part of FSA cannot legally exceed the "cap," regardless of state need or demand.

Implementing JOBS presents further problems. Central is the issue targeting the most difficult groups, particularly the long-term poor. Many of the long-term poor require intensive individual remedial education, job training, numerous health and social services, and carefully supervised job placement. To economize, states and localities are tempted to train and place more readily employable individuals and use cheaper work-placement methods, such as counseling recipients regarding their job search activities. Yet training and placement of the more readily employable are not seen as cost efficient in the long run because members of this group are likely to find employment on their own. State and local administrators of FSA need to foster close relationships with already existing job-training programs. The program established by the Job Training Partnership Act of 1982 (JTPA), which already has close working relationships with the private sector, is one training resource. Because of stringent performance standards set by the government, JTPA has tended to take the most job-ready trainees.

Many critics view workfare efforts as a way of punishing, rather than helping, the poor. Writing in the May 24, 1993, issue of *The Nation*, for example, policy analyst Richard Cloward and political scientist Frances Fox Piven note, as others have, that there is no economically and politically practical way to replace welfare with work when the unemployment rate is hovering around 7 percent and there is a proliferation of low-wage employment. Furthermore, there is little evidence that putting welfare recipients to work would transform family structure, community life, and the alleged "culture of poverty," as welfare reformists such as Mickey Kaus in *The End of Equality* (1992) and Lawrence Mead in *The New Politics of Poverty* (1992) so forcefully assert. In the fall, 1993, issue of *The American Prospect*, policy analyst Laurence Lynn claims that pushing ill-prepared young mothers and older ones with severe disabilities into a deteriorating job market, while seeking to get support from increasingly destitute fathers, two FSA cornerstones, makes no sense. Lynn calls for the end of welfare reform as it was conceived in the 1980's and early 1990's.

Context

Title IV of the 1935 Social Security Act established the federal-state program for aid to dependent children that is now called Aid to Families with Dependent Children (AFDC). In 1962 federal matching funds were made available for states whose AFDC recipients age eighteen and older and living with dependent children participated in community work and training programs if certain conditions regarding health and safety regulations, minimum-wage pay, and income criteria were met. States, however, determined what constituted deductible work expenses. As a result, allowances for work expenses varied tremendously across the country. Some states included child care and work-related taxes such as Social Security, while others did not. Some had flat allowances for work expenses, while others treated them on an "incurred" basis.

The 1967 Social Security Amendments created the Work Incentive Program (WIN) and required that AFDC recipients be referred to the WIN program unless under age sixteen, ill or incapacitated, attending school, needed to be continually present in the home because of the illness or incapacity of another household member, or exempted by decision of the state agency. The 1967 amendments called for services to former (within the previous two years) and potential (within the next five years) AFDC recipients, and they broadened purchase of services by the welfare agency to include private as well as public agencies. Like the 1962 changes, the 1967 amendments were meant to reduce the welfare rolls by preventing family break-up and by encouraging work. Regulations from these amendments authorized twenty-one services, sixteen mandatory. The theoretically expanded target population and the service emphasis diverted congressional intent. Concrete services such as child protective care, legal services, and homemaker services had little bearing on employment but concerned aspects of daily functioning. Competence-enhancing services designed to strengthen family life, such as "family-planning information and counseling," were difficult to monitor and assess in relation to employment. Early studies showed that only 36 percent of AFDC families receiving child care as a service, for example, contained mothers who were working, training, or awaiting training. For the most part, child care services went to families with nonworking and nontraining mothers, many of whom were not AFDC recipients but were, rather, potential recipients.

Services and expenditures increased dramatically between 1971 and 1972. The threat of further increases prompted Congress in 1972 to put a limit on 1973 federal social services payments to the states and to focus on self support rather than on strengthening family life. Only three of eleven services were mandatory. Child care under AFDC was made optional, except for WIN participants. Regulations further restricted eligibility by reducing "former" AFDC recipients to those who had received benefits within three months and "potential" AFDC recipients to those who could be expected to be recipients during the next six months. A coalition of sixteen national welfare organizations formed to oppose the changes. Many denounced deletion of strengthening family life as a goal, and the social service industry objected to the reduction of mandatory services.

On January 4, 1975, the Social Service Amendments of 1974 became law. Title XX of the Social Service Act replaced Title IV-A (the adult social services title) and virtually repudiated the 1972 amendments. Under Title XX, states assumed responsibility for social services, and eligibility for services was expanded to include non-welfare categories such as the working poor and middle-income families. Half of Title XX money had to be spent on welfare recipients. The 1974 amendments placated the social service and welfare organization communities, but they also eroded the goal of the work-through-services strategy regarding AFDC recipients. Throughout the remainder of the 1970's, AFDC service recipients and expenditures accounted for a smaller proportion of Title XX recipients and funds expended, including day care, education-training, and employment.

As the work-through-services strategy receded, national policy sought to encourage work through incentives. The 1962 amendments legislated exclusion of work expenses in the computation of a family's welfare budget, but the states defined such expenses. The 1967 amendments mandated that each state disregard a certain portion of recipients' earnings for the explicit purpose of inducing work. The law stipulated that the first $30 per month of earnings, plus one-third of the remainder, would be exempt as income to be counted toward reducing the assistance payment. (This stipulation is often called the "thirty and one-third disregard.") It affected only families already on AFDC, thereby reinforcing its purpose to encourage those on welfare to work and not to encourage those at work to become eligible for welfare. Studies reported by social worker Mildred Rein show that work effort, as measured by those at work while on welfare and cases closed for employment, did not increase after the implementation of the thirty and one-third disregard. On the whole, increased benefits and reduced income incentives, such as including casual income in determining family income, resulted in decreased work effort among AFDC recipients throughout the country.

Another work-through-incentive strategy, the negative income tax (NIT), found favor in the 1970's. The NIT, however, was aimed at the working poor, not the welfare poor. It was to be attached to the federal income tax system. Those whose income exceeded a certain amount would pay, and those with incomes below that level would receive payment. The intent was to reduce the stigma associated with AFDC receipt and to reduce state discretion and variability regarding AFDC policies and benefit levels. The NIT ideology influenced President Richard Nixon's failed Family Assistance Plan (FAP) in 1969 and 1972, as well as President Jimmy Carter's aborted Better Jobs and Income Program (BJIP) in 1977. The Seattle-Denver income maintenance experiment (SIME/DIME) conducted between 1970 and 1978, showed that the NIT incentive plan reduced work effort but that decreases in work activity could be avoided by combining incentives with job opportunities and work requirements. Theses lessons were incorporated into AFDC work-related demonstration projects in the 1980's and eventually became part of the (JOBS) program of the Family Assistance Act of 1988.

In 1981, federal legislation permitted states to establish a Community Work Experience Program (CWEP) designed to improve the employability of AFDC recipients. In addition, states were permitted to develop and operate a work supplementation program as an alternative to AFDC. Participation was voluntary, but states could vary benefit levels geographically and/or by categories of recipients. Federal requirements regarding treatment of income could be waived under this program. The work-through-requirement employment experiments offered a variety of educational, training, and other services such as health and child care, to AFDC recipients. The mix of services varied from program to program, in part reflecting differences among states and other political subdivisions.

Results of seven WIN and WIN Demonstration studies showed that in most cases, programs lead to consistent and measurable increases in employment and earnings. Positive impacts continued for three years in states where data was available. During the final year of study, earnings gains of 10 to 30 percent per eligible person in the AFDC caseload were found; welfare savings were usually smaller and less consistent than employment gains. There were two notable exceptions. West Virginia experienced higher unemployment than many other areas, and its workfare program did not lead to increased employment and earnings. The Cook County, Illinois, program also resulted in no statistically significant employment gains. Its mix of services, however, was considered quite sparse in comparison with other programs across the country. Aside from monitoring functions, the Cook County program provided little direct assistance. The West Virginia and Cook County programs served as useful reminders of the importance of labor market conditions and of the need to provide at least minimal assistance to get employment results. These lessons were applied in the formulation of the Family Support Act of 1988.

Bibliography

Chilman, Catherine S. "Welfare Reform or Revision? The Family Support Act of 1988." *Social Service Review* 66 (September, 1992): 349-377. This article outlines the major provisions of the Family Support Act of 1988. Discussion revolves around FSA's background and implementation, especially the JOBS program and child-care components, as well as plans for evaluation. It is well-referenced, with sixty-six endnotes.

Gueron, Judith M., and Edward Pauly, with Cameron M. Lougy. *From Welfare to Work.* New York: Russell Sage, 1991. A synthesis of what has been learned from past research on JOBS's predecessors, what is likely to be learned from work-incentive studies, and what important gaps of knowledge will probably remain. Appendices describe ways of defining program costs, with alternative cost estimates and supplemental tables. Includes references and an index.

Marshall, Will, and Martin Schram, eds. *Mandate for Change*. New York: Berkley Books, 1993. This book is a guide to the ideas and themes that undergirded the Clinton presidential campaign of 1992. "Replacing Welfare with Work" by Will Marshall and Elaine Ciulla Kamarck is the tenth of fourteen chapters that address domestic and economic policies. Chapter notes are gathered at the end of the book.

Rein, Mildred. *Dilemmas of Welfare Policy: Why Work Strategies Haven't Worked*. New York: Praeger, 1982. Describes the early work-incentive programs of the 1960's and 1970's and examines work requirements in the light of social services, work incentives, work experience, work requirement, jobs, and other provisions. The book contains a bibliography and index.

United States. Social Security Administration. *Annual Statistical Supplement to the Social Security Bulletin*. Washington, D.C.: U.S. Department of Health and Human Services, Social Security Administration, 1993. Among other things, this text contains fairly detailed summary descriptions of AFDC and FSA provisions, in addition to tables showing the average monthly number of AFDC recipients, total amount of cash payments, and average monthly payments from 1936 to 1991.

Richard K. Caputo

Cross-References

WHITE-COLLAR AND CORPORATE CRIME

Type of sociology: Deviance and social control
Field of study: Forms of deviance

White-collar and corporate crime consist of illegal acts, such as fraud and embezzlement, that are distinguished from other crimes both by the occupational nature of the acts and by the middle- or upper-class character of the white-collar and corporate criminal.

Principal terms
> CORPORATION: a "juristic person," founded on the legal basis of limited liability; since the middle of the nineteenth century the corporation has evolved into the dominant form of business within capitalist societies
> ECONOMIC DEMOCRACY: a political system, synonymous with democratic socialism, that is characterized by cooperative enterprise, central planning and government regulation in the interest of social justice
> ELITES: the leaders or influential persons within any community, institution, or locality; they are commonly viewed as being protective of their status and indifferent to the concerns of the public
> OCCUPATIONS: specific patterns of activity by which persons earn a living and that determine their social status
> ORGANIZED CRIME: collective criminal behavior that is structured in the manner of a legitimate business enterprise, commonly a partnership or a syndicate of interlocking partnerships

Overview

White-collar and corporate crime is the illegal occupational behavior of persons of high social status. Fraud and embezzlement are typical white-collar crimes. Such crime is distinguished from common criminal actions committed by middle- and upper-class persons, such as battery or murder, as well as from illegal occupational actions by "blue-collar" persons, such as fraud by automobile repair men or forgery of checks by sales clerks.

Although the phenomenon has existed as long as modern capitalism has, it was not conceptually defined until the work of Edwin H. Sutherland of the University of Chicago in the 1940's. He was concerned with correcting a popular misconception that crime is largely the result of poverty and hence is mostly a lower-class phenomenon. Sutherland's investigation of the illegal behavior of society's elite broadened the definition of crime and pointed investigation of the causes of criminality in a different direction. He found that white-collar and common felons had two characteristics in common: They held law in contempt and they lacked ethical norms. More important, he focused public as well as scholarly attention on the most distinctive and reprehensible characteristic of white-collar crime: its pervasive, corrupting influence on the socioeconomic, juridical, and political foundations of a democratic society.

Subsequent discussion of this concept seemed to confirm Sutherland's insight that "white-collar" is an appropriate qualifier for a distinctive kind of crime. The privileged social positions of white-collar criminals gives special distinguishing characteristics to their illegal behavior that add to the gravity of their offenses. For one thing, they violate the trust that accrues to them in virtue of their respectability and professional certification. For another, they shirk the obligation of service to society that they owe for their own education, wealth, and elevated social position or power. Hence, there is a qualitative as well as quantitative difference between a clerk stealing three hundred dollars from an employer's office (or forging a check for that amount) and the president of a savings and loan company defrauding clients of two billion dollars.

The term white-collar is also appropriate for another reason. White-collar criminals' privileged social positions often wrongly win for them more lenient treatment by the criminal justice system than they deserve. This favor is contrary to both the spirit and the letter of the law, which knows no distinction between persons. It also perverts the basic principle of punishment—that it be in proportion to the gravity of the offense. Nevertheless, the reality of the law confers enormous advantages upon wealthy and powerful persons, especially in complicated cases of financial crime. Their legal resources are often far greater than those of the prosecutor's office, and their testimony is likely to enjoy greater credence than that of common offenders.

White-collar crimes are not well understood by the public, who sometimes even seem to admire the cleverness of the perpetrators and the wealth they gained. The perpetrators' professional colleagues are inclined to regard them as rogues or mavericks rather than criminals. Social pressure for their conviction, therefore, is less than in cases of comparable gravity involving less privileged persons. If convicted, the sentences of privileged persons are usually much lighter. They enjoy considerable empathy from their peers, both inside and outside the criminal justice system. Newspaper editors, heeding the sentiments of their publishers and advertisers, sometimes declare that the white-collar criminal "has suffered enough" from the stigma that a conviction puts on his reputation. For President Richard Nixon and Vice President Spiro Agnew, for example, it was deemed sufficient punishment that they resign their offices.

There are different varieties of white-collar crime. Common white-collar crime involves persons of high social status acting illegally in the course of their occupations for their personal gain; for example, a lawyer acting as trustee may siphon income from the trust fund into his or her own pockets. Corporate crime, in contrast, involves persons of high social status (serving as officers of a corporation) causing the corporation to act illegally. As officers, they act illegally, but they do so for the corporation's benefit rather than their own.

Not to be confused with white-collar crime is professional crime. The white-collar criminal's occupation is legal, even though it is being practiced feloniously. The professional criminal is a person who pursues an illegal occupation such as counterfeiting. Moreover, white-collar criminals do not regard themselves as criminals; professional criminals do. White-collar crime of the corporate variety also differs from organized crime in a similar way. The corporation's essential purposes (for example, making refrigerators) are legal. Those of an organized crime syndicate are not, even though they may have a legal façade.

Sutherland's concept generated lively controversy that continues to the present day. His critics generally deny that there is any white-collar crime that can be distinguished from common crime, or they alter the concept substantially, removing the characteristic of high status, and call it "occupational crime." Yet despite the efforts of its critics, Sutherland's concept remains dominant in the field.

Applications

How corporate crime operates in real life can be shown by two examples. Michael Milken illustrates criminality in the most powerful, prestigious centers of American finance. In the 1980's, as the brilliant head of the high-yield bond department of the investment firm Drexel Burnham Lambert, he developed the "junk bond" into an enormously successful instrument for speculation in takeover stocks as well as a means of financing daring ventures, such as cable television.

In March, 1989, Milken was indicted by a grand jury on ninety-eight counts of fraud and racketeering. He was the most prominent of several members of the firm, including Ivan Boesky and Dennis Levine, who were implicated in deliberate and flagrant violations of federal securities laws. The firm itself had pleaded guilty in December, 1988, to six felonies and paid a record $650 million in restitution and fines. In February, 1990, the firm went bankrupt.

Milken's battery of lawyers plea bargained with the prosecution for a reduction of the charges to six, to which he pleaded guilty in April, 1990. He was sentenced to pay $600 million in fines and restitution and to serve ten years in prison. He was also barred for life from the securities industry. On March 4, 1993, he was freed after serving twenty-two months in a minimum-security prison, a month in a half-way house, and thirty days at home under police supervision. For the next three years he was ordered to perform eighteen hundred hours of community service. Although he has admitted to six felonies, Milken continues to profess his innocence of any wrongdoing, a view shared by many of his peers in the financial community. He does not consider himself a criminal, nor do they think he is. He exemplifies the truth of Sutherland's contention that among the chief roots of criminality are the sociopathic attitudes of a subculture, be it that of investment brokers or inner-city street gangs.

Milken's case also demonstrates how difficult and costly it is for society to protect itself against modern corporate criminals. Like Milken, they are very clever and operate under dense cover. They also have great resources. Even after allowing for the fines and restitution, Milken had an estimated billion dollars to spend on his defense. The federal prosecutor's office was outmatched and forced to plea bargain.

In contrast to Milken's kind of crime, which deprives people of their property, the case of Film Recovery Systems, Inc., reveals corporate crime that deprives people of their lives and health. In 1983, five officials of the Illinois firm were indicted in the cyanide death of an illegal Polish immigrant worker, Stefan Golab, who was sixty-one years old. They were charged with flagrant disregard for worker safety; for example, they were charged with deliberately removing the labels and warnings on containers of the extremely poisonous chemical used in the process of extracting silver from film.

In 1985 the company's president, Steven O'Neill, the plant manager, Charles Kirschbaum, and the plant foreman, Daniel Rodriguez, were found guilty of murder and reckless conduct. They were fined and sentenced to twenty-five years in prison. This was the first conviction of its kind. In January, 1990, however, it was overturned on a technicality by the state appellate court. In a plea bargain in September, 1993, O'Neill and Rodriguez pleaded guilty to involuntary manslaughter. The former was sentenced to three years in prison, the latter to thirty months of felony probation, four months of home confinement, and five hundred hours of community service. Kirschbaum awaited retrial on the murder charge. In most personal safety or environmental crimes involving large corporations, as in the Ford Pinto case (in which Ford Motor Company was charged in the deaths of three young women), the prosecution is unable to prove criminal responsibility. Film Recovery Systems was unusual in that the company was so small and the crime so blatant that guilt could be reasonably determined.

There is no consensus as to what should be done about white-collar and corporate crime. Some believe that nothing more should be done to fight this type of crime than is being done at present. This perspective seems tacitly to be saying that high-status crime is simply one of the costs of business in a system of free enterprise. More stringent regulation and prosecution, it is argued, would harm the economy and fail to control corporate behavior. A diametrically opposing view holds that corporate crime is systemic and is representative of the inequities inherent in the American system of capitalism. In this view, nothing less than a radical reformation of the economy is needed to eliminate such crime; some people holding this view advocate establishing a system of economic democracy. There is virtually no chance, however, that American society will undergo such sweeping reforms in the near future. A third, more pragmatic alternative involves reforms that would make corporations more accountable to the public and to shareholders, reduce secrecy, deter or punish malefactors, and gain greater compliance with law through better regulation.

Context

Although the sociological concept of white-collar and corporate crime is of recent origin, the illegal behavior that it describes is as old as capitalist society. Among the more spectacular examples from American history is the Crédit Mobilier scandal (1872-1873). Major stockholders of the Union Pacific Railroad formed a construction company, Crédit Mobilier of America, to build for the railroad and gave or sold shares to congressmen, who voted for subsidies for the company.

Serious efforts to police this kind of crime began during the Progressive period

(1900-1917) and revived during the New Deal (1933-1941), when state and federal regulatory bodies, such as the Securities and Exchange Commission (1934), were created. Corporate crime nevertheless continued at a very high level. Edwin Sutherland, in 1949, found seventy major American corporations guilty of 759 felonious acts over a ten-year period, and several of the corporations offended repeatedly. Yet only 20 percent of these acts were prosecuted as crimes. That this persistent criminal behavior went relatively unpunished, he reasoned, was attributable not only to the complexity of financial crime and the virtual immunity of corporations from criminal prosecution but also to the privileged, upper-class character of the criminals. Hence he included in his definition of white-collar crime the social status of the offenders.

The problem has continued to grow. In the 1980's, under the leadership of the Reagan Administration, deregulation cleared the way for white-collar and corporate crime on a scale not before seen in the United States. Banks, savings and loan institutions, investment corporations, and other financial organizations were allowed to operate without effective public oversight.

Between 1981 and 1983, the previously conservative savings and loan industry became a volatile, crime-prone arena for profit-seekers. Regulatory agencies, their powers curbed, were slow to react. Congress averted its gaze, and some of its members became implicated in the debacle. Meanwhile, the Reagan Administration reassured the nation that the economy was merely shaking out dead or inefficient enterprises. By 1988, however, the nation had begun to realize that white-collar crime had occurred on a scale that made Crédit Mobilier look like child's play. The federal government had to design a "bail-out" plan; in 1990 the projected cost to the taxpayer was conservatively estimated at $600 billion. Moreover, the country's largest and most prestigious investment brokers were charged with insider trading and a host of other financial crimes.

The machinery of criminal justice was set into motion against the most conspicuous suspects. Approximately half of the money lost by the savings and loan industry was attributable to criminal acts and much of the rest to reckless incompetence. By the end of 1990, more than 330 persons connected with the savings and loan disaster had been convicted and sentenced to prison for an average of two years. Hundreds more were allowed to plea bargain and were merely fined. Thousands of other criminals undoubtedly escaped unnoticed, since prosecutors lacked sufficient resources for a thorough criminal investigation. Because of increased public awareness, the federal and state governments are trying to upgrade the personnel of regulatory and criminal-fraud agencies, increase their funding, coordinate their efforts, and sharpen their legal weapons.

Bibliography

Croall, Hazel. *White Collar Crime*. Philadelphia: Open University Press, 1992. A careful, well-balanced survey focused on Britain that treats white-collar crime as occupational crime. The author analyzes the characteristics of white-collar crime that are common to the U.S. and other advanced capitalist countries.

Cullen, Francis T., William J. Maakestad, and Gray Cavender. *Corporate Crime Under Attack: The Ford Pinto Case and Beyond.* Cincinnati, Ohio: Anderson, 1987. This objective account of the historic trial of one of the nation's largest and most powerful corporations explains how the Ford Motor Company was charged with being criminally responsible for the 1983 deaths of three young women. The authors place the case in the context of corporate crime.

Green, Gary S. *Occupational Crime.* Chicago: Nelson-Hall, 1990. The author is among the modern critics of Edwin Sutherland's concept of white-collar crime who argue that it is too imprecise. Green develops instead a concept of occupational crime. He distinguishes between the varieties committed by individuals, professional persons, organizations, and representatives of the state.

Groves, W. Byron, and Graeme R. Newman, eds. *Punishment and Privilege.* Albany, N.Y.: Harrow and Heston, 1986. A collection of original papers reflecting a conceptual tension between those who would abolish criminal punishment in favor of civil remedies and those who would increase the punishment of white-collar and corporate criminals. Henry Pontell, Paul Jesilow, and Gilbert Geis argue that existing legal and political institutions cannot control medical fraud and that punishment is not an effective sanction. Authors dealing with other kinds of white-collar crime acknowledge the problem but suggest new kinds of punishment, such as court-ordered shaming, that might prove effective.

Mokhiber, Russell. *Corporate Crime and Violence: Big Business and the Abuse of the Public Trust.* San Francisco: Sierra, 1988. The author discusses thirty-six cases of corporate crime, especially against veterans, consumers, workers, children, women, and the environment. The discussion is aimed at raising public awareness of the enormous and manifold costs of such crime and offers some helpful remedies.

Simon, David R., and D. Stanley Eitzen. *Elite Deviance.* 4th ed. Boston: Allyn & Bacon, 1993. A textbook that marshals much useful information while attempting to demonstrate that white-collar and corporate crime is not simply a matter of individual "bad apples" in the modern American capitalist system but rather a systemic problem that undermines the foundations of American democracy.

Sutherland, Edwin H. *White-Collar Crime: The Uncut Version.* New Haven, Conn.: Yale University Press, 1983. This new version of Sutherland's classic work restores the names of those companies the author considered guilty of white-collar crimes. They had been omitted from the original 1949 edition under legal and financial coercion. A lengthy introduction by Charles Geis and Colin Goff analyzing the life and work of Sutherland significantly enriches the new edition.

Charles H. O'Brien

Cross-References

Corporations and Economic Concentration, 360; Crime: Analysis and Overview, 373; The Criminal Justice System, 380; Monopolies and Oligopolies, 1248; Organized Crime, 1322; Victimless Crime, 2150.

WOMEN IN THE LABOR FORCE

Type of sociology: Major social institutions
Field of study: Economy

Participation by women in the labor force has been increasing steadily since 1950. The majority of women tend to be clustered in a small number of occupations, however, mostly in the categories of sales, service, and clerical jobs. In general, women in the labor force have been underpaid and underemployed and have faced discrimination.

Principal terms

COMPARABLE WORTH: a proposed solution to wage inequality between men and women that would require equal pay for comparable work regardless of a job's title or classification

DUAL LABOR MARKET: the concept that men and women occupy separate labor markets, with women mostly working in service, sales, and clerical jobs, while men work in a wide range of occupations with higher wages and more opportunities

GLASS CEILING: the "invisible" obstacles and impediments confronting women when they try to reach top-ranked and high paying jobs

OCCUPATIONAL SEGREGATION: the separation of jobs by gender, race, or other criteria; in the case of gender segregation, two labor markets are created

PINK-COLLAR GHETTO: a term referring to the concentration of women in traditionally female jobs that have low wages and present little or no opportunity for advancement

SECONDARY WORKER: a married working woman who is viewed as working primarily to supplement a husband's primary earnings

WAGE GAP: the salary differential between men's and women's median incomes

Overview

Increasing numbers of women are participating in the labor force. According to the United States Department of Labor in 1991, 58 percent of all American women were in the labor force at that time. The greatest increase over earlier years was among women twenty-five to thirty-four years of age. There are several reasons for women's increased participation in the labor force. One reason is an increase in educational achievements by women. More women are receiving college and advanced degrees than ever before, which gives them access to more jobs. According to demographer Cheryl Russell in her article "Women's Rights" (1992), women by the early 1990's were receiving half of all master's degrees and about one-third of all doctorates. Women who have postsecondary education are more likely to stay in the labor force after marriage and after childbearing.

Another factor in women's increased participation in the labor force is changes in marital and family patterns. Women tend to stay single longer than in the past. Moreover, married women are having fewer children, and they are waiting longer to have their first child. These three factors—greater postsecondary education, later marriage, and later childbirth—have significantly added to the pool of women workers in the twenty-five to thirty-four age group.

Many women work simply because changes in the economy have made it necessary for many married women to work; it has long been a necessity for single women if they sought autonomy from their families. Living costs, such as housing and food prices, have risen—as have taxes—while wages have stagnated or even decreased. Thus, for most married couples or two-parent families it is necessary to have two incomes to maintain the standard of living it was once possible to attain (in the 1950's and 1960's, for example) with a single wage earner. For single mothers, the situation is extremely difficult. An increasing number of female-headed families live at or below the poverty level. According to professor Susan Basow in her book *Gender: Stereotypes and Roles* (1992), this economic situation is attributable to many factors, including inadequate vocational training, low educational level, lack of adequate child support, lack of affordable child care, and low salaries in traditionally female jobs.

Yet another factor in the increase in women in the workforce has been the growth of industries and occupations that primarily hire women, such as educational, governmental, recreational, and medical services. The United States Department of Labor (1991) reported that three-fifths of all women are employed in clerical jobs, teaching, and nursing.

Though women are moving into the labor force in increasing numbers, they still are concentrated in a small number of female-dominated occupations. This pattern has changed little in the past hundred years, despite a shift from agricultural jobs to textile jobs and then to office work. The few occupational areas in which most women work are relatively low paying and tend to be of low status. Basow argues that the segregation of jobs by gender is even more pronounced than the segregation of jobs by race. The United States Department of Labor reported in 1991 that about three of every four female employees worked in one of three categories: clerical (28 percent); professional and managerial (27 percent), most of which is teaching and administration; and service (18 percent). Even within the same occupational area, women are often given the lowest paying tasks.

Even though women's participation in the labor force has increased since the 1950's, the salary differential between men and women has changed little. Figures for 1991, for example, recorded a woman's income to be somewhere between 65 to 74 percent relative to a man's income. One factor involved in this differential is job segregation, as mentioned earlier. Women are concentrated in a small number of low-paying jobs. Basow estimates that 25 percent of the wage gap between men and women can be attributed to gender segregation of jobs. It also may be that more women than men take time off for child care activities and thus do not build seniority as quickly.

When level of degree, field of study, and work experience are controlled, however, men still earn more than women do. Also, when men and women are employed in the same occupation, men tend to earn more. In *Women and Children Last: The Plight of Poor Women in Affluent America* (1986), scholar of women's studies Ruth Sidel suggests that the subordinate role of women in the workplace is caused by a "family-wage system" under which men are presumed to earn enough to support a wife and children. This leads to women being viewed as secondary workers, working only to supplement a husband's primary earnings.

Another major reason that women's wages have stayed low is that the majority of women are not unionized. Only 11 percent of female workers were unionized in 1986, as compared with 20 percent of men. Trade unions have often tried to keep women out, and even those unions that women have joined in large numbers are usually directed by men. Thus women have assumed few leadership positions in the unions. This is unfortunate, considering that women who belong to unions have advantages over nonunion women, especially regarding the availability of avenues for reporting and fighting sexual harassment. Unions have structured grievance policies for filing complaints of various kinds, harassment among them, and these complaints are generally taken more seriously. Additionally, union women tend to earn 30 percent more than nonunion women workers and have greater access to educational opportunities.

Women's position in the labor force is strongly affected by the conflict that can result from the need to find time for both work and family. Women are often forced to choose between their jobs and their children. Given that most women work because of economic need, such a choice is painful and difficult to make. This conflict is aggravated by the fact that the United States does less than any other economically developed country to accommodate working mothers. United States public policy offers less in terms of job flexibility, maternity leave, and subsidized day care. These deficits in public policies adversely affect women in the workplace and are responsible, in part, for women earning less than men.

The United States has little in terms of laws to ensure infant care leave, for example. It was not until 1993 that the United States government passed the Family and Medical Leave Act, which grants unpaid leave of up to twelve weeks for the birth or adoption of a child or because of the illness of a close family member. This only applies, however, to those who work in companies with fifty or more employees, and it provides only unpaid leave.

Applications

The study of women in the labor force has shown that in general women have been underemployed, underpaid, and discriminated against in the workplace. Women have, however, been making some slow progress in terms of occupation. In the early 1990's, women accounted for one-third of graduating physicians and 41 percent of new lawyers. Within specific professions, women's incomes have moved closer to those of men. For example, women on the police force earn 91 percent as much as men, female psychologists earn 80 percent as much as male psychologists, and female engineers earn 86 percent as much as male engineers. Unfortunately, the status of a profession often changes as its gender composition does. As more women enter a profession, some sociologists have argued, the status of the profession may decline, and men may start leaving.

Various programs, organizations, and possible solutions to inequities have developed from the study of issues related to women in the labor force. Susan Basow discusses one proposal for closing the wage gap between men and women; called comparable worth, it requires equal pay for comparable work. This concept is based on the idea that jobs should be compensated similarly which require similar amounts of education, experience, supervisory responsibility, and skill levels. The proposal of comparable worth would address the issue of the differential valuation of what women and men do.

Among the reasons for women's lower status in the labor force are women's socialization and societal factors such as work and family arrangements, direct and indirect discrimination, and the nature of the work environment. In terms of socialization, girls and boys tend to be socialized into different roles, with different skills and behavioral traits. Females are generally socialized to nurture and care for others, while males tend to be socialized to compete for power and status. Women often feel less comfortable in traditionally male work environments, which tend to be autocratic in terms of management style. Women prefer a more democratic management style. It has been suggested that some women may avoid positions in which they would need to use an autocratic approach to management. A woman might even leave a job because of such a situation, or because of a generally hostile environment. This is beginning to change, however, in that some companies are starting to understand the benefits of different management styles and traits. Much of this change has been prompted by research on women in the labor force and a concomitant recognition of the effectiveness of different management styles.

Traditionally male-dominated blue-collar jobs or jobs in the trades have presented even larger barriers to many women. Women tend to confront considerable resistance and hostility. In spite of the barriers, however, a growing number of women are working in jobs not traditionally held by women. To encourage and promote women in nontraditional jobs, programs have been established. One such program is Wider Opportunities for Women (WOW), based in Washington, D.C., which promotes employment for women in occupations that are more than 75 percent male. WOW encourages women to consider nontraditional jobs not only in the trades but also in a wide range of blue-collar and white-collar jobs. Though many women aspire to nontraditional jobs in the professions, blue-collar work can also offer many opportunities. Work in the trades can pay two to three times as much as clerical work, and a college education is not necessary. For many women, entering a nontraditional job such as a trade can break the cycle of poverty. The wages of a journeyman, a person who has fully completed an apprenticeship in a trade, are enough to support a family, unlike the wages of many traditionally female occupations. Such occupations also offer room for advancement, such as promotion to a supervisory or foreman's position.

Women may need help getting into trade jobs, because the competition is tough for apprenticeship spaces in unionized trades and women sometimes face discrimination. Programs have developed to assist women in this regard. One is Chicago Women in Trades, a group that prepares women for apprenticeship programs by offering preapprenticeship training to give them a head start in the learning process.

Context

Throughout American history, most women have been in a subordinate role to men in the labor force. Women have been mostly known as secondary workers, working primarily to add to a husband's earnings. In *Women and Children Last*, Sidel outlines some of the history of women in the labor force. Around the middle of the nineteenth century, an ideology developed in American society that the home needed the special presence of women. Since the beginning of the Industrial Revolution, production had been moving out of the home; men went to work in impersonal, stressful, and sometimes dangerous places. It became the role of a man to earn money to support his wife and children. Women were to remain in the home, which was supposed to be a haven from the stressful work environment. Before this time, wage labor (as well as the domestic work) was often done at home by women.

During World War I, women began to enter jobs to which they were previously unable to gain access . After the war, however, many of these jobs went back to being predominantly men's domain. Women began entering white-collar jobs as clerks, bookkeepers, saleswomen, and advertising copywriters. In the 1920's, an increasing number of women entered jobs that were seen as consistent with their roles in the home, such as nursing, teaching, social work, and library work.

The situation for women in the labor force changed considerably during World War II. Most gains were made in war industries. Female union membership rose drastically; the image of the new working woman was typified by "Rosie the Riveter," appearing on government posters urging women to work. During this period, it seemed that job segregation by gender might finally be eliminated. Immediately after the war, however, many women were laid off as the veterans returned. The number of women in the labor force continued to increase after World War II, but union membership decreased and once again there was a high degree of job segregation.

Though women's participation in the workforce has increased steadily since World War II, conditions are changing very slowly. There is still a dual labor market. Most women work in a few occupations with relatively low wages and little opportunity for advancement, and they earn less than men, even in the same profession. Women still must confront considerable discrimination in the workplace. There are few supports in American society to help women balance the demands of work and family. Women's secondary status in the labor force is unlikely to change until lawmakers and employers are willing to make changes to support family life as it exists in modern American society. Necessary changes include more affordable child care, structural changes in the workplace to allow flexible hours and parental leave, and the sharing of domestic responsibilities.

Bibliography

Basow, Susan. "Consequences for the Labor Force." In *Gender: Stereotypes and Roles*. 3d ed. Pacific Grove, Calif.: Brooks/Cole, 1992. An excellent introductory overview and survey of women and men in the labor force. Basow looks at how gender stereotypes influence people's work lives.

Blau, Francine, and Marianne Ferber. *The Economics of Women, Men, and Work*. Englewood Cliffs, N.J.: Prentice-Hall, 1986. A good survey of men and women in the labor force. The focus is on the economic elements of men's and women's situations in the workplace. The authors conduct a detailed analysis of the wage differential.

Fuchs, V. R. *Women's Quest for Economic Equality*. Cambridge, Mass.: Harvard University Press, 1988. A well-written and clearly developed book based on the idea that women's responsibility for children is one of the root causes of women's subordinate status in the labor force.

Jacobs, J. A. *Revolving Doors: Sex Segregation and Women's Careers*. Stanford, Calif.: Stanford University Press, 1989. Provides a thorough analysis of the problem of the segregation of jobs by gender and looks at how this affects women's careers.

Schwartz, Felice N. *Breaking with Tradition: Women and Work. The New Facts of Life*. New York: Warner Books, 1992. The author makes the case that the world of business has largely ignored the fact that women rear families and that the talents of many women are wasted because of this. Schwartz argues that many productive women are forced out of the workplace because of outdated corporate policies. A thought-provoking look at the dilemmas of women in corporate settings.

Sidel, Ruth. *On Her Own*. New York: Viking Press, 1990. Addresses the issues of women within a changing society. Sidel discusses how family life is changing and includes an informative chapter on the realities women face in the labor force.

_____. "Women and Work." In *Women and Children Last: The Plight of Poor Women in Affluent America*. New York: Viking Press, 1986. An excellent chapter that discusses women in the labor force. Concisely traces the history of women in the labor force, focusing on the subordinate role of women to men. The author relates the issues involved for women in the labor force and discusses how these contribute to the poor economic circumstances of many women and children. Sidel uses excerpts from interviews with women to illustrate her points.

Anna M. Heiberger Abell

Cross-References

WOMEN IN THE MEDICAL PROFESSION

Type of sociology: Major social institutions
Field of study: Medicine

The number of women in the medical profession has increased substantially since 1965. Female medical students and health care providers tend to be more person- and less science-oriented than their male counterparts, which influences their choice of medical specialties and the way in which they practice medicine.

Principal terms
DISCRIMINATION: the denial of opportunities and rights to certain groups on the basis of their membership in those groups
GENDER ROLE: a set of expectations (norms) about how the members of one sex should behave
PREJUDICE: an unjustifiable negative attitude toward a group and its individual members
ROLE: a set of norms that define how persons in a given social position ought to behave
SEXISM: individuals' prejudicial attitudes and discriminatory behavior toward persons of a given sex; institutional practices that subordinate persons of a given sex
STEREOTYPE: a belief about the personal attributes of a group of people which can be overgeneralized, inaccurate, and resistant to change in the face of evidence demonstrating that it is inaccurate

Overview

During the seventeenth century, a woman's role in medicine was to be either a midwife or a nurse. Throughout the eighteenth and nineteenth centuries, women in the medical field had low status and received much lower pay than did their male counterparts. This situation began to change only in 1847, when Elizabeth Blackwell entered Geneva Medical College in upstate New York; she became the first woman to graduate from medical school. From that point on, women fought their way into the medical profession. In 1960, 405 women and 6,676 men graduated from medical schools in the United States. The percentage of women applicants to medical school increased steadily from 7.3 percent in the academic year 1965-1966 to 40.3 percent in 1990-1991. In 1990, 6,404 women and 10,345 men enrolled in medical school.

Despite making progress in the medical profession, women continue to encounter prejudices and discrimination throughout their training and during their professional lives. Psychologists Marita Inglehart, Donald R. Brown, and Oksana Malanchuk have reviewed the literature concerning these problems. Empirical research shows that female medical students and professionals face significant amounts of sexual harassment and that female physicians in male-dominated specialties such as surgery still face considerable hostility. Analyses of the number of men and women in the various fields of specialization and in the leading positions in medical organizations show that women are more likely to be found in less prestigious and lower-income specialties (such as pediatrics, obstetrics/gynecology, psychiatry, pathology, and family practice) and to be underrepresented in the top positions in medical organizations and medical school facilities. One concrete indicator of sexism toward female physicians is the fact that in 1985, the average annual income of female physicians in the United States was 30 percent lower than that of their male counterparts, regardless of age, specialty, number of hours worked, or numbers of patients seen.

Following female students from the time they enter medical school until the point at which they are established professionally provides an interesting picture of the situation that women face in the medical profession. Inglehart, Brown, and Malanchuk have described various results from an ongoing longitudinal study conducted at the University of Michigan medical school since 1972. When entering medical school, women typically tend to emphasize helping and person-oriented goals, whereas men tend to emphasize financial and political goals. Women also cite person-related reasons for entering the field of medicine more often than men do; men tend to cite the status of medicine and the opportunity to earn a large income as reasons for entering the field. Psychologist Marjorie A. Bowman has shown that women who enter medical school are generally outgoing, independent, and well adjusted, and that they have academic records that are comparable to those of their male counterparts. She indicates, however, that the stress placed on women during medical training and in their professional lives takes a toll on these women.

Inglehart, Brown, and Malanchuk have shown that, ten years after graduation, the women in their study tended to practice less prestigious specialties than men did, they seemed to advance somewhat more slowly than men did, and they were more likely to hold salaried positions than men were. This lack of power and authority in the medical establishment is one major source of stress for female health care providers. Another source of stress is role strain. Role strain can be defined as the conflict caused by having to choose among demands made by different roles. It is interesting to note that most female physicians in the United States are married either to other physicians or to highly career-oriented professionals. Research shows that married female professionals are often responsible not only for their professional duties but also for all the housework and child care in their families. These responsibilities are a major source of stress. A third potential source of stress for women physicians is that they tend to spend more time with each patient and to be more sensitive to personal issues. Such sensitivity to the personal and interpersonal aspects of diseases and the ways in which diseases, death, and dying affect the patient and his or her family can drain a physician emotionally. Research shows that patients are more likely to discuss symptoms of mental illness and emotional aspects of diseases with female health care providers than they are with male providers. Such sources of stress may explain why women physicians have a higher burnout rate and higher rates of alcoholism, drug addiction, depression, suicide attempts, and suicides than do male physicians.

Applications
Knowledge of the experiences of women in the medical profession can be taken into account in the planning of medical education and in discussions of trends in the health care system. In the area of medical education, it is crucial to recognize that women are motivated primarily by person-related values. Purely science-oriented curricula are likely to discourage women and to keep them from living up to their potential. Introducing the "human touch" into medical school curricula will tend to motivate women.

Knowledge of the specific issues that women face in the health professions can be quite useful for medical organizations that are attempting to change the state of the medical profession. The lack of female role models for women physicians is still an important issue. Professional organizations of women physicians (such as the American Medical Women's Association) are, however, gaining influence and beginning to effect changes.

The U.S. health care delivery system is in a period of change. It will be interesting to see how these changes will influence the role of women in the health care professions. Health psychologist Robin DiMatteo provides an excellent overview of 1980's trends in the delivery of medical care in her book *The Psychology of Health, Illness, and Medical Care* (1991). The most important factor motivating change in the U.S. health care system might be the fact that costs have been rising dramatically. It is likely that the health care delivery system will increasingly use primary physicians (such as family practitioners and general practitioners) as gatekeepers, who will attempt to provide optimal care at a reasonable cost. It is likely that the demand for physicians in general practice—a field of choice for many female physicians—will increase. It is also likely that general practitioners will become more influential.

Another trend is the changing pattern of diseases away from infectious diseases toward diseases that are related to lifestyles. Lifestyle-related diseases are preventable, and therefore patient education is a crucial element of preventive medicine. It is a fact that cooperation with health care recommendations depends largely on the relationship that a patient has with a physician. An impersonal, business-like interaction style tends to generate a lower compliance rate than does a style that is characterized by concern for and interest in patients. Female health care providers tend to be person oriented and therefore may be more successful than male health care providers in establishing a basic relationship that is conducive to changing lifestyle-related risk factors for preventable diseases such as coronary artery disease and strokes.

A third trend in the medical field is the growing percentage of older patients, which indicates that the treatment of diseases will shift from the treatment of acute diseases to the treatment of chronic diseases and the providing of maintenance care. In this area also, the more person-related approach of women physicians may be an important factor in providing optimal care.

One factor seems to be common to these three trends toward patient-oriented treatment by physicians. The changing pattern of diseases away from infectious diseases toward preventable, lifestyle-related diseases, for example, points to the significance of motivating patients to engage in preventive activities and to change their lifestyles. Stopping smoking and changing one's diet to include more fiber and less fat are two examples of lifestyle changes that can make a difference in a person's health and life expectancy. The fact that Americans are beginning to live longer means that medical professionals will be treating more patients for chronic diseases that require constant care. Research shows that female physicians tend to be more responsive than male physicians to patients' concerns and that they try harder to promote the psychological and social well-being of their patients than do male physicians. For this reason, women could be instrumental in bringing about an attitude change in the medical profession, tending to treat patients as whole human beings who are responsible partners in the health care process. Such a change may be a crucial factor in making it possible to provide high-quality health care at a reasonable cost.

Context

The increasing number of women in the medical profession can be seen in the context of the changing role of women in the United States since the 1960's. Research has shown that, since the late 1970's, women and men have been entering colleges in roughly equal numbers. The percentage of women who earn a Ph.D., however, is nowhere near 50 percent. At the next level of postgraduate achievement, the proportion of women drops even more, with women being severely underrepresented in professional-level occupations, particularly in the scientific and professional fields. In the field of chemistry in the late 1980's, for example, approximately 10 percent of doctorates were earned by women, but women held only 4 percent of faculty positions. Furthermore, women who hold faculty positions receive, on the average, lower salaries than do men in comparable positions. Women's relative progress in the medical profession must be examined in the context of this gender-based filtering process. Analyzing the way that women entered the medical profession and the gap that still exists between men and women in the field might contribute to a better understanding of the factors that keep women from living up to their potential and succeeding at the same rate as that achieved by men.

Serious concerns have been raised in recent years regarding the future development of the work force in the United States. There may soon be a shortage of qualified personnel in the natural sciences and engineering fields, which may put the United States at a tremendous disadvantage in international competition. One solution to this problem would be to introduce women into these fields in larger numbers. Understanding how women overcome gender stereotypes and sexism when entering the medical profession and how they continue to overcome discrimination in these fields might contribute to the opening up of ways to include more women in other professions.

Bibliography

American Medical Association. *Women in Medicine in America: In the Mainstream.* Chicago: Author, 1991. Discusses the problems that women face in the medical profession. Includes many informative statistical tables.

Bowman, Marjorie A., and Deborah I. Allen. *Stress and Women Physicians*. New York: Springer-Verlag, 1985. This book provides an overview of issues related to stress in female physicians. It also addresses issues of mental health.

DiMatteo, M. Robin. *The Psychology of Health, Illness, and Medical Care*. Pacific Grove, Calif.: Brooks/Cole, 1991. This book provides an excellent overview of health psychology and gives a good description of the issues that women in medicine faced in the 1990's.

Inglehart, Marita R., Donald R. Brown, and Oksana Malanchuk. "University of Michigan School Graduates of the 1980s: The Professional Development of Women Physicians." In *Women's Lives Through Time*, edited by Katherine Day Hulbert and Diane Tickton Schuster. San Francisco: Jossey-Bass, 1993. This chapter reviews the literature on women in the medical profession and provides the results of a longitudinal study of women from the time they entered the University of Michigan medical school to ten years after graduation.

Morantz-Sanchez, Regina Markell. *Sympathy and Science: Women Physicians in American Medicine*. New York: Oxford University Press, 1985. This book provides a historical overview of the way in which women entered the medical profession, along with documentation of women's contributions to medicine.

Marita Inglehart

Cross-References

Gender Inequality: Analysis and Overview, 820; Gender Socialization, 833; Health and Society, 852; Health Care and Gender, 858; The Medical Profession and the Medicalization of Society, 1159; Medical Sociology, 1166; The Institution of Medicine, 1185; Two-Career Families, 2077; Women in the Labor Force, 2185.

THE WOMEN'S MOVEMENT

Type of sociology: Collective behavior and social movements

The women's movement is a social movement whose agenda focuses on obtaining equal rights and status for women in a male-dominated society. Among its goals are that women be free to decide what careers they want to pursue and what lifestyle they want to adopt.

Principal terms
EQUAL RIGHTS AMENDMENT (ERA): proposed as the twenty-seventh amendment to the U.S. Constitution, acknowledging women's equality to men as U.S. citizens; a 1970's symbol of the women's movement in the United States
GROUP CONSCIOUSNESS: the belief that an individual's problems arise from unfair treatment because of the person's group membership and not from the person's inadequacy
MARXIST FEMINISTS: those who pursue equality for women through the use of analytical tools of society propounded by Karl Marx; they see class structure and capitalism as the basic cause of women's problems
NATIONAL ORGANIZATION FOR WOMEN (NOW): organization formed in 1966 to bring women into equal partnership with men so they can participate fully in the mainstream affairs of the nation
SEPARATIST FEMINISTS: those feminists who advocate totally seceding from male-formed structures as the only way for women to achieve true liberty; they call for all-female communes
WOMAN SUFFRAGE: woman's right to vote; especially the drive to enact the Nineteenth Amendment to the U.S. Constitution, ratified in 1920, which gave women the right to vote

Overview

The women's movement—also variously called the feminist movement, women's liberation movement, or women's rights movement—is a transformational social movement that focuses on changing the mostly institutional and social attitudes, beliefs, activities, practices, and identities that form the basis of social life arranged according to an assumed gender hierarchy. Though in the United States the movement gathered momentum after the publication of Betty Friedan's *The Feminine Mystique* (1963), which coincided with the release to President John F. Kennedy of a report by the President's Commission on the Status of Women, the women's movement has a world history that goes back to earlier centuries. During the Enlightenment, for example, Mary Wollstonecraft published a book that advocated women's rights. In *A Vindication of the Rights of Woman* (1792), Wollstonecraft attacked the societal idea that women were created simply to please the male gender. She asked that women be given equal opportunity in social, political, educational, and labor matters.

It was the Industrial Revolution, with its widespread social changes, that caused the women's movement to develop rapidly in Europe and the United States. It opened women's eyes to the fact that their economic dependence on men and their lack of educational, political, and social opportunities were key factors in their subordinate position in society. Various organizations founded and run by women for women arose. Such awareness brought about the nineteenth century movement for woman suffrage, the fight for the abolition of slavery, and the 1848 opening of the Queen's College for Women in London—the first of its kind in higher education for women. Throughout the nineteenth century, American women worked together to address needs and grievances; by the first half of the twentieth century they had won the right to vote, control their earnings, own property, and be employed. Yet the issues of full participation in party politics, the limits placed on women's labor participation, and the traditional notion of woman as naturally destined to be mother, wife, and homemaker lingered. The women's movement in the second half of the twentieth century sought to address these concerns as women in the United States took the lead in fighting for total emancipation.

The period was ushered in by the publication of Simone de Beauvoir's *Le Deuxième Sexe* (1949; *The Second Sex*, 1953), which pointed out that woman's liberation is also man's liberation. It was a precursor to Friedan's major analysis of the condition of women in *The Feminine Mystique*. Reported by many women to have changed the direction of their lives, Friedan's book attacked "deadening domesticity" and the entrapment of woman in the "mystique" (resurgence of ancient or traditional belief and attitude) that woman is different from man in a mysterious way and can achieve full womanhood only in the naturally unique female order of "sexual passivity, male domination, and nurturing maternal love." Friedan suggested that individual women should find some meaningful, fulfilling employment outside the home, be committed to a vocation, make life plans, and develop group consciousness.

Friedan's ideas did not fall on deaf ears. She and other women founded the National Organization for Women (NOW) in Washington, D.C., in 1966, with Friedan as its president. According to its statement of purpose, NOW intended:

> To take action to bring women into full participation in the mainstream of American society now, exercising all the privileges and responsibilities thereof in *truly equal partnership with men*. . . . NOW is dedicated to the proposition that women, first and foremost, are human beings, who, like all other people in our society, must have the chance to develop their fullest human potential.

Other feminist organizations were soon formed in the United States and Europe, especially by younger, more radical women. Groups such as Boston's Bread and Roses, Berkeley Women's Liberation Group, Women's Radical Action Project, New York Radical Women (especially its "Redstockings" group), Seattle Radical Women, and the October Seventeenth Movement rose to prominence. Ranging from Marxist feminists to radical feminists, separatist feminists, and socialist feminists, these women's movements were the first to use the designation of women's (or female) liberation.

A major national organization called the Women's Equity Action League (WEAL), largely made up of professional women, was also formed to focus on legal and economic issues. Other milestones for the movement included the formation of Older Women's Liberation (OWL), the National Women's Political Caucus (NWPC), the Coalition of Labor Union Women (CLUW), and the Nine to Five National Association of Working Women. All these groups incorporated discussions of social, political, and economic equality and sex discrimination into a coherent ideology that held men and governments responsible for discrimination against women and drew an action-oriented plan to ease women's problems.

The goals of the women's movement have varied from country to country, but as reflected in the United States, the agenda includes politics, family planning (including child care, abortion, and contraception), media representation, and language use. The perennial issues of equal education, equal pay for equal labor, and equal involvement in societal decision-making processes are also still on the agenda.

Applications

Though there are ideological differences within the women's movement, such as disagreements about lesbianism and abortion, the women's movement expresses a widely shared social, political, and economic dissatisfaction. In Europe and the United States, women have boycotted major corporations, initiated lawsuits, lobbied legislative bodies, and engaged in demonstrations to make their grievances known and to secure their legitimate rights.

The women's movement functions primarily through its involvement in the political process. Strategy and tactics are coordinated, and the movement engages in a number of political activities. Combining different methods of persuasion and protest in its efforts to change public policy, NOW has worked within and outside the system to bring change. Its arsenal includes deliberate interruption of Senate committees and conferences, writing polite letters, consulting, lobbying and demonstrating, calling for and coordinating strikes for equality, and consciousness-raising among the populace. The movement also tries to influence party politics in favor of women. One of the most visible successes of the movement's intraparty activities was the nomination of Geraldine Ferraro as the Democratic vice presidential candidate in 1984.

Employing these strategies and tactics, the movement has served as a leader for various causes affecting women on the local and national levels. Fighting for equal employment for women, it has closely watched how the Equal Employment Opportunity Commission (EEOC) enforces Title VII of the Civil Rights Act of 1964. It has taken cases to the commission and filed discrimination complaints on behalf of employed women. At the same time, it has devoted energy to attacking sex-segregated employment advertisement. It persistently fought for the Equal Rights Amendment (ERA) until time ran out on the ratification process in 1982. This has enabled women's participation in the labor force to increase tremendously.

When in 1976 a U.S. Supreme Court ruling allowed pregnant women to be excluded from employee health benefits, various members of the women's movement responded with an outcry to Congress. This led to the 1978 Pregnancy Disability Act, which assured qualified women of pregnancy benefits. Working women have since asked for and won other maternity rights, such as flexible work time in recognition of their multiple roles. In 1993 a law was enacted that allows a parent to take a leave of absence from work to attend to a pressing family matter without losing his or her employment.

The issue of abortion has presented the greatest challenge to the women's movement, causing divisiveness, animosity, and heated public debate among members. NOW has worked hard for the repeal of antiabortion laws, defining the issue as "the right of a woman to control her own body" or the "right of women to control their reproductive lives." In the early 1970's, both NOW and WEAL devoted their energy and funding to the fight to make abortion legal, supporting litigation based on the argument that restricting abortion violates the individual's constitutional right to privacy. In 1973, the Supreme Court decided in *Roe v. Wade* that abortion, under certain conditions, was legal. This victory, however, precipitated deep divisions in the movement. Two opposing groups were quickly formed: The National Right to Life Committee (opponents of abortion) and the National Abortion Rights Action League (supporters of a woman's right to have an abortion).

The women's movement has also been active in religious matters, particularly in attempts to expand the role of women in Christian denominations. A common accusation of the movement has been that much of the basis for the oppression of women comes from the Judeo-Christian tradition, and women have formed consciousness-raising groups at various levels to assess and reform the attitudes of the church toward women. Women's studies programs have been established in some Protestant seminaries and church-affiliated colleges. (The Boston Theological Institute is one.) Even in the Catholic church, the women's movement has made itself felt in the National Coalition of American Nuns and through feminist theologians such as Mary Daly and Sidney Cornelia Callahan. The women's movement within Christian churches has focused on three main areas: the ordination of women to church hierarchies, the status and role of women in the church in general, and the biblical and theological interpretation of the female gender.

Context

The women's movement came to prominence in the 1960's along with several other sociopolitical movements. The period was marked, for example, by the antiwar movement, civil rights agitation, and black nationalism. In many voices, these movements called out for equal rights and justice. None existed in a vacuum, and all had impacts on society at large and on various other movements.

The Civil Rights movement, for example, inspired the tactics of the anti-Vietnam War movement. In turn, the experiences of women in both those movements frequently were influential in causing them to examine the role of women in society. Even in those social movements that were struggling to change society, many women found that they were expected to conform to stereotypical female roles. Women became frustrated, then angry, that male leaders wanted them to answer telephones and make coffee (and to be available for sex) while the men theorized, planned strategy, and led demonstrations. Later, as the women's movement gained its own momentum, it found itself divided by other movements. The increased sense of empowerment among gays and lesbians, strongly related to the gay liberation movement, was at least partially responsible for a split within the women's movement (most visibly in NOW) over whether one had to be a lesbian to be a true feminist. The impassioned crusaders at both poles of the abortion issue, sharply focused movements of their own, further divided women.

Since the early 1970's, the women's movement has had profound effects on many fields, including history, sociology, and psychology. It has inspired sociologists to explore the issues of gender stratification and sexism (individual and institutional) in great detail. The oppressive effects on women of patriarchal societies have been examined. Feminist sociology, along with such subfields as feminist psychology and feminist literary criticism, has become a thriving area. The establishment of women's studies programs on many college and university campuses—a direct result of the women's movement—has been instrumental in the growth of these fields.

Truly equal treatment of men and women, as advocated by the women's movement, requires that many of society's myths, values, and beliefs be fundamentally reassessed and changed. Changes must occur in patterns of work and family life and in social behavior, decision making, politics, religion, and education. Even the more personal and private domain of sexuality will be deeply affected. Women's issues as diverse as the provision of day care facilities, the development of a nonsexist vocabulary, and the representation of women and their roles in the mass media, including advertising, are being assessed and debated. The changes wrought by the women's movement have already been profound, and regardless of controversy and backlash, further important changes will occur.

Bibliography

Andersen, Margaret L. *Thinking About Women*. 3d ed. New York: Macmillan, 1993. Introduces the reader to women's experiences in society and provides a comprehensive review of feminist scholarship. Part 3 is especially important in its treatment of feminism and social change. It has a large bibliography and an index.

Barrett, Jane, et al. *South African Women on the Move*. London: Zed Books, 1985. This book by six women focuses on the main experiences of black South African women as individuals and in organizations, and it discusses their form of resistance. Includes photographs.

Beauvoir, Simone de. *The Second Sex*. New York: Knopf, 1952. Mostly an analysis by this French atheistic existentialist of how Christianity has been used to oppress and domesticate women. Should ideally be read with Mary Daly's *The Church and the Second Sex* (1968), which sees how Beauvoir's attack on Christianity could open a dialogue on the possibilities for women within Christianity.

Chapman, Jenny. *Politics, Feminism, and the Reformation of Gender*. London: Routledge, 1993. The book deals with the "scissors problem" faced by women as they are caught between their female gender and their aspirations in the world of men. It offers an international perspective by using case studies from the U.S., Russia, Finland, England, and Germany.

Doely, Sarah Bentley, ed. *Women's Liberation and the Church*. New York: Association Press, 1970. Contains essays written by Catholic and Protestant feminists that look at the women's movement from a theological and religious perspective. It points out the paradox that liberation, which is central to New Testament Christianity, has not been practiced by the church when it comes to women.

Friedan, Betty. *The Feminine Mystique*. New York: W. W. Norton, 1963. A sensitive and provocative work on the syndrome of woman as housewife, mother, and sex object in the United States and the resultant feeling of loss and unfulfillment. Friedan's solution for this syndrome is for woman to seek employment outside the home.

Jaquette, Jane S., ed. *The Women's Movement in Latin America*. Boston: Unwin Hyman, 1989. An analysis of the political role of the women's movement and of women in the transition from dictatorships to democracies in some Latin American countries in the 1980's. The book also tries to bring Latin American experiences to bear on the effort of developing international feminism.

Katzenstein, Mary Fainsod, and Carol McClurg Mueller, eds. *The Women's Movements of the United States and Western Europe*. Philadelphia: Temple University Press, 1987. Focusing on the women's movement in seven countries, the book discusses the convergence and interaction of sociopolitical institutions, gender consciousness, and feminist movements.

Simon, Rita J., and Gloria Danziger. *Women's Movements in America*. New York: Praeger, 1991. The book discusses the achievements, failures, and aspirations of the women's movement and of women in general from the founding of the United States to 1990. Includes a good bibliography and an index.

Yates, Gayle Graham. *What Women Want*. Cambridge, Mass.: Harvard University Press, 1975. Looking at the ideas behind the women's movement in the United States, the book puts the movement in historical perspectives: feminist, liberationist, and androgynous. Includes notes, a bibliography, and an index. Highly recommended.

I. Peter Ukpokodu

Cross-References

Comparable Worth and Sex Segregation in the Workplace, 303; Gender and Religion, 813; Gender Inequality: Analysis and Overview, 820; Gender Inequality: Biological Determinist Views, 826; Gender Socialization, 833; Health Care and Gender, 858; Sex versus Gender, 1721; Sexism and Institutional Sexism, 1728; Women in the Labor Force, 2185; Women in the Medical Profession, 2191.

WORKPLACE SOCIALIZATION

Type of sociology: Socialization and social interaction
Field of study: Agents of socialization

Workplace socialization encompasses two types of socialization. First, it refers to the ways in which a particular society uses a person's job to promote its values, norms, and desired behavior. Second, it refers to the mechanisms and processes used by work organizations to promote their own values, norms, and desired behavior. Generally speaking, workplace socialization is a means of social control.

Principal terms
> NORMS: standards of behavior created and observed by a society or organization
> RESOCIALIZATION: the process of learning the norms, values, and behaviors of a new role
> ROLE: the behavior associated with a social or organizational position
> SOCIALIZATION: the lifelong process of learning norms, values, attitudes, and behaviors appropriate to one's role in society
> VALUES: beliefs shared by members of a society (or organization) of what is good, bad, desirable, undesirable, proper, or improper

Overview

Socialization is a lifelong learning process in which an individual learns the values, norms, and roles of a particular society; a society's shared values, norms, beliefs, and symbols are collectively known as its culture. Societies use various social institutions to promote culture among their members. Institutions used for these purposes are called socialization agents. The workplace is one such agent. In it, a person learns the values and behaviors desired by the employer or that are necessary to perform a job effectively. Similarly, a person's occupation is sometimes used by society to transmit its generally accepted values, norms, and roles.

Sociologist Wilmer Moore has described four phases of workplace socialization. These are career choice, anticipatory socialization, conditioning and commitment, and continuous commitment. According to Moore, occupational socialization begins when a person decides (often early in life) to pursue a particular vocation or career. After a choice is made, he asserts, the person will purposely try to obtain the necessary training and education to obtain such a job.

After getting the job, the person will adjust his or her behavior and values to the pleasant and unpleasant aspects of the job with the help of superiors, peers, informal leaders, and perhaps organizational consultants. According to Moore, later in his or her career, the median person will have achieved a high degree of job satisfaction and will have internalized the norms, values, and role content of the job and will act accordingly. In short, the person will have become successfully socialized.

This socialization process, however, may find resistance from some individuals.

For example, a male police recruit at the police academy may wish to wear long hair. It is an organizational (and societal) norm, however, that police officers should conform to certain codes of dress and appearance. Therefore, peer pressure, superior's orders, application of the police manual, and dismissal threats would make the recruit quit or have his hair cut.

Another aspect of workplace socialization is the external or social aspect. A person's job is frequently used by society to "complete" or enhance a person's socialization during adulthood. For example, in contemporary society people are often socialized in their jobs to avoid drugs and alcohol, to dress appropriately, not to engage in sexual harassment or corruption, and in general to avoid antisocial behavior. Employees who fail to change their conduct could be fired or face sanctions from management. Work organizations generally promote socially accepted values that are consonant with their own.

The workplace is also a resocialization agent. Frequently, organizations have structured processes to change employees' dysfunctional values or behavior. For example, as a requisite to keep a job, a person could be resocialized to avoid laziness and become a productive employee. In the case of jobs that require interaction with the public, people could be resocialized by means of training programs to overcome rudeness or impoliteness in their relationships with peers, superiors, and customers. Organizations use a number of methods to encourage accepted behavior and to limit unacceptable behavior among their employees. Economic bonuses, vacation plans, fringe benefits, career advancement, peer pressure, and other positive reinforcements are often used to promote accepted behavior among workers. On the other hand, organizations also have instruments to avoid undesired employee behavior. Peer pressure, disciplinary sanctions, and dismissals are among the methods used to avoid undesirable employee behavior.

Frederick W. Taylor's *Principles of Scientific Management* (1911, repr. 1982) provides a good example of managerial attempts to resocialize workers. Taylor a businessman, engineer, and writer, believed that businesses were losing considerable money and effort because the managerial methods used in those days promoted "systematic soldiering," or laziness among workers (an undesired behavior). His managerial theory and method (named "Taylorism" or scientific management) were aimed at eliminating these undesired behavioral traits. This was accomplished by studying the ways in which the best workers in each trade performed their jobs (using stopwatch studies) and by training all workers in that trade to perform their job in the same way as the "best man." Workers would obtain economic bonuses for the improvement in their performance using these new methods.

Applications

The study of workplace socialization enables social scientists and students to identify the instruments and processes used by work organizations to mold employee behavior in ways consonant with social and organizational values and norms. Similarly, it provides managers, management consultants, and industrial psychologists with theories and instruments to affect employee behavior in order to increase their productivity and reduce organizational conflict.

For example, many American companies place considerable emphasis on the physical appearance of employees at work. They have, for example, adopted dress codes and grooming codes. By establishing such codes, organizations communicate to their employees the way they should dress and "look" at work. Studies have revealed that close to 70 percent of U.S. companies have dress codes. Although such codes may appear unconstitutional, the U.S. Supreme Court has generally validated dress and grooming codes if they are in accordance with "generally accepted community standards" and are evenhandedly applied. This exemplifies the fact that occupational socialization may serve to reinforce social values.

Similarly, since the early 1980's, as a corollary to former U.S. president Ronald Reagan's "war on drugs" policy, many companies in the United States have adopted rules and processes to eliminate illegal drug use among their employees. Many companies enacted codes against drug use and adopted programs for detection of drug use among their employees. Indeed, according the Bureau of Labor Statistics, 67 percent of large companies in the United States have put in place some kind of drug testing policy. In addition, many of these companies have also established programs to rehabilitate employees with drug abuse problems. The dual dimension of workplace socialization can be easily understood by using these policies as an example. On one hand, companies socialize their workers to stay away from drugs because it is considered antisocial behavior. On the other hand, companies adopt such policies in order to increase productivity and reduce work-related accidents and employee absenteeism.

There are many other occupational areas in which management, management consultants, and informal groups exert their socialization efforts. For example, new employees are strictly supervised and coached until they internalize many organizational norms and rituals. For example, employees are expected to comply with strict work schedules, often having to begin their work at 8:00 A.M. and leave at 5:00 P.M. They are also expected to be productive at work. Many jobs have production and quality standards. The new employee is trained and given an adjustment period to see if he or she can meet such established standards. If this does not happen, the employee could be fired.

Workers are also socialized by informal groups. For example, if a new employee is exceeding her production quota by many units, her peers may let her know that she should slow down a little. Similarly, informal groups could teach a new employee not to "blow the whistle" on fellow workers in certain circumstances. On the other hand, informal group socialization may also make a lazy employee more productive. For example, if an employee's unproductiveness in the assembly line is making all the employees in that unit appear unproductive, the person could be rejected from social activities of the group. Hence, the employee might increase productivity in order to be accepted by the social group.

Professional groups are also agents to occupational socialization. The American Bar

Association (ABA), for example, regulates lawyer socialization in the United States. First an aspiring lawyer has to have a bachelor's degree, and then he or she must continue legal studies at an institution accredited by the ABA. After graduation, the person must pass a state bar exam. Then the behavior and practice of this professional attorney will be regulated by the state and national bars' codes of ethics. Similar situations exist in the medical, nursing, and educational fields.

Another practical application of workplace socialization and resocialization occurs in the management of organizational change. Workplace resocialization is necessary for organizational changes to occur smoothly. For example, in the 1980's, secretaries who were used to using typewriters needed to be resocialized in the use of word processors and computers in order to keep pace with advancements in their profession. The need for change involving resocialization occurs in many fields and for many reasons. Technology is responsible, directly or indirectly, for much resocialization. Physicians, for example, need to be more versed in human relations than they once were because many of their patients are now generally better informed by the media and want their physicians to give them detailed explanations of treatments and alternatives.

The relative importance accorded the study of workplace socialization has markedly increased since the 1960's. The concept has been widely discussed in sociology, psychology, management, and public administration journals under such rubrics as change management and management of organizational culture. Its practical applications have also been widely explored by management. Indeed, the importance of the training department, which is in charge of formal socialization and resocialization efforts in many firms, has increased significantly.

Context

It is almost impossible to determine the historical beginnings of workplace socialization. Some may argue that this phenomenon is as old as work itself. The greatest importance of workplace socialization, however, is its application to companies employing large numbers of workers, and these began with the factories of the Industrial Revolution of the eighteenth and nineteenth centuries. Inventions such as the steam engine and the spinning jenny as well as the use of coke (a more efficient derivate from coal) as a combustible revolutionized the ways in which goods were produced. They made it possible to produce more goods more efficiently.

In the historical period previous to the Industrial Revolution, goods were generally produced in a workshop by an artisan. The artisan, usually a man, was generally self-employed; he owned his own tools and determined his work schedule and tempo. Artisans were experts in a particular craft or trade (for example, shoemaking) and made their goods from the beginning to the end, keeping a close eye on their quality. The guild (an early version of today's unions) determined the cost of goods and consequently the artisan's earnings per unit.

After the Industrial Revolution, work was organized differently. Workers were specialized in the production of only one part of the end product—an approach called the division of labor. Generally, they were not business owners and worked for a wage. Work and workers were more strictly controlled. Management determined when the job would begin and end and set the workers' wages.

The writings and managerial practices of the eighteenth century writer and businessman Robert Owen show an unusual system of workplace socialization and control. In his factories, Owen established a "silent monitor" system, consisting of a small wooden figure with different colors on different sides that hung near each employee. The color that was displayed rated the employee's performance during the previous day and was aimed at making workers adjust their performance to the desired production rate.

Another perspective on workplace socialization was presented by German sociologist and philosopher Max Weber. In his book *Wirtschaft und Gesellschaft* (1922; *The Theory of Social and Economic Organization*, 1947), he explains the legal or bureaucratic form of social domination. From his explanation of this form of domination, it could be inferred that employees in modern organizations are controlled (and socialized) in an impersonal manner through the use of abstract norms and routinized procedures.

In the early 1900's, another interesting perspective on occupational socialization and resocialization was presented by Frederick W. Taylor. As stated before, this author popularized a managerial system (scientific management) that consisted of systematically studying the way in which the "best worker" of each trade performed and then training all employees in that trade in that "one best way."

A very different approach to workplace socialization was studied in the Hawthorne studies during the 1920's and 1930's. These studies revealed, for the first time, the existence of informal groups, norms, and leadership within work organizations. Thus, a very important aspect of workplace socialization consists of the values, norms, and behaviors transmitted and learned through informal groups.

Bibliography

Davis, Keith, and John W. Newstrom. *Human Behavior at Work: Organizational Behavior.* 7th ed. New York: McGraw-Hill, 1985. Presents valuable information related to the topic of workplace socialization. Of special interest are the chapters devoted to leadership and supervision, performance rewards systems, and the individual and the organization. In the former chapter, the author discusses topics such as the use of lie detectors in the workplace, organizational security systems, and drug testing policies and their relation to an employee's right to privacy.

Hersey, Paul, and Kenneth Blanchard. *Management of Organization Behavior.* 5th ed. Englewood Cliffs, N.J.: Prentice-Hall, 1988. Although directed toward a managerial audience, this book provides students of the social sciences with a solid understanding of the theories and principles underlying workplace socialization. Topics such as the role of leadership and the management of change are of special interest.

Merton, Robert K. *Social Theory and Social Structure.* Rev. and enl. ed. London: Free Press, 1957. This book by a famous sociologist is very important for the understanding of workplace socialization. Of particular importance are chapter 4, "Social Structure and Anomie," in which topics such as patterns of cultural goals and institutional norms are discussed, and chapter 6, "Bureaucratic Structure and Personality," in which Merton argues that the occupational socialization offered in most bureaucratic organizations could be dysfunctional for society and the individual. Well written and extensive. Has an index and footnotes but no bibliography.

Roucek, Joseph S., ed. *Social Control.* 2d ed. Westport, Conn.: Greenwood Press, 1970. This book presents a collection of classic essays by Roucek and others on the subject of social control. It provides the reader with a wide frame of reference to understand the phenomenon of workplace socialization: social control theory. Of special interest are chapter 9, "Education," where the author explains how schools and universities shape the behavior of future professionals. Includes notes at the end of each chapter, bibliography, and an index.

Schaefer, Richard T. *Sociology.* 4th ed. New York: McGraw-Hill, 1992. This introductory sociology textbook presents a very well-documented chapter on socialization. It is among the few sociology textbooks that discuss the topic of workplace socialization. Many graphs, photographs, and charts. Includes a bibliography and separate subject and name indexes.

Schein, Edgar. *Organizational Culture and Leadership.* San Francisco: Jossey-Bass, 1985. Schein explains the process of the formation of the norms and values inherent to every organization. In addition, the process of diffusion of this "organizational culture" are fully explored. Finally, the process of cultural change in organizations is explored. Includes a good bibliography and index.

Taylor, Frederick W., and Frank B. Gilbreth. *Principles of Scientific Management.* 2d ed. Easton, Pa.: Hive, 1982. This book, originally published in 1911, provides the reader with a good theoretical and philosophical explanation of Taylor's concept of scientific management. Highly recommended for those interested in workplace socialization, because this school of thought represents the first systematic approach to changing employee behavior in the workplace.

Weber, Max. *The Theory of Social and Economic Organization.* Translated by A. M. Henderson and Talcott Parsons; edited and introduced by Talcott Parsons. New York: Oxford University Press, 1947. A translation of the original 1922 German version. Weber emphasizes the study of social domination. The influences of abstract norms in the process of molding human behavior in society and organizations arise from his explanation of the legal or bureaucratic form of social domination.

Hernán Vera Rodríguez

Cross-References

Aging and Retirement, 47; Alienation and Work, 80; Gender Socialization, 833; Industrial Sociology, 960; Leisure, 1075; Organizations: Formal and Informal, 1316; Social Groups, 1806; Socialization: The Family, 1880; Socialization: The Mass Media, 1887; Socialization: Religion, 1894.

XENOPHOBIA, NATIVISM, AND EUGENICS

Type of sociology: Racial and ethnic relations
Fields of study: Basic concepts; Patterns and consequences of contact

Eugenics refers to the theory that the human race can be improved through controlled or selective breeding. Xenophobia and nativism both gave birth to the eugenics movement and influenced theories about which human characteristics are desirable or undesirable.

Principal terms

ETHNOCENTRISM: the conviction that one's own group or race is superior to all others

GENETIC ENGINEERING: the scientific altering of genes to eliminate undesirable characteristics or produce desirable characteristics in offspring

GENETICS: a branch of biology that deals with the heredity and variation of organisms

NATIVISM: the favoring of native inhabitants over immigrants; the revival or perpetuation of indigenous culture, especially in opposition to acculturation

XENOPHOBIA: fear and hatred of strangers or foreigners or anything strange or foreign

Overview

Members of premodern (traditional) societies often exhibit distrust and fear of any persons not immediately known to them. Social scientists call this unreasoning and seemingly instinctual fear of strangers "xenophobia." Xenophobia manifests itself in modern societies among members of subcultures, religious sects, ethnic groups, and political movements. Because people of similar beliefs and cultural backgrounds often tend to associate largely with one another, they develop little understanding of people with different beliefs and cultural backgrounds. As a result, in a pluralistic society such as the United States, xenophobia develops between Jews and Christians, between African Americans and European Americans, and between the members of many other groups that have limited interaction with people with backgrounds different from theirs.

Often xenophobia leads directly to ethnocentrism, a conviction that one's own group and its culture are superior to all other groups and their cultures. Xenophobia and ethnocentrism form essential elements of "nativism." Sociologists include nativist movements as part of a larger category called "revitalization movements." Revitalization movements usually occur within societies or groups that have suffered stress and whose cultures have suffered disorganization. Such movements aim to better the lives of their members, often at the expense of the members of other groups. Modern examples include the African American separatist movement in the United States, the Nazi movement in Germany during the period between the world wars, the Branch Davidian religious sect of the late twentieth century, the Indian Ghost Dance movement in the western United States during the last quarter of the nineteenth century, and many others. Several nativist movements, fueled by xenophobia, have actively advocated the use of eugenics to revitalize their own culture by eliminating foreign traits from their memberships.

Eugenics is a branch of science that deals with the improvement of the hereditary qualities of human beings through controlled or selective breeding. Eugenicists argue that many undesirable human characteristics (for example, inherited diseases such as hemophilia and Down syndrome) can be eliminated through careful genetic screening of couples planning to marry. Moderate eugenicists advocate the creation of a central data bank of genetic records for entire populations. A person contemplating marriage would be able to investigage the genetic endowment of his or her chosen partner to ascertain whether that person had a genetic weakness.

More radical eugenicists argue that governments should take a direct hand in racial improvement by passing laws forbidding genetically flawed individuals from reproducing. Others insist that such a law is not enough and hold that genetically flawed individuals should be medically sterilized. Eugenicists justify their positions on economic and scientific grounds: They maintain that the human race cannot spare scarce resources to tend to those born with genetic handicaps and that people must somehow compensate for the retrogressive evolutionary effects of modern technology.

According to many eugenicists, the cost of keeping genetic defectives alive through the use of modern medical technology will eventually bankrupt world society. These eugenicists also believe that if genetically unsound men and women are allowed to breed uncontrollably, all of humanity will eventually inherit their debilitating characteristics. Before the rise of modern industrial society and the development of medical science, genetically defective individuals rarely lived long enough to reproduce, which controlled their negative influences on the human gene pool. Today, society not only expends increasingly scarce medical care on these people but also allows them to perpetuate and to spread their genes. The only way to reverse this retrogressive evolution, say the eugenicists, is to control or prevent the reproduction of that part of the world's population that carries dysfunctional genes.

The debate concerning eugenics has taken on a greater urgency with the recent strides that have been made in genetic engineering. This new technology may make possible not only the medical elimination of genetic defects but also the "engineering" of desirable characteristics. It is apparently possible that genetic engineers may in a few decades be able to increase the intelligence of future generations (or decrease it). They may also be able to ensure that progeny will be tall (or short) or fair complected (or dark), to determine their hair color, and even to determine their sex. For some people, these possibilities presage a brilliant future. For others, they conjure up frightening images of an Orwellian nightmare.

Applications

The instances in which governments or societies have implemented eugenics principals have not inspired confidence that eugenics goals will ever be achieved. They have not only failed to eliminate undesirable characteristics in the popuations on which they were tested but also, in virtually every instance, have resulted in abuses that are indefensible in any moral court. Those who have controlled eugenics programs have been influenced in the passage and implementation of eugenic laws by xenophobia, nativism, and outright racism, rather than by sound scientific principals. Two examples should suffice to underscore the failure of eugenics programs to date and the potential dangers posed to pluralistic societies by xenophobia, nativism, and ethnocentrism.

The leading spokesman for the eugenics movement in the United States for many years was Charles B. Davenport. Davenport taught zoology and biology at Harvard University and the University of Chicago in the late nineteenth and early twentieth centuries. His book *Heredity in Relationship to Eugenics* (1911) convinced some scientists and politicians as well as a large group of laypersons that many undesirable human characteristics were hereditary. Davenport argued that not only were diseases such as hemophilia, osteosclerosis, and Huntington's chorea genetically transmitted, but so were other traits, such as insanity, epilepsy, alcoholism, pauperism, criminality, and feeblemindedness. Like many (perhaps most) scientists of his era, Davenport assumed that each "race" had its own characteristics. His own xenophobia showed clearly when he maintained that Poles, the Irish, Italians, "Hebrews," and "negroes" all had peculiar genetic characteristics that would ultimately have a deleterious effect on the American "race." Davenport's nativism and xenophobia prompted him to write that the flood of immigrants then pouring into the United States would result in the population becoming darker complected and more inclined toward violent crime and sexual immorality.

Davenport led a grass-roots nativist movement in the United States that eventually succeeded in passing eugenics laws at both the national and state levels. The Immigration Act passed by large majorities in both houses of the U.S. Congress in 1924 governed who could immigrate to the United States from abroad. Its language made immigration from northern Europe relatively easy, while residents of Africa and Asia found themselves virtually excluded. As several of its supporters (including future president Calvin Coolidge) acknowledged, the Immigration Act was designed to prevent the decline of the "Nordic" race by limiting the influx of members of "inferior" races.

The Connecticut legislature passed the first identifiable eugenics law at the state level in 1896. The law provided a three-year prison term for marriage or sexual relations between the "genetically unfit" if the woman was under forty-five years of age. Although the law was praised by eugenicists, no other states followed Connecticut's lead for almost a decade. In 1905, the Indiana legislature adopted a measure that forbade marriage between "mentally deficient" persons or persons with transmissible diseases. In 1907, Indiana congressmen became the first to enact a law mandating sterilization of mental deficients. By 1917, fifteen more states (mostly in the Midwest) had enacted sterilization laws. Candidates for sterilization included habitual criminals, rapists, epileptics, the insane, drug addicts, and anyone convicted of white slavery. Supporters of eugenics policies also played a role in the passage of the clearly xenophobic state miscegenation laws. More than 15,000 people suffered state-imposed sterilization in the United States before World War II, many of them for reasons recognized as having little or nothing to do with genetically inheritable traits.

In Germany, the nativist movement that implemented eugenics laws had even more repulsive results than did the eugenics-related laws in the United States. Scientists in Germany, especially anthropologists and psychiatrists, began advocating eugenics legislation before the beginning of the twentieth century. They had only limited success before 1933. In that year, Adolf Hitler led his Nationalsozialistische Deutsche Arbeiterpartei (National Socialist German Workers Party, or Nazis) to power. National Socialism was a classic nativist movement: Its adherents advocated the rejuvenation of a defeated nation whose society and culture was in chaos through elimination of the "foreign elements" that had caused its decline. Eugenics seemed to offer scientific validation for the racial theories of Hitler and other Nazi leaders (theories based not on scientific evidence but on xenophobia and nativism). The German Reichstag delegates (who became yes-men for Hitler) adopted immigration and sterilization laws aimed primarily at Jews, Gypsies, and Slavs. Under the Nazis, however, German eugenicists proceeded further than those in other countries ever openly contemplated.

Shortly after the outbreak of World War II, German doctors and directors of medical institutions—apparently authorized by Hitler—began the so-called euthanasia program. In mental institutions, hospitals, and institutions for the chronically ill, doctors began to kill (by neglect, by lethal injection, and by poisonous gas) those persons judged to be "useless eaters." Although it was supposedly terminated after 1941, the program resulted in the deaths of many thousands of people. Some of the personnel involved in the euthanasia program formed the nucleus of the units that carried out the legalized murder of enormous numbers of people in Nazi concentration camps in Poland from 1942 to 1945. Most of the victims were members of races deemed "inferior" by Nazi ideologists: Jews, Gypsies, and Slavs. It is little wonder that many people are fearful of the policies advocated by contemporary eugenicists.

Context

The modern science of eugenics may properly be said to have begun with Sir Francis Galton. A first cousin of Charles Darwin, Galton published many eugenics tracts, two of which were especially influential: *Natural Inheritance* (1889) and *Essays in Eugenics* (1909). In those works, Galton voiced many of what are now the standard arguments of those who favor the implementation of eugenics policies. Almost immediately after the publication of his first work, eugenics societies (almost all of which were arguably nativist in orientation) appeared in most western European nations and in the United States, Canada, Australia, and Latin America. Among the members of those societies were scientists and academics from many disciplines as well as many well-meaning laypersons, most of them clearly influenced by xenophobia. All the areas in which those societies arose were experiencing a rising tide of immigration.

The rediscovery at the beginning of the twentieth century by biological scientists of Gregor Mendel's genetic experiments brought considerable publicity and many new members to the fledgling eugenics societies. Increasingly, these societies began advocating legislation that would use the new science to improve and "protect" the human race. The U.S. eugenicists proved far more successful in convincing legislators of the wisdom of eugenics laws than did their counterparts abroad. Many U.S. states and the federal government adopted legislation advocated by the eugenics societies, often motivated by racism, ethnocentrism, nativism, and xenophobia rather than by sound scientific principles.

Beginning in the 1930's, the affinity between Nazi racial theories and eugenics caused most biological and medical scientists around the world to renounce eugenics policies and experiments. The information about the concentration camps that became known at the many war-crimes trials held after 1945 seemed to have dealt a death blow to eugenicist dreams of a perfected human race. By the mid-1950's, eugenics societies around the world were seemingly bereft of members and influence. Nevertheless, an increasing number of physicians began to recognize the many possible benefits of continued genetic research. During the 1950's, the number of genetic counseling institutes increased from ten in the U.S. and Britain to thirty. A number of medical schools in the two countries began to offer courses in human genetics.

By the 1970's, medical researchers had identified more than 900 single-gene disorders (disorders caused by a sex-linked gene, two recessive genes, or a dominant gene). At least one hundred of those disorders were treatable if detected early enough. Tests for those diseases were much cheaper than were treatments for the afflicted. For example, the disorder called galactosemia occurs when the body is unable to process galactose, a substance derived from milk. The disorder causes mental retardation, cataracts, liver enlargement, and infant death. Those symptoms can be avoided by means of early detection and the implementation of a galactose-free diet. Genetic screening for galactosemia costs less than one dollar per infant.

By the 1970's, genetic researchers had shown conclusively that some ethnic and racial groups were especially susceptible to certain genetic disorders. African Americans are particularly prone to the single-gene disorder called sickle-cell anemia, Ashkenazic Jews to Tay-Sachs disease, and Americans whose ancestors came from the Mediterranean area to Cooley's anemia. The new eugenics/genetics societies in the United States led a movement that resulted in the National Genetic Diseases Act, which funded research into the detection and treatment of genetic disorders. A number of states extended their postnatal screening programs to include many single-gene disorders. Doctors developed a medical procedure known as amniocentesis, which allowed them to identify genetic and chromosomal disorders during the early stages of pregnancy. If an unborn fetus was identified as genetically flawed, parents could elect abortion.

In the 1970's, eugenicists also turned their attention to the population explosion.

They found increasing cause for alarm because most of the human population increase was occurring in the Third World (Africa, Asia, and Latin America) and among the bottom socioeconomic strata of industrialized nations. Fearing for the quality of the human gene pool, many eugenics groups began to advocate and finance "family planning" programs in the Third World and among domestic socially disadvantaged populations. These new programs clearly indicate that the nativism and xenophobia that influenced earlier generations of eugenicists are still operative.

However frightening or enthralling the possibilities opened by genetic engineering may be, the new scientific knowledge and technology in this field will remain. Human beings now apparently possess the ability to determine their own biological destiny, and almost certainly that ability will be used during the next few decades. The extent to which the old flaws of eugenics—racism, xenophobia, and nativism—will influence the implementation of the new technology depends on the groups in society that will control future eugenics/genetics programs.

Bibliography

Davenport, Charles Benedict. *Heredity in Relation to Eugenics*. New York: Holt, 1911. The prejudices and erroneous scientific assumptions of the longtime leading spokesman for the eugenics movement in the United States are clearly evident in this, his most important work. Valuable in understanding the arguments of early eugenicists, but difficult reading.

Galton, Francis. *Essays in Eugenics*. London: The Eugenics Education Society, 1909. In this pioneering work, the founder of modern eugenics pleads his case in heavy Victorian prose. Readers will find genuine insights into complex problems of human biology interspersed with long-discredited racial and genetic positions. Necessary reading for those interested in the history and development of eugenics.

Graham, Loren R. *Between Science and Values*. New York: Columbia University Press, 1981. A thoughtful and provocative exploration of the moral and ethical issues raised by the new science of genetic engineering. Graham is critical of the old eugenics and of the xenophobia and ethnocentrism upon which it was based.

Higham, John. *Strangers in the Land: Patterns of American Nativism, 1860-1925*. New York: Atheneum, 1963. Explores American attitudes toward immigrants from the Civil War to the Immigration Act of 1924. Shows how nativism was given a measure of scientific legitimacy by the eugenics movement.

Kevles, Daniel J. *In the Name of Eugenics: Genetics and the Uses of Human Heredity*. New York: Alfred A. Knopf, 1985. The most thorough coverage to date of the eugenics movement in the United States and England. Clearly demonstrates the influence of nativism, xenophobia, and outright racisim on the leading eugenicists. Also explores the significance of genetic engineering and sociobiology for the future of humankind.

Muller-Hill, Benno. *Murderous Science: Elimination by Scientific Selection of Jews, Gypsies, and Others, Germany 1933-1945*. Translated by George R. Fraser. Oxford, England: Oxford University Press, 1988. Establishes beyond question the relationship between the eugenics movement in Germany and both the euthanasia program and the mass murder in concentration camps. Shows the active participaton in both programs of German biological scientists who accepted eugenics arguments.

Pearson, Karl. *The Scope and Importance to the State of the Science of National Eugenics.* 3d ed. London: Dalau, 1911. This work by Galton's most important successor in England was one of the first to argue for a national eugenics program. Like most early eugenics works, it is filled with the racist assumptions of the early twentieth century.

Pickens, Donald K. *Eugenics and the Progressives.* Nashville, Tenn.: Vanderbilt University Press, 1968. A thorough exploration of the influence of eugenics on politics (or of politics on eugenics). Shows how eugenics laws became popular with the reform movement in the United States and how some politicians used eugenics as a viable political issue.

Robitscher, Jonas, ed. *Eugenic Sterilization.* Springfield, Ill.: Charles C Thomas, 1973. The articles in this book provide an overview of the sterilization programs adopted by many U.S. states. Shows the judicial procedures used to condemn persons to sterilization, the methods of sterilization, and the assumptions upon which sterilization sentences were based, most of them now discredited.

Paul Madden

Cross-References

Annihilation or Expulsion of Racial or Ethnic Groups, 92; Anti-Semitism, 114; Assimilation: The United States, 140; Conquest and Annexation of Racial or Ethnic Groups, 353; Cultural and Structural Assimilation, 405; Internal Colonialism, 1015; Prejudice and Stereotyping,1505; Racial and Ethnic Stratification, 1579; Racism as an Ideology, 1586; Segregation versus Integration, 1707.

ZERO POPULATION GROWTH

Type of sociology: Population studies or demography

Zero population growth (ZPG) refers to the condition of a population whose size is stable rather than growing or shrinking. Beginning in the late 1960's, the term became a rallying cry for people advocating the control of the world's population growth because of predictions that continued growth would create vast ecological damage and would exhaust the world's resources.

Principal terms

AGE STRUCTURE: the composition of a population with regard to the relative numbers of old and young people

BIRTHRATE: the number of individuals born in a defined period; the annual number of live births per 1,000 individuals in a population is called the crude birthrate

DEMOGRAPHIC TRANSITION: a process theorized to affect population growth as industrialization occurs; an industrializing population moves from low growth to high growth and back to low growth

LESS DEVELOPED COUNTRY (LDC): a country with a low level of industrialization and a low standard of living

MORE DEVELOPED COUNTRY (MDC): a country that is highly industrialized and has a high standard of living

PER CAPITA GROWTH RATE: the number of births minus the number of deaths divided by 1,000 per year

POPULATION: a group of individuals of a given species in a defined geographic region

TOTAL FERTILITY RATE: the number of children that women in a given population have (or are expected to have) during their lifetime

Overview

A condition of zero population growth (ZPG) simply means that a population is not growing. Population growth is the change in population over time; it is the number of births minus the number of deaths. Population decrease—occurring when deaths exceed births—is sometimes referred to as negative population growth; therefore, ZPG implies that a population's size is remaining stable.

The growth of the world's population has been slow throughout most of history. Only since the nineteenth century has the human population shown explosive growth. As the world's population has risen above the five billion mark, population control has been viewed by many scientists and policy makers as a critical matter. The call for ZPG initially came from the more developed countries (MDCs); it was spurred on by concerns that the earth will, in the future, be depleted of nonrenewable energy resources such as oil and gas. The trend toward ZPG has spread to less developed countries (LDCs) as well, as rapid population growth has created such problems as severe food shortages.

Even when governments and populations themselves are united in trying to make zero population growth a reality, however, a lag of many years is involved before the goal can be reached. Because of population processes that are already in existence, ZPG cannot be achieved immediately at the time when all parents agree to have no more than two children per family. Three factors in particular are crucial in determining when a population will reach ZPG: the total fertility rate, the population age structure, and migration.

The total fertility rate (TFR) is defined as the average number of children that a woman bears in her lifetime. In the United States in 1992, for example, the TFR was 2.0, which means that each woman in the age group between fifteen and forty-five was expected to have two children in her lifetime. By contrast in India, the TFR was 3.9. Using the TFR, one can calculate the replacement-level fertility for each country, or the number of children a couple must have to replace themselves. The replacement level in more developed countries (MDC's) is 2.1 children; the number is greater than 2.0 because of the mortality of some children before they reach the age of reproduction. Even when a population's fertility rate is no higher than replacement level, it may continue to grow because of the next two factors.

The population growth rate is also a function of the age structure of the population. Population composition can be considered young or old, depending on the ratios of young and old individuals; these ratios give the population what is called its age distribution or age structure. A population with large numbers of young individuals who are either of prereproductive or reproductive age will have a fairly large growth rate because it will have a low mortality rate.

It will take some countries many decades to reach ZPG because of their age structure: They have increasing numbers of females entering the reproductive period. Despite the fact that the total fertility rate is at or below the replacement level, the sheer number of woman entering reproductive age will increase the population. For example, in the United States in the years 1932 and 1965, the birth rate was similar; however, the number of live births in 1932 was 2.4 million, compared with 3.8 million in 1965. Thus, the population showed a larger increase in 1965 than in 1932. When a population starts to grow, it will continue to grow despite reaching replacement-level fertility rates. This phenomenon is called population momentum. It means that a population will show a lag period during which it will continue its growth before it slows down and stabilizes. ZPG will not occur until the number of women entering reproductive age equals the number leaving reproductive age.

The last factor that must be taken into account is migration. Even though a population may reach replacement-level fertility, it may continue to grow because of immigration. The effect of immigration is dependent on who is immigrating, because this may change the population's age structure. Migration may involve young males looking for work in different countries or young females leaving rural areas and moving to the cities, for example. In the latter case, more young females in their reproductive years might skew the age structure and raise the total fertility rate.

Most experts agree that population growth needs to be controlled and the world as a whole needs to reach zero population growth. Voluntary family planning and the long-term societal changes brought about by industrialization have slowed growth rates in the more developed countries. Some have reached ZPG. In the less developed countries, education and changing attitudes and taboos against birth control need to be among the strategies instituted. Even if replacement-level fertility were achieved today, the world population would still grow to more than eight billion people because of the population momentum of the less developed countries.

Applications

In the United States the call for zero population growth is increasing. The U.S. population is still a growing population, having an age structure intermediate between that of a fast-growing and no-growth population. This is partly attributable to the baby boom generation. The U.S. birthrate was quite high in the years between 1946 (post-World War II) and the early 1960's; these were the years of the baby boom. In the 1970's and 1980's, the fertility rate dropped, partly because more women entered the workforce and delayed having children until later in life, and partly because more families had fewer children. Nevertheless, the American population will continue to grow for decades because of the sheer number of baby boomers.

Another reason the population will continue to grow is the influx of people migrating to the United States. The United States annually receives twice as many immigrants as all other nations combined. Despite the lowered fertility rate, therefore, the age structure and immigration will keep the population growing; however, it is projected that the United States could reach zero population growth by the mid-twenty-first century if the replacement level fertility reaches 1.5 children.

Calls for population control in the United States started in the 1960's with the advent of the environmental revolution. In 1968, Paul Ehrlich wrote an influential book entitled *The Population Bomb*, foretelling the fate of the world if the world's population were to continue to grow unchecked. It was realized that with increased population size, there is an increased demand for and utilization of natural resources. The pressure of population growth currently is forcing difficult decisions regarding land usage, timber production, and endangered species in the United States.

The increased call for zero population growth has led to the proliferation of organizations advocating population control. They call for sex education, population awareness, and fertility control. The social ramifications of these policies are great, however, as are the moral and ethical dilemmas involved. The teaching of sex education in schools has been controversial because it is against many people's religious or moral beliefs. No issue regarding family planning has been more polarizing than the debate over whether abortion should be legal. Advocates of what they see as reproductive freedom have been pitted against religious groups defending what they see as the moral rights of unborn children. This controversy is only one of the difficult issues that can come into play when the subject of population control is discussed. A fundamental question is whether reproduction is a personal right and decision.

Organizations such as Negative Population Growth and the Federation for American Immigration Reform (FAIR) have called for the outright banning of all types of immigration to control population growth. Organizations such as FAIR support tighter controls of the United States borders to limit the flow of immigration, legal and illegal. They also want to revise the immigration laws to limit severely the numbers of immigrants allowed legally into the country.

The control of population in the United States may lead to other social problems. The long-term trend in the United States of declining fertility and longer life span translates into an aging population. The number of elderly people is expected to double between 1990 and 2030. This could possibly lead to policies intended to increase the fertility rate. This shift has happened in Singapore and Sweden. In Singapore, incentives for having a third child are a tax rebate of $10,000 and, for a working mother, a rebate of 15 percent of her annual income. Sweden allows maternity leave with pay and has easily available day care. In both countries, these policies have increased the fertility rate.

Another policy to help compensate for an aging population would be to encourage migration of young laborers into the country to support the elderly population. This policy has been instituted in some European countries that were decimated by World War II. There the baby boom did not supply enough workers to enter the labor force in the 1970's and 1980's, so some countries had to recruit laborers. The importing of such a workforce can produce many social issues—for example, what rights and privileges should the immigrants or temporary workers receive? Policies supporting a foreign labor force could lead to backlash, including discrimination and various restrictions on the immigrants.

The trend for zero population growth has already started in some less developed countries. Family planning programs range from purely voluntary to compulsory. The People's Republic of China occupies a position somewhere between an LDC and an MDC. This country, with 1.1 billion people, has more than 20 percent of the world's population. The government has realized that to improve the country's standard of living, there must be control of population growth. During the 1970's the government initiated a fertility reduction campaign, which then became a compulsory policy called the "one-child campaign." The policy led to an increase in infanticide in the rural provinces; if a family's first child was a girl, some parents would allow her to die so they could try to have a son. By the mid-1980's, the government realized that most couples did not want to have only one child, especially if it was a girl. In the rural areas, a son was needed for labor on the farm. The government eased restrictions and allowed couples to have more than one child.

These results teach several vital lessons. Even under an authoritarian government, population control will be resisted if people believe that it is not in their best interest. Even strong economic incentives, such as free medical care and education, may not be enough. Finally, even though China started population control in the 1970's and set a target of 1.2 billion by the year 2000, the country will probably overshoot its target by 20 percent.

Context

The human population has remained small throughout most of history because both birthrates and death rates were high. It was not until the seventeenth century that the human population began to grow significantly. With the advent of complex technology, stable food supplies, the medical advances, the human population was able to show explosive growth by decreasing the death rate while the birthrate remained high.

This phenomenon began to occur in the industrializing nations (MDCs) of Europe in the eighteenth century. A theory known as the demographic transition theory attempts to explain the changes that occur in an industrializing population. Stage one, preindustrialization or very early industrialization, involves both high birthrates and high death rates, so a population's growth is slow. Phase two involves a high birthrate and a low death rate (as technology and modernization lower mortality), so population grows very rapidly. In phase three, population growth decreases as the birthrate slows. One cause of the slowing of the birthrate is the fact that a large number of children, a sign of prestige and a necessity for providing cheap labor in agricultural societies, is a detriment in an industrial society.

The less developed countries are presently in phase two of the demographic transition; advances in medical technology have decreased the mortality rate, but the birthrate is still high, giving an overall high population growth rate. Large families are still the norm. It has been debated whether the demographic transition alone can work in reducing the birthrate in these countries as it has in the MDCs. Many experts conclude that, for a number of reasons, it cannot. First, the necessary economic resources to support the cycle of industrialization are not there. Second, the process took more than two hundred years in the MDCs, and the LDCs do not have that much time before growth needs to be slowed significantly. It has been argued, therefore, that population control will have to come from other means, such as family planning, education, and sustainable economic development.

Calls for population control and zero population growth came in earnest in 1968 when Paul Ehrlich published *The Population Bomb*. Ehrlich warned of the population explosion that was occurring in the less developed countries. These calls have been heeded, and the overall growth rate of the less developed countries has decreased from 2.4 percent to 1.7 percent. Still other countries have achieved remarkable success in slowing population growth with their education and family planning policies.

Yet the world is still far from ZPG. In 1992, 33 percent of the world's population was under fifteen years of age; they will soon enter their reproductive years. Thus, with the population momentum involved, it will be a number of years before the world's population can reach ZPG. Long-term challenges to reaching ZPG include making family planning affordable, accessible, and culturally acceptable. The MDCs also must assist the LDCs in finding a sustainable level of economic development.

Bibliography

Chiras, Daniel D. *Environmental Science*. 4th ed. Redwood City, Calif.: Benjamin/ Cummings, 1994. Chapter 5 covers population growth, fertility, and zero population growth. Chapter 6 deals with control of populations. An easy to read book with many facts, diagrams, and figures. Good bibliographies at the end of each chapter.

Ehrlich, Paul R. *The Population Bomb*. New York: Ballantine, 1968. A good short paperback book that will give the reader some historical context on the population problem as seen in the 1960's. It is easy to read and well worth it.

Ehrlich, Paul R., and Anne Ehrlich. *The Population Explosion*. New York: Simon & Schuster, 1990. A follow-up book to *The Population Bomb*. It not only talks about the population problem but also relates these problems to the environmental changes that are occurring on the planet.

Heer, David M., and Jill S. Grigsby. *Society and Population*. 3d ed. Englewood Cliffs, N.J.: Prentice-Hall, 1992. A short paperback book that is easy to read. It describes population processes, then discusses their impact on society. Takes an international approach.

McFalls, Joseph A. *Population: A Lively Introduction*. Washington D.C.: Population Reference Bureau, 1991. Many facts and figures. It includes good diagrams of age structures and discusses age and sex as well as other parameters and their effects on populations.

Morgan, Michael D., Joseph M. Moran, and James H. Wiersma. *Environmental Science: Managing Biological and Physical Resources*. Dubuque, Iowa: Wm. C. Brown, 1993. Chapters 5, 6, and 7 deal with populations. Chapter 6 covers human populations, and chapter 7 covers methods of population control. Includes boxed essays on social issues relating to populations.

Volpe, E. Peter. *Biology and Human Concerns*. 4th ed. Dubuque, Iowa: Wm. C. Brown, 1993. An interesting biology book that is very easy to read and includes helpful pictures and diagrams. Part 5 discusses ecology and the environment. Chapters 42 and 43 discuss population dynamics; chapter 48 covers the human impact on the environment.

Lonnie J. Guralnick

Cross-References

Demographic Transition Theory of Population Growth, 499; Fertility, Mortality, and the Crude Birthrate, 761; Life Expectancy, 1087; Malthusian Theory of Population Growth, 1113; Population Growth and Population Control, 1421; Population Size and Human Ecology, 1428; Population Structure: Age and Sex Ratios, 1434.

GLOSSARY

Acculturation: The process by which culturally distinct groups understand, adapt to, and influence one another.

Achieved status: The assignment of individuals to positions in society based upon their achievements, such as education or the attainment of some skill.

Acquaintance rape: Rape committed by someone who is known to the rape victim.

Affirmative action: A policy designed to redress past discrimination against minority groups by targeting them for recruitment into jobs and educational institutions.

Age cohort: A category of people born at about the same time who enter various stages of the life cycle together and experience historical events at the same approximate ages.

Ageism: Any ideology that justifies and rationalizes discrimination on the basis of age.

Alienation: An individual's feelings of estrangement from a situation, group, or culture.

Androgyny: The possession of both masculine and feminine social, emotional, or behavioral traits.

Anglo-conformity: The cultural mold that people of English ancestry established in the United States into which others had to fit.

Anomic suicide: Suicide attributed to a breakdown in social regulation or a loss of a sense of belonging.

Anomie: Social condition characterized by the breakdown of norms and values governing social interaction.

Apartheid: The type of segregation that developed in South Africa; separateness was the principle guiding contacts between whites, blacks, and "coloureds."

Ascribed status: The assignment of individuals to positions in society based on intrinsic characteristics, such as birth order, kin network, sex, or race.

Ashkenazi: Diaspora Jews who migrated to the Franco-German area of Europe during the medieval period.

Assimilation: The process by which individuals take on the language, behavior, and values of another culture, as well as the process by which outsiders are incorporated into a society.

Attitude: An evaluation or opinion, regarding a person or thing, that affects one's thoughts, feelings, and behaviors.

Authoritarian personality: A syndrome of personality characteristics that predispose a person to hold extreme views and to act on them.

Authoritarianism: A form of rule in which one person or a small group of people has a monopoly of political power.

Authority: Power accepted as legitimate by the people over whom it is exercised.

Baby boom: An unusually large cohort of individuals who were born between 1945 and 1962.

Bargaining unit: A clearly defined group of employees whose shared common interests warrant their negotiation of labor-related issues as a group.

Behavior: How individuals overtly act in the presence of others; actions that are observable and measurable, including verbal expression.

Bias: The deviation of the expected value of a statistical estimate from the true value for some measured quantity.

Bilingualism: Fluency in two languages.

Biological determinism: The belief that most human behavior is a result of genetic "programming" rather than learning.

Bisexuality: A type of sexual orientation in which the sexual behaviors and feelings of a male or female are directed toward both males and females.

Bourgeoisie: The class of capitalists who own the means of production and distribution and who hire workers for wages or a salary.

Bureaucracy: A formal organization that emphasizes the rational and efficient pursuit of goals through a highly structured and hierarchical network of statuses and roles.

Capital: Money or wealth, including land, factories, and machinery, that has been invested in means of production.

Capitalism: An economic system based on private ownership of property and the means of production; the guiding principle is maximization of profit.

Carrying capacity: The population density of a given species that can be sustained indefinitely in an ecosystem.

Case study: A detailed study of a particular individual, group, organization, or situation; a combination of research techniques may be used to describe the "case."

Caste system: A hierarchical social arrangement in which people are assigned the same status as their parents and have no possibility of changing status through personal achievement.

Censorship: The procedure of suppressing or changing material or expression that the government or another group finds objectionable.

Chattel: A slave; the term emphasized the fact that the slave was property that could be used, moved, or sold at will by an owner.

Child abuse: The psychological, physical, or sexual maltreatment of a person under the age of eighteen in which that individual's welfare, health, or safety is endangered.

Child neglect: Failure on the part of adult caregivers to provide a child with adequate supervision, nourishment, shelter, education, medical treatment, or emotional and intellectual stimulation.

Citizenship: Membership accorded to individuals within a particular nation-state that guarantees certain rights and requires certain responsibilities.

City: A relatively large, densely populated, and diverse human settlement.

Civil rights: Legal rights that have been accorded to all citizens within a political state.

Class: A group of people of similar social rank; largely defined in economic terms, but also often considering such factors as political power and lifestyle.

Class consciousness: An awareness of belonging to a definite socioeconomic class and a conscious sharing of the political interests of that class.

Class struggle: The pervasive range of social conflict that emerges from the antagonistic relationship between social classes that exploit and the classes that are exploited.

Closed shop: Form of labor organization, which the Taft-Hartley Labor Relations Act of 1947 made illegal, that required employees of unionized firms to be union members before they were hired.

Coalition: An alliance among interest groups; may include committees or institutions of the government.

Cognition: The mental activities involved in the acquisition and retention of knowledge, such as thinking, remembering, understanding, perceiving, and learning.

Cognitive dissonance: The theory that individuals try to achieve internal harmony, such as consistency between attitudes and behavior.

Cohort: A group of people who simultaneously share some common social events, with year of birth being one possible social characteristic.

Collective bargaining: The process of a company and a union jointly negotiating wages or salaries, hours, and conditions of employment.

Collective behavior: An activity engaged in by a number of people who are oriented toward the same goal.

Colonialism: A geopolitical phenomenon in which one nation's state power is imposed upon foreign territories, typically for the political, economic, and/or military benefits of the colonizer.

Coloureds: Under apartheid, the designation for South Africans of racially mixed backgrounds.

Coming out: The psychological process of acquiring and acknowledging a gay or lesbian identity—first to oneself, then to friends, family, and others.

Communicable diseases: Diseases capable of being transmitted from person to person; also known as infectious diseases.

Community: Any stable group, such as a neighborhood or professional association, sharing a geographical area and common traits, sense of belonging that shape it into a distinct social entity.

Comparable worth: A proposed solution to wage inequality between men and women that would require equal pay for work of equal value regardless of a job's title or classification.

Compensatory education: Educational programs and experiences designed to help overcome the economic disadvantages and the cultural dissimilarities students may bring to school.

Compositional theory: The theory that urbanites experience as many warm and direct interactions with family, friends, and neighbors as do people in small towns and rural environments.

Compulsory education: School attendance required by law for youths between certain specified ages.

Concentric zone theory: The theory that urban expansion takes the form of concentric circles, in each of which land use is devoted to specific types of activity.

Concept: An abstract idea that mentally categorizes a recurring aspect of concrete reality by identifying its key components and thereby defining it.

Conflict perspective: A theory that views conflict as being a ubiquitous force in shaping arrangements between social classes and competing groups in society.

Conformity: Behavior by members of a society or group that is compatible with the norms and values of that society or group.

Consanguine: Related by blood; having the same ancestry.

Conscientious objector: A status held by a person who, by virtue of his or her objection to war because of religious, moral, or political reasons, does not serve in the armed forces but instead performs alternative government service, serves time in jail, or becomes a fugitive.

Consensus: Unanimous or almost unanimous agreement, usually achieved through persuasion.

Content analysis: Unobtrusive research in which human communications, such as written materials, are used as data.

Content validity: A type of experimental validity determined by whether an experiment actually measures a property that it is intending to measure.

Control variable: Any variable other than the independent variable or the dependent variable that is controlled by the researcher to prevent it from becoming a confound.

Convergence: A process in which the structures of different industrial societies increasingly resemble one another.

Core: In world-system theory, Western European countries, the United States, and Japan, which have specialized in banking, finance, and highly skilled industrial production.

Corporate crime: A type of white-collar crime committed by a group of individuals or a corporation for corporate gain.

Corporation: A "juristic person," founded on the legal basis of limited liability; since the middle of the nineteenth century, the corporation has evolved into the dominant form of business within capitalist societies.

Correlation: A statistical concept that measures how frequently two events co-occur, thereby suggesting either a relationship or a lack of relationship between the events.

Counterculture: A group that is consciously in opposition to the norms and values of the dominant culture.

Credentialism: The tendency in modern societies to require particular academic credentials for entry into certain occupations even though the educational qualifications may have very little to do with the skills actually used in the job.

Crime: Behavior that violates laws prohibiting such behavior and may be punished; often poses a threat to personal well-being and safety.

Crime rate: A comparative tool for reporting crime; it allows population differences and different times to be compared when crime is measured.

Criminalization: The process of converting specific behaviors into criminal behaviors through the passing of criminal laws.

Criminology: The branch of sociology that scientifically studies the various aspects of crime.

Critical theory: A school of thought developed in Frankfurt, Germany, during the 1920's that employed the early humanistic ideas of Karl Marx to criticize positivism and scientific Marxism.

Crowd: A temporary group of individuals who come together for some particular activity, such as Christmas shopping, a sporting event, a film, or a rock concert.

Cultural lag: A term coined by William Ogburn to describe the situation that occurs when a technological invention, device, or process is developed but the social setting cannot keep pace with changes and thus lags behind.

Cultural pluralism: A system in which different ethnic and racial groups can coexist without losing their respective cultural traits.

Cultural relativism: The view that a culture is to be judged by its own standards.

Culture: The beliefs, values, behavior, and material objects shared by a particular people.

Culture of poverty concept: An ideology that maintains that poverty is caused by the defective values and attitudes of those who are poor.

Data: Information collected or observed that is relevant to the research question under study.

Day care: Any type of arrangement that is used to provide care, supervision, or education for children under age six when parents are at work.

De facto segregation: Racial and other forms of social separation that result from informal social mechanisms of discrimination.

De jure segregation: Racial and other forms of social separation that are produced by formal, legal mechanisms.

Decriminalization: Changing the law to legalize something that was formerly illegal.

Deduction: The process of arriving at a specific conclusion or prediction by applying a premise (a general law, hypothesis, or assumption) to a particular case.

Definition of the situation: Individuals' definition of a social interaction by means of explicit or implicit agreement.

Deindustrialization: The closing of industrial facilities in one country or region as a result of the movement of capital to other countries or regions, or to nonindustrial investments.

Delinquency: Behaviors for which a juvenile can be formally sanctioned; collectively, these behaviors include status offenses and those behaviors prohibited under criminal law.

Democracy: A form of government based on the freely given consent of its members; it is characterized by majority rule, protection of the rights of all of its members, and effective control over the exercise of power.

Democratization: The process of moving from an authoritarian to a democratic system.

Demographics: Information that describes certain characteristics of research subjects;

for example, age, gender, marital status, and education level.

Demography: The scientific study of human populations, with an emphasis on the age, sex, racial/ethnic, and socioeconomic structure of society and how the structure changes.

Denomination: A religious group that is often considered a subgroup of a particular religion; Anglicans, Baptists, and Catholics may be considered Christian denominations.

Dependency theory: A theory in which underdeveloped regions are considered "internal colonies" that are dependent on, or controlled by, modern industrial states.

Dependent variable: The observed, consequent, or outcome variable; this variable is the one on which the effects of the independent variable are observed.

Descriptive statistics: A branch of statistics that involves the use of numerical indices to summarize basic characteristics of a distribution of scores, without any attempt causation or to infer other amounts of data.

Desegregation: The elimination of laws or statutes restricting the rights of specific groups to housing and public facilities, especially schools.

Deterrence: A purpose of punishment according to which an offender is punished as an example to discourage other people from committing similar crimes or to discourage the offender from continuing to commit crimes.

Deviance: Action or behavior that is inconsistent with what a particular society defines as normal and acceptable.

Dialectical materialism: The Marxian theory of change that regards knowledge and ideas as reflections of a society's material condition.

Dictatorship: Another term for authoritarianism, or a form of authoritarian government in which power is concentrated in the hands of a single person or a small group of rulers.

Differential association theory: The view that criminal behavior is learned through social contacts.

Diffusion: The geographic spread of ideas, technologies, or products.

Discrimination: The denial of opportunities and rights to certain groups on the basis of some identifiable characteristic, such as race and ethnicity.

Displacement: Loss of employment caused by the disappearance of specific types of jobs; also, the phenomenon in which people are forced to move from their homes by urban renewal, gentrification, highway construction, and the like.

Distributive justice: Justice in the distribution of the "good things" in life, the most critical of which are class, status, and power.

Division of labor: The manner in which work is allocated in society, with increasing specialization of different tasks/occupations leading to a more complex division of labor.

Domestic abuse and violence: Mistreatment, injurious actions, or the abuse of power occurring in the home.

Dominant group: The group that exercises control over societal resources.

Dual labor market: The idea that the labor market is divided into two sectors, one characterized by higher-paying, more stable, and prestigious jobs, the other by less desirable, dead-end jobs.

Dysfunction: A negative consequence that may lead to disruption or breakdown of the social system.

Dysfunctional families: Families that fail to perform important social or psychological functions such as the nurturance and socialization of children.

Ecological fallacy: An error in logic that occurs when a researcher tries to apply a conclusion drawn from one level of analysis (such as social systems) to another level (such as individuals).

Ecology: The relationship between populations and their physical environments.

Economies of scale: Savings in production or marketing costs that are better exploited by large operations than by small ones, up to some ceiling, above which there are no more gains.

Education: The transmission of knowledge by either formal or informal means.

Egalitarianism: A system emphasizing equal political, social, and economic rights for all persons.

Egoistic suicide: Suicide related to the victim's inability to become integrated into society.

Element: The basic unit of a population, such as an individual, household, segment, or social organization, for which information is sought.

Elites: Those groups in society that manage to control the largest amount of social or economic resources and obtain a privileged position in relation to other groups.

Emergent norms: The normative guidelines that direct and control the course of action during mob-induced riots, panics, or similar occurrences and that replace the norms and laws of the governing social order.

Emigration: Leaving one's native country in order to move to a new country.

Eminent domain: The right of the government to take private land for public use as long as the owners are compensated.

Empirical: Based on direct observation and measurement using the physical senses.

Endogamy: The practice or custom of marrying within a particular group to which one belongs.

Entitlement programs: Government payments or services to which individuals who meet certain criteria are "entitled."

Entrepreneur: An investor who undertakes a business venture.

Equal opportunity: A situation in which all members of society have an equal chance of achieving power, social status, and economic resources.

Equal Rights Amendment (ERA): Proposed as the twenty-seventh amendment to the U.S. Constitution, it stated that "equality of rights under the law shall not be denied or abridged by the United States or by any state on account of sex."

Error: With respect to assessment, reliability, and validity, error refers to variation in scores generated by the measurement device when measuring the same thing more than once.

Ethics: The rules and guidelines that regulate the research and work of professionals; ethics in the social sciences are primarily concerned with protecting the rights of the human subjects being studied.

Ethnic group: A group classified according to a perceived common ancestry or common cultural characteristics, such as language, religion, food habits, and folklore, and seen by themselves and others as distinctive.

Ethnic stratification: Structured social inequality on the basis of ethnicity.

Ethnocentrism: The tendency to judge other people's behavior and values on the basis of one's own culture, which is usually considered superior.

Ethnography: The detailed study of a particular society and its culture.

Eugenics: The study of genetics and selective breeding to alter and improve the composition of the human gene pool.

Evolution: Change through a sequence of stages.

Exogamy: The practice of marrying outside a particular group to which one belongs.

Exploitation: An unequal social relationship in which a dominant individual or group acquires a valued commodity from a subordinate individual or group.

Extended family: A household consisting of spouses, their children, and other relatives.

External validity: A quality that enables the generalizing of results from a limited sample of subjects to a larger population.

Extramarital sex: Sexual relations between a married person and someone other than his or her spouse.

Fad: A frivolous trait or activity that temporarily becomes popular within a peer group, only to disappear just as quickly.

False consciousness: A Marxist term referring to beliefs held by the working class that run counter to, or do not further, their best interests.

Family: People related to one another on the basis of blood, marriage, or adoption and who constitute a social system.

Female-headed families: Single-parent families headed by women.

Feminism: A movement whose goal is social, political, economic, and sexual equality of men and women.

Feminization of poverty: The trend under which an increasing percentage of the poor are women, many of whom are supporting children.

Field notes: A written account of the social behavior observed by a field researcher while studying a culture.

Field research: Research in which an observer goes to a culture and either records observations of that culture or participates to some extent in the culture and makes observations based on that participation.

Formal organization: A large collection of people whose activities are specifically designed for the attainment of explicitly stated goals.

Functionalism: A theoretical perspective that proposes that society is composed of various social institutions that work together to maintain a stable social environment.

Functionalist perspective: A theory that focuses on the way the various parts of society work together to maintain stability and order in the social system as a whole.

Gemeinschaft society: Any society characterized by the predominance of face-to-face personal relationships—usually a reference to rural or small-town society.

Gender: A term that refers to the culturally defined (rather than biologically defined) attributes of each sex or to the meanings people give to the biological differences.

Gender roles: Specific patterns of behavior and expectations for each gender; learned through the socialization process.

Gender socialization: Differential child-rearing and other practices based on gender.

Gender stratification: A system in which groups are ranked hierarchically by gender.

Generalized other: Stage in a child's development where he or she takes the role of numerous others in society in general.

Gentrification: The movement of affluent people into poor urban neighborhoods that they hope to upgrade, though in the process they often displace poorer residents.

Gerontology: The study of the biological, psychological, and sociological implications of aging.

Gesellschaft society: Any society characterized by limited, impersonal, and instrumentalist relationships among its people.

Ghetto: An urban ethnic enclave, originally designating Jewish quarters in European cities.

Glass ceiling: The "invisible" obstacles and impediments confronting minorities when they try to reach higher-level, high-paying jobs; the term has most frequently been used to describe discrimination against women.

Global village: A concept of the interconnectedness of human societies, under which social and environmental policies of one community may have far-reaching effects on distant communities.

Grounded theory: A theory that is generated and modified during field research; different from a conventional theory in that theory and data-gathering perpetually interact.

Group: A small number of people who interact over time and establish patterns of interaction and identity and norms governing behavior.

Hate crimes: Crimes of violence toward or degradation of others prompted by extreme prejudice against them, for reasons such as their race, gender, sexual orientation, or religion.

Hegemony: The preponderance of influence and power, especially when wielded by one state or country over others.

Heterosexuality: A type of sexual orientation in which an individual's sexual behavior and feelings are directed toward a person of the opposite sex.

Hidden curriculum: A set of unwritten rules of behavior taught in school to prepare children for academic success and for social relations outside school.

Hierarchy: An organizational system of graded positions, from high to low, that considers such factors as authority, prestige, and income.

High culture: A form of leisure pursuit often chosen by cultural elites.

Historical/comparative method: Unobtrusive research in which historical records and published materials are used as data; typically, more than one data source are analyzed.

Homeless: Those persons who lack the necessary resources and community ties to provide for their own shelter.

Homogamy: The tendency of individuals to marry people with similar social backgrounds.

Homophile: Literally "love of same," this term was employed by homosexual activists in the 1950's as a more positive one than "homosexual," which referred to sex acts.

Homophobia: An irrational fear of or aversion to people with a same-sex sexual orientation.

Homosexuality: A type of sexual orientation in which the sexual behavior and feelings of a male (gay) or female (lesbian) are directed toward a person of the same sex.

Horizontal social mobility: Movement across social ranks of approximately the same status.

Human capital: The talents, skills, and knowledge that may enhance a worker's value in the labor market.

Hypothesis: A statement predicting a relationship between variables; it is a theoretical statement that has been operationalized.

Ideal type: A logical, exaggerated model used as a methodological tool for the study of specific phenomena.

Ideology: A system of beliefs used to justify an existing social arrangement.

Immigration: The movement of individuals from one country to another, with permanent resettlement usually in mind.

In-group: The group to which an individual belongs and feels loyalty.

Indentured servant: An immigrant who contracts to work for a certain period of time in exchange for passage.

Independent variable (IV): A variable that is manipulated in an experiment because it is thought to cause change in another (dependent) variable.

Induction: The process of arriving at a general law, premise, or hypothesis by discovering some similarity across a set of related facts.

Inequality: Disparity in status and opportunity among people and groups within a society.

Infant mortality rate: The rate of death among infants under one year of age.

Inference: The process of making an educated guess about something using either induction or deduction; alternatively, the outcome or conclusion resulting from that process.

Inferential statistics: Techniques used to make estimates about a population based on data collected regarding a sample (a part) of the population.

Informal organizations: Unofficial relations and practices found in all bureaucracies of formal organizations.

Informed consent: A subject's consent to participate in research, based on appropriate knowledge of that research.

Institution: A stable social arrangement, including values, norms, statuses, and roles, that develops around a basic need of a society; a military institution, which wages wars declared by political institutions, is an example.

Institutional discrimination: See *Institutional racism.*

Institutional racism: The way society's institutions operate so as systematically to favor some groups over others with regard to opportunities and resources; often such racism is unintentional, but the discrimination is nevertheless real.

Institutions: Stable social patterns and relationships that result from the values, norms, roles, and statuses that govern activities that fulfill the needs of the society; for example, economic institutions help to organize the production and distribution of goods and services.

Integration: The condition that exists when all people in a society live together freely, experience equality under the law, and have equal opportunities to secure society's rewards.

Intergenerational mobility: The vertical social mobility that is measured by comparing offspring with their parents; the comparison usually entails comparison of the occupational status of parents at a given age with the occupational status of their offspring at approximately the same age.

Internal colony: A community that is subjected to colonial control and is located within the national borders of the colonizer.

Interval scale: A scale of measurement in which equal differences between numbers correspond to equal differences in that which is being measured.

Intragenerational mobility: The vertical social mobility that is measured by observing the same person across time; studies usually entail comparing occupational status at an early stage with status at a later stage.

Jim Crow laws: Statutes that enforced racial segregation in the American South until the Civil Rights movement.

Juvenile delinquency: See *Delinquency.*

Kin group: A social unit in which individuals are related to one another by blood or marriage.

Labeling theory: States that once an individual's behavior has been classified, society will see and treat the individual with respect to that definition, which in turn will cause the individual to conform to the definition; for example, individuals labeled as schizophrenics will be treated by others as mentally ill and will act accordingly.

Labor market segmentation: The division of the employment field into discrete areas, each of which is open predominantly to certain workers on the basis of race, gender, or other characteristics.

Laissez-faire: A doctrine opposing government interference in industry and trade.

Latent function: An unrecognized or unintended consequence.

Laws: Norms that have been formally included in a written legal code.

Legitimation: A set of beliefs, values, and attitudes that attempt to explain and justify existing social conditions and inequalities.

Liberation theology: Theology that makes explicit connections between religious experience and struggles for social justice.

Life course: The biological progression and social sequence of expected behaviors that individuals assume from birth to childhood, middle age, old age, and death.

Looking-glass self: The sense of personal identity that is the image reflected by the "mirror" of other people; it includes both identity and self-esteem.

Low-intensity warfare: Conflicts that are limited in scope, particularly in terms of the weaponry involved; examples are terrorism, guerrilla warfare, and insurgencies.

Macro-level: A concern with large-scale patterns that characterize society as a whole.

Macrosociology: The level of sociological analysis that is concerned with large-scale social issues, institutions, and processes.

Majority group: The group in a society that is socially, economically, and politically dominant.

Manifest function: The intended or obvious consequences.

Manumission: The granting of freedom individually to slaves before formal emancipation.

Marginal man: The individual who stands between two distinct cultures or races but is not at home in either group.

Marriage: A union between two or more individuals that is usually meant to be permanent, is recognized legally or socially, and is aimed at founding a family.

Marxism: A general term for the several schools of sociological thought deriving from Karl Marx, which share notions of social class and material production as pivotal social determinants.

Mass culture: A term initially used to characterize the culture of a modern mass society with its mass media; now often used to mean popular culture. See also *Popular culture.*

Master status: The status (such as father, farmer, or wife) with which an individual identifies most strongly.

Material culture: The tangible products of human society.

Matriarchy: A society ruled by or otherwise under the control of women.

Matrilineal descent: The transmission of authority, name, property, privilege, and obligations primarily through females; also called uterine descent.

Matrilocality: Often associated with primitive agricultural societies, matrilocality refers to family residence patterns revolving around matrilineal kinship groups, including women, their unmarried sons, daughters, and sons-in-law.

Mean: A measure of central tendency that is the sum of all the scores divided by the number of scores, sometimes referred to as the "average."

Measurement: The specific indicators of variables for the purpose of testing hypotheses, developing theory, and discovering the incidence of variables.

Median: The point in a distribution below which lie 50 percent of the scores and above which fall the remaining 50 percent.

Melting pot theory: The belief that individuals from various ethnic backgrounds eventually blend into one homogeneous American culture.

Meritocracy: Any society in which ability and effort are deemed more important than inherited privilege and status in the allocation of cultural, economic, political, and social position.

Micro-level: A concern with small-scale, or individual-level, patterns of social interaction within specific settings.

Microsociology: The level of sociological analysis concerned with small-scale group dynamics.

Migration: Movement from country to country or place to place.

Minority group: Any group that, on the basis of physical or cultural characteristics, receives fewer of society's rewards; a "minority" group can therefore be in the majority numerically.

Miscegenation: Racial intermarriage or cohabitation, including especially sexual intercourse and procreation between whites and either blacks or other people of color.

Misogyny: The devaluation or hatred of women.

Mode: The score in a distribution that occurs most frequently.

Mode of production: The combination of the social relations of production and its sources; capitalism is one example of a mode of production.

Modernization: The gradual change in the social, economic, and political institutions of a society as a result of increasing industrialization, urbanization, and literacy and education, as well as changes in traditional values and beliefs.

Monogamy: A marital relationship in which an individual has only one spouse at a time.

Monopoly capitalism: A type of capitalism in which major sectors of the economy are dominated by a few capitalists or by managers.

Moral entrepreneurs: Persons who attempt to define behavior as deviant; some have official power, but many do not.

Multicultural education: An educational approach that strives for inclusivity and fairness regarding the contributions of all cultures and races, and both genders, to society; it sometimes challenges the dominant culture's views.

Multinational corporation: Typically, a private corporation principally headquartered in one nation and having branch offices and significant economic activities in one or more other nations.

Nationalism: The ideological and political expression of social groupings that seek to advance the interests of their established, suppressed, or emerging nations.

Nativism: The favoring of native inhabitants over immigrants; the revival or perpetuation of indigenous culture, especially in opposition to acculturation.

Nominal scale: A measurement scale in which data are in the form of names, labels, or categories.

Nonresponse bias: An effect that may occur when a significant proportion of a research sample does not return surveys; this nonresponse results in inaccurate survey results if the nonresponders differ from those who responded.

Norm: A rule or expectation about appropriate behavior for a particular person in a particular situation.

Normal distribution: A continuous distribution of a random variable in which the mean, median, and mode are equal; sometimes called a "bell-shaped" curve.

Nuclear family: A unit consisting of a husband, a wife, and their children.

Observer biases: Beliefs or attitudes of a researcher that can alter the outcome of research by interfering with collection of accurate data or objective analysis of the data.

Occupational prestige: The shared value members of a society place on different jobs.

Occupational segregation: The separation of jobs by gender, race, or other criteria.

Occupational sex segregation: The concentration of women in particular positions in the labor force, usually low-paid, low-skilled jobs such as clerical and service work.

Oligarchy: A small group of people who control an organization or rule a society.

Oligopoly: Control over a market by only a few producers or sellers.

Open-ended questions: Questions that permit survey subjects to respond in their own words.

Open marriage: A form of consensual adultery in which both spouses openly engage in extramarital sexual experiences while putting the marriage itself first.

Operational definition: A specific description of a variable that will enable it to be measured; it outlines the precise steps or operations for other researchers to use in assessing the variable.

Oppression: Any unjust act or situation that prevents a person or group from full self-actualization or self-realization; oppression may be mental or physical.

Ordinal scale: A scale of measurement in which data are ordered by rank.

Organization: A group guided by specific goals, rules, and positions of leadership.

Organized crime: Collective criminal behavior that is structured in the manner of a legitimate business enterprise, commonly a partnership or a syndicate of interlocking partnerships.

Out-group: A group composed of people who are not members of one's in-group and are considered outsiders.

Outlier: A value that lies outside the normal range of responses for a particular variable.

Pandemic: A phenomenon of multinational or global proportions, such as a pandemic disease.

Paradigm: In the exemplary sense, a scientific achievement embodying experimental results and theoretical interpretations that serve as a model of how puzzles are to be solved; also the constellation of beliefs, values, methods, theories, and laws shared by members of a scientific community.

Parameter: A measure of a variable taken from a population.

Participant-observer method: A research technique first applied in anthropology but extended to sociology and political science at the University of Chicago in the 1920's whereby the student of an institution or group lives among the people being studied.

Paternalism: The practice by which governing individuals, businesses, or nations act in the manner of a father dealing with his children.

Patriarchy: An institutionalized system of male dominance that is expressed in everyday social practices and their corresponding social ideologies.

Patrilineal descent groups: A form of kinship structure in which family ties are organized with respect to males, making all children members of their father's descent group.

Patrilocality: A family residential pattern that revolves around the male who lives with his wife, his unmarried daughters, and his sons and their wives and children.

Peer group: People who are the same age and are roughly equal in authority.

Periphery: In world-system theory, the exploited former colonies of the core, which supply the core with cheap labor and raw materials.

Phenomenology: An approach that emphasizes the socially constructed nature of knowledge, especially knowledge of everyday life.

Physiognomy: The study of human facial features in the belief that personality and intelligence can be inferred from facial characteristics.

Pluralism: A theory that views power as being dispersed among competing groups in society; also, the maintenance of social equality and respect for the cultures and peoples of different ethnic groups living in the same society.

Pogrom: A systematic persecution and massacre, especially of Jews.

Political action committee (PAC): A political organization whose purpose is to further the goals of a particular special-interest group or political candidate, primarily through fund-raising.

Political economy: A framework linking material interests (economy) with the use of power (politics) to protect and enhance interests.

Political machine: A party organization made up of professional politicians whose primary goal is to win and maintain power; although political machines have existed at different levels of government, in many places, and at many times, historically the heyday of the political machine and the boss has been identified with the late nineteenth and early twentieth century U.S. city.

Polygamy: A marital relationship in which an individual has more than one spouse at a time; sometimes used to mean "polygyny," the form of polygamy in which a man has more than one wife.

Polygyny: See *Polygamy*.

Popular culture: The cultural forms enjoyed by the populace, including the leisure and recreational activities of typical segments of a society.

Population: The entire aggregate of individuals, items, scores, or observations from which random samples are drawn.

Population control: Refers to control over the size, growth, distribution, and characteristics of populations; most often used with respect to population growth.

Pornography: Written and visual materials of a sexual nature that are used for sexual arousal.

Positivism: The view that sociology should model itself in method and theory after the physical sciences and that all knowledge can be hierarchically arranged.

Postindustrial society: A formerly industrial society noted for its manufactured goods that subsequently produces fewer goods than it provides services and information.

Poverty: A condition in which people find themselves lacking the means for providing basic material needs.

Poverty line: The income measure of poverty based on a federal formula that accounts for insufficiency in food, housing, clothing, medical care, and other items required to maintain a decent standard of living for families of varying sizes.

Power: The ability of a social actor (individual or group) to achieve its wishes against the opposition of other social actors.

Power elite: A term used by C. Wright Mills to identify those at the top of the power structure who formulate policy designed to perpetuate their own interests.

Praxis: Practice as distinguished from theory; in liberation theology, praxis is the practical application of church teachings and theology.

Predestination: John Calvin's Protestant doctrine that all individuals are born into (and must forever remain in) one of two groups, the Elect or the Damned.

Prejudice: Arbitrary beliefs or feelings about a certain ethnic, racial, or religious group and about the individuals belonging to that group.

Primary group: A small social group whose members interact frequently with one another on a face-to-face basis, have intimate knowledge of one another, and share emotional ties.

Primary sector: A part of the economy that offers high wages and job security, including industries that are unionized and engaged in monopoly production.

Productivity: The amount of goods produced, or services provided, in relation to the work hours used; fewer hours and more production equals higher productivity.

Profession: A vocational group whose practitioners need higher education and advanced training; a profession typically has clearly defined entrance requirements, certification of competence, and procedures for internal control.

Proletariat: The term used by Karl Marx to define workers, those who survive by selling their labor to the bourgeoisie.

Public opinion: The public's expression of its preferences on issues of public interest or policy.

Push/pull factors: Circumstances that force (push) individuals or groups out of their native country or attract (pull) them toward a particular destination.

Qualitative research: Research that relies heavily on direct observation and descriptive analysis of social interaction, principally to examine the underlying meanings and patterns of these phenomena.

Quantitative research: The numerical examination and interpretation of observations, relying heavily on statistical analysis to evaluate differences in the variability and central tendency of variables.

Race: A conventional way of referring to a population that has been socially defined as being physically different from another population; race is a social reality, but not a meaningful biological one.

Racial discrimination: Behavior, practices, or policies that result in harm, intended or not, to individuals on the basis of their race.

Racial prejudice: The dislike and fear of others based on real or perceived physical differences.

Racism: The ideology contending that actual or alleged differences among different racial groups assert the superiority of one racial group over another.

Random sampling: A method of sampling in which all items in the population have an equal probability of being selected.

Range: The highest score minus the lowest score of a distribution.

Rape: Sexual intercourse as a result of force or threats of force rather than consent; the legal definition varies from state to state.

Rational-legal authority: The legitimization of power by law, rules, and regulations rather than by tradition or personality.

Rationalization: In the Weberian sense, using formal procedures and rules (as in a bureaucracy) instead of informal, spontaneous patterns.

Recidivism: The commission of a criminal act by a person who has previously been convicted for criminal activity and served time.

Reference group: A group or category that people use to evaluate themselves and their behavior.

Reification: The process by which habitual patterns of behavior and categories of thought are apprehended by members of society as if being external to them and having a life of their own.

Relations of production: The structure of economic relations or the way in which people are related to one another in the production process.

Relative deprivation: A theoretical perspective on social movements that states that social movements occur when there is a gap between expectations and objective conditions experienced by members of society.

Relative poverty: Determinant of poverty based on the standards of living in a given society, rather than on some absolute level.

Reliability: The ability of an instrument to measure a variable or construct consistently over repeated measurements.

Religion: A system of communally experienced human thoughts and beliefs about the assumed nature of reality involving some supernatural or transcendent nonhuman deity or principle.

Reproduction: The theoretical proposition that institutions within the capitalist social system reproduce class, gender, and racial inequities to benefit those in positions of power.

Research design: The plan followed by a researcher to structure data collection and analysis.

Research hypothesis: A specifically worded statement or prediction that can be verified or falsified through the collection of data; a tentative answer to a research question.

Resocialization: In the context of total institutions, the deliberate control of a social environment to alter a subject's personality radically.

Resource mobilization: A social movement theory that the success of a movement depends substantially on the ability to organize effectively to obtain necessary resources, such as money, mass media coverage, and the support of influential people and important groups or organizations.

Revolution: A transformation of political, economic, and/or social structures in which a dominant class loses power.

Riot: A relatively spontaneous form of collective behavior that is often characterized by violent and destructive attacks on people and property.

Rite: A ceremony, such as a christening, baptism, marriage, or burial, often recognizing a stage of life; a rite of passage (such as the Jewish bar mitzvah) is an initiation ceremony into adulthood.

Ritual: Prescribed formal behavior, often symbolic, fixed, and solemn, that follows a cultural tradition.

Role ambiguity: Unclear expectations concerning the normative performance of a social role.

Role conflict: A condition that occurs when two or more of a person's roles contain incompatible expectations.

Role strain: A condition that occurs when the expectations found within a single role are incompatible.

Role-taking: Seeing the world from the perspective of other individuals and groups, and directing one's own actions accordingly.

Roles: Behavioral expectations related to positions (statuses) held by individuals in any particular group; identified by related clusters of behavioral norms.

Romantic love: A form of affectional relationship based on interpersonal attraction, emotional attachment, and passion.

Rotating credit association: A method of raising cash, prevalent in some ethnic groups, that involves the continuous pooling and withdrawal of money.

Rumor: False information that moves by word of mouth or, occasionally, through the mass media.

Rural sociology: The systematic study of rural society and the knowledge obtained from that study; currently it is an international discipline.

Sacred: A social classification of phenomena that includes extraordinary and awe-inspiring events and processes distinct from the everyday, mundane aspects of social life.

Sample: A set of items, scores, or observations selected from a population. See also *Random sampling.*

Sampling frames: The actual list of sampling units from which the sample, or some stage of the sample, is selected.

Sampling unit: An element or a set of elements considered for selection in some stage of sampling.

Sanctions: Rewards and punishments for conforming to or violating norms.

Scapegoating: The practice of unfairly blaming a person or category of people for the troubles of others.

Scientific method: A method for acquiring knowledge that is characterized by systematic observation, experimentation, experimental control, and the ability to repeat the study.

Scientific revolution: A historical event during which a scientific community abandons a traditional paradigm in favor of a new one whose worldview, methods, and logical structure are incompatible with the paradigm it replaces.

Secondary sector: The portion of the economy in which wages are low, employment is erratic, and benefits are few, often involving nonunionized, competitive industries.

Sect: A group that has broken away from an existing religious body, usually to maintain its traditional roots.

Sector theory: A theory of urban growth that asserts that urban development proceeds outward from the central business district in wedge-shaped sectors, each containing a particular social class.

Secularization: The process whereby the influence of religious values and beliefs over various aspects of life is reduced.

Segregation: The act, process, or state of being set apart; for example, stringent separation between racial or ethnic groups.

Self-concept: Personal identity; the collection of ideas that one has about oneself and one's nature.

Self-esteem: The affective or emotional appraisal of value regarding the self.

Self-fulfilling prophecy: A situation that occurs when other people's expectations for a person lead him or her to act in ways that confirm those expectations.

Semiperiphery: In world-system theory, the intermediate societies between the core and the periphery.

Sepharidi: Diaspora Jews who migrated to the Andalusian-Spanish area of Europe during the medieval period.

Sex: A term that refers to the physical, biological differences between men and women.

Sex discrimination: Behavior, practices, or policies that, whether intended or not, result in harm to individuals on the basis of their sex, such as denying opportunities and rights to women or giving preferential treatment and privileges to men.

Sex-role stereotyping: Notions that only certain pursuits or behaviors are appropriate for each gender; not based on individual ability or motivation for those pursuits.

Sex roles: Social expectations and norms that are different for each gender.

Sex segregation: The separation of jobs on the basis of sex; sex segregation devalues women's work by paying them lower wages.

Sexism: Individuals' prejudicial attitudes and discriminatory behavior toward persons of a particular sex; institutional practices that subordinate persons of a particular sex.

Sexual abuse: Sexual contact with or exploitation of a nonconsenting individual, including exhibitionism, voyeurism, fondling, sodomy, and rape.

Sexual orientation: The direction of one's sexual feelings and behavior; the term is preferred to "sexual preference," which implies that a conscious choice has been made.

Significance test: A statistical test for determining whether the conclusion based on a sample holds true for the population from which the sample was drawn.

Significant other: Anyone who has or has had an important influence on a person's thoughts about self and the world.

Slave mode of production: An economic system in which slaves were the principal workforce and slavery was central to the overall economic structure.

Social change: Any alteration in the social behavior or institutions of a society that results in important long-term consequences.

Social class: A category of group membership that is generally based on one's position in the economic system with respect to economic resources, income, occupational prestige, and educational attainment and whose members usually share the same attitudes and values and an identifiable lifestyle.

Social cohesion: Forces that bind a society together, in ideological, social, and material aspects, to produce unity and harmony.

Social conflict: The struggle over values and resources between disparate social groups.

Social control: The use of formal and informal mechanisms by society to enforce dominant beliefs, values, and behavior.

Social demography: The scientific study of human populations, with an emphasis on the age, sex, racial/ethnic, and socioeconomic structure of society and how it changes, stressing the importance of the social determinants and consequences of fertility, mortality, and migration.

Social distance: A mode of measuring varying degrees of intimacy, understanding, and influence between individuals and groups in society.

Social ecology: The interactions between geographically separate human societies and between all human individuals or societies and their physical-chemical, biological, and cultural environments.

Social engineering: A process by which government or industry impinges upon a populace in order to achieve specific social ends, such as racial integration.

Social epidemiology: The scientific study of the occurrence and spread of disease, defects, or diseaselike conditions.

Social evolution: Regular change from one form of society to another, following general laws or principles; often associated with progress and with progression through a sequence of stages.

Social gerontology: The area within sociology that focuses on the study of aging and the elderly, with special emphasis on the social determinants and consequences of aging for the individual and society.

Social group: A set of individuals who interact in patterned ways, who share a culture that includes role expectations of how group members ought to behave, and who create a "boundary" by identifying with one another.

Social inequality: The unequal distribution of such things as wealth, income, occupational prestige, and educational attainment.

Social institutions: See *Institutions.*

Social integration: The extent to which the members of a society identify with that society, share its values, and accept its structure.

Social mobility: The movement of groups and individuals within and between social levels in a stratified society.

Social movements: Collective efforts to resist or bring about social change.

Social sciences: The behavioral sciences, including sociology, anthropology, political science, psychology, and economics; these sciences are differentiated from the "natural" or "physical" sciences in that the subject of study is the group or individual behavior of human beings.

Social strain theory: An explanation of the emergence of social movements using the idea that social tensions and/or disequilibrium stimulate the actions of a complaining group.

Social stratification: A structured, hierarchical ranking system with differences in access to social resources; individuals at the top ranks have more access, while those at the bottom lack social resources.

Social structure: Relatively stable patterns of social relationships organized around statuses and roles.

Social support: Instrumental, informational, and emotional support that a person receives from others.

Social theory: An explanatory framework proposed to shed light on some facet of social life.

Socialism: An economic system based on the public ownership of goods and of the means of producing them in a market controlled by the state.

Socialization: The process by which individuals learn the roles, norms, and values of the society to which they belong.

Socialization agent: A source of socialization; the persons or means that instruct or impart information, either formally or informally.

Society: A group of people who interact with one another within a limited territory and who share a culture.

Sociobiology: The study of the biological and evolutionary underpinnings of social behavior; controversial because its biological determinist assumptions sometimes have political implications, especially regarding gender and racial relations.

Socioeconomic status: An individual's socially defined position in society, determined by a combination of factors such as income, occupation, and education.

Sociometrics: The quantitative analysis of social parameters indicative of social change.

Sodomy: An overarching term for sexual deviation; its legal definition specifies anal intercourse or oral-genital contact, either consensual or coerced.

Spouse or partner battering: Physical, psychological, or sexual mistreatment that occurs in a relationship between married couples or among individuals in a sustaining partnership.

Standard deviation: A measure of variability that reflects the average amount of distance the scores of a distribution are from the mean.

State: A powerful institution that holds the legitimate monopoly on the use of force in society.

Statistic: A measure of a variable based on a sample of scores or observations.

Statistical inference: An inference made by applying some basic assumptions and/or laws of statistics to a set of observations.

Status: The socially defined positions occupied by an individual throughout the life course; examples include child, student, or parent.

Status attainment research: The study of whether or not social mobility takes place, including an evaluation of the factors that account for patterns of mobility.

Stereotype: A standardized mental picture held by members of a group that represents an oversimplified, critical, or prejudicial judgment about members of another group; stereotypes are often used to legitimize discrimination.

Stigma: The intense social disapproval and alienation that follow the assignment of a deviant status.

Stockholm syndrome: A condition in which hostages begin to identify or sympathize with their captors.

Strain theories of delinquency: Theories that explain the cause of delinquency by emphasizing the frustration experienced by youths who do not have access to legal methods to achieve success.

Stratification: See *Social stratification.*

Structural: The level of human reality that is directly attributable to the patterns of social organization and that is not reducible to the level of the individual.

Structural differentiation: The notion that as institutions increase in size in terms of the complexity of the functions that they perform, they necessarily form specialized subsystems with distinct responsibilities.

Structural-functionalist theory: The theory according to which society is held together by the sharing of ideals and values; holds that society is a system of interrelated parts.

Structural unemployment: Unemployment caused by a change in structure of the economy, with most workers not expecting eventual reemployment in the same location and industry.

Structured inequality: See *Social stratification.*

Subculture: A group of people who hold many of the values and norms of the larger culture but also certain beliefs, values, or norms that set them apart from that culture.

Subordinate groups: Society's "have-nots" who are disadvantaged compared with other groups.

Sudden infant death syndrome (SIDS): The cause ascribed to the sudden, inexplicable death of an infant of less than one year of age.

Symbol: Something that represents something else, particularly a material object that stands for something invisible or intangible.

Symbolic interactionism: A theoretical perspective analyzing day-to-day interactions among individuals; symbolic interaction theory holds that social life is dependent on an individual's ability to interpret social symbols correctly and to perceive correctly his or her own role in relation to the roles of others.

Taboo: An absolute ban against the performance of a particular behavior; stronger in its meaning than "rule" or "prohibition."

Taylorization: The process pioneered by Frederick W. Taylor of applying scientific management to the labor process.

Technology: Cumulative skills and knowledge applied in environmental adaptation, including such processes as food production.

Tertiary sector: The part of the economy engaged primarily in services, such as banking and retail sales.

Theoretical sampling: A technique in which data collection is controlled by the demands of an emerging theory rather than by an existing theoretical framework.

Third World: A contemporary term for the developing countries as defined through their engagement in the early and intermediate phases of industrialization.

Total institution: A form of social organization where the inmates are isolated from society and have every aspect of their lives controlled by staff, usually for the purpose of changing the personalities of the inmates.

Totalitarianism: A government that exercises nearly total control over individual citizens—a relatively recent and extreme form of authoritarianism.

Totemism: The belief in the power of a sacred plant, animal, or object that symbolizes a particular clan or social group.

Tracking: Putting students into certain curricula (such as technical, academic, or remedial) that control their later options in life.

Traditional authority: Authority based on customs and long-standing practice.

Underclass: A social class at the bottom of the social strata; the poorest of the poor, among whom poverty is an ongoing feature from generation to generation.

Uniform Crime Reports: A yearly compilation of crime based on a count of nine "index" crimes tabulated by local police forces and published by the Federal Bureau of Investigation.

Union shop: A shop in which membership in a union is mandatory for employees thirty days after employment or thirty days after the signing of the union shop's contract, whichever comes later.

Urban legends: Narrative stories that are hearsay and unverifiable and that deal with contemporary urban life.

Urbanization: The process of expansion of urban areas and culture through rural-urban population shifts.

Validity: The extent to which a measurement actually measures what it claims to measure.

Values: Beliefs shared by members of a society or organization of what is good, bad, desirable, undesirable, proper, or improper.

Variable: A trait that can vary in magnitude from case to case.

Verstehen: Empathic (interpretive) understanding; Max Weber's main goal as a social analyst.

Vertical social mobility: Movement upward or downward in the social hierarchy.

Volunteerism: A philosophy encouraging individuals to offer their services free of charge for a good cause.

Voucher: A certificate given to the parents of students indicating the amount of public money that the former may distribute to the schools attended by their children.

Welfare: A general, informal term for government programs, particularly Aid to Families with Dependent Children, that provide payments and services to the poor.

White-collar crime: Crime committed by high-status individuals in the course of their occupations for personal gain.

White flight: The movement of white families from ethnic neighborhoods, and white students' abandonment of urban schools for private or suburban schools.

Workfare: A general, informal term for welfare programs in which the acceptance of payments and services obliges the recipient to prepare for, seek, and accept employment.

Working poor: Those who lack the means for an adequate existence even though they are employed.

World system: According to Immanuel Wallerstein, the modern system of nations and their economies, which is dominated by wealthy capitalist economies.

Worldview: The way an individual or group perceives and conceptualizes the world.

Xenophobia: An irrational fear or hatred of foreigners or others with different appearances or customs.

Zionism: The movement to establish a Jewish state in Palestine.

ALPHABETICAL LIST

SOCIOLOGY

CATEGORY LIST

INDEX

Page ranges appearing in boldface type indicate that an entire article devoted to the topic appears on those pages; a single page number in bold denotes definition of a term in the Glossary.

Mass media socialization, political, 1409-1410
Mass production. *See* Industrial Revolution and mass production.
Mass psychogenic illness (MPI), **1141-1146**
Master status, 334, **2232**
Mate selection, 134
Material culture, **2232**
Matriarchy, 903, **2232**. *See also* Patriarchy versus matriarchy.
Matrilineal descent, **2232**
Matrilineal inheritance systems. *See* Inheritance systems.
Matrilocal residence patterns. *See* Residence patterns.
Matrilocality, **2232**
Mead, George Herbert, 567, 1010, 1196-1197, 1929, 2036, 2040; on significant and generalized others, **1748-1753**
Mead, Lawrence M., 1455-1456
Mead, Margaret, 1722
Mean, 521, 1147, **2232**
Means-tested antipoverty programs, 1478
Measurement, **2233**. *See* Validity and reliability in measurement.
Measures of central tendency, 520-522, 984, **1147-1152**
Measures of variability, 984, **1153-1158**
Median, 521, 1147, **2233**
Medicaid, 966-968
Medical ethics, 892-893. *See also* Euthanasia; Organ transplantation.
Medical profession, women in. *See* Women in the medical profession.
Medical profession and the medicalization of society, **1159-1165**. *See also* Medicalization of deviance.
Medical sociology, **1166-1171**, 1189-1190
Medical versus social models of illness, **1172-1177**
Medicalization of deviance, **1178-1184**. *See also* Medical profession and the medicalization of deviance.
Medicare, 966-968

Medicine, history of. *See* Germ theory of medicine; Hippocratic theory of medicine.
Medicine, institution of, 644-645, **1185-1191**
Meese Commission, 1442-1443
Megalopolis, 253, 2010, 2129
Melting pot model of assimilation, 1375. *See also* Assimilation: the United States.
Melting pot theory, **2233**
Meltzer, Bernard, 2036
Mendelssohn, Moses, 1030
Mental disorders. *See* Deinstitutionalization of mental patients.
Mental disorders, medicalization of, 1180-1181
Meritocracy, 2057-2059, **2233**
Merton, Robert K., 100-102, 105, 787-788, **1498-1504**, 1934, 1991
Metropolis, 2010, 2012, 2129
Metropolitan Statistical Area (MSA), 2012-2013
Michels, Robert, 173
Micro-level, **2233**
Microsociology, **1192-1199**, **2233**. *See also* Interactionism; Symbolic interaction.
Middle-range theory, 1328-1329
"Middleman" minorities, **1200-1206**
Migration, 507, 921-922, **2233**
Miles, Robert, 1553
Milgram, Stanley, 675-678
Miliband, Ralph, 1974
Military-industrial complex, **1207-1212**. *See also* Cold War.
Milken, Michael, 2181
Millenarian religious movements, 512, 514, **1213-1218**
Miller, Dan E., 1668
Miller v. State of California, 1441
Mills, C. Wright, 342, 1491-1496, 1929, 1975
Minority and majority groups, **1219-1225**. *See also* "Middleman" minorities; "Model" minorities.
Minority group, **2233**
Mintz, Sidney, 1243